The Cambridge Companion to Stravinsky

Stravinsky's work spanned the major part of the twentieth century and engaged with nearly all its principal compositional developments. This Companion reflects the breadth of Stravinsky's achievement and influence in essays by leading international scholars on a wide range of topics. It is divided into three parts dealing with the contexts within which Stravinsky worked (Russian, modernist and compositional), with his key compositions (Russian, neoclassical and serial) and with the reception of his ideas (through performance, analysis and criticism). The volume concludes with an interview with the leading Dutch composer Louis Andriessen and a major re-evaluation of 'Stravinsky and us' by Richard Taruskin.

JONATHAN CROSS is University Lecturer in Music and Tutorial Fellow of Christ Church, Oxford. He is author of *The Stravinsky Legacy* (Cambridge, 1998) and *Harrison Birtwistle: Man, Mind, Music* (London, 2000), and is Editor of the journal *Music Analysis*.

Cambridge Companions to Music

Composers

The Cambridge Companion to Bach
Edited by John Butt

The Cambridge Companion to Bartók
Edited by Amanda Bayley

The Cambridge Companion to Beethoven
Edited by Glenn Stanley

The Cambridge Companion to Benjamin Britten
Edited by Mervyn Cooke

The Cambridge Companion to Berg
Edited by Anthony Pople

The Cambridge Companion to Berlioz
Edited by Peter Bloom

The Cambridge Companion to Brahms
Edited by Michael Musgrave

The Cambridge Companion to John Cage
Edited by David Nicholls

The Cambridge Companion to Chopin
Edited by Jim Samson

The Cambridge Companion to Debussy
Edited by Simon Trezise

The Cambridge Companion to Handel
Edited by Donald Burrows

The Cambridge Companion to Ravel
Edited by Deborah Mawer

The Cambridge Companion to Schubert
Edited by Christopher Gibbs

The Cambridge Companion to Stravinsky
Edited by Jonathan Cross

Instruments

The Cambridge Companion to Brass Instruments
Edited by Trevor Herbert and John Wallace

The Cambridge Companion to the Cello
Edited by Robin Stowell

The Cambridge Companion to the Clarinet
Edited by Colin Lawson

The Cambridge Companion to the Organ
Edited by Nicholas Thistlethwaite and Geoffrey Webber

The Cambridge Companion to the Piano
Edited by David Rowland

The Cambridge Companion to the Recorder
Edited by John Mansfield Thomson

The Cambridge Companion to the Saxophone
Edited by Richard Ingham

The Cambridge Companion to Singing
Edited by John Potter

The Cambridge Companion to the Violin
Edited by Robin Stowell

Topics

The Cambridge Companion to Pop and Rock
Edited by Simon Frith, Will Straw and John Street

The Cambridge Companion to Jazz
Edited by Mervyn Cooke and David Horn

The Cambridge Companion to Blues and Gospel Music
Edited by Allan Moore

The Cambridge Companion to the Orchestra
Edited by Colin Lawson

The Cambridge Companion to

STRAVINSKY

....

EDITED BY
Jonathan Cross

CAMBRIDGE
UNIVERSITY PRESS

PUBLISHED BY THE PRESS SYNDICATE OF THE UNIVERSITY OF CAMBRIDGE
The Pitt Building, Trumpington Street, Cambridge, United Kingdom

CAMBRIDGE UNIVERSITY PRESS
The Edinburgh Building, Cambridge CB2 2RU, UK
40 West 20th Street, New York, NY 10011-4211, USA
477 Williamstown Road, Port Melbourne, VIC 3207, Australia
Ruiz de Alarcón 13, 28014 Madrid, Spain
Dock House, The Waterfront, Cape Town 8001, South Africa

http://www.cambridge.org

First published 2003

Printed in the United Kingdom at the University Press, Cambridge

Typeface Minion 10.75/14 pt   *System* LaTeX 2_ε [TB]

A catalogue record for this book is available from the British Library

ISBN 0 521 66330 X hardback
ISBN 0 521 66377 6 paperback

Contents

Contributors

Louis Andriessen is one of the most distinguished living Dutch composers. He teaches composition at the Koninklijk Conservatorium Den Haag.

Craig Ayrey is Lecturer in Music Theory and Analysis at Goldsmiths College, University of London.

Rosamund Bartlett is Lecturer in Russian and Music History at the University of Durham.

Christopher Butler is Professor of English at the University of Oxford and Tutorial Fellow of Christ Church.

Stuart Campbell is Honorary Senior Research Fellow in the Institute of Central and Eastern European Studies and the Department of Music at the University of Glasgow.

Nicholas Cook is Research Professor in Music at the University of Southampton.

Jonathan Cross is University Lecturer in Music and Tutorial Fellow of Christ Church, Oxford.

Kenneth Gloag is Lecturer in Music at Cardiff University.

Anthony Gritten is Lecturer in Music at the University of East Anglia.

Martha M. Hyde is Professor of Music at the State University of New York at Buffalo.

Max Paddision is Professor of Music at the University of Durham.

Anthony Pople is Professor of Music at the University of Nottingham.

Joseph N. Straus is Professor of Music at Queens College and the Graduate Center, City University of New York.

Richard Taruskin is Professor of Music at the University of California at Berkeley.

Arnold Whittall is Professor Emeritus of Music Theory and Analysis at King's College London.

Chronology of Stravinsky's life and works

ANTHONY GRITTEN

Year	Stravinsky's life	Major works
1882	Igor Fyodorovich Stravinsky born in Oranienbaum, east of St Petersburg (5 June [OS])	
1883	Wagner dies (13 February)	
1884		
1885		
1886		
1887		
1888		
1889		
1890		
1891	has first piano lessons; first meets future wife, Catherine Nossenko	
1892	hears his father sing in Glinka's *Ruslan and Lyudmila* (November)	
1893	glimpses Tchaikovsky at the Mariinsky Theatre; Tchaikovsky dies (25 October [OS])	
1894		
1895		
1896		
1897	Brahms dies (3 April)	
1898	composes earliest surviving composition, a Tarantella for piano	
1899		
1900		
1901	commences study of Law at University of St Petersburg; begins private lessons in harmony and counterpoint (November)	
1902	first visit to Rimsky-Korsakov (August); father dies (21 November [OS])	
1903		
1904		
1905	becomes engaged to Catherine (1 August [OS])	
1906	marries Catherine, b. 1881 (11 January [OS]); graduates from University of St Petersburg (May)	
1907	first child, Theodore, born (17 February [OS])	Symphony in E♭, Op. 1 (1905–7) 22 Jan 1908 [OS], St Petersburg *The Faun and the Shepherdess*, Op. 2 (1906–7) 22 Jan 1908 [OS], St Petersburg
1908	daughter Lyudmila born (before Christmas); Rimsky-Korsakov dies (8 June [OS])	*Scherzo fantastique*, Op. 3 (1907–8) 6 February 1909 *Fireworks*, Op. 4 6 February 1909
1909		

(*Cont.*)

Year	Stravinsky's life	Major works
1910	meets Debussy and Cocteau (25 June); moves to Switzerland (late summer); son Sviatoslav Soulima born (23 September, Lausanne)	*The Firebird* (1909–10) 25 June 1910, Paris
1911	visits Rome with Ballets Russes (April); returns to Clarens (September)	*Petrushka* (1910–11) 13 June 1911, Paris *Zvezdolikiy* 19 April 1939, Brussels
1912	hears Wagner's *Parsifal* at Bayreuth with Diaghilev (20 August); meets Schoenberg (4 December) and hears *Pierrot lunaire* (8 December)	
1913	attends performance of Strauss's *Elektra* at Covent Garden (February); works with Ravel on performing version of Musorgsky's *Khovanshchina* (March–April); publishes the first of many polemical articles (29 May)	*The Rite of Spring* (1911–13) 29 May 1913, Paris
1914	moves family to Switzerland (January); birth of last child Milena (15 January, Leysin); Ansermet first conducts Stravinsky's music (2 April); first concert performance of *The Rite of Spring* (5 April, Paris); visits Ustilug and Kiev and collects volumes of Russian folk verse (July)	*The Nightingale* (1908–9 and 1913–14) 26 May 1914, Paris *Three Pieces for String Quartet* 19 May 1915, Paris
1915	inaugurates career as conductor (December); visits Rome (February) and Milan (April), meeting Italian Futurists Marinetti and Russolo	*Three Easy Pieces* (1914–15) 22 April 1918, Lausanne
1916		*Renard* 18 May 1922, Paris
1917	meets Picasso and Gide; Bolshevik revolution (7 November)	*Five Easy Pieces* 22 April 1918, Lausanne
1918	Debussy dies (25 March)	*The Soldier's Tale* 28 September 1918, Lausanne *Ragtime* (1917–18) 27 April 1920, London
1919		*Piano-Rag-Music* 8 November 1919, Lausanne
1920	moves family to Paris (June)	*Pulcinella* (1919–20) 15 May 1920, Paris *Symphonies of Wind Instruments* 10 June 1921, London *Concertino* 23 November 1920, New York
1921	begins pianola transcriptions of his works in Pleyel's studio in Paris (February); moves family to Biarritz (May); begins affair with Vera Sudeikina (14 July); Ballets Russes present Tchaikovsky's *Sleeping Beauty* in London (2 November)	
1922		*Mavra* (1921–2) 3 June 1922, Paris
1923	meets Landowska (25 June); meets Busoni in Weimar (19 August); makes first recording, of *Octet*, in Paris (November)	*Les Noces* (1914–23) 13 June 1923, Paris Octet (1922–3) 18 October 1923, Paris

(*Cont.*)

Year	Stravinsky's life	Major works
1924	meets Lourié while in Brussels (14 January); moves family to Nice (25 September); inaugurates career as pianist (22 May); European concert tour (October–December)	Concerto for Piano and Wind Instruments (1923–4) 22 May 1924, Paris Sonata for piano 16 July 1925, Donaueschingen
1925	makes first North American tour (January–March), meeting Gershwin (7 January); seals first recording contract, with Brunswick Records (14 March); performs at ISCM festival (8 September, Venice)	Serenade in A 25 November 1925, Frankfurt
1926	conducts *The Rite of Spring* for the first time (28 February, Amsterdam); spiritual crisis and religious epiphany (March, Padua); meets Maritain (10 June)	
1927	conducts first full concert, in Paris (10 February), and first broadcast concert, in London (19 June)	*Oedipus Rex* (1926–7) 30 May 1927, Paris
1928	Balanchine first choreographs Stravinsky (*Apollon musagète*, Ballets Russes, 12 June, Paris)	*Apollon musagète* (1927–8) 27 April 1928, Washington DC *The Fairy's Kiss* 27 November 1928, Paris
1929	death of Diaghilev (19 August); first recording of *The Rite of Spring*, conducted by Stravinsky in Paris (7–10 May)	*Capriccio* (1928–9) 6 December 1929, Paris
1930	recordings in Paris (8–10 May); concert tour (October–December)	*Symphony of Psalms* 13 December 1930, Brussels
1931	moves family to Voreppe (16 June); concert tour with Dushkin (October–December)	Violin Concerto 23 October 1931, Berlin
1932	recordings in Paris (6–9 May)	*Duo concertant* 28 October 1932, Berlin
1933	concert tour with Dushkin (February–March)	
1934	given French citizenship (4 June); recordings in London (July); meets Berg, in Venice (11 September)	*Perséphone* (1933–4) 30 April 1934, Paris
1935	second North American tour (January–April); meets Mussolini in Rome (May); recordings in Paris (October); publishes first volume of autobiography	Concerto for Two Solo Pianos (1932–5) 21 November 1935, Paris
1936	failed application for membership in the Académie des Beaux-Arts (January 1936); South American tour (April–June)	*Jeu de cartes* (1935–6) 27 April 1937, New York
1937	third North American tour, with Dushkin (January–May)	
1938	daughter Lyudmila dies (30 November)	Concerto in E♭, 'Dumbarton Oaks' (1937–8) 8 May 1938, Washington DC
1939	wife Catherine and mother Anna die (2 March and 7 June, Sancellemoz); sails to New York (September); gives Norton lectures [nos. 1–3] at Harvard University (October–November)	
1940	marries Vera in Bedford, MA (9 March); moves to Los Angeles (June)	Symphony in C (1938–40) 7 November 1940, Chicago
1941	Disney's *Fantasia* uses excerpts from *The Rite of Spring*	

(*Cont.*)

Year	Stravinsky's life	Major works
1942	listens to radio broadcast of Shostakovich's 'Leningrad' Symphony (19 July)	*Danses concertantes* (1940–42) 8 February 1942, Los Angeles *Circus Polka* (1941–2) 14 January 1944, Cambridge, MA
1943		*Ode* 8 October 1943, Boston
1944		Sonata for Two Pianos (1943–4) 2 August 1944, Madison, Wisconsin *Scènes de ballet* 24 November 1944, Philadelphia
1945	given US citizenship (28 December)	*Symphony in Three Movements* (1942–5) 24 January 1946, New York *Ebony Concerto* 25 March 1946, New York
1946		Concerto in D 27 January 1947, Basle
1947		*Orpheus* (1946–7) 28 April 1948, New York
1948	first meets Robert Craft (spring); appears on the cover of *Time* (July)	Mass (1944–8) 27 October 1948, Milan
1949	Craft joins the Stravinsky household (1 June)	
1950		
1951	makes first trip to Europe since 1939 (August); Schoenberg dies (13 July)	*The Rake's Progress* (1947–51) 11 September 1951, Venice
1952	attends Craft's rehearsals of Schoenberg (February, September); hears Boulez and Messiaen perform Boulez's *Structures Ia* (7 May)	Cantata (1951–2) 11 November 1952, Los Angeles
1953	meets Dylan Thomas (May)	Septet (1952–3) 23 January 1954, Washington DC
1954	European tour (April–June); first televised concert of Stravinsky (Chicago WGN)	
1955	visits Webern's grave (24 April); recordings in Hollywood (28 July)	*Canticum sacrum* 13 September 1956, Venice
1956	visits Lisbon, Barcelona, Naples, Gesualdo, Palermo, Athens, Mycenae, Istanbul (June–September)	
1957	hears Boulez's *Le Marteau sans maître* in Los Angeles (11 March); first TV documentary on the composer (NBC)	*Agon* (1953–7) 1 December 1957, New York
1958	European tour (October–December)	*Threni* (1957–8) 23 September 1958, Venice
1959	visits Japan (April–May); visits Britain and sees Olivier in *Coriolanus* (September); publication of the first of the Stravinsky–Craft *Conversations* books	*Movements* (1958–9) 10 January 1960, New York
1960	tours Latin America (August–September)	*Monumentum pro Gesualdo di Venosa (ad CD Annum)* 27 September 1960, Venice
1961	invited to sit on the editorial board for *Perspectives of New Music*; concerts in Mexico (April); European tour (September–October); Australasian tour (November–December)	*A Sermon, a Narrative, and a Prayer* (1960–61) 23 February 1962, Basle

(*Cont.*)

1962	dinner at the White House (18 January); South African tour (May–June); visits Russia (September–October); recordings in Toronto (November–December)	*The Flood* (1961–2) 14 June 1962, CBS TV (USA)
1963	European tour (April–June); recordings in New York (December)	*Abraham and Isaac* (1962–3) 23 August 1964, Jerusalem
1964		*Variations (Aldous Huxley in memoriam)* (1963–4) 17 April 1965, Chicago
1965	European tour (May–June); recordings in Hollywood (August, October–November); Eliot dies (January)	*Introitus (T. S. Eliot in memoriam)* 17 April 1965, Chicago
1966	European tour (May–June)	*Requiem Canticles* (1965–6) 8 October 1966, Princeton University
1967	last recording (18 January, Hollywood); last concert (17 May, Toronto)	
1968	visits Switzerland and Paris (September–November)	
1969	in hospital in New York (May–June); Ansermet and Adorno die (20 February, 6 August)	
1970		
1971	dies in New York (6 April); given funeral and burial in Venice (15 April)	

Notes:

1 Works are listed in the year of their completion.

2 Dates of premieres are of the first public complete performance of the principal version of the work.

Preface and acknowledgements

Born in the nineteenth century, Stravinsky became one of the dominant creative figures of the twentieth, and his influence is still strongly felt into the twenty-first. The contributions to this volume reflect the range of Stravinsky's impact on many aspects of current musical and musicological life. They offer a broad spectrum of historical, critical and interpretative approaches to the composer and his music: Stravinsky the Russian, the modernist, the neoclassicist, the serialist, the dramatist. The chapters also look at the fascinating ways in which Stravinsky and his ideas have been received by performers, critics, analysts and composers. The final chapter proposes that the twentieth century was indeed 'Stravinsky's century' and that a 'Stravinskian' attitude pervades much recent musical thought and practice.

I owe an enormous debt of gratitude to Kathryn Puffett for her support; indeed, without her help, the Companion might never have appeared at all. I am also immensely grateful for her expert setting of many of the music examples. Michael Downes gave invaluable editorial advice during the final stages of the preparation of this volume. Thanks, too, to Penny Souster at CUP, who has, as always, encouraged and cajoled in equal measure, and to Anthony Gritten for his assistance with the chronological work list. Above all, thanks to Emma who has been there throughout and who makes it all worthwhile.

I gratefully acknowledge the generous financial assistance of the University of Bristol Faculty of Arts Research Fund towards the cost of preparing the music examples.

The music examples from Stravinsky's scores are reproduced by permission of Boosey & Hawkes Music Publishers (London), Ltd., with the exception of the excerpts from the Symphony in C, *Scherzo fantastique* and *Fireworks*, which are reproduced by permission of Schott and Co., Ltd., and the *Piano-Rag-Music*, which is reproduced by permission of J & W Chester/Edition Wilhelm Hansen, London, Ltd. The facsimile of the sketches for Stravinsky's Cantata are reproduced by permission of the Paul Sacher Stiftung, Basel. The excerpt from Debussy's *Nocturnes* is reproduced by permission of Editions Joubert, Paris/United Music Publishers Ltd.

PART I

Origins and contexts

Origins and contexts

1 Stravinsky's Russian origins

ROSAMUND BARTLETT

'A man has one birthplace, one fatherland, one country – he *can* have only one country – and the place of his birth is the most important factor in his life.' These words were uttered by Stravinsky at a banquet held in his honour in Moscow on 1 October 1962.[1] The eighty-year-old composer had returned to his homeland after an absence of fifty years. In the intervening period he had acquired first French and then American citizenship, and developed an increasingly hostile attitude towards his native country and its culture.[2] This hostility had been fully reciprocated by the Soviet musical establishment. Now, as the guest of the Union of Composers, Stravinsky was seemingly performing a complete *volte-face* by wholeheartedly embracing his Russian identity. For Robert Craft, his assistant and amanuensis, this was nothing short of a 'transformation', and he was astonished, not only to witness Stravinsky and his wife suddenly taking 'pride in everything Russian', but to observe at close hand how 'half a century of expatriation' could be 'forgotten in a night'.[3] Craft's diary of the famous visit contains many revealing comments about a composer who was a master of mystification.

Like his younger contemporary Vladimir Nabokov, with whom there are some intriguing biographical parallels,[4] Stravinsky did not care to be pigeon-holed or linked with any particular artistic trend after he left Russia. Above all, because of a sense of cultural inferiority which stemmed from the fact that Russia's musical tradition was so much younger than that of other European nations, he came to disavow his own musical heritage, which necessitated embroidering a complex tapestry of lies and denials. So proficient was Stravinsky in creating an elaborate smoke-screen about who he really was, in fact, that the highly controlled image he projected of his artistic independence remained largely intact for over two decades following his death in 1971. It is an achievement of the painstaking scholarship of Richard Taruskin and Stephen Walsh[5] that in the twenty-first century we can now look behind Stravinsky's cosmopolitan façade to see the carefully concealed but manifestly Russian identity that lies behind it. The extent of the obfuscations and contradictions of Stravinsky's musical persona can be judged from the sheer scale of Richard Taruskin's efforts in unravelling them: his study runs to 1,757 pages, and does not explore works written after 1922. Stravinsky's habit of falsifying his own life story means that we must clearly treat all his pronouncements with circumspection, but his highly emotional and apparently involuntary reaction in 1962 to being back on Russian soil (which he claimed even had a particular smell),[6] nevertheless speaks volumes about the continuing importance of his native origins.

Stravinsky was born on the cusp of two distinct eras, at a pivotal point in Russian cultural history. In 1881, the year before his birth, not only was Alexander II assassinated, but Dostoevsky and Musorgsky died, thus symbolically bringing to a close the era of the Great Reforms, Realist novels and Populism. Alexander II's reign (particularly the earlier part of it) had been a time of relative liberalism compared with the oppressive regime of Nicholas I which had preceded it. The reforms Alexander II had introduced in the 1860s, most notably the long-awaited Emancipation of the Serfs in 1861, had given rise to an upsurge of energy and optimism that was reflected across all sections of Russian society over the course of the following decade. The young radical intelligentsia believed at last the time had come for action (not for nothing was Nikolai Chernyshevsky's 1863 novel of political emancipation entitled *What is to be Done?*), and the arts were dominated throughout the 1860s and 1870s by a preoccupation with ideas of social change and questions of national identity. This was the age of the great novels of Tolstoy, Dostoevsky and Turgenev, and the ideologically charged canvases of the 'Wanderers' – nationalist painters who wished to highlight Russia's acute social problems. This was also a vibrant time for Russian music. As a result of the efforts of Anton Rubinstein, a Conservatoire had finally opened in St Petersburg in 1862, enabling Russian musicians to acquire professional status for the first time (all-important in a society where social position was still defined by a notorious Table of Ranks). Tchaikovsky was one of its first graduates. And at the same time that the Populist-minded artists of the 'Wanderers' group were rebelling against the Western and classical orientation of the St Petersburg Academy of Arts, a nucleus of nationalist composers was already turning its back on the Western and classical orientation of the new Conservatoire. Rather than be trained according to the German model set up by Rubinstein, the five members of the Balakirev circle opted to teach themselves, out of a belief that Russian music should follow its own course. One of those composers was Rimsky-Korsakov, later to become Stravinsky's teacher. Their spokesman was the prolific critic Vladimir Stasov, who waged an unceasing and often cantankerous campaign on behalf of Russian nationalist art from 1847 to 1906, the year of his death.

By the time of Alexander II's violent death, however, Russian culture was already beginning to undergo a sea-change as former radicals and non-conformists amongst the artistic community began to become part of the establishment. Rimsky-Korsakov had been appointed to teach at the St Petersburg Conservatoire in 1871, for example, and the Wanderers later became stalwart representatives of the Academy of Arts. Russia had embarked on a programme of rapid industrialisation and urbanisation, but the pace of reform had slowed, and social unrest consequently increased. When the peaceful attempts of the Populists failed to convince the peasantry of the need for urgent political action, the Revolutionary intelligentsia began to turn its attention to the new working-class organisations that were beginning to spring up in cities across the Russian empire. And their new terrorist methods began to achieve results. Conservative anyway by nature, Alexander III responded to the assassination of his father by bringing to a halt the wheels of progress and by tightening instruments of repression. Thus Stravinsky was born at a time of widespread despondency amongst the Russian population.

The new tsar's chauvinistic policies resulted in the persecution of Jews and other religious minorities, but there was one aspect of his Russification policies that had positive consequences, namely his active promotion of native culture. A century and a half of imperial patronage of Western art forms at the expense of Russian traditions (long considered unsophisticated by comparison, and associated with peasants, therefore inferior) had led to a huge explosion of national consciousness amongst Russian artists in the middle of the nineteenth century. Alexander III was the first Russian tsar to recognise and support native achievements. It was due to his efforts that the first government-sponsored collection of Russian art (now housed in the Russian Museum) was put on public display in St Petersburg in 1898, and he was clearly in favour of the 'revivalist' architecture which quickly became popular. The first major public building project of his reign was the onion-domed Church of the Resurrection, begun in 1882, the year of Stravinsky's birth. Built on the spot where Alexander II was assassinated, its pastiche of medieval Russian styles sits oddly amongst the stately neoclassicism of most of the rest of St Petersburg's eighteenth- and early nineteenth-century buildings, which had of course been specifically designed to emulate the European style and make a deliberate break with Muscovite tradition. This sort of retrogressive orientation was closely allied to Alexander III's reactionary and Slavophile political beliefs. Of far greater value were his services to Russian music. Alexander's decision, also in 1882, to end the monopoly on theatrical production held by the Imperial Theatres and to close down the Italian Opera were to have far-reaching consequences for the performing arts in Russia. As a singer at the Russian Opera in St Petersburg (where he was principal bass), Stravinsky's father was a direct beneficiary of this policy. Stravinsky's own musical development was also indirectly affected as a result. The two most important operas premiered in the year of Stravinsky's birth were Wagner's *Parsifal*, staged in Bayreuth, and Rimsky-Korsakov's *The Snow Maiden*, the latter performed at the Mariinsky Theatre in

St Petersburg, with Fyodor Stravinsky creating the role of Grandfather Frost.

Nicholas I had installed an Italian company in the main opera house in St Petersburg in 1843 (as much for political as for artistic reasons), and lavish sums from the imperial purse were invested in promoting it. Very much second-class citizens, the composers and performers involved with the Russian Opera did not even have a proper stage of their own until the Mariinsky Theatre was built in 1860. It must be said that the repertoire was still not very large at this stage, nor of consistently high quality (with the obvious exceptions of Glinka's operas, of course), but the Russian government had equally done nothing to encourage its subjects to become composers. The fortunes of the Russian Opera started to prosper in earnest only after the accession of Alexander III, when it became the sole company in St Petersburg, and thus the country's premier stage. Fyodor Stravinsky had joined the Russian Opera in 1876, having begun his singing career in Kiev, and it was in the 1880s that he began to receive his greatest acclaim, not only for his powerful voice, but also for his dramatic talents. By the time he stopped performing in 1902, he had developed a repertoire of sixty-four roles, most but not all of which were in Russian opera. He also knew composers like Musorgsky, Borodin and Rimsky-Korsakov, as well as other prominent musicians and critics, many of whom must have come to visit the singer at home. The young Igor Stravinsky thus grew up in an environment which was steeped in Russian music. Stasov and Dostoevsky also paid calls.[7]

Apart from his fine voice, Fyodor Stravinsky was famous for his extensive library of valuable books and scores (held to be one of the largest private collections in Russia), and for the painstaking way in which he researched his roles. All of this inevitably rubbed off on his son, who would have probably heard his father rehearse at home and who also had the benefit of being able to attend operatic performances at the Mariinsky on a regular basis from a young age. It is not surprising that the theatre became something of a second home for Stravinsky while he was growing up, as his family's apartment was situated right next door to it. The 1890s and early 1900s were the Mariinsky Theatre's golden years: operas by Russian composers had become its staple repertoire,[8] and there was now, for the first time, an impressive roster of performers, producers and set designers to stage them. Stravinsky was able to become closely acquainted with what are now the classic masterpieces of Tchaikovsky, Glinka, Borodin, Musorgsky and, of course, Rimsky-Korsakov. 'Sitting in the dark of the Mariinsky Theatre, I judged, saw, and heard everything at first hand', he later recalled, 'and my impressions were immediate and indelible'.[9] He would subsequently have a direct involvement with Rimsky-Korsakov's last operas.

Stravinsky's family came from the nobility, but it is important to recognise that this was a class that differed from its Western European counterpart by encompassing small-scale landowners without titles and (by the end of the nineteenth century) *haute-bourgeoisie* as well as Counts and Princesses. Only in Russia could one automatically join the nobility by being promoted to a certain position in the Table of Ranks (as happened with Dostoevsky's father). Stravinsky's social background was relatively privileged without being particularly aristocratic. While the young Nabokov was driven to school by a chauffeur from the family mansion, for example, Stravinsky walked across town from a rented apartment. His parents also rented their summer dachas; although the family was able to stay at the country estates of their relatives and were later affluent enough to travel abroad, they had no property of their own, however modest, to retreat to at the end of the season. It is also worth pointing out that pursuing a career on the stage as a singer in Russia had only begun to acquire social respectability at the end of the nineteenth century. Both Shaliapin and Ershov, two of Russia's other great pre-revolutionary male singers, were of lowly origins, and Fyodor Stravinsky had originally planned to join the Civil Service, following a training in law. It is indicative that he and his wife also wanted their son Igor to become a lawyer rather than a professional musician, and he studied law at St Petersburg University from 1901 to 1906. But as with Tchaikovsky, who half a century earlier had been destined for a career in the Ministry of Justice, the urge to write music proved ultimately too strong to resist.

Stravinsky had his first piano lessons in 1891, when he was nine years old. This was also the year in which he met his first cousin Ekaterina Nosenko, who was later to become his wife. Then, when he was a university student, he began to study music theory privately. Musically speaking, however, the pivotal year for Stravinsky was 1902, the date of his earliest surviving compositions. At university Stravinsky had become friends with Rimsky-Korsakov's son Vladimir, and through him met the composer while they were on holiday in Germany that summer. After Stravinsky's father died of cancer at the end of 1902 at the age of fifty-nine, Rimsky-Korsakov – just one year younger – became a kind of father figure to him. There was something of an inevitability to this development. Fyodor Stravinsky studiously recorded details of the cost of each of Igor's music lessons, along with every other family expense, and his son seems to have inherited his love of precision,[10] sending dutiful letters to his parents during summer vacations when they were apart.[11] Stravinsky did not, however, have a particularly affectionate relationship with his father (he was closer to his mother, though that relationship was difficult too), and neither of his parents encouraged his musical ambitions. Rimsky-Korsakov did not formally become Stravinsky's composition teacher until 1905, having persuaded him that enrolling at the Conservatoire, where Rimsky had now been teaching for thirty years, would at this point be counter-productive. In the meantime, however, Stravinsky started to receive informal tuition from him, and to attend the musical soirées at his apartment which became a weekly fixture from 1905 onwards.

Cultural life in St Petersburg by 1905 had undergone another sea-change since the time of Stravinsky's childhood. He was not exaggerating when he later remembered the city as a stimulating and exciting place in which to have grown up,[12] as his coming of age coincided with the birth of Russian Modernism – the movement to which he himself was to make such an enormous contribution. Alexander III's Russification policies had positive consequences for the fortunes of Russian opera in the 1880s, and the abolition of the Imperial Theatres' monopoly had led to the foundation of important new companies such as Savva Mamontov's Private Opera in 1885, and later the Moscow Arts Theatre, directed by Stanislavsky and Nemirovich-Danchenko. In general, however, the reign of Alexander III was one of the bleaker periods in Russian culture, typified more by repression and stagnation than by innovation and dynamism. The apathy and disillusionment of the period is captured well in the short stories of Chekhov, the very modesty of their form indicating the diminution of the intelligentsia's hopes and dreams following the era of the great reforms. The Russian musical scene also lacked dynamism and innovation. The main symphony concert series, which had been inaugurated by the Russian Musical Society in 1859, was now becoming increasingly reliant on the classical repertoire, for example, and was beginning to lack freshness. The wealthy art patron Mitrofan Belyayev promoted contemporary composers at the 'Russian Symphony Concerts' he founded in 1885, an enterprise of inestimable value in consolidating a national musical tradition that was now well and truly established, but Arensky, Lyadov, Glazunov and Rachmaninov hardly belonged to the avant garde. As Walsh has commented, the enterprise succeeded, ironically, in truly institutionalising Russian music,[13] which had hitherto prided itself on its anti-establishment stance. As a bastion of the musical establishment, and now the *éminence grise* of the St Petersburg Conservatoire where he had been professor since 1882, Rimsky-Korsakov certainly did not use his position as Belyayev's main adviser to change its orientation.

Everything was to change after the death of Alexander III in 1894, although his successor Nicholas II was hardly less reactionary. The cultural revival that was now instigated was prompted to a certain extent by a desire to escape from a depressing political reality that was clearly going to worsen and partly by the simple and inevitable need to strike out in a new direction. Music was in fact the last art form to be affected by the winds of change that now began to sweep through Russian cultural life, but ironically it was music which – through the agency of Stravinsky – was to contribute Russia's most significant contribution to the Modernist movement. Signs of the dawning of a new age in the arts came with the production of Tchaikovsky's operatic masterpiece *The Queen of Spades*, premiered in 1890 at the Mariinsky. A loyal subject of Alexander III, Tchaikovsky willingly conformed to the dictates of the Imperial Theatres, which commissioned the opera, and *The Queen of Spades* represents, in many ways, the apotheosis of the Russian 'imperial style'. It is also, however, a work whose hallucinatory subject-matter, nostalgic mood and stylistic pastiche align it with the preoccupations of the new generation of artists that emerged in the closing years of the nineteenth century. Their rebellion against old forms and their championing of the new were accompanied by an explosion of creative talent across all the arts on an unprecedented scale at the beginning of the twentieth century and is now rightly regarded as a kind of Russian 'Renaissance'. Stravinsky, of course, was at the epicentre of this movement, which saw Russian artists for the first time becoming leaders of the avant garde. Along with Kandinsky, Malevich and, to a lesser extent, Skryabin and perhaps Bely, he was one of the key Russian figures of the period who was destined to change the very language of art.

Russian Modernism began in the middle of the 1890s as a reaction against the relentless utilitarianism that had dominated all the arts in the preceding period in favour of aestheticism. Concern with ideology was jettisoned to be replaced by an interest in individual experience and beauty, which was expressed at first in small, lyrical forms rather than the grand canvases of the Realist period. The narrow Russian focus of much of what was produced earlier was exchanged for a new cosmopolitan outlook. There was also, in the aftermath of Nietzsche and the 'death of God', a liberation from the stifling Victorian mores of the 1880s and a cultivation of amorality and the occult. The earliest practitioners were a group of poets who called themselves Symbolists, but who were quickly labelled Decadents by their detractors. Led in Moscow by Valery Bryusov and Konstantin Bal'mont, they drew their inspiration from French writers such as Baudelaire and Verlaine. In St Petersburg the leader of the new movement was the writer Dmitry Merezhkovsky, who published an influential article in 1893 that pinned the blame for the general decline in literary quality at the time on the didacticism of the Populist age and called for culture to be revived through a concern with metaphysical idealism and spiritual experience.

The torchbearers for this artistic renewal were the eclectic young artists and sexually liberated aesthetes of the 'World of Art' group, also based in St Petersburg, who wished precisely to bring Russian culture out of the doldrums. Convinced that the quality of modern Russian art was now on a parity with that of Western Europe, their leader, Sergey Diaghilev, organised a series of international exhibitions beginning in 1898, which the ageing Stasov was quick to condemn as decadent. Diaghilev had anticipated this reaction. When soliciting work for his first exhibition, he had addressed the problem directly: 'Russian art at the moment is in a state of transition', he wrote to prospective exhibitors. 'History places any emerging trend in this position when the principles of the older generation clash and struggle with the newly developing demands of youth.'[14] Later in 1898, the group launched a lavishly illustrated and expensively produced journal under the title *The World of Art* which acted, amongst other things, as the first major platform for the Symbolists. Diaghilev, Benois and their colleagues had eclectic tastes also where music was concerned. They worshipped Tchaikovsky, but they were also the first non-musicians in Russia to champion Wagner in the pages of their journal, regarding him as a founder of the Modernist movement in Russia, as he had been elsewhere. As well as publishing articles on Wagner's artistic ideas and methods, Diaghilev began to review the first Russian stagings of his music dramas at the Mariinsky Theatre, and Benois was invited to design the first production of *Götterdämmerung*.

In the initial period, the members of the World of Art group focused mainly on the visual arts. At first, Diaghilev had attempted to forge a career in music, but after being discouraged by Rimsky-Korsakov when he showed him his compositions, and having been turned down as a member of the august Russian Music Society, whose dull concert programmes he had hoped to revitalise, he decided to focus in the immediate term on art. In the meantime, two other members of the group, Alfred Nurok and Walter Nouvel, took up the challenge of bringing music under the World of Art canopy by founding the 'Evenings of Contemporary Music' in 1901. The aim was to acquaint the St Petersburg public with new music, consciously espousing a more radical programme than the rival Chamber Music Society.[15] As Taruskin has pointed out, the music that was performed at the concerts was hardly the most outré, since the most popular composers were Franck, D'Indy and Reger, while the most avant-garde Russian composers represented were Vasilenko, Senilov, Rebikov and Catoire.[16] Other living Russian composers whose works were performed included Rachmaninov, Tcherepnin and Glazunov. The Moscow-based Skryabin, who had most in common with the aesthetics of the Symbolist movement, was largely ignored. It was nevertheless here that music by Ravel, Fauré and Strauss was first introduced to Russian audiences and composers, while Debussy, Schoenberg and Reger were invited personally to attend performances of their works. And it was here that Stravinsky's music was publicly performed for the first time, on 27 December 1907.[17]

The nineteen-year-old Stravinsky had, in fact, taken part in the very first concert of the Evenings of Contemporary Music, on 20 December 1901, according to a notice in a contemporary music journal,[18] and from then on he attended at least some of the concerts organised each season,[19] but his loyalties lay very much with Rimsky-Korsakov's circle after he was welcomed into its midst the following year. For this group, the Evenings of Contemporary Music represented the opposition. Rimsky-Korsakov attended their concerts when music by his pupils was performed, but he was in general hostile to the whole enterprise and its modernist and dilettante outlook, particularly since he had no direct involvement. Nurok did not, for his part, conceal his low regard for Rimsky-Korsakov's conventionality, the conservatism of the Belyayev concerts, and their already somewhat ossified aesthetic position.[20] A kind of half-way house was provided by the important new concert series founded by the conductor Aleksandr Ziloti in 1903, which premiered music by Strauss, Mahler and Schoenberg, amongst others. In 1909 Ziloti also conducted the first performances of Stravinsky's *Scherzo fantastique* and *Fireworks* at one of his concerts. Nevertheless, the contemporary music scene in St Petersburg in the early 1900s was certainly not as vibrant as, say, activities in literature at the time.

Just as Stravinsky was beginning his official tuition with Rimsky-Korsakov in 1905, his teacher began to host weekly musical soirées every Wednesday. These meetings provided an important forum for Stravinsky to meet other musicians, discuss ideas and hear informal performances of new compositions, including his own. In 1905 the ideas discussed were inevitably dominated by politics, as the year began with the infamous 'Bloody Sunday', when a peaceful demonstration by workers was greeted with gunfire and over a hundred people were killed. Stravinsky remained largely unaffected by the 1905 Revolution (this was also the year he became engaged to his cousin), but his teacher became directly caught up in the turbulent events. Amid public outcry, Rimsky-Korsakov was dismissed from his post for supporting Conservatoire students who had gone on strike to call for reform. Although musically he represented the forces of conservatism, Rimsky-Korsakov occupied a relatively left-wing position politically, and he was eventually successful in demanding autonomy for the Conservatoire administration. Despite the political factors, the atmosphere of the Rimsky-Korsakov 'Wednesdays' was still extremely tame by comparison with the infamous *jours-fixes* held across town on the same night by the Symbolist poet Vyacheslav Ivanov, which also started in 1905. These attracted a broad spectrum of St Petersburg's leading modernists (including Walter Nouvel and several other musicians), who would congregate at midnight in Ivanov's orotund top-floor apartment (known by all as 'The Tower') and sit up until dawn participating in learned discussions on mysticism, poetry readings and impromptu musical and theatrical performances. Stravinsky was only two years younger than one of the salon's most celebrated habitués, the poet Alexander Blok. Another of its regular attendants, however, was Sergey Gorodetsky, two years younger than Stravinsky and a poet who first came to public attention with a collection of poetry published in St Petersburg in 1907 entitled *Yar'*. Gorodetsky in some ways provides a point of intersection between the opposing worlds of Rimsky-Korsakov and the World of Art, with which Stravinsky became irrevocably associated in 1910. Stravinsky chose to set two of the poems from Gorodetsky's collection to music in 1907 and 1908, and it is these two songs for mezzo-soprano and piano (*Two Songs*, Op. 6) which first exhibit signs of the direction the composer would later follow. Rimsky-Korsakov instinctively recognised this embryonic gesture towards musical independence by condemning the first song, set to the poem 'Spring', as 'contemporary decadent-impressionist lyricism' which contained 'pseudo-folksy Russian lingo'.[21]

Gorodetsky later went on to become a decidedly conformist member of the Soviet literary establishment (in the 1920s, for example, he completed a new translation of the libretto of *Die Meistersinger*), but in 1907 he was part of an 'experimental spiritual and sexual collective' at the Tower,[22] and one of the more adventurous members of the avant-garde community in St Petersburg. His collection *Yar'* contains some of the first modernist poetry to be inspired both thematically and stylistically by Slavic mythology and folklore, as exemplified in the two poems chosen by Stravinsky, whose settings partially match Gorodetsky's achievement. As Taruskin points out, folklore in Russian music had traditionally been regarded as an intrinsic part of a work's content. To establish a musical style based on folklore was unprecedented, and 'to borrow artistic elements created by the people so as to create an art that was unintelligible to them seemed an implicit mockery'.[23] With these two Gorodetsky songs, Stravinsky unconsciously made his first tentative steps into the unknown. It was with the first of these songs that he made his public debut at the Evenings of Contemporary Music in December 1907.[24]

Until Rimsky-Korsakov's death in 1908, Stravinsky remained a relatively docile pupil who was not yet fully aware of the artistically sterile environment in which he was serving his musical apprenticeship. Apart from the time he spent in his teacher's apartment, he regularly accompanied him to opera performances at the Mariinsky and shared at that point his antipathy towards ballet. At the end of the following year, however, Stravinsky was already at work on the *Firebird*, his first ballet commission for Diaghilev. It soon became apparent that the sophisticated and cosmopolitan milieu which Diaghilev and his associates inhabited, mostly abroad in Paris, was a more natural Russian environment for Stravinsky. Like Diaghilev and the other key members of the World of Art group, Stravinsky identified strongly with the city he grew up in precisely because of its international and aristocratic character.[25] It is telling that Diaghilev had to cajole Rimsky-Korsakov into taking part in his 'historical concerts' in Paris.[26] Apart from the memories of some unfortunate concerts he had conducted there in 1889, Rimsky-Korsakov had no wish to associate himself with anything decadent, and had no desire to meet any of the latest French composers.[27] Stravinsky soon relished being part of the European avant garde, but he never relinquished his love for his native city. 'St Petersburg is so much a part of my life that I am almost afraid to look further into myself, lest I discover how much of me is still joined to it', he confessed in *Expositions and Developments*. 'It is dearer to my heart than any other city in the world'.[28] When considering Stravinsky's Russian origins it is significant that he grew up in imperial St Petersburg. Like Vladimir Nabokov, he never once visited Moscow when he was growing up, and first saw the city on his celebrated return to Russia in 1962. Old Slavonic Moscow had remained a quiet provincial backwater throughout the nineteenth century, and it was only at the end of the first decade of the twentieth century that it suddenly began to vie with St Petersburg as a centre of the Russian artistic avant garde. Stravinsky also adored his native city, of course, because of its physical beauty. As Mikhail Druskin has commented, there is a correlation between the 'bright, solemn, spacious' proportions of its neoclassical architecture and the economy and simplicity of the neoclassical style Stravinsky was later to adopt.[29]

By the beginning of the twentieth century, St Petersburg could match any other European capital for elegance and refinement. Its cultural life was greatly enriched by contact with Paris, Vienna and Berlin, cities to which there were fast train connections, and Russian society opened up still further following the 1905 Revolution, which led to an easing of censorship. The ascendancy at this time of the Mariinsky Theatre, which was beginning to hold its own with the world's leading opera houses, with appearances by singers and conductors from abroad and a superb native company, is emblematic. From 1906 onwards, Diaghilev began triumphantly to export Russia's cultural legacy to the West before striding boldly into history by commissioning the unknown Igor Stravinsky to write scores which drew from, transformed and transcended the Russian background he had been brought up in.

As Richard Taruskin has so amply demonstrated, it was only when Stravinsky came into contact with the World of Art circle that he first started to consider Russian folklore as source material for his music. A small but important role here was played by his friend Stepan Mitusov, who became the librettist of his first opera *The Nightingale*. Four years older than his friend, Mitusov was a well-read 'intelligent amateur', in the words of Stravinsky,[30] who followed the latest artistic trends in Europe with a keen eye. He was also a good friend of the Rimsky-Korsakov family: his own family lived in the same building and he had studied at the university with the composer's sons. Mitusov got to know Stravinsky when he was sent by Rimsky-Korsakov to study harmony and counterpoint with Vasily Kalafati. The two first met in 1898, but their friendship began properly in 1903, and the two met regularly at the Rimsky-Korsakov apartment. As an amateur enthusiast, Mitusov was not bound by the same loyalties as Stravinsky, and according to one Russian critic it was he who took Stravinsky clandestinely to attend Evenings of Contemporary Music concerts.[31] It was also at his apartment in 1904 that Stravinsky made the important acquaintance of the painter, archaeologist and writer Nikolai Rerikh (Roerich), who had been a friend of Mitusov since 1899.[32] Six years later Stravinsky and Rerikh began to collaborate in the creation of the epoch-making *The Rite of Spring*, first performed in 1913.

In *The Rite of Spring* Stravinsky presented Russian folk life with a greater authenticity than any other composer before him. It was the apotheosis of the neo-nationalist style cultivated by the artists and aesthetes of the World of Art group that so captivated Western audiences. Unlike the nostalgic and conservative aesthetic fostered by Alexander III, which had produced such backward-looking buildings as the Church of the Resurrection (a *faux* St Basil's which was completed in 1907), the neo-nationalism of the Russian avant garde was inspired by the desire to create something new. It had begun in the 1870s, as a desire to preserve native crafts in the face of encroaching capitalism and urbanisation, at the artists' colony set up at Abramtsevo, the estate of Savva Mamontov, a merchant who had made his millions building railways in Russia.[33] The first neo-nationalists, in fact, were artists linked to the Wanderers movement. Soon, however, particularly at the other important artists' colony set up by Princess Tenisheva in the 1890s at her estate in Talashkino, native folklore came to be seen more as a stylistic resource with which to regenerate art and infuse it with a vigour and energy that was commonly felt to have been lost.

Stravinsky was the first Russian composer to turn to folklore as a source for stylistic renewal and experimentation, but it was only some time after he began working with Diaghilev and the World of Art group in Paris that he started consciously exploiting its potential. In so doing he moved abruptly away from the 'academic' and 'de-nationalised' style of composition that characterised much of the Russian music written at that time. Ethnographic colour – as artistic content – had been the cornerstone of nationalist aesthetics of the 1870s, but by this time had come to be regarded as distinctly outmoded.[34] It was Diaghilev's genius to perceive that native style, made part of a modernist aesthetic, was an essential ingredient if Russia was to come into its own and contribute something new to world culture, and this was a vital factor in the creation of the Ballets Russes, in whose success Stravinsky was to become such a linchpin. And, after his first commission to write the score to *Firebird* in 1909, it inspired the development of a neo-nationalist orientation in Stravinsky's music that would later explode with *The Rite of Spring* and culminate in the composition of *Les Noces*, the representation of the Russian peasant wedding, where even the intricate oral rules followed by folk singers are scrupulously replicated.

For *Firebird*, Stravinsky wrote music to a scenario already planned by Fokine which fused several Russian fairy tales involving mythical firebirds. The resulting score was an assimilation of 'contemporary Russian idioms'[35] which was perceived as Russian-influenced in France and as French-influenced in Russia. It was almost the last composition Stravinsky wrote in Russia and was still quite conventional in its treatment of native folklore. *Petrushka*, Stravinsky's second ballet for Diaghilev, premiered in 1911, was a transitional work, and the composer had much more of a hand in its planning through his collaboration with Alexander Benois. Although Petrushka had part-Italian origins in Pulcinella (he became Punch in England), and in the ballet became a *commedia dell'arte* Pierrot figure, he was based on the Russian puppet-show character who was traditionally part of the time-honoured Shrovetide festivities. Stravinsky contributed to the creation of authenticity in the representation of the Shrovetide revelries by suggesting the introduction of traditional Russian mummers, even though his knowledge of them almost certainly came only from seeing his father perform in Serov's *The Power of the Fiend* at the Mariinsky Theatre when he was growing up. The opera features a Russian Shrovetide scene with mummers in its fourth act.[36]

It was with the score of *Petrushka* that Stravinsky found the way forward out of the musical *cul de sac* in which he had found himself as a protegé of Rimsky-Korsakov. It teems with borrowed urban and rural folksongs from a wide array of collections, and also – more significantly – the first examples of Stravinsky's deliberate adoption of folkloric style to create something entirely new and distinctive of his own. An important role here was played by musical ethnographers, in particular Yuly Melgunov and Evgeniya Lineva, who undertook to collect folksongs in a much more rigorous and authentic manner than had been the case before, by attempting to transcribe the complete performances of songs as performed by entire groups rather than by individuals.[37] Lineva's use of the phonograph in the three collections of transcriptions she published between 1904 and 1909 for the first time enabled the study of the musical form of Russian folksong, and revealed the depersonalised nature and simplicity of its performance. Her work, which followed on from Melgunov's pioneering methods in exploring the counterpoint of folksongs through their *podgoloski* (the harmonically variant reproductions of the main tune performed by the chorus), undoubtedly exerted a major influence on Stravinsky. The neo-nationalist approach that Stravinsky took in the composition of the score of *Petrushka* was unprecedented in Russian music, and was to lead to an abrupt and irrevocable break with the upholders of the Rimsky-Korsakov school, who henceforth viewed Stravinsky as an apostate. In a review of the score's Russian premiere in 1913, Rimsky-Korsakov's son Andrey condemned the work as 'deliberate and cultivated pseudo-nationalism'.[38]

In July 1911, after the successful premiere of *Petrushka* in Paris, Stravinsky resumed work on the score that would become *The Rite of Spring*, and travelled to Talashkino to work with Rerikh on its scenario. Rerikh, a close friend of Princess Tenisheva, was one of the artists associated with the World of Art movement, and had achieved international prominence when invited by Diaghilev to design the sets and costumes for the *Polovtsian Dances* (the second act of Borodin's *Prince Igor*), which were presented as part of the first Ballets Russes season in Paris in 1909.[39] In keeping with the interest amongst the Russian literary and artistic avant garde in pagan Russian culture which had, amongst other things, produced Gorodetsky's *Yar'* in 1907, Rerikh was fascinated by the ancient past of the Slavic peoples, and their rites and customs were the inspiration behind most of his painting and essays at this time. When Stravinsky had started planning *The Rite of Spring* in 1910, it was therefore natural for him to ask Rerikh to become his collaborator.[40]

In characteristic fashion, and out of an intense desire to dissociate himself from his Russian background and ally himself instead to the European avant garde, Stravinsky later denied the presence of authentic folk material in the score, but these scenes of pagan Russia, which celebrate the sacrifice of a young maiden, were from the beginning intended to be as ethnographically accurate as possible. Appropriate folksongs were assiduously researched in published collections (including the 1877 anthology compiled by his former teacher Rimsky-Korsakov), noted down from singers or gathered from friends like Stepan Mitusov and then absorbed into Stravinsky's compositional processes. What finally emerged was a musical texture whose sources are not immediately recognisable in the score.

Stravinsky's great innovation was thus to combine Russian elements from his musical upbringing with the essential stylistic features of native folklore, in order to approach nationalism from a modernist standpoint.[41] The result was the composition of scores whose structure is consistently based on the principles of *drobnost'* (the idea of a work being the sum of its parts rather than driven by an overarching idea), *nepodvizhnost'* (the accumulation of 'individualized static blocks in striking juxtapositions')[42] and *uproshcheniye* (the reduction of any organic development between the different sections of a work, producing an impression of immobility).[43] Stravinsky successfully broke with the linear progression and logical development of Germanic musical tradition by deliberately turning his back on it. He had, in the words of Artur Lur'ye (Arthur Lourié), stopped trying to pour Russian wine into German bottles, and cut his ties with Europe.[44] Russian composers had in fact traditionally balked at the concept of complying with German symphonic form, but the phenomenon has its counterpart in the other arts. A refusal to adhere to traditional 'Western' genres is, after all, a hallmark of Russian literature, which begins with Pushkin, author of a novel in verse. Tolstoy regarded Russian literature as being totally different from Western literature and after his crisis rejected traditional Western genres in favour of creating his own. Perhaps there is even a correlation with the quality of *nepodvizhnost'*, furthermore, in a novel like *War and Peace*, constructed by the accumulation of dozens of discrete short chapters in which the work's central ideas are often repeated. As 'verbal icons' of his religious view, as Richard Gustafson has so compellingly argued them to be,[45] the thematic structure of Tolstoy's literary works is often far from linear. The same is true of the works of Nikolai Gogol, especially his novel (which he called a 'poema') *Dead Souls*. It is interesting in this regard to recall the seminal ideas of the theologian and art historian Pavel Florensky about the 'reverse perspective' of icons, which Mikhail Druskin brings into his discussion of Stravinsky's treatment of time and space.[46] Druskin draws an analogy between the structure of Stravinsky's works and the simultaneous multidimensionality of Cubism. In identifying the replacement of a linear process of development in his music with the 'mutual relating of different planes and volumes, the single vanishing point by a multiplicity of "horizon-levels", unicentral, object-centred composition by multicentral',[47] Druskin also demonstrates a fundamental similarity with the system of reverse perspective that is a cornerstone of the icon-painting tradition in Russia. Boris Uspensky defines it thus:

> the system of reverse perspective arises from the viewer's (i.e. the artist's) adopting a number of different positions. That is to say, it is connected with the dynamic of the viewer's gaze and the consequent total impression obtained . . . the opposition between linear and reverse perspective can be connected with either the immobility, or on the other hand, with the dynamism of the viewer's position.[48]

Florensky observed that reverse perspective is 'multi-central', in contrast to 'linear' perspective, which is 'unicentral'.[49] Surely much fruitful enquiry could be conducted into the impact of folkloric style on Russian art and literature coterminous with or preceding Stravinsky's most 'Russian' works. Similarly, a more detailed exploration of the impact of such cardinal aesthetic principles as reverse perspective on Stravinsky's works, perhaps in the context of Russian literature, might further help to define what is intrinsically Russian about them.

The sense of Russia as being fundamentally 'different', neither European nor Asian, fuelled Stravinsky's creation of a new musical language, and it also underpins the ideology of the Eurasian movement to which the composer was close in the early 1920s. It was a movement that arose out of the acute sense of loss felt by the first generation of Russian emigrants. The basic idea of Eurasianism was that Russia had erred by following a process of Westernisation with Peter the Great's reforms. World War I and the 1917 Revolution were the inevitable consequences of the 'identity crisis' that naturally followed as soon as Russia had started on a path that was alien to her destiny. But, in typical Slavophile fashion, the Eurasianists believed Russia had a unique mission to rescue the degraded and corrupt West, because of its 'healthy barbarism'.[50] Russian Orthodoxy lay at the heart of Eurasianism, and the final element of Stravinsky's Russian origins that must be considered is his religious orientation. Stravinsky was baptised into the Russian Orthodox faith, but like most members of the Russian intelligentsia did not have a particularly devout upbringing. It was only when he was in emigration in the 1920s that he turned back to his mother church. In a famous letter written to Diaghilev in April 1926, Stravinsky claimed not to have fasted for twenty years but that he now felt a 'mental and spiritual need' to do so.[51] He had lived next to the Russian Orthodox church in Biarritz in the early 1920s, and started dating his compositions according to the festivals in the Orthodox church calendar.[52] He started to wear a crucifix and collect icons. Stravinsky's friendship with the Eurasian Pyotr Suvchinsky (Pierre Souvtchinsky) reinforced his new religiosity, which was accompanied by regular attendance at mass and regular fasting. As Walsh has argued, there was a strong linguistic reason for Stravinsky's reconversion to the Orthodox Church, which first resulted musically in a setting of the Lord's Prayer in 1926. Stravinsky maintained that Russian had always been the language of prayer for him,[53] but more generally it was increasingly the strongest link he had with the country he could no longer visit – that is to say, the Russia of his pre-revolutionary St Petersburg. In a newspaper interview during his visit to the Soviet Union in 1962, he perhaps unwittingly revealed how deep his Russian origins lay by drawing an important connection between the language in which he thought and spoke and the language in which he expressed himself in his music.[54]

2 Stravinsky as modernist

CHRISTOPHER BUTLER

One way of characterising the modernist period might be to say that it was the age of Picasso, Stravinsky and Joyce: geniuses who brought about revolutionary changes in the procedures for their arts and publicised them from Paris, so contributing to the myth that it was the avant-garde capital of Europe at that time. Other capitals were home to great geniuses as well – Kandinsky, Schoenberg, Mann – people who, while quite different from Stravinsky, were also very influential modernists and were well out of his cultural range. Indeed, to understand them, we would be moved towards modernist considerations to which Stravinsky was deeply antipathetic. His 'rivalry' with Schoenberg (whether it was actual or invented by defenders of the atonal, such as Adorno) is not nearly so important as his intellectual differences from him, including his refusal to write the kind of music that 'develops', as it does within the German tradition. But it is the modernist tradition in France – that of Debussy, Proust and Matisse – which influenced at least the early Stravinsky. This was a world that grew out of the Symbolist tendencies so strongly supported by Diaghilev and his circle in Russia[1] and one that produced works such as *Fireworks*, *Zvezdolikiy*, *The Firebird* and, most obviously, *The Faun and the Shepherdess*, influenced as it was by Debussy, Ravel and Dukas.

It is this belonging to a particular tradition which is most important for understanding Stravinsky as a modernist: as we shall see, there were plenty of inspiring modernist ideas, and Stravinsky was highly resistant to many of them (to the potential of the unconscious and the irrational, for example). Stravinsky, very like T. S. Eliot, was immensely conscious of the past, and exceptionally well placed to be aware of contemporary avant-garde activity in all the arts, but he nevertheless selected a very conservative tradition in which to work. He is a conservative innovator. This seems paradoxical only if you think, wrongly, that a socially critical, leftist avant garde is central to modernism, and forget the contribution of conservative modernists such as Pound, Eliot and Lewis in England, and Valéry, Cocteau and Claudel in France.

These differences do not seem to have mattered much to Stravinsky, whose commitments (to a sense of Russia, to orthodox religion) lay well outside the worldly politics that sometimes gripped friends of his, such as Picasso. In any case, his composing life, as it most dramatically came into contact with the public, was formed in the context of a hardly radical or critical institution, the Diaghilev ballet. Those critics of modernism who use 'bourgeois' as a term of criticism or disapprobation should see the dandified and obsessively money-conscious Stravinsky as a prime target.

There is a well-known drawing of Stravinsky by Picasso, made in May 1920, which depicts him in the style of Ingres.[2] The composer of *The Rite of Spring* is shown here in anything but a primitivist or avant-gardist mode. He looks like the conformist that he is. But Picasso has chosen the right mode in which to portray him. For both artists changed their styles in the 1920s, after revolutionising the languages for their arts before the War with their most radically avant-garde works. They moved on, from the invention of Cubism (on the part of Picasso and Braque) and the startling rhythmic complexities and violence of *The Rite of Spring*, to a new, neoclassical style. Quite apart from their everyday friendship and co-operation (on *Pulcinella*, for example), it is this willingness to change styles which unites them. This stylistic metamorphosis after radical beginnings is the sign of the extraordinary fashionability of modernism after the war, and signifies for many observers the compromise of artistic by social values.

Stravinsky was perpetually sensitive, in many ways, and not just as a man of the theatre, to the demands of patrons and of audiences. He was always inclined to communicate his position, his intentions, and his nationalist and religious commitments to an audience, and with some clarity, whether in the concert hall, the lecture theatre (through Roland-Manuel) or in conversation (through the person of Robert Craft). His very lucidity, even if occasionally borrowed from others, is a great disguiser of any internal conflict. He is at the opposite pole from the Expressionist artists of his time, such as Kandinsky and Schoenberg.

Like Picasso and Joyce, he is a great shape changer and, like them, he uses Greek mythology as one of his central justificatory escapes from orthodox religion to public drama. After *The Rite*, the solitary, isolated, self-imposed attempt to revolutionise the very language of music from within was not for him. Indeed, it took him a long time to show any sympathy for such aims as they manifested themselves in Schoenberg and, more discreetly, in Webern, who no doubt seemed to be far less Expressionist in his aims, and in his 'language less heavily founded in the most turgid and graceless Brahms'.[3] Schoenberg's (self) portrait, with its great red glare of the visionary in the eyes, is the kind of act of self-exposure that Stravinsky would have found inexcusable. And, so far as I know, he never shows much sympathy for Expressionist art, despite the violence of *The Rite*, and perhaps comes near to it only in thinking of Chagall as a possible designer for a revival of *Les Noces* and in his early reactions to *Pierrot lunaire*. He is not, to that extent, a dedicated avant-garde artist.

By upbringing, training and perhaps inclination a man of the theatre, Stravinsky was what we would call a dedicated networker, whose talents once he came to Paris were immediately recognised in the triumph of *The Firebird*. He then plays through *The Rite* on the piano with Debussy; his close friends include the musicians Ravel, Satie, Schmitt and de Falla, the writers Cocteau, Gide, Claudel and Valéry,[4] the painters Picasso, Léger and Derain. And they work with or for him: hence, for example, Picasso's design for the cover of *Ragtime* comes about through the mediation of Cendrars for the Éditions de la Sirène. His many conversations with Craft, which until the recent publications of Taruskin and Walsh have very much controlled the image that Stravinsky wanted to project of himself, are often anecdotal memories of closely knit groups of his friends.[5] And with fame, the metropolitan, modernist, cultural village of Paris was opened to him (offering opportunities undreamt of in the feuding and provincial St Petersburg). Some of these opportunities were rather unlikely ones, such as when Blaise Cendrars asked him to write music for a proposed film about Quixote directed by Abel Gance, and when in 1922 Picabia wanted him to set his play *Les Yeux chauds*.[6] But Stravinsky generally avoided any connection with movements like Futurism (while being amused by it) and Surrealism. This modernist metropolitanism meant that Stravinsky, as an already well-read and sophisticated artist, continued to be closely and discriminatingly aware (at least by his later account) of French developments in all the major arts.[7]

A close attention to the visual arts was one of the advantages of working for Diaghilev, and Stravinsky co-operated with some of the greatest artists of his time in staging his works, from the designs of Golovine and the Bakst costumes for *Firebird* and the Benois décor and costumes for *Petrushka*, to the Matisse designs for *The Nightingale* (which he did not like).[8] Benois describes Stravinsky as being deeply interested in painting, architecture and sculpture. But the stage designs with which he was most familiar were rarely avant-garde, and his co-operation with writers such as Cocteau and Gide also kept clear of real avant-garde aesthetic considerations (despite Cocteau's impresario-like activities) and has an air of compromise. He never set avant-garde poetry, for example, in contrast to a composer such as Poulenc. His most advanced text is probably that for *Les Noces*, which he compares to the work of Joyce: he tells us that it is 'a suite of typical wedding episodes told through quotations of typical talk ... As a collection of clichés and quotations of typical wedding sayings it might be compared to one of those scenes in *Ulysses* in which the reader seems to be overhearing scraps of conversation without the connecting thread of discourse.'[9] He was well aware of the politics of some of the advanced writing of his time. But then it is typical of modernist artists that they often worked within quite closely knit groups, as did the circles round Picasso and Braque, Gertrude Stein in her Paris apartment, Virginia Woolf in Bloomsbury, and Pound and Lewis in London at the time of the Vorticist movement. On the other hand, Stravinsky never belonged to a modernist movement such as Imagism or Dada or Surrealism, or Schoenberg's Society for Private Musical Performances; and in his neoclassical period he did not need to ally himself to Les Six. On the other hand, the Ballets Russes as a whole should be seen as a modernist group, even if it is less obviously experimental than, say, Futurist theatre groups.[10]

And, of course, Stravinsky was making a living. Students of modernism have recently become (rather too disapprovingly) interested in its economic underpinnings;[11] and it is important for our understanding of Stravinsky that he had to make a transition from a considerable dependence upon a famous, aristocratic, extravagant and very well-advertised, if not always solvent, institution, which attracted extraordinary patronage (Diaghilev, for example, playing off Misia Sert and Coco Chanel), towards another source of patronage. He finally found this, like so many others, in the United States, a country described by Auden as 'so large, / So friendly, and so rich'.[12]

Thanks to Diaghilev and his extraordinary talent for bringing together a unified 'team' right across the arts, Stravinsky became, with *The Firebird*, 'a major figure in the world of music overnight'.[13] To achieve this, it is necessary to work in an artistic mode that thrives on publicity. That is exactly what Stravinsky had. As a man of the theatre and later of the concert hall, he developed a career that could always be based upon the pragmatic needs of a particular audience in a particular place, and on giving pleasure. (The situation was very different for Schoenberg and his followers.)

His early music had characteristics, well adapted to the theatre, that – much modified – were to be sustained after his recognition as a major composer; that is to say, he had an extraordinary stylistic adaptability. Of course, *The Firebird* and *Petrushka* are unique; but they show an extraordinary eclecticism in their influences. This is, perhaps, what you would expect in a ballet and opera tradition that embraced the work of Borodin, Tchaikovsky, Rimsky-Korsakov and (even) Glazunov. Stravinsky developed his language by working through such influences and metamorphosing them (Picasso-like) within masterpieces, but he only really begins to come within the modernist rather than the symbolist paradigm in the (to me, doubtful) early montage techniques of *Petrushka*. Here, folk influences combine with the popular mixture of high and low art (in his inclusion of Viennese and popular urban tunes) which is so typical of later modernism. We are close to the world of Toulouse-Lautrec, Seurat, Satie, Debussy, early Picasso and others. As Glenn Watkins puts it, 'Stravinsky's techniques in *Petrushka* differ from Satie's only in detail; both imply vernacular and pseudo-vernacular sources projected by overlap and intercut, and both embrace a nostalgia without tears'.[14]

Stravinsky's career as a composer of expensive-to-produce ballets as well as of concert music has to be understood, then, as driven by the need for a popular adaptability, for serious patronage and for large fees, as well as by independent aesthetic considerations (hence, for example, the piano concerto that he wrote for himself to play in exclusivity for five years). But it is nevertheless difficult to show in other than banal cultural materialist terms exactly when or how such monetary considerations affected his aesthetic decisions, for he was a composer whose inner artistic convictions were to prove to be very far from worldly, even as he maintained a way of life and an outer appearance that were entirely fashionable and, indeed, dandified. Stravinsky's relationship with money requires quite a deep psychological explanation, which is offered without Freudian oversimplification by Walsh.[15]

Stravinsky as revolutionary?

The rich Parisian network sketched above (which could be paralleled elsewhere, though with less *éclat*) ensured that you could be a modernist by association (in the way that figures such as Cocteau, Anna de Noailles, Gleizes and Metzinger, Auric and Tailleferre were). These 'fashionable' modernists could promote and adapt styles invented by others.

Stravinsky is a genuine revolutionary (much as he disliked the idea), but only up to a point. That is what makes him like Picasso, Schoenberg, Apollinaire and Joyce, who also moved through the extraordinarily successful adaptation of available late-nineteenth-century or symbolist modes (such as Picasso's post-Impressionist and Blue Period paintings, Schoenberg's *Pelleas und Melisande*, Apollinaire's more symbolist poems, and Joyce's Chekhovian *Dubliners*), to the production of a startlingly innovatory work, which revealed completely new possibilities for the basic techniques of their art. Picasso did this with the *Demoiselles d'Avignon* (1907), Joyce with the opening pages of *A Portrait of the Artist as a Young Man* (1914), Schoenberg with the last movement of his Second String Quartet (1908), and Stravinsky with *The Rite of Spring* (1913).

He thus came through to the prototypically modernist avant-garde 'scandal' of *The Rite*, which was in its way as unpredictable as the other examples cited above (though Stravinsky's implausible 'I was the vessel through which *Le Sacre* passed' has all the marks of a fashionable, anachronistic, post-Surrealist explanation which transfers the impulse for innovation into the unconscious or the dreaming faculty). Nor was *The Rite* really scandalous, despite the noisy manifestations at its first performance, which were vital side-taking publicity of a kind that has done yeoman service for many more or less 'avant-garde' works. This kind of row was what Futurists counted on; but shocking your rivals, the bourgeoisie, or the merely ignorant, does not get you very far. For success and later influence, you need to impress an artistically informed intelligentsia, and that is exactly what the Ballets Russes, and *The Rite of Spring* – which was very soon widely performed as a concert work – could do.

It was soon applauded and accepted everywhere, and it had to be, precisely because it presented something new, which, however much it might have been detested by conservatives, would have seemed to any well-informed consumer of contemporary art to demand precisely the same kind of attention as the other works that were even then seen as part of the artistic avant garde. This is for precisely the same reasons as apply to Picasso, Joyce and Schoenberg; for the *Rite* was like nothing else in 1913. It would be clear that something had changed irrevocably, and a newly available technique would become apparent (as it was to Eliot, in proclaiming a new post-Einsteinian 'mythical method' for literature after reading Joyce, which he adapted for 'Gerontion' and *The Waste Land*). Stravinsky had taken apart the very basics of the language of the art involved, as is most obvious in the still extraordinary treatment of rhythm in the *Rite*. In it, dissonance for once does not rob music of movement. The need for harmonic movement is overridden.

> Where a chord is so dissonant that the ear cannot sense a possible resolution, the music stands still. Stravinsky's achievement, and it was unprecedented, was to give a crucial structural importance to rhythm instead of harmony, and to use the tension of dissonance to fuel this powerful engine still further.[16]

This development in the *Rite* was as radical as the taking apart of perspectival relationships in Cubist painting, and the disruption of logical ordering and 'normal' syntax in the newly disjunctive writing of such as Apollinaire, Marinetti and other Futurists, Joyce and Eliot, whose 'The Love Song of J. Alfred Prufrock' (written 1909, published 1915/17), was the work by which Pound in 1914 recognised that Eliot had 'modernised himself all on his own' – just as Stravinsky had. But it is important to note that Stravinsky later emphasised that his work was not so much revolutionary, as an extension of the past.

> in music advance is only in the sense of developing the instruments of the language – we are able to do new things in rhythm, in sound, in structure, we claim greater concentration in certain ways and therefore contend that we have evolved, in this one sense, progressively. But a step in this evolution does not cancel the one before.[17]

There is, of course, more to be said about *The Rite*; but the internal, technical nature of Stravinsky's 'revolution' needs to be emphasised – finely adapted though it may have been to an orgiastic ritual in the theatre – with yet another erotically engaging sacrifice of the female, to succeed those in *Salome, Elektra* and Schmitt's *Tragédie de Salomé*. For Stravinsky was not one of those artists and intellectuals who, in being affected by the widespread late-nineteenth-century propaganda against past lies in favour of the 'Modern', were encouraged (by Nietzsche among others) to see themselves as *critics*, and so divorced from and marginal to the society in which they lived. It is not clear that Stravinsky as a good, landowning bourgeois with an extraordinary loyalty to a large dependent family, however cranky or useless or reactionary (not surprising given their position after 1917), would have had much time for that modernist strain that runs from Flaubert through Ibsen and Freud, which lays bare bourgeois self-deceptions. (There are no significant references to Freud that I can find in any of Stravinsky's extant writings or conversations. An amazing omission.)

In *The Rite*, Stravinsky is not trying to say something radically new and challenging about sex or women or the social order; it was always intended to be a viscerally exciting work, with all the attendant sensationalism involved in its post-Polovtsian (if more clumsily choreographed) group uproar round the human sacrifice of an attractive young girl. But he might well have been aware of the strong relationship between Roerich's treatment of the scenario and fashionable modernist ideas of myth, primitivism and tribal art, and so *The Rite* is one of the key works for the modernist interest in the 'primitive'.[18] It comes after the *Demoiselles*, and it is the contemporary of Lawrence's *The Rainbow*, with its lyrical appraisal of the sexual appeal of an African statue; its thirteen pictures or stations, plus two preludes, enact, not for the last time in Stravinsky's work, a public ritual of a kind which, many were coming to think in this period, must be the primitive basis and origin of drama as a genre.

This radically new language is not really exploited by Stravinsky to the same extent in later works: the nearest he comes to it is in the *Three Pieces for String Quartet* of 1914, although again the second movement looks back to the turn of the century, in that it is inspired by the movements of the clown Little Tich. Even here there is a connection to the world of Toulouse-Lautrec and Debussy. Not a few attempts have been made to see these *Three Pieces* (and other works of Stravinsky) as somehow related to other movements in the arts of the time – the obvious radical innovation being that of Cubism. So Watkins sees the first of the *Three Pieces for String Quartet* as 'a virtual demonstration piece, a *reductio* of Cubist premises'.[19] But this is a typical example of the attempt to make what are no more than analogies, between ambiguous referentiality in painting and its apparent counterpart in music, and music without text does not even attempt to refer to particulars in the real world. Similarly analogical is the claim that this music superimposes three essential layers, which are allowed to be independent (like the conflicting points of view in a Cubist painting) through 'different phraseological lengths, variable periodicity, and independent tonal orientation . . . until they locate a logical terminating point'.[20] Stravinsky certainly knew about some versions of Cubism, in the work of Goncharova, Laryonov, Malevich, Picasso and others. But the Russian artists associated with Diaghilev did not have any 'shared commitment to the premises of Cubo-Futurism' in anything but a very selective sense.[21]

The argument for the Cubist character of any of Stravinsky's work thus depends upon some pretty loose analogies – we can see, for example, that Cubism and *The Rite* and 'Prufrock' are all disruptive of previously acceptable single types of ordering, as in narrative; that they juxtapose rather than put in logical order; and that they (perhaps) also contest the idea of a single ordered viewpoint on the world, though how a piece of music can express that without text is difficult to explain (the analogy between a conflict of keys and a conflict of 'viewpoints' is popular). Watkins is nevertheless surely right to say that the 'conscious movement towards simultaneous non-alliance in matters of harmony, rhythm, phraseology and cadence appears as an increasingly observable fact of musical life' in Schoenberg, Stravinsky, Ives, Debussy and Ravel.[22] For him and for many others, this is like the 'relativity' of time and space in Cubism, where we have conflicting points of view of the same object, which are 'simultaneous', at least in the sense that they are to be seen together on the same two-dimensional surface). This lack of a background narrative order (for which the most obvious musical analogy is harmonic progression) is most obvious in the *Symphonies of Wind Instruments*, which certainly comes closest to a collage-like juxtaposition of its musical sections.

Stravinsky as traditionalist

After *The Rite*, Stravinsky quickly developed into another kind of modernist, typical of the post-war period, in which there was a change from the pre-war avant-garde formal experiments (which established the techniques of atonality, Cubism and the juxtapository stream of consciousness) to an adaptation of modernist technique to the production of a whole variety of socially acceptable, indeed fashionable, styles. Picasso, for example, was much berated by John Berger for giving in to this socialisation,[23] and we can see in the work of such figures as Dufy, Derain and the Delaunays a kind of 'jazz modern' style whereby modernism became acceptable to the luxury consumer. The trajectory of the Diaghilev ballet after *Les Noces* – in producing work like *Les Biches*, *Le Train bleu* and *Les Matelots* – can be seen in the same light. Modernist techniques were superimposed, in an allusively sophisticated kind of way, to quite obvious and often popular subject-matter: as, for example, in much of the work of Stravinsky's friend Cocteau, who was a talented modernist imitator and trivialiser (his addition of a little trail of 'cubes' to his sketch of Stravinsky playing *The Rite* on the piano shows the extreme adaptability of 'modernist' styles of representation to the popular caricature or cartoon). Goncharova's backcloth for the 1926 revival of *The Firebird* is similarly well adapted, to look like an easily legible Klee cityscape, with some Slavonic onion domes thrown in. The Diaghilevian theatre as spectacle thus democratised, popularised and synthesised a number of available modernist styles.

The most obvious example of Stravinsky's own mixture of styles and rapprochement between high and low in art is perhaps his *Ragtime*. It is a descendant of Debussy's 'Golliwogg's Cake-Walk'; and jazz themes recur in Stravinsky through to the *Ebony Concerto* of 1945. This adaptation of a popular music which was easily to be heard in Paris in this period,[24] is also to be found in works by Poulenc, Milhaud and others. Given the extraordinary celebrity of Josephine Baker and her colleagues in the famous *Revue nègre*, Stravinsky might well have thought that he was producing an amusing essay on a different kind of 'primitivism', that of the 'negro'. Stravinsky thought he had 'the idea of creating a composite portrait of this new dance music' in a concert piece, as other composers had done for the waltz,[25] and his phrase reveals the way in which his music can be thought of as a parallel to the juxtapository construction of collage in much contemporary painting. This putting bits of things together into 'constructions' (rather than developing them, by harmonic progression or by extended narrative) is typical of the arts of the twenties. For Adorno this is an 'infantile phase' of Stravinsky's composition. In the *Piano-Rag-Music*, 'anxiety before dehumanisation is recast into the joys of revealing such dehumanisation, and, in the final analysis, into the pleasures of that same death wish whose symbolism was prepared by the much hated *Tristan*'. It is a '*danse macabre*' round the 'fetish character' of consumer goods.[26] This ludicrous judgement is a fine example of the incongruities that arise if you try to ensnare Stravinsky – and his putative intentions and subconscious motivations – in a mixture of Freud and Marx.

Ragtime, *The Soldier's Tale*, *Pulcinella* and *Mavra* reflect the stylistic pluralism, and the interest in the popular arts, that existed in the 1920s. Stravinsky is very like Picasso in the same period, who moved from the pre-war primitivism of the *Demoiselles* and the 'analytic' or 'hermetic' cubist style, through collage towards (by 1915) a far more accessible 'synthetic' mode, full of Harlequins and clowns, and then beyond that, to an Ingres-like reproductive classicism (just as in *Pulcinella*), which can be seen in his portrait of Stravinsky – and in his portraits of Diaghilev ballerinas, one of whom (Olga Kokhlova) he married.

Stravinsky's surprising contribution to this regressive Harlequinade (once more to meet the theatrical demands of Diaghilev) was the (re)composition of *Pulcinella* from work originally attributed to Pergolesi, with costume designs by Picasso. It was classical, clear, not at all Russian, and French rather than Germanic, and so came perilously close to the mere pastiche of other ballets of the period, which were also spiced-up arrangements of previous music, such as Respighi–Rossini's *La boutique fantasque* and Tommasini–Scarlatti's *The Good-Humoured Ladies*. Constant Lambert (himself not above the popular style) hated this development:

> a composer with no creative urge and no sense of style can take medieval
> words, set them in the style of Bellini, add 20th century harmony,
> develop both in the sequential and formal manner of the 18th century,
> and finally score the whole thing for jazz band . . . These scrapbook
> ballets were of course only a more grandiose and theatrical presentation
> of the scrapbook taste which is considered so modern and 'amusing'
> when applied to interior decoration.

Lambert saw the Stravinsky of *Pulcinella* as 'like a child delighted with a book of eighteenth-century engravings, yet not so impressed that it has any twinges of conscience about reddening the noses, or adding moustaches and beards in thick black pencil'. The result, for Lambert, is 'a complete confusion between the expressive and the formal content of the eighteenth-century style . . . like a savage standing in delighted awe before those two symbols of an alien civilisation, the top hat and the *pot de chambre*, [Stravinsky] is apt to confuse their functions'.[27]

These later critical reactions did not of course prevent *Pulcinella* from being of immense importance for a change in Stravinsky's aesthetic – the point at which he thought he had taken on a quite new kind of motivating idea – for he called it his 'discovery of the past, the epiphany through which the whole of [his] late work became possible'.[28] What saves *Pulcinella* from being mere pastiche and puts it into the mainstream of Stravinsky's modernist works is an astringency, an irony and detachment which are already characteristic of his works from *Petrushka* on, and which extends itself into all the stylistic parodies of this period. As Walsh puts it:

> In 1917 it would still have been possible to look at Stravinsky's work and
> grade it as, on the one hand, the 'real' Stravinsky of the *Pribaoutki* and
> the Russian ballets, and on the other the casual derivative Stravinsky of
> the easy pieces. In 1918 it no longer makes sense to separate these styles;
> they have all become part of the essential artist, the mixing up of tonal
> and modal allusions every bit as much as the jostling of modern popular
> dances, archetypal marches and folk ditties . . . The ironic effect of these
> colliding planes, so different from the calm objectivity of *The Wedding*, is

directly associated with the work's moralising tendency. As we listen to the 'Chorale' in the *Soldier's Tale*, it is hard to resist that sense of superior knowledge carefully avoided in *The Wedding*, which comes from the parodying of a solemn observance.[29]

This detachment and humour is a formal and emotional characteristic which is shared by modernists in other arts, notably in the tradition through Laforgue and Apollinaire to Eliot, who in 1920 temporarily abandoned free verse for neoclassically strict quatrains in adapting Gautier.

Stravinsky is at his most witty and charming, and his most obviously neoclassical, in the Octet. He uses a visual analogy for this work: 'My Octet is a musical object. This object has a form and that form is influenced by the musical matter with which it is composed. The differences of matter determine the difference of form. One does not do the same with marble that one does with stone.'[30] In this and later works one can hear Bach given the inflections of jazz, Handelian slow introductions, toccata-like passages and so on. All this has the self-conscious, academic, reactionary (but not in this case as in so many others in France, nationalist) sense of the wish to go back to a better order for inspiration. Stravinsky in this period becomes more and more like T. S. Eliot, as a classicist and then as a Christian. Both men 'reconverted' in 1926, partly for reasons that are consistent with their (declared) conservative aesthetic.[31] And Stravinsky, in writing music that is extremely allusive, was also preoccupied with the thought that even when a composer follows earlier forms and is anti-Expressionist and anti-Romantic, he can still have, as Eliot put it, 'a personality to express': 'In borrowing a form already established and consecrated, the creative artist is not in the least restricting the manifestations of his personality. On the contrary, it is more detached and stands out better, when it moves within the limits of a convention.'[32]

It thus came about that the idea of a European canon was tied to a general modernist technique of allusion, and of an interrelationship between pictures, texts and music which was central to the thinking of many modernists. When Eliot tells us, in his famous essay on 'Tradition and the individual talent', that 'we shall often find that not only the best, but the most individual parts of [a poet's] work may be those in which the dead poets, his ancestors, assert their immortality most vigorously',[33] he could be speaking for Stravinsky, Picasso, Joyce, Schoenberg and many others. In the post-war period, this aesthetic meant for Stravinsky a joining of a European tradition (and to some extent, the temporary exclusion or suppression of Russian influences). As his immensely cultivated and allusive later conversations show, he would rather have prided himself on this newly extended 'historical sense' as prescribed by Eliot, which involves

a perception, not only of the pastness of the past, but of its presence; the
historical sense compels a man to write not merely with his own
generation in his bones, but with a feeling that the whole of the
literature of Europe from Homer and within it the whole of the literature
of his own country has a simultaneous existence and composes a
simultaneous order. This historical sense, which is a sense of the timeless
as well as of the temporal and of the timeless and the temporal together,
is what makes a writer traditional.[34]

This does not mean succumbing to any 'influence', a word which can too
often give a false impression of passivity. It is really a matter of paradigm
adaptation, and that is exactly what neoclassicism involved, in music and in
painting.

Eliot (much influenced by current conservative French thought) asserted
in his rather later 'The function of criticism' (1923) that classicists 'believe
that men can not get on without giving allegiance to something outside
themselves'. This kind of doctrine was immensely influential in Europe after
the war, though it was prepared for by writers like T. E. Hulme well before it:

Here is the root of all romanticism: that man the individual is an infinite
reservoir of possibilities; and if you can so rearrange society by the
destruction of oppressive order then these possibilities will have a
chance and you will get Progress.
   One can define the classical quite clearly as the exact opposite to this.
Man is an extraordinarily fixed and limited animal whose nature is
absolutely constant. It is only by tradition and organisation that
anything decent can be got out of him.[35]

This something outside (easily compatible, too, with the Christian view of
'original sin') could also secure a kind of impersonality in art, and was for
many modernists in England and France a peculiar mixture of inherited
myth and orthodox religion, both conceived as belonging to the society
represented in the work of art. Stravinsky is no exception here. He creates
rituals in his works which seem to take place quite independently of his
own subjective position; indeed, he uses alienation effects (such as the pianos on stage in *Les Noces* and the narrator in *Oedipus Rex*) to secure this
detachment. He took pride in the fact that the former work is 'perfectly homogeneous, perfectly impersonal, and perfectly mechanical'.[36] The peasant
band of earlier versions has given way to something far more traditional and
abstracted. This aim at a basic archetype, rather than at nineteenth-century
local detail and sentiment, is typically modernist. (It can also express nostalgia for a lost communitarian unity, and this, for Stravinsky, was only to
be reconstructed, at some cost, in Orthodox religion.)

After *Les Noces* this sense of permanence was to be found in the revival of Greek myth in detached, Apollonian modernist modes. Like Joyce,

Stravinsky prefers the myth of timeless repetition, basic human beliefs, and some none too forcefully expressed, rather purified emotions in these later ballets. (Thus *The Fairy's Kiss* hardly rises to the full Tchaikovskian passion, though *Apollon musagète* brilliantly implies it.)

Oedipus Rex fits into a French modernist tradition of its own. (For example, Milhaud had provided music for Claudel to *Agamemnon* (1913–14), *Les Choephores* (1915) and the *Eumenides* (1917–22).) *Oedipus* completes one trilogy, with *The Rite* and *Les Noces*, and leads towards another, from *Apollon musagète* through *Orpheus* to *Agon*. Its use of formulae from Handel oratorios, crowd scenes from the Bach Passions and so on is as suppressed as are its echoes of Verdi. It is a curiously creaky work, in which the narrator's explanations are peculiarly condescending, the use of Latin no doubt *très catholique* (old style, another 'universal authority') – but all the same a huge barrier to comprehension (though its meaning in English is often bathetic) – and the orchestration odd (one can sympathise at times with Schoenberg's thought in 1928 that it is 'a Stravinsky imitation by Krenek').[37] Stravinsky's literary discrimination failed him here, as it was later to do with Gide, but he had admired Cocteau's *Antigone* and so asked him to do the libretto for *Oedipus*, which was then put into Latin by Jean Daniélou. It is a work which, partly because of its allusions to other works, parades its own restraint. Stravinsky makes a rather teasing general remark about his ideals in this respect in his *Poetics of Music*:

> What is important for the lucid ordering of the work – for its crystallisation – is that all the Dionysian elements which set the imagination of the artist in motion and make the life-sap rise must be properly subjugated before they intoxicate us, and must finally be made to submit to the law; Apollo demands it.[38]

This third sacrifice is at the opposite extreme to that of the *Rite*, and it leads on to similar restraints in *Apollon musagète*, the *Symphony of Psalms* and *Perséphone*.

Stravinsky and Picasso and many others, in all the arts and in all the main capitals of modernism, thus became traditionalist, conservative modernists, and turned away from the experiments of Cubism and Futurism and early Expressionism to neoclassicism. Paul Dermé and Pierre Reverdy indicate some of the considerations that were involved, the former claiming that 'a period of exuberance and force must be followed by a period of organisation, stocktaking, and science, that's to say a classicist age',[39] and the latter that 'the moment came [in 1916] when one could talk about aesthetics . . . because the period was concerned with organisation, with the mustering of ideas, because *fantasy gave way* to a greater need for structure'.[40] This post-1918 reappraisal of the artist's relationship to the past opened up a new aesthetic – of allusion, of relativistic contrast between cultures, and of the combination of their values – in an attempt to reconcile the apparent chaos of the modern world to a classical order; hence the kind of historical reconstruction we find in Joyce's *Ulysses*, which is at once a compendium of eighteen available experimental styles, and (for Eliot and others) an attempt to bring order through myth to 'the immense panorama of futility and anarchy which is contemporary history'.[41] This was, of course, only one tendency within modernism in general. It is clear from the fortunes of Dada after the war and Surrealism from at least 1922 on that the attempt to transform consciousness through various forms of Expressionism and the anarchism of fantasy was not going to go away. Picasso was soon drawn into these movements; Stravinsky kept well clear.

There are many conflicting causal explanations for this shift away from what could be seen as a dominant Cubist aesthetic. Kenneth E. Silver, for example, depends on the idea that the reaction against effects of the war included a turn towards a conservative defensive nationalism, which expressed itself in the adaptation of earlier styles.[42] He says of Picasso, for example, that he turned to neoclassicism to escape criticism of his non-participation in the war, and so distanced himself from Cubism and aligned himself with values associated with the Mediterranean tradition. But this fails to notice his continued Cubism during the war, notably in the *Seated Man* of 1916; his exhibition of the *Demoiselles* in 1916; and most particularly his Cubist costumes for *Parade* in 1917, let alone the animated Cubism of his work for *Le tricorne* in 1919. Convincing though Silver's view may be for many French artists, it hardly applies to the fast-becoming-French but expatriate figure of Stravinsky, whose move towards classicism of all kinds must, I think, be explained in terms of a religious conservatism.

Other, more severe, leftist critics see these changes as a failure of nerve, as we move from revolutionary Cubism to pastiche to neoclassicism as the 'counterfeit Other' of the truly modern. Hence, also, Adorno's attack on Stravinsky for retaining tonality in a mutilated form, in contrast to Schoenberg's heroic pioneering of the twelve-note technique. For Marxist critics like Rosalind Krauss,[43] Stravinsky's music and Picasso's neoclassical work are equally 'fake', a 'borrowed music of the pastiche'. This makes it difficult to rationalise Schoenberg's reliance upon classical models as well in this period. And, although the contrast between linguistic radicalism and stylistic accommodation may well be a valid one, it takes some very odd assumptions about art, and distorted views of the historical development of modernism, to see the latter as a betrayal of the former, particularly when one considers the major works (including Schoenberg's own) that attempt a synthesis of the two. Stravinsky and Picasso both compromised, much to the benefit of the enjoyability and intelligibility of their work. For some others who took the same route – Chirico, Severini, Derain – the same could not be said.

Nevertheless, for some interpreters of modernism the invention of new ('bourgeois-free') systems of meaning is of the essence, and any retreat from that is a betrayal of what they see as 'the modernist project': *the* modernist project, as if there could be one, except as prescribed by them. Liberal pluralists tend to retort that there can and should be no such thing as 'the' modernist movement or 'the' inner (progressive) tendency of an epoch. One can give the impression that there is such a tendency only if one also takes on a good deal of implausible Hegelian Marxist baggage.[44] Claims to have discovered, or attempts to defend, a 'central' or essential tradition in modernism are no more than politickings *with* modernism, and have very little to do with the making of an empirically well-founded historical analysis of its very various manifestations. In the cases of Stravinsky and Picasso, we have two modernist geniuses who expressed themselves by taking more than one approach to art. And their changes of style were just as provocative to those who thought that there should be a modernist orthodoxy in the 1920s as they are to those who hanker after the same kinds of doctrinal certainty today.

A third phase?

As Stephen Walsh points out, much of Stravinsky's work in America was consolidatory.[45] After the Second World War, Stravinsky addresses the legacy of the past in two ways: both involve consolidation. In *The Rake's Progress* he summarises the neoclassical method in a moralising masterpiece, and then (for whatever reason to do with the presence or absence of Schoenberg, and/or of Robert Craft) he goes back to look at another stylistic path not followed, into serialism, by yet again constructing his own – Webernian, medievalising, scrupulously clear – tradition in which to work. As he does so, he finds that he can use the once new twelve-note language of the 1920s in a way that manages to be extraordinarily conservative, and to offer no consolation whatsoever to the progressivist camp, who had always so much disapproved of him.

His position as a modernist, by the time he came to write *The Rake*, was an equivocal one, as was that of his collaborator. Both had left far more radical experimental works behind them, such as Auden's *Orators* (1932). Though they hardly knew one another to begin with, they had both returned to orthodox religious belief under the pressure of politics, and both had an equivocally accepting and critical relationship to the American culture in which they were honoured and often well-remunerated guests. What could they say, in 1948, in the wiser, post-war phases of both their careers? It had been their fate as modernist classicists to become classics themselves. They both could play with tradition, make some comment on modernism, look for a final internal *rappel à l'ordre* and try to make some kind of moral statement – of a more or less disguisedly theological kind – by putting the Devil into Hogarth, and making his Rake a Don Giovanni, as we can see in the graveyard scene and in the moralising limericks of the final quintet. Stravinsky here follows Mozart, after using Bach for *Dumbarton Oaks* and other works, and even Beethoven in his Symphony in C.

Agon makes a Greek trilogy with *Apollon musagète* and *Orpheus*, as Balanchine wished. It makes an appraisal of the history of music, tonal and atonal, and dancing, side by side. Like *Ulysses* (and like *Wozzeck*), it is a kind of encyclopaedia: twelve-note series and diatonic scalic patterns, ostinato, Baroque dance types, canon, ritornello are all here. The 'plot' is no more than a game or contest – there is no story, and the dancers' rehearsal costume emphasises the different disciplines of its parts, which are required for a competition before the gods. It moves from one style to another as its technique changes towards serialism. (It is rather like the comparative narrative ease and realism of *Ulysses*' opening episodes, whose elements are then combinatorially disrupted in the later ones.) In Lincoln Kirstein's original proposal, suggesting that Stravinsky look at the *Apologie de la danse* by de Lauze (1623), he asks for a competition of 'historic dances' before the gods, in which 'the dances which began quite simply in the sixteenth century took fire in the twentieth and exploded'.[46] Watkins cites Luciano Berio as seeing *Agon* as 'a "short history of music" that performs a lucid, but tragic autopsy on itself under the pretext of a game'.[47] All this – the lack of a controlling narrative, the game-like construction and the self-conscious self-referentiality, the assembly of a 'funhouse' of available techniques – could be thought to be quite postmodern.

Agon makes a wonderful contribution to the canon of abstract ballet by adapting neoclassical disciplines within a serialist environment.[48] Stravinsky likes the economy of Schoenberg's method, although he allows repetition and uses rows shorter than the prescribed twelve notes, but he likes even more the economy of Webern's sound world, which fits with his earlier compositional methods. Eliot similarly uses the abstract, musically derived structures of *Four Quartets* to make his own combinatorial *art poétique*. Even as Stravinsky is, so to speak, working from inside, in one modernist tradition of utopian formalism (following a language alone into its combinatorial possibilities), he is also, like Schoenberg and Berg, looking to classical forms to hold the whole thing together – not Brahms but French ballet music, which also emancipates him into the rhythmic drive and interest that so often eluded the second Viennese school.

Stravinsky, then, is three types of modernist. Firstly, he is an avant-garde scandal-maker who produces an initially unintelligible discordant master-piece which provokes all sorts of outraged reactions, is immediately recognised for its originality and its contemporaneity, exerts a huge influence, and now sounds positively tuneful. Secondly, he is a fashionable style-changer who can also be austerely traditionalist, in the sense defined by a key figure such as T. S. Eliot. He is a composer who can transform any style in all sorts of ways, from minor melodic and harmonic modification (as he did for Pergolesi) to imitation (in *Apollon musagète* and *The Fairy's Kiss*) to total transfiguration by moving from one musical language to another (to serialism in *Agon*). This makes for a level of allusion and deviation that allies him to many other literary modernists, and to many painters, notably Picasso, who paraphrased works from the past. Thirdly, he is possibly a be-lated progressive, influenced perhaps by the new sound world of composers such as Boulez, who takes on serialism after the death of Schoenberg.

Adorno was right – at least about Stravinsky's social conformity, if that can be thought of as something which is not just disablingly 'bourgeois', but a pragmatic response to the disciplines of the ballet or the ritual demands of religion. It is these external demands which made it impossible for Stravinsky to follow the excessively self-centred methodical obsessions of so many of his rivals. He could not see himself as an avant gardist devoted to the 'new language' approach and to 'progress'. If we put aside the political premises upon which Adorno and his allies base their arguments, we can see that there are *two* traditions within modernism here, of a kind that liberals (rather than Marxists) would be inclined to tolerate, indeed encourage, for producing their own dialectic. One centres on a 'progressive' avant garde, where 'progressive' is understood to have some of the Hegelian Marxist overtones of an historical progress towards social emancipation, whose true nature can be revealed to the initiated in philosophy or theory or the relevant technical language. Artists in this tradition are like those utopian philoso-phers who want to clean up ordinary language, making it more logical, more 'scientific'. Other artists see the different languages of art as inherently so-cial, as Wittgensteinian language games, and even as competing discourses of power related to particular institutions. For this group, innovation will have a great deal to do with the untidy historical development of all those institutions and their rivalries and co-operations. Who would have thought, looking at the secularist emancipatory aims of so many in the modernist avant garde of the 1890s, that so many undoubtedly innovatory modernists would have turned out to be Christians or fascists? Like Stravinsky, they looked to something bigger outside themselves, whereas artists in the other tradition are far more inclined (and most particularly since the advent of postmodernism) to obey the theoretical imperatives of the critical guardians of avant-garde orthodoxy. Their results are often brilliantly innovatory. But Stravinsky was never one of these. And so he has very little to teach post-modernists that they want to hear.

3 Stravinsky in context

ARNOLD WHITTALL

Stravinsky as context

The eloquent conclusion of Richard Taruskin's monumental study of *Stravinsky and the Russian Traditions* has quickly become the most widely quoted, generally accepted declaration of Stravinsky's significance for twentieth-century compositional practice:

> To the extent that terms like *stasis, discontinuity, block juxtaposition, moment* or *structural simplification* can be applied to modern music – a very great extent – and to the extent that Stravinsky is acknowledged as a source or an inspiration for the traits and traditions they signify – an even greater extent – the force of his example bequeathed a *russkiy slog* [Russian manner] to the whole world of twentieth-century concert music. To that world Stravinsky was not related by any 'angle.' He was the very stem.[1]

Taruskin's purpose is to assert that once, in *Petrushka*, 'Stravinsky at last became Stravinsky'[2] by transforming his own defining Russian context, he could be seen as 'one of music's great centripetal forces, the crystallizer and definer of an age', whose 'work possessed a strength of style, and his oeuvre a unity, that could accommodate an endless variety of surfaces'.[3] It is a powerful argument, and its appeal might even have been strengthened by Taruskin's subsequent emphasis on the deplorable morality of Stravinsky's sympathy for fascism and anti-semitism – a general lack of democratic fervour that allegedly infiltrates even the exuberant rituals and ultimate sublimity of *Les Noces*.[4] Just as a warts-and-all Wagner can be deemed even more fundamentally central to the cultural life of the nineteenth century if the canker at the heart of the later music dramas is conceded,[5] so an 'all-too-human' Stravinsky (to complement that modernist Stravinsky who 'stressed the ritual at the expense of the picturesque'[6]) has a redoubled claim to provide the ultimate frame of reference for all that matters most in the music of the modern age. Yet is it really credible that any one composer should merit such lofty pre-eminence? Is it not in the nature of twentieth-century music that it has many different stems?

The need to complement the Stravinskian *russkiy slog* with other stimuli, other traditions, when seeking to account for the richness and variety of twentieth-century music, is acknowledged by many commentators. For example, Jonathan Cross concludes that 'it is important to remind ourselves that Stravinsky and modernism are not synonymous – it is, at the very least, inappropriate to view the entire century through Stravinsky-tinted spectacles'.[7] But not only are Stravinsky and modernism not synonymous. It cannot be the case that the purely formal factors to which Taruskin refers in his grand peroration represent the whole Stravinsky. Taruskin's emphasis on features of structural design seems to imply that the expressive, trans-national consequences of such procedures are relatively unimportant when it comes to defining Stravinsky's musical identity, the source of his greatness and influence. Yet, as the later stages of this essay will argue, it is difficult to consider such aspects of Stravinsky's creative world as his relation to long-established genres like lament and tragedy, or his concern with the aesthetic polarities symbolised by Apollo and Dionysus, in ways that give a *russkiy slog* any kind of unchallenged priority.

A very different 'stem' for essential aspects of twentieth-century modernism is celebrated by Schoenberg in his essay 'National music' (1931). Here the emphasis is on continuity with past masters of art music, something utterly different from that 'whole, bizarre notion of inventing a new, hyper-modern style out of the fragmented elements of an antique folk music' which Stephen Walsh attributes to Stravinsky at the time of *Renard* (1915–16).[8] The 'teachers' celebrated by Schoenberg were Bach, Mozart, Beethoven, Schubert, Brahms, Wagner, Mahler, Strauss and Reger. 'My originality comes from this: I immediately imitated everything I saw that was good.' But, cru-cially, imitation promoted transformation: 'If I saw something I did not leave it at that; I acquired it, in order to possess it; I worked on it and ex-tended it, and it led me to something new.' And Schoenberg ended the essay with an eloquent plea for recognition as a progressive legitimised by his sensitive and creative relation to the past. 'I am convinced that eventually people will recognize how immediately this "something new" is linked to the loftiest models that have been granted us. I venture to credit myself with having written truly new music which, being based on tradition, is destined to become tradition.'[9]

The tendency to regard the two distinct traditions – the Russian and the Austro-German – as enforcing a polarisation between Stravinsky and Schoenberg has played a significant role in twentieth-century musical historiography.[10] But the main point of this essay is that – at least after 1918 – the two traditions promoted shared aesthetic attitudes to modernism. To put it another way, the importance of Stravinsky within the 'whole world' of twentieth-century composition is enhanced when we not only consider him in relation to Russian traditions – central though those undoubtedly were, especially in the earlier years – but acknowledge Viennese, Austro-German traditions as well, and the ways in which these also explore the fundamental modernist continuum between extremes of connection and disconnection. (That further off-shoots from the central tree of modernism appear later in the twentieth century is not directly relevant to the discussion that follows.)

Conversations and comparisons

It is tempting to conclude that Stravinsky sought to divert attention from the predispositions, especially with respect to compositional genres, which he shared with modernists from other musical traditions, by the apparent clarity and openness of his comments on those predispositions. Some sense of his awareness of ways in which German and Russian polarities might converge can therefore be read into his treatment of aesthetic topics at a time when neoclassicism was making the subject of associations between old and new a very immediate one.

The possible relevance to Stravinsky of Nietzsche's ideas about the conflict between Apollonian discipline and Dionysian anarchism – first mentioned in his ghosted *Autobiography*[11] – can be downplayed if those ideas are regarded merely as a means of reinforcing proto-modernist precepts (especially about structural discontinuity and textural stratification) which Stravinsky inherited from the Russian past. Nor does the mere mention of Nietzsche as the source of the Apollo/Dionysus metaphor justify any claim that Stravinsky's music begins to display explicitly Germanic expressive qualities as a result. There would always be a stylistic gulf between Stravinsky's Russian way of ritualising exotic, symmetrical modality by passing it through those 'fragmented elements of an antique folk music',[12] and the Germanic impulse to intensify, at times to expressionistic extents, the increasingly chromatic tendencies embodied in that Bach-to-Reger tradition to which Schoenberg referred. What is intriguing, when comparisons between Stravinsky and his German contemporaries are attempted, is the very allusiveness and ambiguity of relations between their different approaches to parallel generic, expressive contexts: yet, as we shall see, there are technical similarities, as well as stylistic disparities, in the way these composers deal with archetypal emotional states such as loss and regret.

In the *Poetics of Music* lectures (1939), Stravinsky was content with the lofty assertion that Schoenberg was 'a composer evolving along lines essentially different from mine, both aesthetically and technically'.[13] More considered comparisons between himself and his Austro-German contemporaries had to wait until those later years when the role of oracle or sage (as opposed to active antagonist or collaborator) came more naturally. But the Stravinsky–Craft enterprise, offering the composer the chance to 'comment on the popular notion of Schoenberg and Stravinsky as thesis and antithesis',[14] was little more than a disingenuous premise to set up the idea that 'the parallelisms are more interesting'.[15] After tabulating a series of thirteen alleged 'differences' between himself and Schoenberg (including such evidently absurd over-simplifications as 'Stravinsky: diatonicism / Schoenberg: chromaticism'), *Dialogues* focuses on the 'more interesting' parallelisms. These include 'the common belief in Divine Authority', 'the common exile to the same alien culture, in which we wrote some of our best works', and the point that 'both of us are devoted to The Word'. It is difficult to see how any of these parallels, not least those indicating Stravinsky's belief that his attitude to serial composition owed more to Schoenberg than to Webern, are anything more than a mischievous attempt to reinforce the 'arbitrary' thesis/antithesis notion they are apparently meant to undermine. Such uneasiness could well have its origins in Stravinsky's irritation with the kind of arguments about convergence with Schoenberg promoted by critics as early as 1914. In a review of that year, N. Y. Myaskovsky declared:

> the foundations of his harmony apparently have much in common with the harmonic thinking of Arnold Schoenberg. The latter, of course, is a German, is far more intricate, the texture of his work is considerably more complex and refined, but on the other hand Stravinsky has the edge in his powerful blaze of temperament. One circumstance deriving from this parallel is absorbing: travelling different paths – Schoenberg from Wagner, touching Mahler in passing; Stravinsky from Rimsky Korsakov and Scriabin by way of the French – the two have come nevertheless by almost identical results.[16]

Having quoted these comments, Taruskin cannot resist a footnote observing that 'justification (or condemnation) of Stravinsky's music by superficial comparison with Schoenberg's has been a persistent strand in twentieth-century critical and analytical thinking',[17] a pretext for repeating his hostility to Allen Forte's account of the atonal components of *The Rite of Spring*.[18] The possible existence of 'superficial' comparisons of Stravinsky and Schoenberg does not automatically justify the rejection of all comparisons – especially less superficial ones. Even so, it is only after 1918 that the varieties of convergence between Stravinsky and his Austro-German contemporaries considered here become salient.

Taruskin would probably claim that Pierre Boulez's views are no more adequate than Forte's. Boulez discusses the sense in which, though Stravinsky and Schoenberg had very different attitudes to tradition, 'the result is the same: both composers reinstate dead forms, and because they are so obsessed with them they allow them to transform their musical ideas until they too are dead. Their musical invention has been virtually reshaped by old forms to the point where it suffers and dries up.'[19] For Boulez, as for Taruskin, it is matters of form which are decisive, and – for Boulez, at least – there can be no possibility of worthwhile musical expression being built on such flawed foundations. (It is worth noting the sediment of a Cageian experimental aesthetic in Boulez's draconian polarisation of forces in musical history. For Cage, no less than for Boulez, neoclassicism was a betrayal of the progressive impulse, not the fulfilment of something fundamental to modernist aesthetics.[20])

For Boulez, there is no doubt that, after such early masterworks as *Erwartung* and *The Rite of Spring*, both Schoenberg and Stravinsky allowed consciousness of History to inhibit the continuation of true progressiveness. Boulez could find no validity in a neoclassical modernism that played off old against new, despite his willingness to concede that, in Berg's case, 'a sense of continuous development with an enormous degree of ambiguity'[21] is to be admired rather than deprecated. Boulez asserts that 'Stravinsky also largely deprived himself of the resources provided by the evolution of the musical language, and he therefore found himself on a more primitive plane of invention with virtually no access, more importantly, to the formal complexities characteristic of the late-romantic period.'[22] This inability to discover any ambiguity, any complexity, in Stravinsky's music after the *Symphonies of Wind Instruments* (at least until the serial years), and therefore to find any relevance for such works as context for post-war 'new music', tells us more about Boulez's own creative hang-ups than Stravinsky's. But it also demonstrates the incompleteness of concepts of modernity which deal solely with matters of form: as if, in the case of *Symphonies of Wind Instruments*, its significance were wholly coextensive with its anticipations of Stockhausen's 'Momentform'.[23]

It can certainly be argued that, in his suppression of Dionysian, expressionist qualities in his more Apollonian neoclassical works of the 1920s and 1930s, Stravinsky was at his most distant from the Schoenbergian mainstream, in which the two complementary qualities – Apollonian order with regard to form, Dionysian intensity with regard to expression – strove to achieve a sustainable equilibrium. Schoenberg's avoidance of the explicitly chant-like or chorale-like materials often used by Stravinsky was a vital element in his preservation of an expressionist dimension during the inter-war decades, and Apollonian serenity is extremely rare. Perhaps Schoenberg comes closest to its spirit in 'Verbundenheit', the sixth of the *Pieces for Male Chorus*, Op. 35, composed in 1929,[24] just at the time of Stravinsky's own most wholehearted 'sacrifice to Apollo'.[25] Even when such obvious differences of emphasis are acknowledged, however, it is important to realise that very different expressive qualities can be embodied in similar compositional techniques and textures, and it is through such technical similarities that a degree of shared expressive atmosphere between Stravinsky and his contemporaries can be sensed.

A modern *espressivo*

Given Stravinsky's fabled capacity for appropriating elements of other composers' principles and procedures, it is always instructive to analyse his expressions of lack of empathy. None is more understandable – or relevant to my present argument – than this:

> If I were able to penetrate the barrier of style (Berg's radically alien emotional climate) I suspect he would appear to me as the most gifted constructor of form of the composers of this century. He transcends even his own most overt modelling. In fact, he is the only one to have achieved large-scale development-type forms without a suggestion of 'neo-classic' dissimulation. His legacy contains very little on which to build, however. He is at the end of a development (and form and style are not such independent growths that we can pretend to use the one and discard the other) whereas Webern, the Sphinx, has bequeathed a whole foundation, as well as a contemporary sensibility and style.[26]

The fact that so much music composed since 1960 refutes Stravinsky's sweeping claim that Berg's legacy 'contains very little on which to build' is powerful evidence for the partial nature of Stravinsky's own importance to music since his death. The 'otherness' of Berg clearly struck deeply, and in another comment Stravinsky was more specific about his personal resistance. He singled out the 'direct expression of the composer's own feelings' in the 'orchestral flagellation' of *Wozzeck*'s 'D minor' Interlude, declaring that 'what disturbs me about this great masterpiece and one that I love, is the level of its appeal to "ignorant" audiences'. In one of his most artfully revealing comments on his own expressive ideals, Stravinsky continued as follows: 'Passionate emotion' can be conveyed by very different means than these, and within the most 'limiting conventions'. The Timurid miniaturists, for example, were forbidden to portray facial expression. In one moving scene, from the life of an early Zoroastrian king, the

> artist shows a group of totally blank faces. The dramatic tension is in the way the ladies of the court are shown eavesdropping, and in the slightly discordant gesture of one of the principal figures. In another of these miniatures, two lovers confront each other with stony looks, but the man unconsciously touches his finger to his lips, and this packs the picture with, for me, as much passion as the *crescendo molto* of *Wozzeck*.[27]

As I have argued elsewhere, Stravinsky could hardly have been expected, in the 1960s, to recognise that the alternative modernity of Berg (compounded of constructivism and expressionism) might provide a no less valid legacy than his own devotion to 'the most limiting conventions'.[28] Others had similar problems of perception, and the fact that Boulez (for one) advanced from reservations about Berg, which parallel Stravinsky's, to an acceptance of Berg's importance as an authentically modern voice provides further support for the view that Stravinsky's would be one legacy among several within a late-century context of pluralities and polarities. At the same time, however, this contextualising of Stravinsky invites consideration of the degree to which his own music undermines assumptions about its incompatibility with Austro-German modernism. To this extent, the composer was perfectly correct in suggesting to Craft that the similarities ('parallelisms') between himself and Schoenberg were 'more interesting' than those 'thesis/antithesis' oppositions.

From polarity to convergence

In addition to reminding us that 'Stravinsky and modernism are not synonymous', Jonathan Cross notes the dangers of proposing an 'opposition between the non-developmental, non-narrative objectivity of Stravinsky and the subjective, Expressionist continuity with the Romantic tradition in Schoenberg'.[29] But no less problematic is any implication that Stravinsky himself, after 1914, lost all contact with subjectivity, continuity and other remnants of traditions very different from those with which his later style was most directly concerned. It is not the case that, after *The Rite of Spring*, Apollo entirely eliminates Dionysus, or that (neo)classicism promotes synthesis at the expense of continuing, unresolved dialectic. Rather, the Stravinskian context – the ways in which his compositional style evolved over more than half a century between *Petrushka* and *Requiem Canticles* – intersects with those of other composers, and is not absolutely, inherently different. The reasons for this circumstance are complex, and much to do with that pervasive aesthetic polarity between divergence and convergence in relation to tonal, harmonic centres which is outlined in the *Poetics of Music*.[30] Although *Poetics* appears to confine the relevance of polarity to the realm of purely musical 'language', its role is no less salient when matters of form and genre are brought into play.

It has long been a commonplace of twentieth-century music histories to note that the pre-1914, avant-garde formal initiatives of such compositions as Schoenberg's *Erwartung* and Webern's sets of orchestral pieces, Op. 6

and Op. 10, were not followed up with significant determination until the appearance of a new avant garde after 1945. But it is one thing to note the extent to which, between 1918 and 1945, Stravinsky, Bartók, Hindemith, Schoenberg, Berg and others dedicated themselves to preserving the formal attributes of traditional genres – symphony, concerto, string quartet and so on – leaving it to Webern and Varèse to carry more radical attitudes forward; it is something else to demonstrate that these 'conservative' attitudes had lost all contact with the progressive modernism that preceded them. They had not. Not only do Stravinsky's various vocal and instrumental works – even those called symphony or concerto – 'remake the past' in ways that help to define their inherent modernity; they allude to past modes of expression (and with as much pleasure as anxiety) in ways that reinforce their generic links with tradition, at the same time as they proclaim, stylistically, their distance from tradition.

Broken chords and lyric tragedy

While an essentially 'linguistic' study of this phenomenon in Stravinsky could focus on such continuity-establishing factors as the presence of broken chords or outlined triads – comparing the ending of *Petrushka* with the Postlude from *Requiem Canticles*, for example – a generic traversal of the same ground will highlight the composer's resourceful exploitation of allusions to dance and song, and to contrasts between dynamic and lyric *topoi*.

Stravinsky believed that melody was 'the summit of the hierarchy of elements that make up music',[31] and the Stravinskian melodic style never abandoned that element of formality which remained his greatest defence against the fierce explosiveness of Germanic Expressionism. Stravinskian lyric expressiveness is never more formal, or more deeply felt, than in the context of lament. Nevertheless, it is when sorrow and regret are presented in ways that distance them from the formalised ceremonies of the liturgy that 'order' – which, Walsh declares, was 'the watchword in his life and in his music'[32] – is most forcefully challenged.

No composition is more crucial in demonstrating the range of Stravinskian lyricism than *Oedipus Rex*, and Walsh's commentary on the opera-oratorio suggests what some of the useful terms for a comparison with other dramas might be: he writes, for example, of the work's opening as 'a gesture of panic and despair', and of its final stages that 'the atmosphere is one of terror and theatrically real catastrophe, not the commemorative or prophylactic disaster of the Stations of the Cross or the Burial Service'.[33] As Walsh demonstrates, such features are not inconsistent with the use of chant-derived thematic material, not least because at the opening of

Oedipus such material can be felt to establish a further allusion, to Verdi. But the emotional language of Walsh's interpretation – 'the numbed anguish of the plague-ridden Theban people', 'the image of Oedipus's moral blindness could hardly be more poignant',[34] coupled with references to the composer's achievement of 'a more disturbing irony', and to the 'dramatically telling picture of self-assurance gradually undermined by the Truth'[35] – offers ample evidence of the vital respects in which this work invites interpretation and understanding in terms no less relevant to music dramas whose style and aesthetic context could not be more different. Most striking of all is Walsh's discussion of the first scene of Act 2, with Jocasta's aria brilliantly conveying 'the richness and complexity of the drama of great souls brought low by human frailty', and of 'the fear and even panic', the 'sense of suppressed violence', of Jocasta's duet with Oedipus.[36]

If all this does little more than underline the sense of Dionysian forces at work in what is often categorised as a stylised and statuesque ritual, it serves its purpose. The nearest Stravinsky comes in *Oedipus* to the luminously restrained, Apollonian lyricism he employs in several subsequent works is the famous moment of the King's acknowledgement of the terrible truth, 'Lux facta est', with its descending B minor arpeggio. Walsh neatly touches on the sense of multiple meaning – ambiguity, enrichment? – at this moment,[37] and this is an important nuance, since the 'sacrifice to Apollo' which can be found in *Oedipus*'s immediate successor, the ballet *Apollon musagète*, does not involve replacing tension and divergence, with resolution and convergence along the lines of the kind of simplistic tabulation employed in *Dialogues*. Rather, the tensions and divergences are less Dionysian, less assertive, less disruptive. It was the ending of *Apollon*, not that of *Oedipus*, which was provocatively described by the composer many years later as the nearest he ever came to the truly tragic:

> if a truly tragic note is sounded anywhere in my music, that note is in *Apollo*. Apollo's birth is tragic, I think, and the Apotheosis is every bit as tragic as Phèdre's line when she learns of the love of Hippolyte and Aricie – 'Tous les jours se levaient clairs et sereins pour eux' – though, of course, Racine and myself were both absolutely heartless people, and cold, cold.[38]

Tragic or not, that ending certainly reshapes those very ambiguities – between D major and B minor – which embody the terrible enlightening truth in the opera-oratorio. The ending of *Apollon musagète* will be discussed in more detail later on. For the moment, it is enough to observe that these passages in *Oedipus* and *Apollon* both indicate the degree to which certainty, tinged with sorrow, summons up a musical expression in which celebration and lamentation co-exist.

Those comments from *Dialogues* suggest above all that, for Stravinsky, 'tragic' implies a state of unknowing innocence, a peculiarly human kind of vulnerability in which hope and optimism, both destined to be confounded, are at their most pure. If this is so, then I would be encouraged to reinforce my own reading of a tragic dimension in the otherwise barbaric 'Sacrificial dance' of *The Rite*, a reading scorned by Taruskin as missing the main point of this musical celebration of the 'subhuman'.[39] I would also see this aspect as evidence of the way in which Stravinsky's still very Russian music can be aligned with wider aesthetic as well as formal concepts in the still-evolving vortex of musical modernism. By the time we get to *Oedipus* and *Apollon musagète*, of course, the modernist context is very different from what it had been in 1912, and to compare the ending of *Oedipus* with that of *Wozzeck* – the most powerful near-contemporary Austro-German demonstration of the tragic vulnerability of innocent optimism – is certainly not to discover startling evidence of absolute stylistic or formal convergence. The parallelism is in the shared generic allusion, and the reliance of both composers on the particular emotional impact of ostinato. Seekers after similarity might also be struck by the role of G as a concluding centre for both *Wozzeck* and *Oedipus*, although Berg's post-tonal stratification is very different from Stravinsky's more homogenous modality.

This comparison, blending formal and hermeneutic aspects, highlights the open-ended play of difference and similarity that such interpretative discourse facilitates. The similarities of *Affekt* between the two works, and the degree to which the spirit of loss and regret is conveyed through focus on ostinato, do not override the complementary differences of texture and style, or of dramatic context. Neither differences nor similarities are absolute, but interdependent, interactive.

Forming laments

To the extent that Stravinsky, even at the height of his neoclassical phase, does not shy away from such representations of loss and regret, he shares fundamental aesthetic contexts with Schoenberg, Berg, Janáček, Bartók and Britten – to name only the most obvious near-contemporaries. It is not that Stravinsky stands for different things; rather, he expresses similar things in different ways. In my judgement, it is his capacity for what Walsh, in connection with the 'Lacrimosa' from *Requiem Canticles*, terms 'intense lyrical outpouring'[40] that does most to establish significant links between Stravinsky and other composers who have nothing to do with Russia and its specific musical traditions. At the same time, however, consideration of this topic takes us back to what is most personal to Stravinsky, namely the very individual way in which his view of 'the spirit of lamentation' is inextricably bound up with 'monotony – the sense of perpetual recurrence ... and the simple inevitability of the cycle of birth, life and death'.[41] On this matter, Walsh's comparison of *Les Noces* and *Threni*, brief though it is, is especially important.

Most other scholars, working from within the established traditions of theory-based analysis, have shared Taruskin's preference for what amounts to an essentially formal context (though normally without the detailed perspectives on the music's Russian aura which are Taruskin's speciality). For example, both Martha Hyde and Chandler Carter make stimulating observations, but they do not extend beyond the refinement of our understanding of Stravinsky's modernist techniques. Hyde, writing about the start of the slow movement of the Octet, homes in on a central Stravinskian characteristic, that 'allusion to a dominant-tonic cadence' which is allusive rather than actual simply because

> octatonic structures intrude and block an authentic tonal cadence; octatonicism here remains superimposed over a D-minor tonality, both octatonicism and tonality maintaining their identities despite their superimposition. The inevitable ambiguities this superimposition creates are essential features of the theme. The clash of diatonic and octatonic elements creates an equilibrium that resists fusion or synthesis.[42]

Similarly, Carter, in his telling analysis of the 'Duettino' from Act III, scene 3 of *The Rake's Progress*, demonstrates that 'the subtle play and inherent ambiguity between the tonal and the non-tonal can be sensitively gauged without dismissing or ignoring the role of either'. Such music demands 'a pluralistic analytical approach ... to unlock the mysteries and delights of works in which play with style substitutes for play within a style'.[43]

Both Hyde and Carter have much more to say about these topics, but a quite different way of exploring modernist ambivalence is found in the following:

> In surprising ways [the work] seems to *remember* and then abandon the musical language of its historical antecedents. Passages that employ harsh, strident dissonance give way to ones that evoke the sweetness of tonality, only to reemerge and begin the process again. Passages where the shape of musical phrases have only the most tenuous connection to [the composer's] precursors give way to ones whose phrase shapes have clear connections to the past ... In sum, within the [work] a radically new musical discourse confronts a host of historical references.[44]

This statement could obviously be applied to a wide range of twentieth-century works, but the fact that Michael Cherlin is writing about

Schoenberg's String Trio of 1946 naturally raises the question of whether the kind of analytical contexts he establishes for this composer might also prove relevant to Stravinsky. Cherlin develops a pair of rhetorical tropes – *imperfection* and *distraction* – in order to bring an expressive dimension to bear on the 'old/new' dialectic of his initial formulation. '*Distraction*... describes the ways in which an anticipated musical trajectory, such as phrase completion or thematic continuation, is disrupted, and the dramatic and emotional sense of that disruption as well. *Imperfection*... conveys a sense of incompletion, which in our context is the result of a *distraction*. Thus the two tropes, distraction and imperfection, work as a pair, with the former leading the latter.'[45]

Cherlin believes that these tropes 'generalize well and can be used to inform interpretations of most of Schoenberg's music, as well as that of other composers'.[46] This is undoubtedly true, and it is clear that their propensity for generalisation is due in large part to their comprehensiveness. Both *imperfection* and *distraction*, as defined above, embody oppositions, while also – from a more Stravinskian perspective – acknowledging the Schoenbergian tendency to give Dionysus priority over Apollo. It would indeed be absurd to argue that the technical parameters and expressive qualities of such 'distraction' and 'imperfection' as we might detect in Stravinsky are identical to Schoenberg's. Yet Chandler Carter's discussion of 'subtle play... between the tonal and non-tonal' is evidence of strategies that link the two composers, and the specific consequences of the type of rhetorical play discussed by Cherlin, creating (in Schoenberg's String Trio, and many other pieces) 'an equilibrium that is suggested and negated throughout the work',[47] is very much the kind of modernist dialogue in which Stravinskian and Schoenbergian qualities begin to converge.

Marking the genre

Full exploration of the analytical consequences of this topic would therefore proceed from form to rhetoric. In the area of form, Cherlin's comment, with respect to Schoenberg's Trio, that 'the evocations of tonality, built into the tone row, imply and then deny closure',[48] might seem to rule out parallels with any of Stravinsky's works before the mid 1950s. Yet we need only recall Hyde's analysis of the Octet movement, or look at other discussions of Stravinskian closure which observe the inherent ambiguity of the processes at work (as in Rehding's study of the *Symphonies of Wind Instruments*[49]), to be aware that the basic principle of calling tonality (as a means of ensuring satisfyingly unambivalent completion) into question is fundamental in both instances, however different the atmosphere or style of the works cited. It is nevertheless precisely to that difference of atmosphere, of style, that the rhetorical or hermeneutic analysis must most decisively address itself. For Cherlin, the expressive character of Schoenberg's Trio is determined, in large part, by the way the composer treats one particular generic allusion, to the waltz. Building on what is known about the autobiographical impulse behind the Trio – Schoenberg's near-death from a heart attack and his avowed intention of embodying this experience in the composition – Cherlin argues that the musical imagery in general, and the waltz allusions in particular, reflect the recognition of an ultimately plural if not ambiguous sense that, in the ultimate human struggle between life and death, both states can be associated with peace and fulfilment. 'With the emergence of the waltz, the listener first apprehends the potential for repose and balance that the returning fragments will cumulatively suggest as the work unfolds'; and it is 'the contrast of those fragments with the other musical material in which they are embedded' that 'brings the tropes of distraction and imperfection into particular relief'.[50]

Cherlin believes that 'Schoenberg's music exemplifies the kind of art that gains density of meaning through conflicting forces'.[51] To the extent that those forces have no need to move from coherent equilibrium to integration, synthesis or unambiguous closure, Schoenberg's 'kind of art' is modernist; and so is Stravinsky's. Nevertheless, Schoenberg makes use of old/new dialogues to explore aspects of more lyrical, more regular, more traditionally tonal and romantic allusions as set against the expressionistic disruptions of music that places such allusions into the most powerful relief. Stravinsky (at least after *The Rite of Spring*) uses old/new dialogues in a more restrained, Apollonian fashion. Yet in a work contemporary with the Schoenberg Trio – the ballet *Orpheus* – the culminating progression from the violent 'Pas d'action', in which 'the Bacchantes attack Orpheus, seize him and tear him to pieces', to the serene 'Apotheosis' in which Apollo 'appears . . . wrests the lyre from Orpheus and raises his song heavenwards', shows that the contrast between Dionysian disruption and Apollonian order is still palpable. Though Stephen Walsh argues of *Orpheus* that 'even its violent episodes are played with restraint', and that 'the killing and apotheosis of Orpheus stand for the taming and ordering of those orgiastic elements which music took over from the Dionysian rituals of primitive culture', Daniel Albright discusses the work in terms of its 'desperation, ecstasy' and 'madness'.[52] Even if 'expressionistic disruptions' are replaced with 'objective' mechanistic patterning, this is set against a kind of lyric expression, and a concern to allude to matters of life and death, as potent in its way as Schoenberg's, or Berg's.

Conflicting forces

Writing of the *Symphonies of Wind Instruments*, Stephen Walsh says that the work 'had distilled the ethnic style into a kind of pure formal essence, of which it really did seem true to say that "the play of musical elements is the thing"'. Walsh refers to 'Stravinsky's image of a music that ruthlessly excludes anecdote and nuance, a music which, so to speak, proves the primacy of form by refusing to admit anything not demonstrably (and in the most primitive sense of the word) "formal"'.[53] The distillation which the *Symphonies* represents does not exclude certain very palpable generic allusions – to song, dance, celebration, lament – whose presence, far from the accidental results of the composer's failure to enforce his own logic of abstraction, are essential aspects of the music's integration of form and content. Even in the *Symphonies* we can sense Apollo constraining Dionysus, not ensuring his total absence, and this remains Stravinsky's governing 'tone' thereafter. If *The Rite of Spring* is Stravinsky's most explicit demonstration of a conjunction between Dionysus and modernism, then such later works as *Orpheus* exemplify, not so much a whole-hearted rejection of modernism, as a refined and complex conjunction between modernising and classicising impulses.

In the light of the comments about the Apollonian principle that occur in Stravinsky's *Autobiography*, we might expect the ballet *Apollon musagète* to offer unambiguous illustrations of the composer's preference for 'studied conception over vagueness, the rule over the arbitrary, order over the haphazard'.[54] In spirit, the ballet's concluding movement, 'Apothéose', in which Apollo is led by the Muses to Parnassus, is indeed worlds away from the corybantic frenzy of *The Rite of Spring*'s 'Sacrificial dance'. Yet, as the *Poetics* confirms, Stravinsky's understanding of Apollonian classicism did not require him to abandon the techniques of polarisation, and of dialogue between convergence and divergence, which had served the Dionysian spirit of *Petrushka* and *The Rite* so well. Apollo's demand, the lectures state, is that 'for the lucid ordering of the work... all the Dionysian elements which set the imagination of the artist in motion must be properly subjugated before they intoxicate us, and must finally be made to submit to the law', with the consequence that 'variety is valid only as a means of attaining similarity'.[55] This would appear to rule out modernist multiplicity, and yet the music of *Apollon musagète*, while obviously much smoother in rhythm and more consonant in harmony than that of *The Rite*, as well as less 'nationalist' in melodic character, indicates very clearly that Stravinskian similarity need not mean *stability*, in the sense of traditionally classical unity and resolution.

Polarity in the 'Apothéose' (Ex. 3.1) is represented most basically by the tonal centres of D and B which are both implied by the two-sharp key signature, and it is as unsatisfactory to interpret what happens as a clear-cut progression from D major to B minor as it is to argue that the two tonics are irreconcilable opposites. The final chord, certainly, is one of B minor, but the context in which it occurs renders its status as tonic less stable than would be the case if that context were more conventionally diatonic.

Another, no less important aspect of the dialogue between convergence and divergence here is the interaction, and also the preserved separation, between the various textural strata. This is of considerable importance to the character of the final section of the 'Apothéose', from one bar before fig. 101. In the upper stratum, the first violins, doubled two octaves lower by the first cellos, repeat the final motivic unit of the main melody, whose lyric character is fundamental to the grave serenity of the musical atmosphere – Stravinsky's uniquely 'cool' spirit of tragic vulnerability and loss. This motive decorates the central B with notes which, if considered as arpeggiating a chord, create a sense of dissonance, even though, separately, both F♯ and G find consonant support in the lower voices. The lowest stratum (which could be subdivided) comprises the ostinatos in second cello (with its initial six-beat pattern) and in double bass (with its initial four-beat pattern). Although these lines finally converge on an agreed progression from G to B, they spend most of the six bars in question offering distinct perspectives on their shared Ds and Bs. The second cellos retain the D-supporting As and F♯s, while the basses have only a G which, in a conventional diatonic context, would support D as tonic more strongly than B. The third, central stratum, in second violins and violas, begins in step with the four-beat ostinato in the bass. While its principal pitches – D and F♯ – have obvious relevance to the prevailing polarities, the linear unfolding of the actual ostinato figures, in which the upper and lower neighbours of F♯ are prominent, contributes significantly to the special, destabilised harmony. This third stratum also supports the opposition between symmetric (B/F♮) and asymmetric (B and F♯) features at the end, something to which Stravinsky could have recourse even when his music was not officially octatonic.

So far this analysis has followed through the implications of a Taruskin-style formal stock-taking. But switching to a more Cherlinesque view of rhetoric allows us to note the expressive force of the contrast between the 'mechanistic' ostinatos of the lower strata and the fined-down lyrical melody of the upper stratum. The mood is not as ritualistically funereal as in several other Stravinsky finales – for example, that of *Requiem Canticles*, discussed below – and there are less explicit generic allusions behind this processional music than for the earlier movements of the ballet. But it would be wholly inadequate to speak of 'a kind of pure formal essence', in which 'the play of the musical elements is the thing'[56] and we willingly exclude – joyfully or otherwise – the kind of nuances of expression which derive from the associations which the music sets up with those precedents and precursors

Ex. 3.1 *Apollon musagète, '*Apothéose'

Ex. 3.1 (*cont.*)

it cannot hope to escape. It was, after all, this closing section of *Apollon musagète* that provoked the greatest admiration in some of the composer's most sceptical critics. For Boris Asaf'yev, 'the hymn is itself justification for the whole work. Listening to it, one forgets the motley mosaic and eclecticism of the other pages of the score';[57] and Prokofiev declared that, 'on the very last page of the work... he has shone and managed to make even his disgusting main theme sound convincing'.[58] As Walsh notes, 'in *Oedipus Rex* and *Apollo*, neoclassicism was openly making its peace with the irrational, with passion and fear, and, at the end of *Apollo*, with a mysterious, otherworldly purity that Schloezer was quick to see as an intimation of the sacramental'.[59]

Schloezer's view was that, after *Apollon musagète*, Stravinsky 'can no longer give us anything but a Mass'.[60] Nevertheless, one does not have to reach for association with the genres of sacred music to find a sufficiently resonant context for an ending whose processional solemnity reaches back through features of the Serenade in A and Piano Concerto to memories of the majestic, march-like transitions in *Parsifal*. The models of Stravinsky's two earlier B-centred conclusions – *The Firebird* and *Les Noces* – establish a link between that tonality and solemn processional music, though both are far more conclusive in their cadencing than the 'Apothéose'. There is indeed a 'sacramental' quality to the 'mysterious... purity' of *Apollon*'s ending: and this might even be felt to reinforce the fundamental quality of separation between celebrants (dancers) and spectators. It is the spectators' sense of loss which the sorrowing quality of the music depicts, while at the same time it represents the transfiguring apotheosis of Apollo and his attendant Muses. However, given the particular spirit that Stravinsky associated with the dithyramb – as most explicitly in the finale of the *Duo concertant*, which is more Apollonian than Dionysian – it is perhaps this elusive yet numinous genre which fits most closely with the qualities to be heard in *Apollon*'s 'Apothéose'.[61]

This analysis, as far as it goes, only hints at the kind of topics that could be involved in an appropriately detailed study of those musical elements which connect Stravinsky to his contemporaries. For example, the fining-down of thematic content, supported by various ostinatos, in the 'Apothéose' suggests the closural technique defined by Schoenberg as 'liquidation',[62] and the *dolce* ending of Schoenberg's String Quartet No. 3 (1927) – contemporary with *Apollo* – is by no means remote in technique or character from the Stravinsky work, despite its twelve-note basis. Both the thematic fining-down and the ostinato-based accompaniment effect an ending which is far from decisively closural in the traditional, classical sense.

Such similarities are far from invariable, of course, and the ways in which these composers create endings that are more decisive than dissolving (Schoenberg's Variations for Orchestra, Stravinsky's *Symphony of*

Psalms) also reinforce differences of tone and spirit. As already pointed out, Schoenberg's contrapuntal propensities ensured that he only rarely fined down his textures to the chorale-like simplicity which was so important to Stravinsky. Although the wistful mood of the Third Quartet's ending is comparable to the regretful sublimity of *Apollon*'s 'Apothéose', for an instance of Schoenberg's ability to embody expressions of loss and sorrow in ways quite different from Stravinsky's, one need look no further than the overtly emotional ending of *Moses und Aron* (Act 2).

Cherlin's consideration of that 'density of meaning through conflicting forces' in Schoenberg is no less relevant to a music of preserved polarities rather than resolving synthesis, like that of *Apollon*. It is nevertheless worth repeating my earlier comment at this point: 'what is intriguing, when comparisons are attempted between Stravinsky and his German contemporaries, is the very allusiveness and ambiguity of relations between their different approaches to parallel generic, expressive contexts'.[63] Nor do 'allusiveness and ambiguity' diminish when Stravinsky's later, twelve-note compositions are brought into the picture.

Ritual and regret

The similarity/difference relation of Stravinsky to Schoenberg is arguably never more resonant than in Stravinsky's last twelve-note movement, the Postlude to the *Requiem Canticles*, and the specific allusions to lyrical and ritual celebration that it embodies. Much interest has already been shown in the generic and semiotic aspects of this music, especially its associations with chorale and dirge. But it is no less salient to suggest that, even in this relatively simple structure, the funereal character of the music has binary rather than singular connotations. In particular, I do not hear the sustained horn line as especially integrative or supportive. To me, it has an almost romantic tone, an echo of lyric lament against the impersonal, ritual bell sounds, and we can hear both the opposition and the interaction, a specifically modernist sense of order as structurally relevant to the circumstances Stravinsky had established in this work. Some will prefer the interaction, even perhaps to the extent of feeling that the movement resolves in favour of a single, F-based sonority. Others will prefer the preserved equilibrium between incompatible strategies, promoted by the mediation of the chords in harp, piano and flutes.[64]

The Postlude is the ultimate demonstration of Stravinsky's rejection of Austro-German *espressivo* in all its fractured and frantic glory. The blend of the lyrical and ritualistic in the Postlude, its combination of a sense of regret with quiet celebration of eternal Christian truths, recalls that concluding, 'cold' apotheosis of *Apollon musagète* which, for Stravinsky, best represented his own personal sense of the tragic spirit, and the feature which, above all, defined his distance from Schoenbergian rhetoric. The post-expressionist trope of 'imperfection and distraction' might therefore appear to have little power here. Yet that basic sense of tension between the centrifugal and the centripetal which underpins Cherlin's reading of Schoenberg's language in the String Trio is a factor in Stravinsky's Postlude as well, as the horn's outlined F minor triad unfolds against the atonal processional chords. Once again, comparable techniques serve radically different styles of expression. So, while it will not do to fine down the complex and intriguing interactions between these composers to a slogan like Mikhail Druskin's – Stravinsky's 'ideal was . . . "unstable stability", as opposed to Schoenberg's which might equally be described as "stable instability" '[65] – the rewards of considering the two in terms of what they share as well as of what divides them are undeniable.

This chapter has argued that it is valuable to consider Stravinsky in a context that does not focus exclusively on his Russian past, or his personal, self-determined 'present', but on the possibility of dialogues, between him and other major composers, that point to a shared nexus – flexible, multivalent, interactive – of 'topical' and generic associations. There is a no less fundamental sense of composers coming after Stravinsky building on features directly relevant to those dialogues: composers like Carter, Maxwell Davies and many others, whose debts to Stravinsky seem to facilitate an engagement with that wider ethos of stylistic attributes in which what is opposed yet complementary invites and stimulates further exploration – amounting, it might even appear, to a late-century mainstream. And even with composers for whom Stravinsky's tone of voice seems to have little relevance – Ligeti, Kurtág – connections can be traced by way of comparable generic concerns, with lyric lamentation, for example. Like the Table of Comparisons with Schoenberg in *Dialogues*, such 'connections' might be felt to offer little more than a rudimentary sense of difference. But they are important nevertheless as a means of guarding against any tendency to categorise composers solely by means of their 'individual' traits within an otherwise open-endedly 'plural' culture. In the end, Stravinsky is a great composer because he survives these comparisons with his individuality enhanced, and not because his individuality renders comparisons irrelevant.

PART II

The works

4 Early Stravinsky

ANTHONY POPLE

When one examines the earliest works of a great composer, it is almost inevitably with hindsight that one does so. Hearing the earlier works through the portal that the later, more well-known works supply can be a strange experience, through which hindsight often hardens into self-reassurance. Does one hear a familiar foretaste of this here, a pre-echo of that there? Is there a discernible quality to the early works that is evident to us today, but which contemporary listeners seem to have overlooked? Such questions are easy to ask and carry a hint of smugness, but, conversely, is anything to be gained by turning the presumptions around – by dwelling, for example, on the ordinariness that allowed the composer's contemporaries to remain unaware of the genius in their midst? Surely not: for such inversion merely preserves the same impoverished agenda in negative.

Questions of style impinge on the assessment of 'early' works in ways that demand examination in the present context. Consider the early works of Mozart as an alternative case to those of Stravinsky: as Charles Rosen has famously argued, the received idea of the 'classical style' is defined for us today by the mature works of Haydn, Mozart and Beethoven, rather than by the music of their many accomplished contemporaries.[1] It is not that Mozart's music is recognised as similar to that of, say, J. C. Bach, Kozeluch and Kraus, and can be measured against it, revealing Mozart's 'superiority'. On the contrary, in fact: the works of these other composers, and many more, are liable to be heard against the yardstick that our familiarity with Mozart's work provides, and so to be regarded as inferior. Listening to Mozart's own earliest, childhood works provides much the same experience, for the same reason. One important distinction between Mozart's and Stravinsky's eras, however, is the comparative homogeneity of style in the former period, as opposed to the evident diversity of the early twentieth century. The sheer variety of late nineteenth- and early twentieth-century music means that hearing Stravinsky's early works in relation to those of his contemporaries and predecessors, and of course in relation to his own later compositions, is a complex business.

Add to this the fact that the mature Stravinsky is well known as a magpie consumer and purveyor of musical styles, and the plot thickens further. One factor which emerges as much from the study of his earlier works as from the late ones is his persistent use of other music as models: in doing so, he managed – by and large – to avoid resorting to *self*-parody in the way that many less impressive composers of the twentieth century were inclined to do. The seeds of this were certainly sown in his early twenties.

Family beginnings

Before that, Stravinsky's very earliest compositions constitute no more than a modest trace of his constant but unambitious engagement with the art of music – an engagement that was conditioned above all by family circumstances. Music naturally formed part of the leisured life of a member of the landowning class to which the Stravinskys belonged; but as the son of the most feted Russian operatic bass of the day, the young Igor Fyodorovich's musical life was fuller than most. He attended the opera 'five or six nights a week',[2] and also went to rehearsals; he got to know the performers, was well placed to meet prominent composers, and became familiar with both the standard Russian repertoire and the latest trends. But one must not imagine that this was a professionalised sphere of activity to which Stravinsky gained easy access at an early age: on the contrary, the strain of amateurism that was ingrained in nineteenth-century Russian musical life was still very much apparent, and the young Stravinsky's own activities as a musician were dilettantish – rooted for the time being in the leisured world of his mother's family rather than in his father's work.[3] His first surviving composition, the fragmentary *Tarantella* for piano (1898), seems to have resulted from an attempt to write down one of many improvisations which the enthusiastic but untutored teenager made at the piano.[4] As he explained ten years later, 'I improvised endlessly and enjoyed it immensely, [but] I was unable to write down what I played. I ascribed this to my lack of theoretical knowledge.'[5]

Considerably more accomplished technically is the Pushkin song 'Storm Cloud', dated 25 January 1902 (OS), which is well shaped and makes coherent if rather obsessive use of enharmonic progressions. A harmonic summary of part of the song's central section is given in Ex. 4.1: note the progression in bars 23–5, initially from an A minor triad to an F minor triad, whose A♭ is enharmonically reinterpreted as G♯ in the following diminished seventh chord, which in turn resolves to another A minor triad; the same pattern is immediately repeated in sequence from bar 27. The basic outline of this progression has, in fact, already been heard in the tonic key of E minor within the principal material of the song (at bars 8ff) and is hinted at in the accompaniment to the opening melody (bar 5) – all of this suggesting not so much that Stravinsky was using the progression as a device to unify the song, but that he was using the song as an opportunity to practise using the progression. The distance in accomplishment between the *Tarantella* and

Ex. 4.1 'Storm Cloud' (1902), bars 23–38, harmonic summary

'Storm Cloud' reflects the fact that Stravinsky had been taking tuition in harmony since November 1901 with Fyodor Akimenko, a pupil of Rimsky-Korsakov.[6] Stravinsky would later write that 'Until I began to take lessons in harmony from Akimenko, you might say that I ripened in ignorance.'[7]

Richard Taruskin's opinion that Akimenko would have taught Stravinsky using Rimsky-Korsakov's *Practical Course in Harmony* is surely justified, and indeed it was not long before Rimsky himself was offering encouragement to the young Stravinsky, whose music ('Storm Cloud' perhaps included) he saw for the first time in the summer of 1902. But he was not yet ready to offer tuition, even to the son of the great opera singer: for the time being, Stravinsky continued his studies under Vasily Kalafati, another Rimsky pupil, who (according to Stravinsky's later recollection) demanded 'the usual exercises' of him and was 'scornful of the "interesting new chords" that young composers care about most'.[8] One may surmise that it was for the painstaking but conservative Kalafati that Stravinsky composed the Scherzo in G minor for piano (1902) – an undistinguished work, somewhat reminiscent of Tchaikovsky, which occupies but a single page of manuscript.[9]

At home with the Korsakovs

After his father's death in November 1902, the Rimsky-Korsakov circle became Stravinsky's home from home, not least because relations with his mother became strained on account of her disapproval of his musical activities.[10] He had got to know the fifty-eight-year-old composer's sons, Andrey and Vladimir, at university, and became a regular attender of the fortnightly musical evenings held in the Rimsky-Korsakov household. Stravinsky's role in these gatherings seems often to have been that of court jester: he later recalled that 'In my University years ... I composed many comic songs',[11] and these were certainly appreciated by V. V. Yastrebtsev, a devotee of the musical evenings, who noted on 6 March 1903 (OS) that 'Stravinsky entertained us with very charming and witty musical jokes of his own invention'.[12] Also into this category fall the so-called Cantata for the sixtieth birthday of Rimsky-Korsakov (1904)[13] and the song 'Conductor and Tarantula' (1906).[14] Another song, 'How the Mushrooms Prepared for War' (1904), acquired in Taruskin's view particular significance as a souvenir of these early days for the aged Stravinsky, containing as it does a multitude of references to his father's vocal repertoire[15] – and yet it is also reasonable to observe that the song's stylistic borrowings from Musorgsky, Borodin and others (including Rimsky-Korsakov himself) were in the first instance part and parcel of a humorous approach taken for the benefit of an audience steeped in knowledge of the musical originals. With hindsight, this aspect of Stravinsky's musical apprentice years seems rather more exciting, by and large, than the fruits of his formal studies. Yet at the time it must have been more important to him that his serious work was successful. The Piano Sonata in F♯ minor (1903–4) and Symphony in E♭ (1905–7) record this stage in his development.

The Sonata marked the culmination of his work with Kalafati, though according to Stravinsky it also incorporated 'many suggestions by Rimsky-Korsakov'.[16] In contrast to the older styles parodied in 'How the Mushrooms Prepared for War', its principal models were the contemporary Russian heavyweights Glazunov and Skryabin.[17] In Taruskin's words, 'The sonata's high-gloss finish is little short of amazing only five or six years after the *Tarantella*',[18] yet in old age the composer could not – or more likely *would* not – recall his youthful work in favourable terms, famously calling it 'fortunately lost' and feigning a belief that it had been an 'inept imitation of late Beethoven'.[19] Only the fact that the whereabouts of the manuscript were at that time (1962) unknown allowed Stravinsky to publish these comments unchallenged; but when the work resurfaced in Russia a few years later and was printed after the composer's death, it became clear that his characterisation of it had been false. The work is in four movements, the third and fourth of which are played without a pause – and, as Taruskin points out, both this feature and the tempo pattern of the four movements is taken from another sonata in F♯ minor, Skryabin's Third (1898).[20] But as one frequently finds in Glazunov's music, form and content seem to arise separately: in terms of its musical substance, Stravinsky's sonata seems little more than an imitation (inept or not) of Glazunov and Tchaikovsky. This was not, then, a student work engaging in parody of classical models so as to gain basic technical competence, but a serious attempt to work in the contemporary Russian manner.

By showing proficiency in the Glazunovian style, however superficially, Stravinsky was establishing himself in a way that promised to satisfy a deep emotional need. Glazunov was half a generation older than Stravinsky: precocious and fabulously gifted, he had responded to Rimsky's teaching by picking up the musical traits of his teacher's generation and deploying them in a fluent succession of works, many of which were cast in conventional forms. Though history has been unkind to Glazunov, his successful career was a beacon for the younger Rimsky pupils – far more so than that of the indolent Anatol Lyadov – and Rimsky evidently saw the makings of a musical dynasty in the succession from himself to Glazunov to those of Stravinsky's age. The prospect of admittance to this dynasty at the head of the 'young Korsakovians' was alluring for Stravinsky, whose own family relationships were far from close, except with his younger brother Goury.[21]

The Symphony in E♭ promised to be the work with which Stravinsky would establish these credentials. Completed under Rimsky's tuition, it was his designated Op. 1 – though it took so long to appear that Op. 2 was actually finished first. Stravinsky's private lessons with Rimsky took place weekly, beginning in the autumn of 1905 and ending only with the older man's death in June 1908;[22] prior to this, in the summer of 1904, Stravinsky had studied orchestration with Rimsky – who used the simple but profound technique of giving pupils his own music in short score and, in due course, having them compare their orchestrations with his.[23] The Symphony was, in fact, sketched between these dates, probably during the first nine months or so of 1905.[24] Perhaps Stravinsky thought he could make quick progress on his own: the account he gives in his *Autobiography* of his studies with Rimsky-Korsakov seems intended to suggest a constructive and well-ordered progression.[25] However, as Taruskin has established, when Rimsky saw the draft of the Symphony, he instigated far-reaching changes.[26] These affected the first movement in particular: Stravinsky's stilted opening theme was over the course of several laborious attempts turned into something that at least had the potential to set in train a symphonic argument, though both the theme and the movement as a whole remain far from inspired, even in the final version. Comparing this music with Glazunov's (particularly his Eighth Symphony, in the same key) serves to emphasise that the older man was a master of the idiom he had established – his ear, his technique and his orchestration far outshine Stravinsky's. None the less, many passages in the young composer's Op. 1 possess considerable charm – the second movement, a scherzo, is the high point – and this was a quality appreciated by its earliest audiences.[27] What is more, Glazunov's expressed opinion was that the work was 'very nice, very nice'.[28]

A voice of his own

In guiding Stravinsky's revision of the Symphony in E♭, Rimsky-Korsakov seems to have constantly encouraged Stravinsky to improve on his own weakest inventions by following specific models. Thus, it might at first sight seem strange to read in Yastrebtsev's reminiscences, in an entry dated 4 November 1907 (OS), that:

> In Rimsky-Korsakov's opinion, Igor Stravinsky's talent has not yet become sufficiently defined. For example, in the fourth movement of his First Symphony, he is still imitating Glazunov too much, and in his new songs (to words by Gorodetsky) he has embraced modernism too zealously.[29]

What are we to make of this? For one thing, it confirms the inordinately slow progress of Stravinsky's Symphony, which had only recently been completed, for the Gorodetsky songs were to be his Op. 6 – and that is not to say that all the intervening works had been finished either! Above all, it indicates that Stravinsky was, now, by no means Rimsky's star pupil in the older man's eyes, though he might at one stage have seemed the natural leader of the 'young Korsakovians'. This position had been taken over in the meanwhile by Maximilian Steinberg (1883–1946), whose role as the 'creative heir' of Rimsky-Korsakov was symbolised by his marriage to Rimsky's daughter, Nadezhda, in the summer of 1908; within a few months, Glazunov and Steinberg would be to the 'Korsakovians' what Rimsky-Korsakov and Glazunov had been before Rimsky's death. Glazunov certainly felt that Stravinsky had some basic deficiencies in ability and technique,[30] but one wonders whether Rimsky might have kept faith with Stravinsky if he had been a quicker pupil.

In fact, despite the slow progress of his Symphony, Stravinsky continued with a sequence of assignments akin to those undertaken by composition students at the St Petersburg Conservatoire – which is to say that his Sonata and Symphony were to be followed by vocal music and opera.[31] His Op. 2 was a cycle of three songs for mezzo-soprano and orchestra to words by Pushkin, *The Faun and the Shepherdess* (1906). Once again the debt to Glazunov is inescapable – the opening of the first song seems to have been virtually lifted.[32] Certainly this first song, and to some extent the second, come across today as more tender and successful essays than the Symphony

Ex. 4.2 'Spring', Op. 6, no. 1, bars 9–11

in essentially the same contemporary Russian vein. But there is also a hint, in the unmistakable Wagnerisms of the third song, that Rimsky's ambivalence towards Stravinsky was beginning to be matched by the pupil's developing interest in styles beyond the models approved by his teacher. Indeed, the first of the Gorodetsky songs – the one which, in Rimsky's view, 'embraced modernism too zealously' – is striking in its expansion of Stravinsky's harmonic thinking. In response to the poet's highly charged religious-erotic image of a novice nun – a bell-ringer's daughter – lamenting her lost love at the cloister gates, the piano begins with a crazed imitation of pealing bells. The phrase leading to the first vocal entry is shown in Ex. 4.2: as the left hand descends through a cycle of perfect fourths, the busy right-hand figuration rises in contrary motion to suggest an alternation of dominant ninth chords and bi-triadic combinations at a major third's distance (e.g. D major underpinned by Bb). The freedom of the harmonic progressions throughout the outer sections of the song is evidence that these advanced harmonic archetypes were merely a background to Stravinsky's invention; in contrast, the song's central section uses mock folksong to embrace a pastoral mood, still with religious-erotic overtones. This was certainly not music for a comfortable 'at home' with the Korsakovs.

The second song – composed in August the following year, after Rimsky's death – confirms Stravinsky's modernism by exploring a musical vein that one finds a few years later in some of the early songs of, for example, Lourié and Prokofiev. Wistful in tone, it is less strikingly adventurous than the first song but oozes confidence on the part of the composer. Often the music focuses on a pedal note, and many of its haunting sonorities result from adding a minor sixth to the major triad, or a raised leading note to the minor triad. Sometimes these combinations are reversed, and in general the use of major harmony as *variant* of the minor – developing the mood without relieving it – lends the music a particular piquancy. Strangely, the Four Studies for piano, Op. 7, which seem to have been completed in the autumn of 1908, are backward-looking by comparison: their reliance on Skryabin's early style as a model is far from convincing.[33]

Almost hidden amidst Stravinsky's early output of shorter pieces is one which sounds uncannily like something he might have written twenty years later: the *Pastorale* for vocalise (wordless voice) and piano. This brief song without words was composed for Nadezhda Rimsky-Korsakov in October 1907. Its engaging lightweight manner and lack of an opus number tell us that it belongs with Stravinsky's extra-curricular music – the 'very charming and witty musical jokes of his own invention' that amused Yastrebtsev and the others. Taruskin suggests that the *Pastorale* was written in playful imitation of some of the harpsichord music in French Baroque style that Stravinsky probably heard Wanda Landowska perform in St Petersburg earlier that year.[34] Many commentators have remarked on the apparently prophetic nature of this piece: certainly it gives food for the thought that in working his way towards his neoclassical manner through the humour of *Renard, The Soldier's Tale* and *Pulcinella*, the later Stravinsky may to some extent have returned, virtually unnoticed, to that side of his earliest musical personality with which the 'Korsakovians' were most comfortable.

Scherzo fantastique, Op. 3 (1907–8), *Fireworks,* Op. 4 (1908)

In the two orchestral works that followed the belated completion of his Symphony, Stravinsky achieved an early plateau of style that points firmly in the direction of *The Firebird*. Both the *Scherzo fantastique* and *Fireworks* are showy, programmatic pieces, with strong rhythmic characterisation and a sense of energetic movement. Unless one imagines that *The Firebird* came from nowhere, then these two scores, particularly the *Scherzo*, must be understood as the ballet's musico-dramatic point of departure. But it suited Stravinsky's purpose to disguise this: he sought to cover up, or at least occlude, the programmatic basis of the *Scherzo fantastique* in Maeterlinck's book *La Vie des abeilles* (The life of bees) even before the work's first performance early in 1909 – though the inspiration he took from the play is evident from his letters to Rimsky-Korsakov.[35]

Whereas critics in the decades around the turn of the twentieth century argued endlessly about the comparative merits of 'absolute' and 'programme' music, many composers hedged their bets, as the young Stravinsky did here. The music was composed with a programmatic basis but presented to the public under a classically generic musical title ('scherzo'), qualified by the suggestion that the work embodies 'fantasy' – which was evidently a quality to be admired – and without divulging the composer's reliance on an existing source. It was a method which also removed the obligation to give credit to the author of his inspiration – in this case, Maurice Maeterlinck. None the less, the *Scherzo fantastique* was firmly associated with bees a few years later when it served as the score for a ballet entitled *Les Abeilles* that was produced at the Paris Opéra in 1917. On this occasion, since neither

Stravinsky nor Maeterlinck had given his permission for the adaptation, both could appear to be outraged. The score was then published with a prefatory note that seems to correspond with the ballet's scenario – which was derived, as it happens, from Maeterlinck's *La Vie des abeilles* – but again without acknowledging Maeterlinck explicitly.

After all this, one can perhaps forgive the older Stravinsky's attempts to deny that Maeterlinck's book had ever played a part in the work.[36] Taruskin has characteristically sought to restore the original detail to this picture, by outlining correspondences between the book and the music,[37] but so strong is the musical imagery that even the score's prefatory note – later disowned by Stravinsky – is enough to guide the listener. After a brief introduction, the busy string music that opens the first main section of the work is easy to associate with the buzzing of bees around the hive. As the music develops, Stravinsky unveils many of the characteristic devices that would reappear in *The Firebird*. Chief amongst these is the artificial scale of alternating whole tones and semitones, known today as the octatonic scale: for example C–Db–Eb–E–F♯– G–A–Bb (other versions begin on C♯ and D, but the next higher example, on Eb, turns out to be exactly the same as the version on C, owing to the internal symmetry of the scale itself). The word 'octatonic' could, in principle, be applied to *any* eight-note collection, but present-day usage signals the fact that in the intervening years this particular scale has come to be so widely shared by musicians that no other eight-note configuration is likely to be confused with it. In the early twentieth century, on the other hand, non-diatonic collections with a well-defined musical character tended to go under various names alluding to their use by certain composers, or their supposed origins in non-Western musical exotica. In Russian musical circles of this time, what we now call the octatonic collection was known as the 'Rimsky-Korsakov scale'; and by this was understood not only the bald eight notes but also a whole repertoire of usages, most if not all of which were imbibed by his pupils through his harmony text. Indeed, other enharmonic devices were included under this rubric, the common feature being the division of the octave into equal intervals: two tritones, three major thirds or four minor thirds.[38] The use by Debussy and other French composers of the scale of six equal whole tones was a further step in this direction.

It was typical of Rimsky-Korsakov that those passages in his works that invoked these devices tended to use them relentlessly in sequence, and that they would be set against a generally more conventional background of the kind that was absorbed and developed by Glazunov. Thus, in Rimsky's music, they generally remain tricks of the trade: the idea of bringing them into a modernist framework was not what he had in mind. Nor indeed was it yet in Stravinsky's, although the ingredients were in place. Keeping contrasted elements separate was something he would famously return to in the block-like architecture of, say, the *Symphonies of Wind Instruments*,[39] but at this stage in his career it served to delay a linguistic synthesis that would become fully evident for the first time in *The Rite of Spring*. The octatonic scale includes many conventional sonorities – four each of major and minor triads, dominant, diminished and half-diminished sevenths – and it was common practice to cycle through these in upward or downward sequence.[40]

Stravinsky had learned the additional effectiveness that was to be gained from combining upward and downward sequences within a complex orchestral texture, as shown in Ex. 4.3: here the horns (later trumpets) move upwards in tritones, whilst the flutes and celesta move downwards in figures that outline successive major triads. Other sources are apparent in the contrasting middle section of the work, particularly Wagner in his *Meistersinger* vein. The work, then, is something of an odd mixture, but as even the aged Stravinsky was forced to acknowledge, it is 'a promising opus three'.[41]

In his dedication of *Fireworks* to Maximilian and Nadezhda Steinberg, one can see Stravinsky with his Op. 4 still clinging to a place in the Korsakov circle. The work is both shorter, and simpler in structure, than the *Scherzo fantastique*: its hyperactive outer sections buzz even more than the *Scherzo*'s 'bees', and in much the same style – though here perhaps it is the incessant spitting and popping of small incendiary devices that is meant. As in the *Scherzo*, much of the substance lies in the orchestration: indeed, when Stravinsky illustrates louder explosions, rockets and so forth, the effect is so onomatopoeic as to be almost comical. The central section of the work again moves beyond the Rimskyan orbit, this time looking not towards Germany but to France, and specifically to Paul Dukas, a composer whose influence was far wider among his contemporaries than his present-day profile might lead one to expect. The opening figures of his tone-poem *The Sorcerer's Apprentice* (1897) clearly provided a model for the slower music that interrupts the fireworks (fig. 9 of the score); the scintillating yet still relaxed music that follows (Ex. 4.4) is perhaps the most accomplished musical passage Stravinsky had composed to date.

Stravinsky had earlier interrupted the composition of *Fireworks* to compose a short orchestral piece in memory of Rimsky-Korsakov. Completed within the space of a few weeks after Rimsky's death in the summer of 1908, the *Chant funèbre*, Op. 5, was performed after some delay on 17 January 1909 (O.S.) and reviewed sympathetically in the press.[42] Assessing extant accounts of Stravinsky's work in the context of other funereal tributes by Glazunov and Steinberg (together with an earlier example by Rimsky-Korsakov himself), Taruskin has suggested that the *Chant funèbre* is likely to have quoted both from the Orthodox liturgy and from Rimsky's own

Ex. 4.3 *Scherzo fantastique*, fig. 7

Ex. 4.4 *Fireworks*, fig. 13

work.[43] The combined presentation of these two elements – liturgical chanting and melodic tributes – was indeed described by Stravinsky in his *Autobiography*: 'all the solo instruments of the orchestra filed past the tomb of the master in succession, each laying down its own melody as its wreath against a deep background of tremolo murmurings simulating the vibrations of bass voices singing in chorus'.[44] Unfortunately, the music of the *Chant funèbre* was never published, and the subsequent disappearance of the manuscript sources leaves us with no way of knowing very much about a piece that Stravinsky in old age was to recall as 'the best of my works before the *Firebird*, and the most advanced in chromatic harmony'.[45]

The Nightingale, Act 1 (1908–9)

After vocal music in Stravinsky's student curriculum came opera, in the shape of a proposed three-act work based on Hans Christian Andersen's tale *The Nightingale*. As one might have expected, Stravinsky's work was conceived firmly within the genre represented by Rimsky-Korsakov's fantastical operas – so much so that Stravinsky and his librettist, Stepan Mitusov, actually developed their scenario under the direct tutelage of Vladimir Bel'sky, who had written the librettos of Rimsky's most recent operas, *The Legend of the Invisible City of Kitezh* (1903–5) and *The Golden Cockerel* (1906–7).[46] The outline of Andersen's story is well known: the Emperor of China, having learned of the beauty of the nightingale's voice, sends his courtiers to fetch the bird to his palace so that it may sing to him, but is then persuaded by a group of Japanese envoys to prefer the warblings of a mechanical bird which they present to him; as he lies mortally ill, however, the Emperor finds strength through his renewed appreciation of the loyal nightingale, and through this change of heart he is saved from certain death.

Although it seems likely that Stravinsky was able to show some musical sketches to Rimsky before the latter's death,[47] the composition of the first act did not begin in earnest until the latter part of 1908, and was completed in Ustilug in 1909, before Diaghilev's urgent commission for *The Firebird* caused the opera to be put to one side and changed the course of Stravinsky's career for ever. In line with principles developed by Rimsky in his own operas, there is an underlying duality in the music of the *The Nightingale*, Act 1. The exotic and the magical – personified in Stravinsky's opera by the Chinese courtiers and the nightingale's wondrous voice – are given chromatic music that frequently centres on the octatonic scale, whereas the down-to-earth human sphere – represented by the peasant fisherman – is associated with diatonic, folksong-like materials. Although this brief description risks oversimplifying a remarkably rich musical language, the basic distinction it outlines is useful to bear in mind as one traces Stravinsky's development from this point through the famous Diaghilev ballets. In *The Firebird*, the fairy-tale characters inhabit a world of princesses, demons and magical creatures entirely in line with Rimskyan subject-matter and are treated accordingly; in *Petrushka*, the puppet characters magically come to life against the backdrop of an Easter fair busy with humanity of all kinds, allowing these same musical archetypes to mingle and interact variously; in *The Rite of Spring*, the scenario of a pagan fertility rite endows the human characters themselves with magical and mysterious qualities – a synthesis to which Stravinsky responds by transforming diatonic folksong material into that work's richly chromatic, often dissonant sound-world.

Whilst the Rimskyan influence is certainly strong in *The Nightingale*, other sources of Stravinsky's inspiration are also very apparent. As one might expect, the non-Rimskyan traits in *The Nightingale*'s music are most evident in those sections which, though chromatic, are not octatonic. Most famous among these is the very opening (Ex. 4.5a), which is akin to the opening of Debussy's 'Nuages' (from *Nocturnes*, 1897–9, Ex. 4.5b) – though this in turn appears to have been lifted more or less directly from a song in Musorgsky's cycle *Sunless* (1874, Ex. 4.5c). As Taruskin has noted in detail, Debussy's work also seems to be the source of some of Stravinsky's orchestration in the opening pages of the opera.[48] Further points of reference beyond Stravinsky's earlier models are Tcherepnin – whose style Taruskin identifies as providing Stravinsky with a musical entrée into the artistic circles where he would shortly find Diaghilev[49] – and some very obvious debts to Skryabin. The Skryabin in question, however, was not at all that of the somewhat insipid early- and middle-period music Stravinsky had drawn on in composing his Piano Sonata and Four Studies, but the theosophically charged and musically advanced Skryabin of *The Poem of Ecstasy* (1905–8). By this time it is clear that Stravinsky was abreast of his older contemporary's most adventurous musical developments – a familiarity, even admiration, that would last at least until Skryabin's death in 1915.[50] In *The Nightingale* the influence is fresh and undigested: towards the end of the nightingale's first burst of song, the music of the orchestra is so close to a passage in *Ecstasy* as to suggest plagiarism (see Ex. 4.6). In contrast, the diatonic Fisherman's song – a recurring musical frame that characterises the rustic scene inhabited by 'simple' people who treasure the nightingale as a living example of nature's magic – represents the other pole of the human–magical, diatonic–chromatic double axis on which the opera's approach to musical dramaturgy is based.

The Firebird (1909–10)

Stravinsky's future was sealed at the first performance of the *Scherzo fantastique*, which was given under the baton of Alexander Siloti on 24 January 1909 (OS) in St Petersburg.[51] The impresario Sergei Diaghilev

Ex. 4.5
a Stravinsky, *The Nightingale*, opening

b Debussy, 'Nuages' (*Nocturnes*), opening

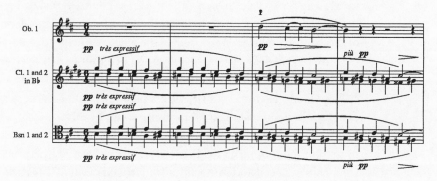

c Musorgsky, 'The useless, noisy day has ended' (*Sunless*), bars 16–17

(1872–1929) was present and, like the conductor and several critics, was
evidently impressed by Stravinsky's score. Diaghilev had been a central figure
in the artistic circles that surrounded and supported his journal *Mir isskustva*
(The World of Art) for more than a decade; he had honed his extraordinary
talent as an impressario in the annual presentations of Russian arts, music,
opera and ballet to Parisian audiences that started in 1906. In these he used

Ex. 4.6 Stravinsky, *The Nightingale*, Act 1, fig. 23

the best talent available to bring Russian art based on Russian folk culture to Western audiences: even the inevitable aesthetic compromises implied by such an enterprise produced works significantly different from the self-consciously Westernised art of, say, Tchaikovsky.

Diaghilev needed some orchestrations for his next season, i.e. the summer of 1909, and he commissioned Stravinsky and Steinberg, among others, to provide them. He intended his creative team – flexible in its membership, but with some favourite key players: the choreographer Mikhail Fokine and the designer Alexander Benois, for example – to put together a ballet based on the folk legends of the firebird and the evil magician Kastchei for the 1910 season. The music was to be composed by Tcherepnin, who actually began work on the score before withdrawing.[52] At this point, Diaghilev commissioned the score instead from Lyadov, whose recent tone-poems *Baba-yaga* (1904), *The Enchanted Lake* and *Kikimora* (both 1909) give ample

Ex. 4.6 (*cont.*)

evidence that he could, in principle, have composed something along the lines that Stravinsky would eventually provide. But Lyadov in turn, and not untypically for him, failed to deliver – he may never even have responded to Diaghilev's letter[53] – and Diaghilev, with time fast running out, had to look elsewhere. It seems likely that others were sounded out; likely, too, that Stravinsky, by coincidence, showed the completed first act of *The Nightingale* to Diaghilev at around this time in an attempt to interest him in that work, and that the two of them may have discussed the 'firebird' project at that

Ex. 4.7 *The Firebird*, opening motive

stage.[54] At any rate, Stravinsky began work on the score in the autumn of 1909, possibly making use of material originally sketched for Act 2 of *The Nightingale*,[55] and shortly afterwards received the formal commission for it.

The commission made Stravinsky's difficulties with Korsakovians irrelevant and allowed him to escape from reliance on their support, bringing him firmly into a new circle of colleagues, many of whom collaborated on *The Firebird*. Among these, in addition to Fokine, Benois and Diaghilev himself, were the folklorist Alexei Remizov, the designer Leon Bakst and the painter Alexander Golovine.[56] The scenario was adapted from a number of folk tales: in the garden of Kastchei's castle, the firebird's beautiful flight attracts the attention of the prince Ivan Tsarevich, who chases the bird, entering inadvertently into Kastchei's domain. The firebird asks to retain her freedom in exchange for a feather, which will bring him luck. As he is about to leave, thirteen princesses enter the garden, where they play by night with the golden apples that are to be found there. As dawn rises they rush away, and the thirteenth princess, with whom the prince is now in love, warns him not to follow, or Kastchei will turn him to stone like twelve other knights before him. Undeterred, he enters the kingdom of Kastchei, and is inevitably captured; remembering the feather, he summons the firebird, who entrances Kastchei and his subjects and lulls them to sleep. Then the firebird shows the prince an egg, which if broken will kill Kastchei; as he does so, the monstrous kingdom disappears, the twelve suitors return to life and Ivan Tsarevich and his princess are united.

There are a number of recurring musical figures, the most pervasive of these being the motive that begins the work (see Ex. 4.7). This motive spans the tritone – an interval at the heart of Rimskyan exotic harmony – and is sufficiently malleable to find a place in octatonic, whole-tone and even diatonic contexts, according to the articulation of its chromatic group of three notes. It is frequently presented in conjunction with its inversion, and is often, though not exclusively, associated with the firebird herself. The prince is assigned folksong-like materials (some genuine folksongs are included), and the princesses also inhabit an essentially diatonic world, albeit with chromatic inflections. Kastchei and his fearful subjects are presented through the full panoply of post-Rimskyan chromaticisms and interval cycles, though their music is quite different in character from that of the also magical firebird – a distinction that is embodied above all in the orchestration. The firebird's dance provides a glittering example: the musical substance is again close to Skryabin's *Poem of Ecstasy* in its core of dominant-quality chords held above a bass that constantly moves by tritone, but the orchestration dances far more effectively than Skryabin's, with fluttering divisi strings, pointillistic high woodwind figures (including piccolo and D clarinet), brassy effects on horns and trumpets, artificial harmonics in the strings, three harps and celesta all making their mark. The entire dance is an intricate tapestry of small figures – it scarcely holds together in Stravinsky's own recording[57] – which forms a remarkable complement to the sight of a prima ballerina apparently on the verge of flight.

The music of *The Firebird* is often heard in one of the three suites that Stravinsky drew from the score. The first was prepared in 1911 simply by extracting suitable sections; in 1919 more music from the ballet was included and the whole suite arranged for reduced forces; the 1945 suite is again longer and once more re-orchestrated. Stravinsky later said that these re-orchestrations amounted to his own 'criticisms' of the original,[58] but there is little doubt that his principal motive in making the 1945 suite, at least, was an attempt to earn royalties from a version that would be subject to international copyright laws. The ballet score deserves to be known in its entirety: some of the music that was omitted from the suites – notably the apparition of Kastchei's subjects, which has more than a hint of *The Rite* about it – is at least as strong as the material that was included. Stravinsky himself, however, seems never to have conducted the full ballet score in live performance.

Two Poems of Verlaine, Op. 9 (1910), Two Poems of Bal'mont (1911), Zvezdolikiy (1911–12)

Some comment on the smaller works composed at the time of the Diaghilev ballet scores is in order. The two pairs of songs to words by Paul Verlaine (Op. 9,[59] 1910) and Konstantin Bal'mont (1911) are less significant in Stravinsky's development than the Gorodetsky songs had been, but to some extent served as bridges respectively from *The Firebird* to *Petrushka*, and from *Petrushka* to *The Rite*. The Verlaine songs developed Stravinsky's fluency in moving between the diatonic and chromatic spheres – the latter category frequently represented by chords of the ninth, giving the harmony a French flavour in keeping with the poetry. The Bal'mont settings, on the other hand, pursue the modernism of the first Gorodetsky song to a point where one can glimpse the combinations of tendril-like woodwind melodies against ostinato backgrounds that would feature so strongly in the slower

Ex. 4.8 *Zvezdoliki*, motto theme

dances of *The Rite*; indeed, the symbolism of Bal'mont's words seems to have been subordinated to this musical development.

Standing between these settings and *The Rite* itself is an imposing short work for male-voice chorus and large orchestra, also to words by Bal'mont. *Zvezdolikiy*, together with *The Rite of Spring*, represents Stravinsky's deepest involvement with the neo-Slavic symbolist movement represented not only by Gorodetsky and Bal'mont but most potently by his collaborator in *The Rite*, Nicolas Roerich. The title of this work is generally translated into French as *Le Roi des étoiles* and from there into English as *The King of the Stars*; the personage in question is the sun-god to whom the chosen maiden sacrifices herself in *The Rite of Spring*. The work opens with an octatonic–diatonic motto theme for unaccompanied voices (Ex. 4.8), which reappears in yet richer harmony, and in monumental orchestration for woodwind and brass, several times as the work proceeds. Stravinsky dedicated the score to Debussy, who accepted the dedication graciously while noting (correctly) that the music would be extraordinarily difficult to perform.[60] Reminiscing about this in his seventies, Stravinsky suggested that *Zvezdolikiy* 'remains in one sense my most "radical" and difficult composition'.[61]

The Nightingale, Acts 2 and 3 (1913–14), *The Song of the Nightingale* (1917)

In conclusion, we should note that when Stravinsky returned to *The Nightingale* after working on the three famous Diaghilev ballets, he was inevitably faced with a problem of stylistic continuity. To some extent this was minimised by the change of scene from the Russian countryside (Act 1) to the Chinese court (Act 2), whose splendours would always have demanded a glittering musical response. This was something he could now provide on a more lavish scale than he might earlier have envisaged: the opera's second act bursts onto the stage with immense energy, and the music of the mechanical Japanese nightingale – which, perhaps surprisingly, bears little relation to the *Three Japanese Lyrics* (1912–13) – is as intricate as clockwork itself. Stravinsky sought to preserve some musical connection with the first act by using the Fisherman's song as a concluding refrain to both Acts 2 and 3. It is stretching the point only a little to say that the extended gestation period of the *Nightingale* music was not quite over even now, for a few years later still, in 1916–17, Stravinsky conjured from the score of the opera a symphonic poem, *The Song of the Nightingale.* The issue of the opera's stylistic fault-line was sidestepped in the symphonic poem by the simple expedient of basing it solely on the music of the second and third acts – though the Fisherman's song, in orchestral guise, ends the symphonic work also.

One illuminating aspect of the later acts of the opera, and thus also of the symphonic poem, can best be understood with reference to the extended gestation of another piece, the ballet *Les Noces*, on which Stravinsky began work in 1914. This production was to have followed directly in line from *Petrushka* and *The Rite of Spring* in being based on Russian folkloric custom – in this case a peasant wedding ceremony[62] – and was also at first intended to extend Stravinsky's orchestral palette beyond even that of *The Rite*. Suffice it to say that war intervened, and that after a number of attempts to find a more modest but at the same time convincing medium for the music, Stravinsky eventually (in 1923) allowed *Les Noces* to emerge with a characteristic scoring of voices, four pianos and percussion. This ensemble was far removed from the 'super-*Sacre*' orchestra he had at first imagined, and which Diaghilev would surely have given him in peacetime circumstances.[63] The result is that the opening of Act 2 of *The Nightingale* (and thus also of *The Song of the Nightingale*) remains the best indication we have of the immediate consequences of *The Rite* for Stravinsky's orchestral technique. Thus, taken together, the opera and its companion-piece trace for us the young composer's journey from Korsakovian magic to the powerfully glittering modernism that was his to command by the time he left Russia for good.

5 Russian rites: *Petrushka, The Rite of Spring* and *Les Noces*

KENNETH GLOAG

The development of Stravinsky's musical language from *Petrushka* through *The Rite of Spring* to *Les Noces* represents Stravinsky's emergence as a modernist composer. In these three works, definitive Russian subject-matter and content is articulated in an increasingly radical language. The expression of Stravinsky's Russian inheritance within the context of modernism – common ground shared by these three works – is the subject of this chapter.

Petrushka

Petrushka, as is well known, was conceived in the aftermath of the success of *The Firebird* and repeated the earlier work's collaborative context: it was written for Diaghilev's Ballets Russes.[1] Following the public success of *The Firebird*, *Petrushka* provides what Richard Taruskin describes as 'Stravinsky's process of self-discovery'.[2] This self-discovery takes the form of a recently acquired technical confidence in conjunction with a new-found modernism. Stephen Walsh has written that 'the emergence of Stravinsky as a modernist, with an individual manner unlike any other, can be dated with some precision to his early work on *Petrushka*'.[3] This 'individual manner' consists largely in the adaptation of borrowed materials, a process which immediately suggests a relationship between past and present and sets up points of reference. At the same time, however, the redefinition of this material generates a sense of distance from its original context. This is evident in the opening moments of the score. The initial gesture of the first of the four tableaux consists of the 'Street vendors' cries' in the flutes, a gesture that is directly invoked by the ballet scenario. This, the first of many borrowings and recollections, is defined by the rising fourth between A and D, but this gesture forms part of a common currency rather than reflecting a specific source. As Taruskin suggests, 'There is no reason to think that Stravinsky would have needed to consult a scholarly tome to obtain appropriate vendors' cries for setting the fairgrounds scene at the opening of the first tableau.'[4] In extra-musical terms, this simple opening gesture evokes the fairground context of the ballet scenario, while its musical function is

Ex. 5.1 *Petrushka*, first tableau, fig. 2

to establish D as the focal point of the harmony. This is supported by the D minor key signature. At fig. 1 the cellos join the texture with a theme that begins on B♮ and rises through D to E. While this rising gesture echoes the initial rise of A to D, this focus on B♮ and E goes some way to undermining the implied stability of D minor. The co-existence of the two thematic statements, along with the two distinct points of implied harmonic focus, are an early indication of juxtaposition, but it also challenges the seeming simplicity of the initial A–D gesture by putting it in an unfamiliar context. Such moments help generate the ongoing sense of tension that pervades the work.

At fig. 2 the first overt reference to a recognised folk-based source occurs, with the lower strings presenting a thematic idea derived from the 'Song of the Volochnobiki', a folksong with which Stravinsky would have been familiar from Rimsky-Korsakov's published collection, and the first of several such references in this first tableau (Ex. 5.1).[5] As Ex. 5.1 demonstrates, the lower strings focus on G, signifying a departure from D and providing a point of textural contrast to the flute of the 'Street vendors' cries'. This new focus on G cannot be viewed as a modulation from the initial D; neither pitch is surrounded by any sort of functional harmonic movement that could be equated with the conventions of the tonal tradition, though they do enjoy a sense of priority that provides a certain reflection of that tradition. These thematic and textural juxtapositions provide the first evidence of Stravinsky's concern with a quite basic formal discontinuity, which is reinforced by the return of the 'Street vendors' cries' (fig. 2^{+3}, flutes) before the more extended realisation of the folk-based material from fig. 2 on its return at fig. 3.

These opening moments can be seen to put in place certain factors that are paradigmatic for the work as a whole: formal, textural and thematic juxtapositions, the focus on specific pitches rather than on functional tonal relationships, the redefinition of historical materials. These factors, both in isolation and in interaction with each other, substantiate the definition of this music as identifiably modernist. They reflect the dislocation between Stravinsky's relationship to inherited Russian tradition and the context within which he was now working, though a line cannot be drawn between the two. What is most notably radical about this music is the extent to which the modernity of the material is formed on an appropriation and reinterpretation of the past.

The second tableau confirms the paradigm described above, but here there is no overt borrowing of identifiable historical material (Russian folksong and popular elements). The absence of such material tends to emphasise the modernity of this section of the score and goes some way to differentiating it from the work as a whole. But, as Taruskin's analysis demonstrates, the entire tableau can be analysed through reference to octatonic collections, a construct which can be seen to form an integral part of Stravinsky's Russian inheritance.[6]

The opening moments of this tableau provide the most notable and widely discussed event in the work, with the collision between C major and F♯ major triads providing a moment of dramatic tension, as well as a unique and significant structural event. It is the C major element that is established in the eight-bar introduction, which effectively resolves onto the C major triad (Ex. 5.2a). However, at fig. 95 the C and F♯ triads are sounded simultaneously, in a moment that has often been used to illustrate the notion of polytonality (Ex. 5.2b). In a seminal essay, 'Problems of pitch organisation in Stravinsky', Arthur Berger demonstrates that both these elements can easily be subsumed within a single octatonic collection;[7] the implications of such an interpretation are treated extensively by both van den Toorn and Taruskin.[8] However, this interpretation, based on hearing

Ex. 5.2 *Petrushka*, second tableau

a

b

the two elements as emerging from a common source – while it does dispense with the dubious concept of polytonality – tends to ignore the unarguable tension that results from the individual identities of the elements and the collision between them, the significance of which is extra-musical.[9] As the tableau unfolds the C and F♯ major triads exert an ongoing influence on the surrounding material. Indeed, their relationship seems to be of precisely the sort to which Stravinsky was referring in an often-quoted remark about polarity:

> our chief concern is not so much what is known as tonality as what one might term the polar attraction of sound, of an interval, or even a complex of tones . . . it is easy to see that the drawing together and separation of poles of attraction in a way determine the respiration of music.[10]

The subsequent musical material is largely defined by C and F♯ as 'poles of attraction', with the music gravitating towards one or the other of these two poles or, in some instances, both. Whether or not one chooses to hear these poles as situated within an octatonic framework, what is most relevant is that these triads – whose identity reflects past conventions and traditions – are at one and the same time octatonic subsets and residual emblematic reflections of common-practice tonality. They are now conceptually distinct from the functions and purpose that gave a precise meaning to such elements within an earlier tonal context.

The tableau subdivides into four sections. The first, as already indicated, is defined initially by the clarification of C at fig. 94^{+3}, with the working out of C and F♯ extending to fig. 101^{+4}. At fig. 102 there is a direct change of texture and the introduction of a D major key signature, though the focus on D that is implied by the key signature and the repetitions of the D/A dyad in the piano part is subverted by the repetition of G♯ in the upper range of the piano in conjunction with the piccolo. As in the first tableau, changes of texture are significant in the simultaneous confirmation and denial of a pitch centre. At fig. 104 there is another sudden change of texture and the introduction of a key signature of one sharp; the extended repetition of E in the bass indicates an E minor tonality. However, as with the previous tonal implications, there is no sense of tonal progression or preparation. After a great deal of movement the music finally arrives on F♯ (at fig. 118^{+2}) as the concluding event of the tableau. These four points can now be seen to have punctuated the tableau, the most dramatic changes of texture coinciding with a new focus on a specific pitch. As Taruskin's analysis shows clearly, they combine to form a 'progression' from C through D and E to F♯[11]:

94^{+3}	102	104	118^{+2}
C	D	E	F♯

Although this chain of moments of focus could be conceived as providing a source of unification for the tableau, the fact that each moment exists in its own right rather than as a direct consequence of the previous moment subverts this possibility. We see and hear this chain as providing a path and, by implication, a sense of coherent structure across a series of largely discontinuous moments, rather than as forming points of connection that draw all the moments together within a unified whole.

In the third tableau, material is absorbed from a distinctly different source; here Stravinsky borrows from the waltzes of Joseph Lanner.[12] This now complicates the process of borrowing, which, up to this point, has been concerned specifically with Russian folk-based material. Nevertheless, the Russianness of the previous borrowings helps lend a sense of 'otherness'

Ex. 5.3 Folk source for the melody in *Petrushka*, 'Wet-nurses' dance'

to this moment, with a wonderful sense of irony which is effective at this particular stage of the ballet scenario. This moment of otherness relates back to the earlier challenge of tonal function. In this instance, although the sound world of the Lanner waltz is seen as the 'other' in relation to the Russian context, the Russian identity itself is challenged through its close proximity to the very different material of the Lanner waltzes.

The fourth and final tableau provides a return to specifically Russian materials; here Taruskin has identified six specific borrowings from folk sources.[13] Perhaps the most striking example is the melody played by the oboe in the 'Wet-nurses' dance' (see Ex. 5.3).[14] This is one of the most literal uses of a folk melody in the work. Although there is a distinct sense of melody and accompaniment, Stravinsky surrounds the melody with an orchestral texture which is rich in detail and motion. The sense of movement implied by the orchestration is, however, effectively suspended by repetitions of A (in the cello) and C (in the viola) as the bass of the texture, and the harmony is, in effect, static. The texture is further complicated by the fact that the folk melody, though set quite literally and thus immediately identifiable, is nevertheless subjected to a process of fragmentation. The first statement (fig. 171–171[+2]) breaks off at fig. 172, the horn enters at fig. 173[+1] with another, shorter, fragment of the melody, and it is not until fig. 174[+2] that the melody is finally expanded, both durationally and texturally.

Although in his analysis of the second tableau Taruskin demonstrates the importance of the octatonic collection, van den Toorn's discussion of the work makes it clear that it is possible to hear large sections from other parts of the score as being basically diatonic.[15] The 'Danse russe' from the first tableau, for example, is clearly defined through a diatonic framework, while at the same time generating its own internal sense of polarity. This will become clear through the consideration of Ex. 5.4a and b, which provides a reduction of the beginning and concluding harmonic events of the 'Danse russe'.

The sense of polarity evident within this section of the score is generated by the large-scale shift from the initial vertical harmony F, G, A, B, D – the diatonic triads of G major and D minor, with G clearly functioning as the 'root' of the harmony (Ex. 5.4a) – to the concluding vertical statement of C, E, G, and A, a harmony which is also based upon the convergence of triads, in this instance A minor and C major, though it is C which now

Ex. 5.4

a *Petrushka*, 'Danse russe', beginning

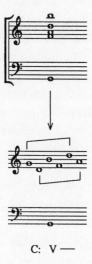

C: V —

b *Petrushka*, 'Danse russe', concluding events

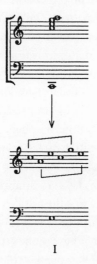

I

c *Petrushka*, 'Danse russe', melodic contour

clearly provides the harmonic bass (Ex. 5.4b). This shift implies a large-scale
movement from G to C with the accompanying tonal implication of a progression from V to I in C. It is also possible, however, to see C and G as
poles of attraction and the movement from beginning to end as a shift from

one pole to another. This polarity, and its tonal implications, provide a framework for much of the diatonic-based material that is evident within this section of the score. Enclosed within the two poles provided by the initial and concluding vertical harmonies are other pitch centres that enjoy localised priority but which, as the music unfolds, exist in parentheses to the main poles of attraction.

These salient pitch centres, which are defined through their prominent placement in the texture and often reinforced through timbral and durational emphasis, are combined and interpreted in various ways, but they continually highlight the structural and syntactic significance of the diatonic collection (in Allen Forte's nomenclature, set 7-35[16]), with the A♯ at fig. 69 being the only element foreign to this collection. Not only does the projection of this set reinforce the significance of the diatonic collection, it is also a G major scale. This G implication can now be related to the implied shift from G to C as part of a general diatonic framework. The melodic contour of the 'Danse russe' is also of interest, as it illustrates Stravinsky's concern with the emphasis of specific pitches; in this instance the initial melodic material continually returns to B within a repeating circular melody (Ex. 5.4c). This melodic focus on B connects with the G-based harmonic context to reinforce the diatonic framework. Other sections of the score reflect a diatonic framework as well. For example, the trumpet solo from fig. 135 of the third tableau is built on an F major scale, eventually leading to the E♭ of the Lanner waltz at fig. 140 (see Ex. 5.5).

Although these moments of sustained diatonicism suggest a certain conventional harmonic vocabulary, there is little direct relationship to functional tonality. While it is possible to suggest a harmonic model that effectively leads from the trumpet's F scale (fig. 134) via a dominant seventh (fig. 139) to the E♭ tonality of the waltz (fig. 140), the aural realisation of such a model is subverted by the change of texture and the resulting sense of distance. Any hint of a conventional harmonic progression is further complicated by the temporary nature of the E♭, which is quickly followed by the change of key signature to B major at fig. 143 and the introduction of the second waltz segment.

This brief discussion of *Petrushka* has centred on certain aspects that imply a questioning of the coherence of the work as a whole. The appropriation of borrowed material has a tendency to give a hybrid identity to the musical materials, while the juxtaposition of textural and pitch events tends to question continuity, as well as the unity of form and content that one would normally assume. But Stravinsky gives his diverse materials a sense of coherence. Even if there is little sense of formal continuity, one feels a logic and inevitability in the sequence of events, with even the most surprising

Ex. 5.5 *Petrushka*, figs. 134–7, trumpet solo

departure seeming, retrospectively, to find its place in that sequence. If this seems to suggest a coherence founded as much on difference as on similarity, it is the mediation between the two – a process that emerged from the interplay of past and present and that is suggested by the ballet scenario – that becomes the defining characteristic of this highly individual work.

The Rite of Spring

The third of Stravinsky's ballets for Diaghilev's Ballets Russes Paris seasons, *The Rite of Spring*, enjoyed an initial reception which immediately situated the work at the forefront of the new challenging epoch of modernism. While much recent writing on the work has tended to reveal substantial continuities with the Russian tradition, the work still has a unique aura, one that resonates with images of innovation and change while simultaneously reconstituting a historical Russian mythology. Although this interaction between past and present was clearly present in *Petrushka*, it is intensified in *The Rite of Spring*. As a result, *The Rite of Spring* defines itself in relation to *Petrushka*, but the relationship between the two works has to do with their differences from each other as much as with any pattern of stylistic continuity.

The distance between *Petrushka* and *The Rite* can be most clearly seen through a consideration of form and structure. *Petrushka* is a sectionalised

Ex. 5.6a Folk source for the opening melody of *The Rite of Spring*

Ex. 5.6b *The Rite of Spring,* opening bassoon melody

score, with each of the four tableaux containing clearly defined divisions and subdivisions that question the presumed continuity of musical form. *The Rite of Spring,* while ultimately resisting the drift towards the incoherent, takes the preference of the discontinuous over the continuous to a new extreme. Each of the two parts of the ballet, 'Adoration of the earth' and 'The sacrifice', consists of several distinct parts, each of which has its own descriptive title and identity. This sectionalisation challenges any notion of continuity.

This is clearly evident from the opening moments of Part One of the score. The Introduction, with its evocative bassoon solo, states a readily identifiable folk source; the implications of this borrowing are discussed by both Morton and Taruskin (Ex. 5.6a and b).[17] The 'Augurs of spring' section, which follows (fig. 13), provides a dramatic contrast to the slow-moving Introduction. After the initial bassoon solo, the texture of the Introduction expands and the movement increases, so that by fig. 11 the music seems to be moving towards a climax. However, the Introduction effectively ends when the music stops at fig. 12. Here Stravinsky inserts a short transitional passage that both recalls the bassoon solo and anticipates the 'Augurs of spring' ostinato pattern (fig. 12^{+3}). While this moment of recollection and anticipation is effective, it tends to negate the impact of the 'Augurs of spring' and provides a connection – a continuity – between the two sections.

The 'Augurs of spring', with the famous chord combining F♭ major and a dominant seventh chord built on E♭, is generally accepted as being the first musical idea Stravinsky put down for the work.[18] The significance of this section is in its repeated statements of this chord, which establish the importance of repetition and the harmonic stasis that results. Although the Introduction and the 'Augurs of spring' are sharply contrasting in character, a sense of harmonic stasis was present already in the earlier section. The initial bassoon melody revolves around A and C, with the first accompaniment consisting of C♯ rising to D in the horn.[19] It is not until fig. 7 that an effective bass to this fluid yet static material emerges. At this point the solo cello has a repeated C, which is later replaced by the sustained B♭ in the double bass at fig. 8. Following the sudden change of texture at fig. 9, B is now repeated as the bass of the texture (fig. 10, double bass) and continues towards fig. 12 and the recollection of the bassoon solo. These three pitches – C, B♭, B♮ – provide moments of localised focus and reference and indicate a certain harmonic context, but it is difficult to identify a specific function for them within some larger progression. B is not the goal of a linear motion that began with C; it is merely the point on which the Introduction effectively stops.

The opening of Part Two (Introduction) reaffirms the idea of a static harmonic framework. The simple oscillation of harmonies prevents a forward momentum. Again there is a sense of focus on a specific pitch (D), which provides some degree of harmonic reference (see fig. 80ff). The main thematic idea of the section that follows, 'Mystic circles of the young girls' (fig. 80^{+2}, fig. $81^{+1/2}$ etc.), is anticipated in the Introduction, but this seems to be more a repetition than a transformation. Although the second version is at a new pitch level, its identity remains intact. There is, however, a distinct change of function. In the Introduction, the first fragmentary statement of this material interrupts the static harmonic texture, and there is a clear sense of juxtaposition, with fig. 82 bringing a return to the texture of fig. 80. In contrast, in the 'Mystic circles' section, the material is expanded (but not necessarily transformed) into a recognisable melodic shape, which makes its folk-like quality more apparent.

The importance of contrast and juxtaposition is reinforced once again at the end of the 'Mystic circles' section, where the repeated chord of the famous concluding bar in 11/4 seems to bear very little relationship to either what has come before or what comes next. The following section, 'Glorification of the chosen one', is marked by a *vivo* tempo indication, and the resulting sense of energy and momentum is in sharp contrast to the static nature of the opening moments of both the Introduction and the 'Mystic circles'. However, the latter concludes with an accelerando and an ascending scale passage, both of which seem to anticipate the section to come. The 11/4 bar interrupts this anticipation.

The opening of the 'Glorification of the chosen one' is marked by pitch repetitions; these produce a static harmonic bass, in contrast to the sense of momentum that is implied by both the tempo and the orchestration. Here it is A that is repeated as the bass, but the focus on G elsewhere in the texture combines with this to create a distinct image of a dominant seventh harmony

Ex. 5.7 *The Rite of Spring*, 'Glorification of the chosen one', figs. 104–5

on A (a harmonic configuration that can be understood to originate from the octatonic collection; see Ex. 5.7). However, given the radical nature of both context and material here, it is no surprise that this harmonic implication does not progress to a resolution on D. Rather, it is repeated throughout the section without any sense of movement or progression, and the next section, 'Evocation of the ancestors', focuses on D♯ rather than D♮ as the sustained bass of a new texture.

Given the heightened use of juxtaposition and discontinuity, clearly the question of closure is rendered somewhat problematic. This is evident from the final moments of both Part One and Part Two. The conclusion to Part One is defined by the sudden cessation of the music during a crescendo, but this signifies neither harmonic arrival nor closure. The material simply stops on a vertical harmony, seemingly at random, a gesture which suggests interruption rather than closure. While this provides a dramatic, accumulative and therefore climactic gesture, the ending of Part Two seems to provide a rather arbitrary concluding gesture to the work as whole, providing neither the drama of interruption nor the satisfaction of resolution.

Although it is entirely feasible to accept *The Rite of Spring* as defined through these sudden changes of texture and juxtapositions of material, and therefore to consider the resulting discontinuity on its own terms, particularly as this can relate to the wider fragmentary nature of modernist culture, there has always been, and perhaps always will be, a seemingly irresistible impulse to seek out possible underlying consistencies and continuities that could bring the work together and reduce the significance of the discontinuous to the level of the musical surface. This impulse, somewhat paradoxically, emphasises the extent to which the 'urge to fragmentation' is ultimately resisted in much modernist culture and thought. The search for consistency leads van den Toorn to state that 'the vocabulary of *The Rite* consists in large part of 0–2 whole-step reiterations, (0 2 3 5) tetrachords, major and minor triads, dominant-seventh chords, and 0–11 or major-seventh vertical interval spans'.[20] All of these constructs can be generated from an octatonic collection. Thus, this suggestion provides an octatonic consistency which, by implication, resonates with the work's Russian background. Taruskin shares this perspective with van den Toorn and, following an extended survey of the work and its background, revisits the problems surrounding the absence of a harmonic and/or thematic unity, concluding that:

> This harmonic cell [0 5 11 / 0 6 11] functions in *The Rite* as another veritable *Grundgestalt*. It is in fact the closest thing one can nominate to a global unifier of this tonally enigmatic score. And such a nominee is indeed an analytical necessity; for while no obvious surface harmony, no theme, no progression, no key can be said to unify *The Rite* over its entire span, its tonal coherence and integrity are impressively evident to the naivest ear.[21]

This configuration [0 5 11 / 0 6 11] is derived from the octatonic collection, consisting of the 'outer notes of the upper tetrachord plus the lowest note of the lower one: (0 6 11); or, reciprocally, the outer notes of the lower plus the topmost note of the higher: (0 5 11), the inversion'.[22] Taruskin provides a convincing selection of examples to demonstrate the operation of this configuration in various contexts. Among these, his Ex. 12.31 (my Ex. 5.8) provides an illustration of its linear deployment. But do his examples signify the existence of a *Grundgestalt*,[23] a concept and terminology appropriated from the theoretical vocabulary of Schoenberg and one that implies derivation and transformation as much as it does repetition? In this instance, it is clear that there is a certain process of repetition in operation, but this does not necessarily suggest that there is an ongoing development of this material across the work. While Taruskin indicates that any such consistency need not imply a unity, his passing reference to a 'tonal coherence' is surely provocative, suggesting as it does some form of tonal background to the work as a whole, a suggestion that raises fundamental questions concerning the most appropriate historical and theoretical location for the work.

Ex. 5.8 Richard Taruskin, *Stravinsky and the Russian Traditions* (1996), Ex. 12.31

The tonal/atonal dichotomy, which is most clearly expressed in the polemical exchange between Taruskin and Forte,[24] raises issues concerning the recurring themes of this brief discussion, which has tended to highlight seemingly simplistic binary oppositions such as unity/fragmentation, continuity/discontinuity and past/present, all of which effectively restate the same problem: the relationship between modernism and tradition. The addition of tonal/atonal to this sequence merely adds another dimension to this recursive paradox. However, Arnold Whittall has suggested a concept that would appear to have the potential to unlock the seeming circularity of these binary oppositions. His interpretation provides for an approach centring on the role of conflict as represented most crucially by 'focused dissonance'.[25] To view dissonance as the conceptual and perceptual opposite of consonance would seem to be merely to restate another binary opposition, but by privileging dissonance over consonance it is possible to view the perceptually dissonant framework of the work as normative, with consonance shifted to a role which, while subordinate, effectively complements the newly privileged status of dissonance. While consonance is decentralised, it retains a meaningful relationship to dissonance, though not necessarily its historical one, where its function was the resolution of dissonance. As Whittall says, 'The "norm" of *Le Sacre* is not one in which predominant dissonances imply unheard consonant resolutions – and it follows that such "imagined" resolutions are unnecessary.'[26] This remark can be related back to Ex. 5.7 from the 'Glorification of the chosen one'. In this instance the dissonant 'dominant seventh' on G does not resolve to the conventional consonance on D, nor does it 'imply unheard consonant resolutions'.

It follows that the shift in the perceived relationship between consonance and dissonance allows for an interpretation that could perhaps correspond more closely to initial responses to the work, thus highlighting its modernity over its relationship to tradition without necessarily losing sight of the value of its traditional background. While it may be difficult to know exactly what Stravinsky meant in his claim that 'very little immediate tradition lies behind *The Rite of Spring*',[27] the work is still a powerful reflection of the Russian tradition, partly, of course, because of the evocative subject-matter of the ballet, but also because of the appropriation of musical materials from that tradition. As already indicated, in its appropriation of folk materials into a distinctively modernist context, *The Rite of Spring* tends to question rather than to synthesise the relationship between past and present. This is a process it shares with *Petrushka* but develops in its own way.

The identification of folk sources, first indicated in relation to the opening bassoon solo, has become a major concern within research on *The Rite of Spring*. The identification of specific sources provides a framework for situating the work, allowing us to view its radical identity as emerging from a specific tradition rather than as representing unmediated opposition to that tradition. As Arnold Whittall has written, '*Le Sacre* may be one of the most crucially radical modern masterpieces, but it needs the perspective of tradition for its nature as well as its effect to be comprehended.'[28] This view of a background of tradition is further emphasised by Taruskin:

Stylistically, it scarcely needs to be emphasized, *The Rite* is hardly retrospective. All the same, the echoes are a reminder that the ballet was written out of – not against – a tradition, and that its stylistic innovations relate to and extend that tradition.[29]

On a technical level, we can hear the work's normative dissonance as constructing a difference from traditional conventions, but in order to give meaning to this departure we must retain some image of the tradition from which it departs. In other words, the innovative radical modernism of this work has to be seen to emerge from a background that includes Stravinsky's Russian inheritance, which sustained its own problematic relationship with convention and tradition.

Les Noces

Like *Petrushka* and *The Rite of Spring*, *Les Noces* is based on definitively Russian subject-matter, with much of its musical material also having been derived from Russian folk sources.[30] The public ritual of the wedding ceremony provides a certain parallel to the public setting of *Petrushka*, but the image of sacrifice implicit in this latest ritual also provides a certain resonance with *The Rite of Spring*. In contrast to the two ballets, however, *Les Noces* is defined as 'Russian choreographic scenes'. Also in contrast to the earlier works, the compositional process of *Les Noces* was more extended and problematic. It was begun in 1914 and therefore could be seen to follow directly on from *The Rite of Spring*. However, because of difficulties involved in defining the instrumental ensemble, the work did not receive its first performance until 1923. In retrospect, the final ensemble of four pianos and percussion now seems inevitable, but in fact the process towards this decision was far from straightforward. As Stravinsky himself later recalled:

> I began the composition of *Les Noces* in 1914 (a year before *Renard*) in Clarens [Switzerland]. The music was composed in short score form by 1917, but it was not finished in full score until three months before the premiere, which was six years later. No work of mine has undergone so many instrumental metamorphoses. I completed the first tableau for an orchestra the size of that of *Le Sacre du printemps*, and then decided to divide the various instrumental elements – strings, woodwinds, brass, percussion, keyboard (cimbalom, harpsichord, piano) – into groups and to keep these groups separate on the stage. In still another version I sought to combine pianolas with bands of instruments that included saxhorns and flügelhorns. Then, one day in 1921 . . . I suddenly realized

Ex. 5.9 *Les Noces*, first tableau, thematic materials

that an orchestra of four pianos would fulfil all my conditions. It
would be at the same time perfectly homogeneous, perfectly impersonal,
and perfectly mechanical.[31]

Homogeneous, impersonal and mechanical: three qualities that become definitive for the work. The homogeneous is reflected in the sense
of collective identity in the subject-matter and in its representation through
the choral writing. The impersonal is reflected by the fact that 'individual roles do not exist in *Les Noces*, but only solo voices that impersonate
now one type of character and now another',[32] while the mechanical is represented by Stravinsky's latest deployment of ostinato effects and rhythmic
impetus.

The work consists of four tableaux. However, although these are intended
to follow each other without a pause, the recurring concerns of juxtaposition
and discontinuity are again in evidence. In the opening of the first tableau
the notion of juxtaposition is evident in the simple alternation of thematic
materials (see Ex. 5.9):

fig.	1	2	4	7	9	10
theme	A	B	A	B A	C	D

This process of repetition, in which the initial material returns, obviously brings to mind the conventions of a rondo pattern. However, rather
than resulting in a process of addition or accumulation, the refrain-like

treatment of the material actually interrupts any meaningful sense of forward momentum.

The initial theme (A) is identified by Taruskin, as is much of the work's material, as being derived from a folk-based source. As well as forming part of a long-range process of repetition, this theme also contains its own internal repetitions, with the repeated returns to E providing a certain focus on this pitch. The repetition of the B–D–B gesture further generates a degree of familiarity. The simple nature of the work's materials is evident as well in the second theme (B), which is also marked by the repetition of E, but now preceded by F♯–F♮. The focus on repeated pitches is reinforced by emphatic rhythmic repetitions. Theme B, for example, consists of a constantly repeated rhythm that disallows any sense of forward momentum. Theme C (fig. 9) also features its own internal repetitions, the initial E–C♯ gesture always returning in the same rhythm. Although the continued focus on E implies a continuity throughout all the themes, there is also a striking sense of contrast, which is reinforced by the change of texture and accompaniment.

The thematic material of the later stages of the score retains many of the musical characteristics of the opening gestures. The fourth tableau begins with a clear focus on D♭, as the music circles round and turns back onto this note (figs. 87–90), providing a parallel to the concentration on E in the first tableau. This D♭ is reinterpreted as C♯ at the conclusion of the vocal line in the final moments of the work (fig. 134). The D♭/C♯ focus provides a degree of continuity throughout the final tableau, though, as in the first, this continuity is often called into question by the many changes of texture and thematic material.

Rhythm and metre were clearly a significant factor in both *Petrushka* and *The Rite of Spring*, but *Les Noces* elevates this dimension to a new level, defined through simplification. This simplification reflects the work's Russian folk origins, but its austerity also generates a modernist sense of being different. Rhythm and metre now become structural in their own right, and rhythm can be defined as structural on its own terms. As Stephen Walsh suggests, 'where *The Rite of Spring* had laid stress on rhythm as something extraordinary and sensational, *The Wedding* [*Les Noces*] asserts the normality of rhythm as a medium for musical expression and structure'.[33] The themes discussed above would be unimaginable separated from their characteristic rhythms, while the rhythms have the potential to function independently of the other musical parameters.

Although *Les Noces* may at times seem to be overshadowed by *Petrushka* and *The Rite of Spring* and remains a highly idiosyncratic work, it still forms an integral part of Stravinsky's Russian period. In its own way, it remains definitive of this stage of his career, redefining its Russian identity in the aftermath of the earlier ballets and providing an effective summation of Stravinsky's Russian style. As van den Toorn concludes:

> however novel or exceptional we choose to consider the instrumentation or the 'cantata-ballet' scheme of *Les Noces*, there can be little doubt that its musical substance is decisively 'Russian'. Indeed, without *Les Noces*, a 'Russian' period becomes scarcely imaginable...[34]

6 Stravinsky's neoclassicism

MARTHA M. HYDE

Introduction: neoclassicism

In his homage to Stravinsky, Milan Kundera explains that Stravinsky's experience of forced emigration triggered a change in his musical style no less reactionary than irrevocable.[1] Also an émigré, Kundera sees emigration as a wound – the 'pain of estrangement: the process whereby what was intimate becomes foreign'. Stravinsky, like any émigré artist, suffered estrangement from the 'subconscious, memory, language – all the understructure of creativity' formed in youth. Leaving the place to which his imagination was bound caused a kind of ripping apart. Kundera believes that emigration erased Russia for Stravinsky. After that, his homeland became the historical landscape of music, and his compatriots were the composers that populate that history. Kundera describes the advent of Stravinsky's neoclassical style as a metaphorical recognition – and achievement – of a new home with the 'classics' of European music:

> He did all he could to feel at home there: he lingered in each room of
> that mansion, touched every corner, stroked every piece of the
> furniture; ... [from] the music of ... Pergolesi to [that of] Tchaikovsky,
> Bach, Perotin, Monteverdi ... to the twelve-tone system ... in which,
> eventually, after Schoenberg's death (1951), he recognized yet another
> room in his home.[2]

Where Kundera sees reverence in Stravinsky's appropriation of history, Stravinsky himself described it as more compulsive and aggressive – a 'rare form of kleptomania'.[3] Whatever attitude we ascribe to it, Stravinsky's appropriation of the past was a genuine artistic engagement, seeking to create modern works by reconstructing or accommodating past styles in a way that maintained his own integrity and identity in the history of music.

In the following discussion, I want to explore four principal strategies that Stravinsky employed in his neoclassical works to accommodate the past. The task is made difficult, first, by the number and variety of works Stravinsky composed during his neoclassical period (roughly from 1920 to 1951) and, second, by confusion about the term 'neoclassicism', in the context of early twentieth-century music and in Stravinsky's own work.

Consider, for example, the differences in scholarly accounts of the origins of neoclassicism. Some scholars attribute the ambiguities of the term to semantic change, nationalistic prejudices, and the polemical torsion inevitable among composers vying to create a niche for themselves in the overpopulated state of the repertoire. Others believe that neoclassicism evolved as a reactionary ploy triggered by the social and political convulsions of the Weimar Republic. Still others – taking a Freudian and formalistic stance – adapt Harold Bloom's 'anxiety of influence' to revise radically the term's usual meaning.[4]

No less confusing are scholarly accounts of what constitutes the 'essence' of Stravinsky's neoclassical style. Too often the confusion results from squabbling about first sightings – when and where Stravinsky first uses triads and major scales, tonal bass lines and dominant–tonic cadences, tonal centres or classical forms. Such sightings clearly have a role in a full description of Stravinsky's neoclassicism, but remain inconclusive if not interpreted in a broader context. The necessary context emerges, I argue, when one recognises that these technical devices almost always concern imitation in some sense of the word: imitation of classical rhythm, phrase structure, harmonic progressions, tonal centres and the like. Analyses of Stravinsky's neoclassical works have tended to isolate specific features, but to lack a theory of imitation that would help identify and categorise imitative resources and effects – that would, in other words, help us to give content to the term 'neoclassical'.[5]

Whenever any kind of secular canon-formation occurs – whenever any choice is made of authorities or models for new artistic creation – T. S. Eliot's question 'What is a classic?' becomes inescapable.[6] A classic is a past work that remains or becomes relevant and available as a model, or can be made so through various techniques of accommodation. Stravinsky's neoclassical pieces invoke earlier classics in a much broader sense than merely music in the style of Haydn or Mozart. What makes a classic in this broader sense is being *chosen* as a model for some sort of anachronistic engagement, some manner of imitative crossing of the distance that divides the new work from its model. This act of choosing is precisely what Kundera portrays by picturing Stravinsky wandering in the mansion of musical styles, choosing which objects to appropriate and which rooms to inhabit.

Perhaps we can agree at the outset that neoclassicism, in any of the arts, involves an impulse to revive or restore an earlier style that is separated from the present by some intervening period. The Renaissance created itself by breaking one historical continuity in order to repair another broken continuity. That is, the Renaissance created the Middle Ages by recognising that the Middle Ages had broken or fallen away from 'classical antiquity'.

Any neoclassicism does the same, rejecting a prevailing period style in the name of restoring an earlier, more authentic, still relevant – and therefore classic – style. That is precisely what happened when early twentieth-century French composers (joined later by Stravinsky) repudiated Romantic music because, in their view, it had abandoned the classical virtues to revel in Teutonic excess, obscurity and subjectivity. A neoclassical aesthetic thus reaches across a cultural and chronological gap and tries to recover or revive a past model. By doing so, it clears ground for modern artists by devaluing intervening styles.

To speak very broadly, there are two modes of returning to the classics, two routes giving access to models acknowledged as classical. The first is philological or antiquarian and the second – and for the history of the arts the more important – is translation or accommodation. Translation and accommodation both grapple with anachronism because they cannot avoid the incongruities that arise from linking different times or periods.[7] Reading our own concerns and needs into the classics, we recognise the classics advancing to meet us on the path we are following. There are several modes of accommodation – modes of accessing the past – but for Stravinsky the most important is what, for lack of a better term, I call 'metamorphic anachronism'. This specific mode of accommodation involves various kinds or strategies of imitation.

A brief digression may help to clarify what I mean by anachronism. As I use it, the term does not imply any kind of failure or mistake. Musical anachronism is rooted in the recognition that history affects period style and that period style affects composition. This is not controversial; we are all willing to assume that pieces are datable on internal evidence. But this recognition of historical change also suggests that pieces will become 'dated' in the negative sense, that is, that they will eventually sound 'out of date'. Music, like the other arts, can incorporate or exploit this capacity for datedness, but only by juxtaposing or contrasting at least two distinct styles. This contrast or clash of period styles or historical aesthetics is the simplest definition of anachronism.[8]

Anachronism can be used in art in a number of different ways, but the type of anachronism most relevant to a neoclassical aesthetic is one that 'confronts and uses the conflict of period styles self-consciously and creatively to dramatize the itinerary, the diachronic passage out of the remote past into the emergent present.'[9] This is the type I call 'metamorphic anachronism', borrowing from geology where metamorphic rocks fuse or compress the old into the new. In music, metamorphic anachronism deliberately dramatises a historical passage – bringing the present into a relationship with a specific past and making the distance between them meaningful.

When anachronism – that is, the conflict between period elements in a piece of music – is meaningful, then a phoenix springs from the ashes. When it is not, then only a corpse emerges, shrunken and mummified from the tomb, though perhaps ornamented with modern trinkets. The main question is not whether anachronism has been avoided, but whether it has been controlled. If not, then no itinerary between past and present is opened, no genuine renewal occurs, and the impulse to revive the past is abortive or trivial.[10]

One mode of controlled anachronism – parody – is usually distinct from a genuine neoclassical impulse, but is nonetheless relevant to several of Stravinsky's works that are sometimes mistakenly described as his earliest experiments in neoclassicism. Composed between 1917 and 1920, just as Stravinsky began to explore compositional techniques that later mark his neoclassical style, these pieces include 'Three dances' from *The Soldier's Tale* (Tango, Waltz, Ragtime), *Ragtime* for eleven instruments, and *Piano-Rag-Music*. While these pieces are Stravinsky's first to be based on contemporary popular dances and do feature more prominently the usual major and minor scales, they nonetheless seem better described as parodies or satires, for their effect derives from making that which has become too familiar appear unfamiliar – or at least barely recognisable. In these pieces, Stravinsky seeks not to revive a past tradition, but playfully to mock popular conventions.

Stravinsky's *Piano-Rag-Music* bears out this view, especially in its ending, which surely pokes fun at contemporary infatuation with jazz improvisation and rags (see Ex. 6.1). Building up to an extended climax of improvisatory flourishes, the piece suddenly subsides to an exhausted, motoric vamp that abruptly breaks off for no apparent reason, as if the performer abandons the piece for lack of inspiration or interest.[11] Particularly surprising is how Stravinsky uses irregularly spaced dotted lines in place of bar lines, for it throws into question the regular metrical patterns of the rag form. Poking fun at the fashion of combining improvisation with a metrically rigid form, Stravinsky concludes with a spent motivic fragment – as if asking a question that, as yet, has no answer. Such parodic or satiric imitation deliberately teases our expectations, replacing the familiar with an absurdly distorted reconstruction, and is ordinarily – though perhaps not categorically – incompatible with neoclassicism.

If anachronism is controlled and not parodic, if the impulse to revive is successful, how are we to describe the imitative process? I find it useful to identify four broad strategies of imitation that Stravinsky employs in his neoclassical works, each of which controls anachronism in a different manner while implicitly portraying one perspective on history.[12]

Ex. 6.1 *Piano-Rag-Music* (1919 edition), ending

Eclectic imitation

Stravinsky's first and most frequent type of imitation in his neoclassical works is what I call 'eclectic imitation'. This characterises works in which allusions, echoes, phrases, techniques, structures and forms from an unspecified group of earlier composers and styles all jostle with each other indifferently. Such an eclectic mingling features prominently in Stravinsky's early neoclassical works, which often use both diatonic and octatonic pitch structures and self-consciously imitate classical phrase structure, simple dance patterns, various tonal forms and baroque contrapuntal textures.[13] Eclectic imitation treats the musical past as an undifferentiated stockpile to be drawn on at will, and it permits the kind of brilliant manipulation of new and old that produced a number of Stravinsky's most important works, including the Octet, Concerto for piano and wind instruments, Sonata for piano, Concerto in D for violin and orchestra and *Oedipus Rex*. Stravinsky himself acknowledged the eclecticism of this mode of imitation, borrowing a term from Kurt Schwitters to describe *Oedipus*. 'Much of the music is a *Merzbild* [construction of random materials], put together from whatever came to hand.' *Oedipus* included 'such little games as . . . the Alberti-bass horn solo accompanying the Messenger', as well as 'the fusion of such widely divergent types of music as the *Folies Bergères* tune' that occurs when 'the girls enter, kicking' and frequent use of 'Wagnerian 7th chords'. Stravinsky defends this procedure by asserting that 'I have made these bits and snatches my own, I think, and of them a unity. "Soule is form", Spenser says, "and doth the bodie make."'[14] Stravinsky's allusion to Spenser, who wrote the first English epic in a made-up language designed to seem archaic, highlights his own playfully serious use of anachronism.

Eclectic imitation is a process by which sources and models are compiled. Rather than a well-organised museum, tradition becomes a warehouse whose contents can be rearranged and plundered without damage or responsibility. At its weakest, of course, this kind of eclectic imitation simply sports with anachronism or wallows in it, but when used precisely and deliberately it can create a vocabulary of a new and higher power – a power that gains strength from rhetorical skill, although not necessarily from a unified or integrated vision.[15]

Octet

The Octet for wind instruments, written in 1922 and often cited as Stravinsky's first neoclassical masterpiece, is a particularly successful example of eclectic imitation. Its effect derives from a rhetorical confrontation between various classical forms – set forth in Baroque-like textures – and the composer's idiomatic use of diatonic and octatonic pitch structures. Stravinsky pointed towards these historical models when he commented that the Octet was influenced by the terseness and lucidity of Bach's two-part Inventions and by his own rediscovery of sonata form.[16] Of the numerous imitative strategies at work in this piece, the most telling is the clash of diatonic and octatonic pitch structures to create an analogue for tonal closure (or cadence).

One clear example occurs at the opening of the second movement ('Theme and Variations'), whose form features a theme and an initial variation that recurs in a rondo-like design.[17] Ex. 6.2 shows an abridged reduction of the complete variation theme. The theme's first part, presented by the flute and clarinet at fig. 24, uses seven of eight pitches from an octatonic scale and stresses A as the central pitch class. The octatonic scale, labelled Collection III, appears at the bottom of Ex. 6.2. Typical of octatonic structures in Stravinsky's neoclassical works, this theme exploits the [0,1,3,4] tetrachord which here structures the initial contour of the theme, using the pitches A, B♭, C, C♯. The second part of the theme, presented by the second trumpet at fig. 25, begins with a transposition of this same tetrachord on C, thereby making use of D♯, the last remaining pitch of Collection III. The

Ex. 6.2 Octet (1952 version), 'Tema con Variazioni': reduction and analysis from van den Toorn (1983)

theme then continues with the tetrachord's return to the central pitch A by the first trombone three bars before fig. 26.

However, beneath the theme (beginning at fig. 24) there appears an accompaniment that unambiguously alludes to a diatonic structure that stresses D and implies a kind of pseudo D minor reference. The bassoons' ascending bass line moves stepwise up from D to an implied dominant, A, and then returns to D, suggesting a I–II–V–I harmonic progression. But neither D nor the tonic triad (D, F, A) is part of Collection III, the octatonic collection that structures the theme. Consequently, among other ambiguities Stravinsky forges a bond between the variation theme and its accompaniment that creates the *allusion* to a dominant–tonic relation. The allusion is consummated in the final bar (fig. 25^{+6}) by what sounds like a cadential dominant-to-tonic resolution on D, in which the variation theme's last pitch, F♯, neatly unites Collection III with a traditional Picardy-third closure of the implied D minor tonality.

Apart from the 'Theme and Variations' form and its conventional texture of melody plus accompaniment, the imitative strategies in the Octet that one can call neoclassical derive from the joining of diatonic and octatonic structures. The bond is loose, with only some elements held in common, but the overall effect alludes to a dominant–tonic cadence that delineates the form of the theme and hence that of the movement. However, the allusion is only approximate, for octatonic structures intrude and block an authentic tonal cadence; octatonicism here remains superimposed on a D minor tonality, with both octatonicism and tonality maintaining their identities, despite their superimposition. The ambiguities that inevitably result are essential features of the theme. The clash of diatonic and octatonic elements creates an equilibrium that resists fusion or synthesis. No definite meaning emerges from the superimposition since, for their effect, both must maintain their independence; here, clashing elements function primarily as rhetorical counters.

In the variations that follow, Stravinsky varies his means of exploiting the clash between tonal allusions and octatonic collections, but continues to use them as rhetorical counters. For instance, in the final variation (Var. E), a stunning finale to the movement and reportedly the composer's favourite, Stravinsky creates a fugato texture in which the theme, still consisting of pitches from Collection III but now with an angular Baroque contour, is answered at the dominant G♯ by pitches from Collection I (suggesting a 'real' rather than 'tonal' answer) (see Ex. 6.3). Here the tonal allusion relies not on a bass line (as in the theme), but merely on a single note, the implied dominant that initiates the fugal 'answer'.

Eclectic imitation in the Octet extends well beyond the clash between tonal and octatonic vocabularies. Indeed, Stravinsky employs extraordinarily varied means to sustain a delicate rhetorical balance between tonal allusion and reality. In the first movement, for instance, he dispenses with the octatonic collection and instead manipulates texture to mimic the sections of a classical sonata form. He then constructs contrapuntal progressions that join these sections together in a way that significantly alters the form. Essential to the altered form, however, is that its meaning resides only in the relationship it creates with the classical model that has been evoked.

Eclectic imitation in the Octet works in several ways. First, no synthesis between old and new is sought, since their effect relies on a precise

Ex. 6.3 Octet (1952 version), 'Tema con Variazioni', Variation E

balance between them; the new is superimposed on the old, and both function as rhetorical counters by maintaining their independence. Second,
the anachronisms introduced so freely – jumbling together features of
baroque and classical styles – work to create only the illusion of various
tonal structures. Keys, cadences, modulations, and the like all lack essential
tonal elements that would provide the organic or developmental integrity
of form required in 'authentic' classical pieces.

While non-organic or non-teleological forms characterise Stravinsky's
neoclassical pieces, they also characterise pieces from his earlier Russian
period, although these earlier pieces seldom use tonal imitations. Commonly termed 'moment form' and often cited as Stravinsky's most
significant innovation in his early Russian works, these forms exploit fragmentation, discontinuity, and abrupt changes in textures and rhythms. The
discrete sections or moments are often marked by ostinatos or short motives
whose repetitions vary, but rarely develop in a traditional or 'classical'
manner.[18]

Perhaps by 1917, when Stravinsky was living in Switzerland and unable
to return to Russia, he found it futile to extend moment form beyond its
achievement in such pieces as *The Rite of Spring* and *Les Noces*. In any case,

Stravinsky's new reliance on imitating tonal procedures also coincides with greater formal continuity than in his Russian works; more regular or periodic phrase structures appear, coupled with far fewer abrupt discontinuities in texture and rhythm. But because the tonal imitations supported by this greater continuity still remain allusive – not quite whole – Stravinsky's neoclassical forms still lack the organic or teleological development typical of authentic classical pieces. In his neoclassical forms, just as in his Russian works, discrete sections seem to begin and end without the compelling internal logic that we take for granted in classical compositions.

While greater continuity is a feature of Stravinsky's earliest neoclassical works, these works also rely on new means of articulation. In place of sharply defined, but disconnected *vertical* moments, Stravinsky's more continuous textures now comprise simultaneous, but sharply defined *horizontal* layers. More importantly, these horizontal layers – like the earlier vertical 'moments' – often seem to achieve their rhythmic or harmonic effect only to the extent that they remain disconnected from or independent of one another. As in tonal music, Stravinsky's neoclassical pieces usually allow the bass to govern overall harmonic direction. However, in this case the bass does not strictly control the internal structure or movement of the higher voices or lines. That is, the higher lines progress in the same general direction as the bass, but do so independently. And when the various lines do become momentarily aligned or synchronised, the effect usually signals a formal event such as the beginning or end of an extended phrase or section.

Mavra

In his neoclassical works, Stravinsky invents new means of articulating independent lines or strata above what we can only loosely call a functional bass line. One early and particularly successful instance appears in the opening aria from *Mavra*, completed one year before the Octet. Dedicating *Mavra* to Pushkin, Glinka and Tchaikovsky, Stravinsky for the first time explicitly identifies the past classical tradition that he seeks to revive or re-engage. He believes this tradition to have been prematurely cut off by those responsible for Russian modernism, the Russian Five, and in particular by his teacher Rimsky-Korsakov.[19]

Whether for professional, artistic or political reasons, Stravinsky associated Russian modernism with German culture, the atrocities of the First World War, and the revolutions that forced him into exile. In his public statements, Stravinsky aligned himself with Tchaikovsky, the 'Latin-Slav culture' and the 'Austrian Catholic Mozart' against the 'German Protestant Beethoven, inclined toward Goethe'.[20] Musical evidence of this new alignment first becomes explicit in Parasha's aria, the Russo-Italian bel canto aria that opens *Mavra* (see Ex. 6.4).[21]

Ex. 6.4 *Mavra*, Parasha's aria (piano-vocal score)

The aria presents Parasha, the young heroine, dreaming of her lover, Mavra, as she sits at the window embroidering. Most striking in this aria – especially in the light of Stravinsky's earlier Russian works – is what appears to be a functional (tonal) bass line (cello, double bass, tuba), which uses a rigid four-beat ostinato pattern alternating between three beats of tonic and one beat of dominant (3+1: TTTD). Such a banal ostinato, no doubt, is meant to suggest both the repetitive nature of Parasha's task and her distracted sense of confinement. Above the bass, off-beat chords (horns) appear to accompany the bass, but in fact unfold a tonic–dominant ostinato that spans six beats (3+3: TDD+TDT), thereby contradicting the bass's four-beat tonic-dominant pattern. Against these two conflicting out-of-phase strata, the melody unfolds a third – an asymmetrical pattern that complements the alternating notated metres of 3/4 and 5/8, meant to portray Parasha's uncontrolled romantic fantasies. Most importantly, the asymmetrical melody uses a bel canto style, infused with Russian gypsy folk gestures and mixing together old and new stylistic features. What is old – yet new to Stravinsky – is the appearance of a tonal B♭ minor scale with a functional leading note that can accommodate an authentic tonal cadence. What is new is how Stravinsky articulates form by joining these three non-aligned, independent strata in a way that blocks or delays cadential resolution of the dominant until the end of the aria's first section (two beats before fig. 3). Only at this single point does the leading note (melody) finally become aligned with the bass's dominant, thereby signalling an upbeat/downbeat cadential resolution to the following tonic. (Immediately after this cadence, the second section begins with an abrupt modulation to G minor.) In Ex. 6.4, the cadential alignment both articulates form and confirms that among the three conflicting strata or lines, the bass line – as in classical tonality – is primary.

The technique of constructing textures by layering simultaneous but independent strata creates a striking effect that Stravinsky continues to refine and develop in later neoclassical works. In textures that rely on tonal formulas or gestures, the effect often involves making the familiar sound foreign – but not so much as to block recognition of the tonal allusion or gesture. Typically, simultaneous but dissociated strata vary in the way they relate to one another. As Jonathan Cross argues, Stravinsky de-familiarised the familiar, not by removing 'past music . . . from its original context – that much is self-evident; rather, by placing familiar objects in new contexts he enables us to see them in new ways.'[22] But these new ways 'have the effect of changing tonality, with its associated phenomena of rhythm, phrasing and harmony, from a process into a system of gestures which constantly alludes to, but does not pursue, the logic which the listener expects of them.'[23]

Most importantly, Stravinsky's technique of layering strata enables him to sustain or re-create in a neoclassical idiom the rhythmic vitality of movement that so characterises his earlier Russian works. In Parasha's aria, for example, the teasing delay of metrical alignment among the three strata creates a voluble, buoyant metrical effect whose eventual synchronised resolution mimics the kind of build-up and release of tension common to tonal music – but that nonetheless avoids the authentic metrical and harmonic structures on which tonal music relies. In his larger neoclassical forms, Stravinsky's method of co-ordinating independent strata to sustain long-range rhythmic structures often assumes a more allusive and complex form.

Concerto in D

In the Concerto in D for violin and orchestra, Stravinsky articulates discrete textural layers through new and varied means. Most often, layers are identified by one or more unique features, such as a distinct combination of motive, interval, pattern of chords, rhythm, register, instrumentation, collection of pitches or pitch centre. While Stravinsky still delineates forms by synchronising constituent layers so as to converge on a single event or sonority, the layers now proceed with greater internal independence. In other words, layers have greater temporal dissociation and fewer points of synchronisation. To create a particularly dramatic effect, such as a climax or formal reprise, Stravinsky often intensifies the temporal dissociation of the layers by intensifying the conflict among their implied metres. One good example occurs in the three-part form of the Concerto's first movement, where temporal dissociation and metrical conflict among textural layers create a climax that signals the end of the movement's first part and the beginning of its second.[24]

Reverential imitation

Similar techniques for creating continuity, rhythmic movement and layered articulation characterise – but perhaps to a lesser extent – a second, quite different type of imitation that I term 'reverential imitation'. In some of Stravinsky's earliest and most famous neoclassical works, reverential imitation follows the classical model with a fastidiousness arising from consciousness of historical discontinuity. In one sense, the imitation proceeds as if it were reverently transcribing a hallowed text, but nonetheless adorns it with modern affectations. The most obvious candidate is *Pulcinella*. Unlike the Octet or the Violin Concerto, *Pulcinella* relies not merely on borrowed styles, but on borrowed music: two *opere buffe* and several instrumental pieces that Stravinsky incorrectly assumed were composed solely by Pergolesi.[25]

Pulcinella

Except for the borrowed popular idioms used in the ragtime pieces and dance movements of *The Soldier's Tale*, *Pulcinella* represents Stravinsky's first major composition based on pre-existing material. For this reason critics have seen it as signalling the onset of his neoclassical style. Despite this common view, much of the borrowed material is left unchanged, rather than recomposed in a modern idiom, and Stravinsky's additions resemble an elegant gloss more than an original composition. Some have therefore convincingly argued that *Pulcinella* is best described as an arrangement – even given its vitality and immense popularity. In other words, because *Pulcinella* fails to present a genuine conflict of period styles, failing also to control musical anachronism, it more closely resembles an artful arrangement than an authentic neoclassical piece.

The lack of a genuine conflict of styles arises from Stravinsky's reproducing the original harmonies largely intact, along with their implied tonal progressions and voice leading. Onto this classically tonal structure, Stravinsky superimposes modern ornaments and orchestral effects, adding devices such as diatonic dissonances, extended ostinatos, brilliant orchestration, altered phrase lengths, and so on. However dazzling, these devices seldom threaten the original tonal idiom.

The Fairy's Kiss

A better illustration of Stravinsky's reverential imitation is *The Fairy's Kiss*, an allegorical ballet inspired by the music of Tchaikovsky. Taking the opportunity to pay 'heartfelt homage to Tchaikovsky's wonderful talent',[26] Stravinsky organised the ballet around borrowings from Tchaikovsky's piano and vocal music. But unlike *Pulcinella*, these borrowings are extensively re-composed and often strung together by lengthy passages wholly of Stravinsky's making. *The Fairy's Kiss* sounds less a pastiche than it might, because Stravinsky faithfully reproduces Tchaikovsky's style in seamless blending of borrowed materials with their newly composed surroundings. Originality here serves to evoke the older composer, to impersonate his style almost with reverence and fidelity. Stravinsky, in fact, mimics both strengths and weaknesses in Tchaikovsky's style. Re-creating Tchaikovsky's distinctive orchestration, for example, Stravinsky also adopts his often rigid phrase structures. This reverential stance has caused some critics to argue that the ballet lacks all irony, and hence the stylistic jostling between old and new that neoclassical works require.[27] This assessment seems misguided, but it does respond to the mode of imitation employed in the piece, which seeks to recreate reverentially the classical model.

Confronted with a short excerpt from *The Fairy's Kiss*, most listeners would guess Tchaikovsky as the composer, but any extended excerpt introduces doubt. One reason is that exact repetition – a stylistic fetish in Tchaikovsky's music – is assiduously avoided. In *The Fairy's Kiss*, themes rarely repeat without variation. Ex. 6.5 shows one of Stravinsky's borrowings, from Tchaikovsky's 'Zimniy vecher' ('Winter Evening'), Op. 54, no. 7. Tchaikovsky repeats this passage three times, without alteration, to separate the song's stanzas. In *The Fairy's Kiss*, the passage serves as the primary borrowing for the D minor Allegro sostenuto that makes up most of Tableau I. Ex. 6.6 shows two of its repetitions, both varied with an imaginative abandon rarely, if ever, found in Tchaikovsky. Whether Stravinsky is offering a gentle critique of Tchaikovsky's music, or merely succumbing to personal preference, is of little consequence, for Stravinsky's stylistic alterations still respect the boundaries of Tchaikovsky's tonal style. Anachronism may ruffle the surface, but the essential style remains intact. In this piece, reverential

Ex. 6.5 Tchaikovsky, 'Zimniy vecher' (Winter evening), Op. 54, no. 7, bars 34–44

Ex. 6.6

a *Divertimento* (arrangement of *The Fairy's Kiss*, trans. for violin and piano by Stravinsky and Druskin), 'Sinfonia', bars 79–85

b *Divertimento*, 'Sinfonia', bars 121–6

imitation allows Stravinsky to celebrate rather than control anachronism, as though any major alteration of the model might damage its integrity.

There is, however, a potential defect in *The Fairy's Kiss* that frequently surfaces in reverential imitations. This defect results from viewing the model as accessible, but beyond significant alteration or criticism, and may be heard as a lack of irony. This kind of reverent reproduction of a model

Ex. 6.7 *Divertimento*, 'Sinfonia', bars 239–56 (ending)

has difficulty functioning transitively, for the reproduction almost always succumbs at least occasionally to idioms that are alien or unbecoming to the original, and whose violations of the original's norms threaten to break out of artistic control. Consider, for example, the newly composed passage that Stravinsky uses to conclude Tableau I, shown in Ex. 6.7. Few would hear Tchaikovsky as the composer of this music. With its clashing dissonances, irregular phrasing, truncated repetitions and, most important, an ambiguous tonality that seems to balance two competing tonal centres, A and D, this passage is quintessential Stravinsky. As if Stravinsky's impersonation of the earlier composer drops away momentarily (perhaps deliberately), this example exposes the abyss that separates the modern composer from his model. Just this sort of momentary lapse in style often breaks loose in reverential imitations. Uncontrolled, such lapses seem to violate essential norms of the model. In this instance, the recreated tonal Tableau must accommodate – or at least co-exist with – an ending whose structure is antithetical to tonality, which will invariably startle an attentive listener.

The authenticity of Stravinsky's return to Tchaikovsky bears historical scrutiny, for 1928 marked the year that Stravinsky spoke most vehemently against modernism, which he believed was implicated in the social upheavals and destructions of World War I. In an article published in 1928, Arthur Lourié, Stravinsky's associate in the 1920s, describes Stravinsky as the 'conservative and reactionary element' in contemporary music, who seeks 'to affirm unity and unalterable substance' amidst the ceaseless flux and disintegration of modern culture.[28] While 'the order to return to Bach', he continues, has only recently been the vogue, it has had its day. 'The musical heritage of the nineteenth century, so recently rejected, has acquired new recognition, it is being called upon to influence contemporary music.' It becomes clear, in fact, that Lourié is describing Stravinsky's re-engagement with Tchaikovsky, Russia's most 'classical' composer and the premier composer of imperial Russia. This re-engagement began with *Mavra* in the early 1920s and now continues with *The Fairy's Kiss*. Lourié describes *The Fairy's Kiss* as 'a natural reaction against modernism', but Taruskin more aptly intuits that 'this gentle music was the fruit of crises, of disillusion, and, it seemed, of exhaustion'.[29] The crisis passed by the end of the decade and bore fruit in the 1930s with a new creative vitality that consolidated the innovations of the previous decade. While the works of the 1930s may seem less radical, many none the less represent Stravinsky's most refined neoclassical style.[30]

Heuristic imitation

A third type of imitation which I call 'heuristic imitation' characterises a number of Stravinsky's neoclassical works that often follow most closely specific classical or baroque forms. Perhaps because heuristic imitation seems to emerge from eclectic imitation, it is sometimes difficult to judge which label better describes the imitative mode of a particular piece. Not infrequently, different movements from a single piece make use of different types. Difference here is one of degree. Stravinsky's eclectic imitations usually do not achieve a cultural or historical continuity that transcends the anachronisms so freely introduced. Because their past is fragmented, jumbled and, in effect, de-historicised, they have difficulty mediating between past and present. They tend to ignore the problem of anachronism or to play with it within a hospitable texture, but seldom confront it directly. Thus, Stravinsky's eclectic imitations seldom arrive at a deeper, more dramatic conflict and engagement with the past. When a deeper engagement does occur, I call it heuristic imitation.[31]

   Stravinsky uses heuristic imitation to accentuate rather than conceal the specific link he forges with the past. Heuristic imitation advertises its dependence on an earlier model, but in a way that forces us to recognise the disparity, the anachronism, of the connection being made. Heuristic imitation dramatises musical history by relying on the datedness of musical styles for aesthetic effect. Stravinsky uses heuristic imitation to position

Ex. 6.8

a Beethoven, Symphony no. 1 in C major, movement I

b Stravinsky, Symphony in C, movement I

himself within a specific culture and tradition, thereby opening a transitive dialogue with the past that allows him to take – and take responsibility for – his place in music history.

Symphony in C

The Symphony in C places itself squarely within the classical symphonic tradition by reproducing – at least at the outset – essential features of a classical symphony. The more obvious of these features are the title (which implies a C tonality), four movements following the traditional order, a classical orchestra, diatonic harmonies with only modest dissonance, metric regularity, relatively simple textures and – most importantly – a first movement whose sections mimic those of a classical sonata form (i.e. an exposition with two themes, a development and a recapitulation). By using such recognisable features, Stravinsky advertises his classical model, but does so without actual thematic quotation.

The success of heuristic imitation, which necessarily juxtaposes two clashing styles, lies in Stravinsky's ability concisely to mimic formulae that instantly evoke classical genres. The economy and strength of these formulae can then absorb or accommodate stylistic elements that clash or seem foreign to it.[32] A good example is to be found in the first theme of the Symphony's first movement, which advertises not only its classical model but a likely composer as well. Ex. 6.8 compares the first theme of Stravinsky's Symphony with that of Beethoven's First Symphony (also in C). Notice how Stravinsky's theme, like Beethoven's, consists of a repeating motive comprising the same three notes (C, G, B) with only an occasional occurrence of a fourth note (E) to fill out the triadic harmony. Moreover, in both themes the rhythmic pacing of the repeating motive intensifies in the middle of the

Ex. 6.9 Symphony in C, first movement, bars 1–10

Ex. 6.10 Symphony in C, first movement, bars 24–33

theme and then subsides towards the end. The stylistic imitation continues in the following phrase, where Stravinsky, like Beethoven, repeats the theme one step higher, on D, to round off the movement's first period.

Stravinsky continues to imitate the style and form of a classical symphony but, as the movement progresses, the listener increasingly senses elements that disrupt its classical purity. These elements work in two ways: first, they advertise the datedness of the older model; and second, they recast or translate the older model into a modern vernacular. In other words, the disruptive elements work together to create an integrated style that not only competes with or challenges the original, but also updates it. Through this process, Stravinsky reveals a particular historical perspective – a specific route from past to an emerging present; as the disruptive, modern elements become more integrated, they also become more powerful and gradually weaken the classical structures from which they derive.

To illustrate how this process works, we need to return to the beginning of the first movement, which opens with a stately 'Beethovenesque' introduction, one that presents the three-note motivic cell (B–C–G) which Stravinsky uses to generate the movement's first theme (see Ex. 6.9). While the listener probably hears the opening in the key of C major, there is none the less a subtle dissonance or ambiguity of key that makes itself felt. First, the motive could articulate E minor as well as C major. Three features create this ambiguity: 1) since the motive, played in unison, is not harmonised, pitch C does not appear in the bass; 2) pitch B (and not C) is repeated and occurs on the single downbeat, while pitch C occurs only once as a quaver off-beat; and 3) the placement of pitch B on the downbeat allows it to be heard either as an embellishing pitch (an appoggiatura to C) or as a harmonic pitch (itself embellished by C as an incomplete neighbour note). Consequently, the pitch B can function in either of two important ways: either as the leading note of C major or as the dominant of E minor. Notice that the tonal ambiguity between C major and E minor intensifies in bars 3–4 where the second bassoon starts as if to end the phrase with an expected bass motion from the tonic to the dominant of C major, but is cut off prematurely by the timpani's repeating B in the lowest register. Moreover, both the tonic and dominant chords are clouded by their own leading notes in the first bassoon and horns. As a result, the phrase ends in bar 4 with a dominant chord on G that includes F♯, the one pitch that differentiates the scale of E minor from that of C major.

On the surface, the twenty-five-bar introduction seems to unfold in a typically classical fashion. The principal motive appears in varied forms, suggesting conventional thematic development, and a dramatic crescendo (repeating ascending scales) creates an extended upbeat that leads as a downbeat into the beginning of the first theme. But, below the surface, various details in the introduction continue to undermine C major and work together to further the suggestion of E minor. For example, the three-note motive is transposed to E at bar 7 (D–E–B); the concluding scales that lead into the first theme all contain an F♯; and the dominant chord that precedes the first theme contains both F♮ and F♯ (bars 24–5).

One might anticipate that the introduction's tension between C major and E minor will be resolved by the principal theme, but it is not. As shown by Ex. 6.10, the first theme (as in the introduction) excludes C from the bass, relying instead on a quaver ostinato consisting of only two notes, E and G, the only notes held in common between a C major and an E minor triad. Notice, too, how often motivic gestures that seem to articulate a C major triad are subtly undermined by accompanying figures that strongly imply an E minor triad (for example, compare violins 1 and oboe 1 in bars 29–33). The first theme, then, not only fails to resolve the tonal ambiguity, but significantly nourishes it. By this point, the attentive listener will suspect that what at first seemed a mild tonal dissonance in fact represents an essential component of the movement's thematic material.

Lack of convincing harmonic progression is another means by which Stravinsky undermines classical tonality in the Symphony, thereby creating an effect of tonal immobility or stasis. For example, the first period of the exposition (bars 26–52) seems conventionally structured by a large-scale harmonic progression of I–II–V–I. But this progression resides only on the motivic surface. Rather than one harmony progressing to the next, the harmonies seem merely to follow in largely unprepared and unmotivated series of static blocks whose boundaries are smoothed over by inconsequential motivic gestures. Consider, for example, the bridge passage (bars 38–42) that supports the harmonic 'progression' from C major (I) to D minor (II). This passage hardly functions as a bridge, for it does not actually bring about a convincing tonicisation of D minor. As Jonathan Cross argues, 'though the descending lines might smooth over the edges separating the two harmonic areas, the two statements [of the principal theme] are essentially juxtaposed without any mediation'.[33] Only the surface gestures suggest a transition, while the harmonic progression itself seems dysfunctional. The passage mimics the rhetoric of a tonal form, but lacks an authentic sense of harmonic motion.[34] Instead of progressing, the harmonic areas remain self-contained, not unlike the discrete harmonic blocks that structured Stravinsky's earlier moment forms.

Lack of convincing harmonic progression – with the resulting harmonic stasis – destabilises other essential components of a classical sonata form, in particular a coherent thematic development. Sonata form requires that the contest between the two key areas in the exposition be resolved through thematic development; motives and themes cannot merely vary, they must

Ex. 6.11 Durational symmetry and form in the Symphony in C, movement I

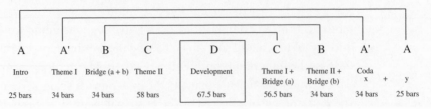

develop organically or teleologically. If there is no convincing thematic development, then the recapitulation of themes in the sonata's final section cannot effectively resolve the form's dramatic contest between key areas. But tonal themes cannot develop effectively without coherent harmonic progression; they may vary, but the variations will not (as a group) develop organically. This is precisely the effect Stravinsky creates in the Symphony's first movement. Most of the movement's thematic material does derive from the initial three-note motive, but harmonic stasis prevents development and creates instead the effect of an arbitrary or undirected succession of motivic variations.

Just as Stravinsky undermines the thematic development that is characteristic of sonata form, so too does he tamper with the ordering of its sections. Again, formal deviations become more prominent as the movement progresses. The first deviation comes in the bridge section that introduces the second key area of the exposition. Consisting of two distinct parts, *a* and *b*, the bridge section ends with a strong emphasis on D major (V of V), which lures the listener into expecting the traditional second key area of the dominant – in this case, G major. But instead of G major, the second theme enters abruptly and without preparation in F major, the subdominant. Coherent harmonic progression is blocked, but this time the unexpected goal also disrupts the dramatic rhetoric of the form itself.

Other formal surprises intrude (such as an oddly abbreviated development section), but the key deviation – the one that makes coherent those that have preceded it – occurs in the recapitulation. Now, the second part of the bridge section (*b*) comes at the end of the second theme. Its dramatic rhetoric here serves to introduce the coda, a section that is not essential to sonata form. Moreover, the coda comprises two discrete sections (*x* and *y*), whose combined length approaches that of the development section. The dramatic character of the bridge's *b* section, as well as the unusual length of the coda, both work to create a competing form for Stravinsky's 'sonata' movement – a balanced arch with strict temporal proportions. As shown by Ex. 6.11, the durations of the form's sections and their constituent parts form a symmetry: A–A′–B–C–D–C–B–A′–A. The repositioning of the bridge's *b* section in the recapitulation, then, is the key to this temporal symmetry. Unlike classical sonata form, this form highlights the development section as centre or fulcrum.

How can we be sure that these progressive alterations in form are part of Stravinsky's design? The most convincing answer comes in the middle of the development section (bar 181), exactly halfway through the movement, where the principal theme reappears for the first time with a tonally *unambiguous* accompaniment squarely in E minor. The accompaniment now omits F♮ and includes both F♯ and D♯, the leading note of E minor. In conventional terms, the listener probably hears this premature reappearance of the theme as a false recapitulation; but, from our perspective, the theme with its new E minor accompaniment provides a large-scale thematic articulation of the movement's basic polarity between C major and E minor.[35]

Rather than the decisive resolution of tonal conflict that occurs in classical sonata form, Stravinsky's form produces its effects by blocking tonal resolution; C major and E minor do compete, but in the end they maintain a static equilibrium or polarity that is temporally balanced and made convincing in an elegantly symmetrical form. In updating the classical symphony, Stravinsky has invented a new means of achieving the classical values of order, clarity, balance and formal beauty. No longer controlled by the demands of functional tonality, organic development, and the resolution of tonal conflict, Stravinsky's new symphony achieves formal elegance by balancing absolute temporal durations – perceived and measured by blocking the progressions of functional tonality – and by sustaining a delicate equilibrium between conflicting tonalities.[36]

The first movement of Stravinsky's Symphony in C has a twofold dramatic function: 1) to advertise the piece's historical model, and 2) to portray the passage of this model through time, leading the listener by progressive stages from a tonally uncontested classical sonata form to Stravinsky's idiomatic neoclassical vernacular. This miniature historical journey progresses, as does the form itself, from mere traces of tonal ambiguity within a seemingly conventional sonata form to whole-scale tonal polarity within a temporally symmetrical form. The Symphony's first movement singles out a classical model, one separated from Stravinsky by a cultural divide, and then reinvents it. The movement thus invites specific comparison of two traditions; it proclaims an inheritance that it puts to a new use. The movement enacts a historical and cultural journey from a specified past into an emerging present. Through this acting out of passage, what I call heuristic imitation exhibits its own cultural awareness and creative memory. Because this imitative strategy defines itself in relationship to a specific model, it sketches far more explicitly than eclectic imitation its own etiology, its own historical passage and artistic emergence.

By invoking the past so explicitly, however, Stravinsky also makes the work vulnerable to comparison with the past and to criticism for being merely derivative. Indeed, many of Stravinsky's critics during the 1920s and 30s did make just this sort of criticism of his new neoclassical style. Stravinsky's use of heuristic imitation has, however, a unique tension or ambivalence. While each type of imitation nourishes some ambivalences more than others, heuristic imitation is most vulnerable in the fictive nature of its diachronic passage. Stravinsky takes sonata form as his model, but succeeds only to the extent that we can accept the historical itinerary he follows. This kind of neoclassical piece does not compete against its model; it pretends to be a direct descendant of the model, the natural heir to its cultural authenticity. The strength of heuristic imitation is its ambition to enact a specific historical and cultural journey, but its distinctive limitation is an incompleteness or fictiveness in the purported relationship between the simpler model and the more complex contemporary one – that is, between cultures too distant or estranged for their relationship to be entirely free of make-believe.

Dialectical imitation

A fourth and final type of imitation that characterises Stravinsky's neo-classical works can be termed 'dialectical imitation'. This type of imitation remedies the lack of exchange or contest in heuristic imitation through a more aggressive dialogue between a piece and its model.[37] Dialectical imitation is often historically and culturally aware, acknowledging anachronism but exposing in its model a defect, irresolution or naivety. At the same time, dialectical imitation invites and risks reciprocal treatment – a two-way dialogue, a mutual exchange of criticism, a contest between specific composers, pieces and traditions. Dialectical imitation implicitly criticises or challenges its authenticating model, but in so doing leaves itself open to the possibility of unfavourable comparison.

How can a piece imitate and sustain a dialogue with another piece or a past tradition? How can a piece enter a contest with its model? Or, put differently, how can a piece reveal an artist making sense of – telling the story of – his or her place in the history of music? In poetry the devices are better understood, but nonetheless require interpretation. Poets can use echoes or allusions to earlier poems or traditions that they both invoke and transform. The echo invites the reader to notice how changed that tradition is from what it was in the earlier poem. This technique is repeatable; poetic echoes can recall earlier echoes, initiating a sequence of traditions and transformations.

In each instance, the echo or allusion suggests the newer poem's place in a history of styles, modes and values. But the imitation is dialectical because the older poem seems to demand – and be granted – a say in locating the newer one.

The Rake's Progress

Stravinsky's most successful use of dialectical imitation is in his last neoclassical composition and his only full-length opera, *The Rake's Progress*. The *Rake* enjoys a unique position among Stravinsky's neoclassical works for several reasons. With one short exception, it is the only music Stravinsky composed with a text on romantic love. Absorbing most of the composer's creative energy over a period of three years (1948–51), it is also Stravinsky's longest work and among the very few that did not originate in a commission or a clear prospect of performance. Its libretto, written largely by W. H. Auden, represents one of the most literary texts in all opera.[38] Stravinsky took his title and inspiration from a series of eight engravings published by William Hogarth in the 1730s. These moralising tableaux depict the progress of a rake from self-indulgent hedonism to degradation, madness and death. Stravinsky and Auden changed the order of Hogarth's tableaux, reinterpreted their detail, and added much new material, including significant allusions, both literary and musical, to Goethe's *Faust* and Mozart's *Don Giovanni*. Largely through these allusions Stravinsky engages in a transitive dialogue, a dialectical exchange, with his chosen classical models.

The opera depicts Tom Rakewell, who unexpectedly receives a sizeable inheritance and leaves his fiancée, Anne Trulove, in the country to pursue fortune and adventure in London. He is accompanied until almost the end by a Mephistopheles character, Nick Shadow, who represents the Jungian darker side of Tom's character. After a series of ill-fated adventures, which include whoring, marrying a bearded circus freak, and squandering the last of his money on a machine to manufacture bread from stone, Tom owes his soul to Nick Shadow. Supported by Anne's faithful love, Tom outwits Nick in a game of cards and survives. But Nick's final curse as he sinks into Hell causes Tom to lose his sanity. Anne visits Tom in Bedlam, surrounded by madmen, and discovers that he responds only to the name Adonis. After a climactic love duet, Anne sings Tom to sleep with a lullaby, bids him a final farewell and departs. Tom awakes to find that his Venus has vanished; he dies, presumably of a broken heart, tormented and mourned by the madmen.

In a programme note written in 1965, Stravinsky explains that he 'chose to cast *The Rake* in the mould of an eighteenth-century "number" opera, one in which the dramatic progress depends on the succession of separate pieces – recitatives and arias, duets, trios, choruses, instrumental interludes'. He continues by identifying specific composers that he imitates, and one that he does not:

> In the earlier scenes the mould is to some extent pre-Gluck in that it
> tends to crowd the story into the secco recitatives, reserving the arias for
> the reflective poetry, but then, as the opera warms up, the story is told,
> enacted, contained almost entirely in song – as distinguished from
> so-called speech-song, and Wagnerian continuous melody.[39]

Beyond this general description, Stravinsky says little about the many classical allusions that he and Auden insert into the opera, nor about their intended meaning. We do know that Stravinsky and Auden worked together closely in shaping the libretto and that Stravinsky was highly satisfied with Auden's work. He chose Auden as his librettist because of his gift for versification, but they proved to have a much deeper rapport. '[A]s soon as we began to work together', Stravinsky wrote, 'I discovered that we shared the same views not only about opera, but also on the nature of the Beautiful and the Good. Thus, our opera is indeed, and in the highest sense, a collaboration.'[40] That *The Rake* concerns itself with the meaning of 'the beautiful and the good' is beyond doubt, but the richness and complexity of that meaning, created largely by its allusions to past works and traditions, has generated a lack of consensus among critics about what exactly the meaning is.

This lack of consensus is clearest in the fact that, for almost fifty years since *The Rake*'s premiere in 1950, critics have debated the fate of its hero, Tom Rakewell. Like Goethe's Faust, Tom employs a satanic servant as he pursues a life of debauchery, but then at the last moment seems to avoid damnation. Unlike Faust, whom angels carry aloft to heaven, Tom ends his life in Bedlam among madmen, believing himself to be the mythical Adonis, lover of Venus. Where *Faust* makes us ask *why* Faust is saved after all the harm he has done to others, *The Rake* makes us ask whether Tom, though clearly saved from damnation, is redeemed and, if so, in what sense. This question can be explored in a number of ways, but here I choose only one, which illustrates the interpretative uses of the idea of dialectical imitation. I want to explore Tom's redemption, first by showing how, at the end of the opera, Stravinsky employs time as a symbol for the rake's progress, and second by suggesting how the libretto reveals Tom's fate by placing time in the context of Goethe's *Faust*. *The Rake*'s engagement with *Faust* sets the stage for dialogue between these two great works – that is, for Stravinsky and Auden's neoclassical masterpiece of dialectical imitation.

In large measure, the meaning of the opera hinges on the final scene and particularly on Tom's fantasy that he and Anne are Adonis and Venus.

Should Tom's mythologisation of himself and Anne be understood as an episode of syphilitic madness or as a transcendent identification with the divine? The scene gives strong support for both interpretations. Like the final Hogarth engraving, the final scene of *The Rake* depicts the horrors of eighteenth-century asylums, with hallucinating men taunting one another and dying of syphilis. Even though Tom asks for forgiveness and repents of his 'madness', he dies apparently without understanding his own life. Unsurprisingly, many critics argue that any redemption in this context can only be ironic. Joseph Kerman, reviewing the opera's American premiere, recommended that unless Auden and Stravinsky intended to deny Tom's redemption, they should re-compose the ending to make Tom's fate clearer.[41] Geoffrey Chew finds the final scene clear enough, but only by superimposing the context of twentieth-century Christian existentialism.[42]

A common approach to interpreting Tom's final fate has been to follow his 'progress' in earlier scenes – to ask what motivates him, what he learns from his adventures, and how his character develops. Again, contradictory interpretations seem plausible, mainly because Stravinsky and Auden relentlessly invoke earlier models that sharpen Tom's character through ironic contrast. The Faust legend, for example, diminishes Tom. Faust's bargain with the devil figures, not his evil, but his striving to transcend the limits of human desire. Tom Rakewell, by contrast, is weak, indecisive, and so naive that he fails to recognise his demonic servant until the last moment. Stravinsky invokes classical models in the music to achieve similar contrasts. As Joseph Straus has shown, when Tom confronts his fate in the graveyard, Stravinsky imitates key features of the music that sends Mozart's Don Giovanni to hell.[43] The allusion reminds an audience how irresolute and cowardly Tom has been when compared with Don Giovanni, whose insatiable desires drive him resolutely on to the end. Tom typically responds to his escapades with astonishment, boredom or remorse – responses that could equally reflect enlightenment or confusion. Trying to interpret Tom's 'progress', then, leads to a similar question: is it a path of enlightenment to some sort of redemption or a path of degradation to some sort of purgatory?

Given the apparent weakness of Tom's character and the fact that his repentance occurs in the context of his insanity, it seems safe to say that an argument for Tom's redemption involves a leap of faith. The most compelling reason for making that leap is that the final scene contains some of Auden's most beautiful verses set to music conveying a convincing sense of fulfilment. In Tom's imagination, the final love duet takes place in a mythological paradise, the gardens of Adonis, where their communion will be complete and eternal:

Rejoice, beloved: in these fields of Elysium
Space cannot alter, nor Time our love abate;
Here has no words for absence or estrangement
Nor Now a notion of Almost or Too Late.

The music half convinces us – against our better judgement – that this imagined paradise is as real as the walls of Bedlam and that the relationship between hero and heroine is ultimately made good, redeemed by a love that transcends the sordid facts of this world. But, at the same time, we have the sense of being duped by beauty. Modernists like Auden and Stravinsky, we think, would never seriously accept this sort of nineteenth-century operatic cliché. Still, the music gives us hope where the drama offers none.

How does Stravinsky create the extraordinary musical effect of the final scene? One unique feature of the final two scenes is that, for the first time, themes begin to reappear. Earlier, except for a few short echoes of previous tunes, Stravinsky – true to his Mozartian model – avoids repeating themes. Significantly, the only two repeated themes recur together, and one of these structures the final, ecstatic love duet between Anne and Tom. The other, the one that Stravinsky labels a Ballad, is remarkable solely for its banality. These two themes transform one another in successive repetitions to portray a transformation of Tom's character, a transformation that gains meaning largely through its imitative dialogue with *Faust*.

The Ballad appears first using its most conventional accompaniment.[44] On stage, the auction of Tom's possessions is ending, and the voices of Tom and Nick are heard from the street. Having lost all of his money on the bread machine, Tom and Nick throw to the wind their few remaining cares and responsibilities. Tom's progressive escape from duty seems to have reached its most absurd end; both Stravinsky and Auden echo this existential predicament by indulging in extremes. Auden's silly verses, in strict iambic metres, are metrically repetitive and mechanical:

If boys had wings and girls had stings
    And gold fell from the sky,
If new-laid eggs wore wooden legs
    I should not laugh or cry.

Stravinsky's little tune is equally silly – the most metrically rigid and harmonically predictable in the entire opera.

The Ballad returns in the next scene, in the graveyard, when Nick sings alone to demand his wages or Tom's soul (see Ex. 6.12). Only now does Tom begin to wonder about his servant's identity and intentions. But just before Nick sings the Ballad and Tom acknowledges his suspicions comes a four-bar

Ex. 6.12 *The Rake's Progress*, Act 3, scene 2, 'Duet', figs. 163–166^{+3}

introduction that presents the second theme which Stravinsky significantly reuses to structure the final love duet. I will call this the 'flutter' motive, and here its changing, irregular metre suggests Tom's growing apprehension and fear.

Were it not for its banal memorability, we would scarcely recognise that Nick is singing the same tune that he last sang for the jaunty street song. In fact, much of the chilling effect results from the ironic tension between the triviality of the tune and the ultimate seriousness of Nick's claim:

> A year and a day have passed away
>> Since first to you I came.
> All things you bid, I duly did
>> And now my wages claim.

Ex. 6.13 *The Rake's Progress*, Act 3, scene 2, 'Aria', figs. 206–9

The Ballad now appears exactly transposed to G major, but important changes occur in the accompaniment, where Stravinsky subtly undermines the metre of the passage. What before had been bar-length arpeggiations are now gradually expanded and repeated without regard to metre.

The Ballad recurs a final time at the next dramatic climax, just after Nick descends to hell, having lost the card game and therefore Tom's soul. But as Nick descends, he condemns Tom to madness. Tom, now insane, sings the Ballad the following morning (see Ex. 6.13). It is spring, and his open grave is covered with a green mound upon which Tom sits smiling like an innocent child, putting grass on his head and proclaiming himself as Adonis. The dramatic effect gains force by the close juxtaposition of the Ballad, first portraying Nick's evil and now Tom's innocence. Again,

Ex. 6.14 *The Rake's Progress*, Act 3, scene 2, 'Duet', figs. 249–52

Stravinsky creates this new effect by recomposing the accompaniment, re-placing the rolling arpeggiations of the earlier settings with the flutter motive that haunted Tom's entrance into the graveyard. Each phrase of the Ballad that Tom sings is interrupted at irregular intervals by various repetitions of the flutter motive, thereby undermining the clear metrical structure of the Ballad.

Thus, with each recurrence of the Ballad, the sense of metre progressively dissipates. As the curtain slowly falls, the flutter motive repeats at irregular intervals. Just as Tom has lost the ability to measure time with his loss of sanity, so too does the Ballad tune lose its metre. A new sense of time takes over, both dramatically and musically. I want to return to how Stravinsky uses time and metre to convey dramatic meaning, but first need to discuss the climactic love duet that follows in the final scene.

While Stravinsky's music changes the way we perceive time in Tom's final presentation of the Ballad, Auden waits to create the same effect until the ec-static reunion of Tom and Anne in Bedlam (see Ex. 6.14). His verses, quoted above, portray a new sense of time: no longer rigidly measured by Nick's year and a day, time now enjoys a sense of immediacy or fullness, one that rejects the notions of almost or too late, of absence or estrangement. Time is no longer cyclic and repetitive, but linear, non-cyclic and ever-evolving: 'Here has no words for absence or estrangement / Nor Now a notion of Almost or Too Late.' For a brief moment, Tom and Anne seem to be joined as fate intended them to be. The music highlights the connection between Tom's insanity and this ever-evolving, utopian vision by again using the metrically unpredictable flutter motive, this time with the lovers themselves joining the accompanying wind instruments. This is when Tom falls asleep and Anne leaves, making it clear that she will not return.

Several things seem clear about time as a symbol in these passages. First, the Ballad, with its rigid, repetitive metre, is associated with Nick Shadow. As Nick gradually loses his hold on Tom, the Ballad gradually loses its metrical effect. Once Nick has disappeared, the Ballad is never heard again. Second, as Tom's sense of dread and fear intensifies, so does his awareness of repentance, and both are linked to the growing dominance of the flutter theme, which culminates in Tom and Anne's final love duet. Dramatically, Stravinsky uses the flutter theme to contrast and compete with the Ballad; musically, he uses metre to portray this contrast or competition.

Perhaps in response to the text, which speaks of a fullness or abundance of time, the love duet itself seems metrically rich or complex, overflowing with a sense of metrical possibilities. It sustains a sense of immediacy by delaying any clear sense of downbeat; the music seems to balance precariously on a continuous upbeat, which never finds its anticipated downbeat. The effect is not an absence of metre, but the opposite; one hears the theme structured by an ever-changing abundance of metrical paths. And exactly this sense of abundance, of sustained anticipation, creates a sense of immediacy unique to the dramatic climax of the opera.

Most listeners quickly grasp how contrasting themes portray competing impulses in Tom Rakewell's character and how time or metre comes to symbolise the outcome of the competition. But what does that symbol mean, and how does it relate to Stravinsky's chosen classical model? Here one of Auden's essays, 'Balaam and his ass', written while he was working with Stravinsky, may help.[45]

Auden takes up the traditional issue of why Faust is saved. Faust's redemption depends on Goethe's ideas of cyclic, repetitive time versus non-cyclic, linear or progressive time.[46] Goethe describes Mephistopheles as a spirit of denial, who expresses and acts upon his sense of the ultimate futility of being. In the final climax of the work, Mephistopheles declares that time is a series of meaningless and empty circles:

> What use these cycles of creation!
> Or snatching off the creatures to negation!
> 'It is gone by!' – and we can draw the inference:
> If it had not been, it would make no difference;
> The wheel revolves the same, no more, no less.
> I should prefer eternal emptiness.[47] [11598–603]

Thus, for Mephistopheles time is meaningless because it is repetitive rather than creative. No progress can occur in any direction; to go round in a circle is to go nowhere.

If evil is understood as a process of negation, then it is both destroying and denying, and the ultimate good becomes creativity, bringing into existence things that did not exist before. Faust's restless striving towards the infinite implies linear movement through time. When making his deal with Mephistopheles, Faust stipulates when his soul will be forfeited:

> If ever I stretch myself on a bed of ease:
> Then I am finished! Is that understood?
> ...
> If ever I say to the passing moment
> 'Linger a while! Thou art so fair!' [1692–3; 1699–1700]

Faust's stipulation, at bottom, turns on the different ways of understanding time – immediate and endlessly becoming versus repetitive and cyclic. If ever Faust ceases striving and wants time to stop, if ever he wants to halt its linear flow, then his time is up: 'The clock may stop, its hands may fall, / And that be the end of time for me!' (1705–6). The root question of Goethe's *Faust* is 'Whose view of time will triumph – Mephistopheles's or Faust's?'

In 'Balaam and his ass', Auden opens his discussion of *Faust* with the phrase, 'Das verfluchte Hier' [the accursed present], and then gives his own interpretation of the nature of Faust's indefatigable striving that generations of critics have seen as the reason for his eventual redemption:

> The story of Faust is precisely the story of a man who refuses to be
> anyone and only wishes to become someone else . . . [What Faust strives
> to reject] is that immediate actual moment, the actual concrete world
> now, . . . and [what he strives for is] the same world seen by memory and
> imagination as possible . . . All value belongs to possibility, the actual here
> and now is valueless, or rather the value it has is the feeling of discontent
> it provokes . . . Faust escapes Mephisto's clutches because he is careful to
> define the contentment of his last moment in terms of anticipation.[48]

To Mephistopheles, the spirit of denial, creation is most hateful, even the anticipation of creation. In Auden's view, Faust escapes damnation not only because he strives relentlessly, driven by dissatisfaction, but because his striving is coupled with anticipation – by engaging the world by memory and imagination, as 'what might have been once and may be yet'.

Auden's comments on *Faust* help resolve the ambiguity of the progress of his and Stravinsky's *Rake*. The conventional association of Mephistopheles with cyclic, repetitive time suggests one reason why Stravinsky chose to give Nick Shadow music to sing that is metrically rigid and repetitive and why Auden gives his spirit of denial the nonsense lines, 'If new-laid eggs wore wooden legs, I should not laugh or cry.' Without too much effort, we also can see how the flutter theme that comes to represent Tom's fate can represent a transcendence of repetition and cyclical time. But what about the idea that Faust saves himself not through mere striving, but through striving motivated by anticipation and imagination?

Here it will be useful to return to the original outline of the opera that Stravinsky and Auden prepared together over a ten-day period in the autumn of 1947.[49] While many details were added later, the initial shape of the opera hardly changed in the final version, perhaps because of the extraordinary rapport between the composer and librettist. In the crucial graveyard scene, where the Ballad and flutter motive first appear together, the original outline calls for the Hero (Tom) and Villain (Nick) to play dice on a grave. After the Hero declares that he is bored, the Villain asks him what more he desires – Pleasure? Glory? Power? The hero rejects each of these and declares instead he desires the Past. The Villain is pleased with this response, for the Hero seems to know what Nick makes explicit at this point in the final libretto, that 'return' to the past – that is, repetition – is impossible:

> The simpler the trick, the simpler the deceit;
> That there is no return, I've taught him well,
>   And repetition palls him;
> The Queen of Hearts again shall be for him the Queen of Hell.

In the original outline, the Villain then commands the Hero to continue playing the game which the Hero loses. Just as the Villain declares that the Hero's time is up, Anne's voice is heard in the distance. The Hero declares with great excitement: 'No, there is still another thing – the future!' and he then commands the Villain to play again. The Villain refuses and proceeds to lose the game, as well as Tom's soul. In this first draft, the reason that Tom escapes damnation is made explicit: at the crucial moment, he, like Faust, does not want to return to the past; he wants the future to resume or repeat 'what might have been once and may be yet'.

In the final version, the reason is less explicit, for Tom's lines are: 'Return! and Love! / The banished words torment.' Nick then declares: 'You cannot now repent.' Again Tom cries, 'Return O love.' But Tom is interrupted by Anne singing in the distance: 'A love that is sworn before Thee can plunder Hell of its prey.' Tom then continues: 'I wish for nothing else. / Love, first and last, assume eternal reign; / Renew my life, O Queen of Hearts, again.' And on that line, Tom wins the game. Because Auden deleted the word 'future' in the final text, most critics have gone astray by interpreting Tom's line, 'I wish for nothing else', to mean either 'I wish for nothing at all' or 'I wish for nothing else than to have Hell plundered of its prey' (that is, his soul). But a third meaning is more consistent with the original text: 'I wish for nothing else' than for 'love to assume eternal reign, and thereby to renew my life'. This interpretation points to Auden's understanding of why Faust is saved – because 'he is careful to define the contentment of his last moment in terms of anticipation, . . . the same world seen by memory and imagination as possible.'

Some might object to the parallel with Faust, since this is not Tom's last moment. He still has one more scene to go and appears to be insane for the whole of it. Auden's imitation of the Faust legend ends when Tom defeats Nick. Everything following has no obvious literary precedent. What dramatic function, then, does the final scene serve? Why should the music of the last scene convey so strong a sense of fulfilment? And if fulfilment suggests redemption, why does Tom – unlike Faust – nonetheless suffer a tragic fate? The answers to these questions are crucial, for if the view presented here of Stravinsky and Auden's imitative strategy is correct, then *The Rake*'s final departure from Faust accommodates and furthers a dialectical exchange – a two-way dialogue that promotes mutually critical reflection on both *The*

Rake and *Faust*. The final love duet, as described above, speaks of a full-ness or abundance of time in music that seems metrically rich or complex, overflowing with a sense of metrical possibilities. With the text in mind, the significance of its most remarkable feature – that all possible metres (2/8, 3/8, 4/8) seem equally plausible – becomes clearer. The duet locks our attention with a sense of presentness or immediacy; while we sense metre, we cannot grasp the metrically repeating downbeats we need to de-fine a specific metre. In Auden's words, Faust is saved because he strives for a world 'seen by memory and imagination as possible', as 'what might have been once and may be yet'. Tom's tragedy, then, depends on his sentence to insanity because it robs him of memory and therefore the ability to bring the past into an anticipated present. We can now understand how the love duet portrays musically this tragic dilemma. It promises or anticipates mul-tiple metres, but falters in its 'memory' of the past metrical events needed to define any one metre. In other words, the metrical past never satisfies an anticipation of a metrical present. This view of the interrelated literary and musical features of the final duet explains why Anne leaves Tom and why Tom dies singing a final melody that alludes to Monteverdi's *Orfeo*. That allusion, of course, furthers the dialectical exchange with Faust by evoking another work in which tragedy lies in the inability both to return and to progress.

Conclusion

Stravinsky's neoclassical style culminates in *The Rake's Progress*. Perhaps sensing that he could never surpass *The Rake*'s accomplishment, Stravinsky abandoned his neoclassical style in 1951 and, until his death in 1971, used primarily serial procedures. And perhaps because of this abrupt change, historical assessment of Stravinsky's neoclassical works has been and re-mains mixed. By the time he had completed *The Rake*, critics were la-belling Stravinsky's neoclassical style as reactionary, in opposition to Schoenberg's serialism, which they thought more progressive. Stravinsky found it increasingly difficult to ignore this assessment. With greater histor-ical perspective, more recent critics have significantly revised this appraisal by judging Stravinsky's neoclassical style as the harbinger of musical post-modernism. Like the earlier assessment that rested on simplistic opposition between Schoenberg and Stravinsky, the current view distorts unless care-fully qualified.

In general, critics who find here the origins of musical postmodernism point to Stravinsky's use of pastiche, which many identify as the signature of the postmodern across every art form. Others use the term 'collage', which seems not to differ significantly from 'pastiche' (in Fredric Jameson's usage) as the most powerful and unifying device in twentieth-century art. This notion that Stravinsky's use of pastiche or collage provides some sort of continuity between musical modernism and postmodernism is not implausible, but can easily lead to a false conclusion – that because postmodern collage or pastiche revels in ambiguity, diversity, and ahistoricism, its seeming presence earlier in Stravinsky's neoclassical works *necessarily* serves the same ends and should be interpreted in the same way. *The Rake* should provide a reasonable test case for this argument, both because it is his final and richest neoclassical piece and because its extravagant musical and literary allusions have led critics to cite it as Stravinsky's clearest use of pastiche. If we understand pastiche as Jameson does (the random imitation or cannibalisation of dead styles, using all the masks and voices stored up in an imaginary museum of a now global culture), then surely *The Rake* seems a plausible candidate. Few pieces of twentieth-century music contain as many literary and musical allusions. While I have focused mainly on the allusions to Goethe's *Faust* and Monteverdi's *Orfeo*, a complete list would include *The Beggar's Opera, Don Giovanni, Così fan Tutte, Don Pasquale*, philosophical themes plucked from Nietzsche and Kierkegaard, as well as a mixture of Classical and Baroque harmonic and contrapuntal forms. On one level, then, *The Rake* seems to exemplify a definition of pastiche as the random imitation or cannibalisation of dead styles and works.

The key element in the usual definition of postmodern collage or pastiche, however, is randomness. Random juxtaposition of allusions scrambles any sustained historical reference, creating instead a surface best described as synchronic or ahistorical. In superficial reaction against modernism's negation of history, postmodernism revels in a facile nostalgia that deploys multiple historical styles and allusions to create diverse and contradictory meanings. Here, too, *The Rake* might be judged a likely candidate because even a cursory glance at its critical history shows a persistent debate about its coherence, and in particular about the meaning of its final scene. But, as I have shown, stylistic pastiche in *The Rake* does not end in joyful ambiguity and irresolution, as it would if Stravinsky were really a postmodernist *avant la lettre*. Clearly, Stravinky's dialogue with *Faust* creates less ambiguity and more integration of meaning than could be characterised as postmodern. I hope also that, at this stage of my argument, no one would willingly assume that the echo of Monteverdi is just one more element of a playful pastiche. An analysis of *The Rake* that merely lists echoes and allusions is misleading, not so much about Stravinky's importance as a progenitor of musical postmodernism, which is undeniable, but because of a natural tendency to interpret causes in terms of their effects. If we rest content with a postmodern view of the play of allusions in *The Rake's Progress*, then we will miss its serious and sustained engagement with models in our musical and literary tradition. We will, in short, underestimate its 'neoclassicism'.

7 Stravinsky's theatres

JONATHAN CROSS

... good or bad,
All men are mad;
All they say or do is theatre.
BABA, 'EPILOGUE', *THE RAKE'S PROGRESS*

In his Bloch Lectures given at the University of California at Berkeley in 1995, the British composer Jonathan Harvey presented his ideas on *The Rake's Progress*, a work he described as being 'aware of its own derivativeness'. *The Rake*, he argued, is 'the most explicit manifestation of self-effacement', its meaning deriving 'not from authorship, but from formal pattern-play and ingenuity'.[1] While such a view determinedly underlines the 'proto-postmodern' tendencies in Stravinsky, it is also interesting that it echoes strongly Stravinsky's own aesthetic as articulated in the 1930s (via his various ghost writers) in such public statements as the *Autobiography* and the Harvard lectures. In the *Poetics of Music*, Stravinsky proclaims that 'It is through the unhampered play of its functions . . . that a work is revealed and justified.' With specific regard to *The Rake*, Stravinsky observed that it is

> ... emphatically, an opera – an opera of arias and recitatives, choruses and ensembles. Its musical structure, the conception of the use of these forms, even to the relations of tonalities, is in the line of the classical tradition.[2]

The 'line of the classical tradition' is extended back as far as early Italian opera in the Prelude, to Bach and Handel in the Bedlam scene and as far forward as echoes of Donizetti and Verdi. And Mozart is heard everywhere: *Così fan tutte* and *Don Giovanni*, especially. *The Rake* thus alludes to virtually the whole of operatic history. Indeed, whatever the main narrative themes of the work (love, greed, power, loss of innocence, madness and so on), *The Rake's Progress* is, at heart, an opera about opera ('aware of its own derivativeness'). Harvey concluded that 'because no-one is telling us anything, what it means (and many of us probably register that it has deeper meaning than most twentieth-century operas) seems objective, immutable, above merely individual opinion'.[3]

This goes some way in explaining why rite, ritual, myth and formal theatres of all kinds were so attractive to Stravinsky. He was drawn to theatres where the collective was emphasised over the individual, where objective representation was preferred over subjective expression. In terms of his theatre, this concept is most succinctly articulated in a comment he made about the character Oedipus: 'My audience is not indifferent to the fate of the person, but I think it far more concerned with the person of the fate, and the delineation of it which can be achieved in music.' In *Oedipus Rex* he focused 'the tragedy not on Oedipus himself and the other individuals, but on the "fatal development" that, for me, is the meaning of the play'.[4] The role of music in the theatre, for Stravinsky, was therefore not one of reinforcing emotions (he claimed he abhorred verismo) but of articulating a framework, of helping to universalise individuals' actions and experiences. Greek tragedy was one important source of such thinking. In Aristotle's analysis, 'The plot . . . is the first essential of tragedy, its life-blood, so to speak, and character takes the second place.'[5]

Igor Stravinsky virtually grew up in the theatre. His father Fyodor was one of the greatest operatic bass-baritones of his day and, as Stephen Walsh points out, Fyodor's twenty-six-year career coincided with a flowering of Russian opera. He made his debut at the Mariinsky Theatre in St Petersburg in April 1876, and took roles to great acclaim in, among other works, Musorgsky's *Boris Godunov*, Glinka's *Ruslan and Lyudmila*, Borodin's *Prince Igor*, Rimsky-Korsakov's *The Snow Maiden* and Tchaikovsky's *Enchantress*, as well as in the major non-Russian repertoire from Mozart to Bizet.[6] Igor had access to all his father's opera scores. He was taken to the Mariinsky from a very young age to see ballet and opera, and it made a deep impression on him. He would sit in his father's box and he was 'soon in the theatre five or six evenings a week. The Mariinsky Theatre was for him almost a "second home".'[7] Another key influence was that of Rimsky-Korsakov and his circle.[8] Aside from composition lessons with Rimsky-Korsakov, Stravinsky also assisted him with his later operas – for example, he helped with the score of Act 3 of Rimsky's opera *The Legend of the Invisible City of Kitezh*, premiered at the Mariinsky in February 1907. It should hardly be surprising, therefore, that Stravinsky's first major public work for the stage – the ballet *The Firebird*, premiered at the Paris Opéra on 25 June 1910 by Diaghilev's Ballets Russes – was such a theatrical success for a young and relatively inexperienced composer.

Throughout his creative life, from his early lyric tale *The Nightingale* to the late musical play *The Flood*, by way of numerous ballets, dance scenes, burlesques, an opera buffa, an opera-oratorio and a fully-fledged opera, not to mention abortive dalliances with film and a never-to-be stage project with Dylan Thomas, Stravinsky engaged with a broad range of dramatic genres. He collaborated with some of the most important writers (as librettists), artists (as set designers), directors and choreographers of his time: among them, W. H. Auden, Jean Cocteau, André Gide, Léon Bakst, Henri Matisse,

Pablo Picasso, George Balanchine and Mikhail Fokine. And even in his non-stage works one finds a deep-rooted fascination with the dramatic dimension of ritual, whether in the religious rituals of the *Symphony of Psalms* and *Canticum Sacrum*, or the ritualised formality of the *Three Pieces for String Quartet* and the *Symphonies of Wind Instruments*. Indeed, in the case of the latter two examples, critics have proposed interpretations based on concrete dramatic/ritual models: the *Three Pieces for String Quartet* as direct response to Cocteau's ideas for his aborted *David* ballet project,[9] and the *Symphonies of Wind Instruments* (in memoriam Claude Debussy) as a stylised representation of the *panikhida*, the Russian Orthodox office of the dead.[10]

In order to explore further the nature of Stravinsky's theatre and to provide an interpretative context, I adopt here two categories borrowed from Peter Brook: 'rough' theatre and 'holy' theatre.[11] Rough theatre Brook identifies with popular, folk and street theatre, circus, pantomime and cabaret. Such theatre was clearly of fundamental importance to Stravinsky: puppetry and the *commedia dell'arte* (*Petrushka*, *Pulcinella*), Russian itinerant folk entertainers (*Renard*, *The Soldier's Tale*), rustic Russian rituals (*Les Noces*). Its roughness results in an immediacy lacking from more institutionalised kinds of theatre, and it is characterised by a boldness and directness of presentation; a breakdown of the distinction between actors and audience; a utilisation of a wide range of performing spaces, often open-air, and rooted in the community; it dispenses with the paraphernalia of formal theatre, working with the minimum of props, costumes, set and so on; it is usually ritualised and stylised in presentation; and actors, singers, dancers and musicians are usually in constant view. In other words, rough theatre represents a continuity with a much older tradition of pre-literate theatre. An interest in such theatre was endemic in the earlier years of the twentieth century, as was a looking outwards to oriental theatre, particularly that of Indonesia and Japan. Artaud, Brecht, Cocteau, Jarry, Meyerhold and Pirandello, for example, were all exploring new kinds of immediate, non-naturalistic, non-narrative theatre by drawing, in part, on ancient, folk and non-Western sources.[12] Stravinsky's collaboration with Cocteau is especially significant in this regard.

The other category from Brook that I adopt is that of holy theatre. The theatre, Brook argues, 'is the last forum where idealism is still an open question: many audiences all over the world will answer positively from their own experience that they have seen the face of the invisible through an experience on the stage that transcended their experience in life'.[13] He gives Artaud's 'Theatre of Cruelty', alongside Happenings and the work of Samuel Beckett, as twentieth-century examples of holy theatre. Artaud's theory of the theatre shares many aspects with the rough theatre: for example, his interest in

Balinese theatre; his prescription that stage and auditorium should be abandoned to enable direct contact between actors and audience; his rejection of narrative, realistic theatre. But Artaud also proposed moving away from a theatre dependent on text and towards one more concerned with myth, ritual and magic, with something metaphysical, sublime. This is why Balinese theatrical productions offered Artaud an important model: there 'is something of a religious ritual ceremony about them, in the sense that they eradicate any idea of pretence, a ridiculous imitation of real life, from the spectator's mind.'[14] A holy theatre, by Brook's definition, 'not only presents the invisible but also offers conditions that make its perception possible.'[15]

This ritual dimension clearly underlies many of Stravinsky's works and is at its most obvious in major stage works spanning his entire creative life: *The Rite of Spring, Les Noces, Oedipus Rex, Agon*. Ritual is concerned with the expression of the collective, of the community, as in ancient ceremonies and acts of religious worship; it transcends the mundane through repeated and repetitive actions; it is symbolic rather than representational; it is stylised and is often associated with a special place and language separate from the everyday. For these reasons, ritual is not primarily concerned with linear time or narratives and it cannot easily represent contemporary events. Myth (broadly defined) thus becomes an important part of many rituals because it represents a collective heritage – in Jungian terms, myths and their archetypal characters express directly the collective unconscious. Stravinsky's general musical characteristics of repeating rhythms, regular pulse, ostinatos, static pedal points and symmetries, of limited melodies and non-developmental structures, are ideally matched to the presentation of ritual.

The two categories of the 'rough' and the 'holy' intersect and overlap in fascinating ways. But, to begin with, I shall look in closer focus at three of Stravinsky's stage works that seem to embody these categories in 'pure' form: 'The Tale About the Fox, the Cock, the Tomcat and the Ram' (later a 'Goat' in C. F. Ramuz's French translation) – better known simply as the burlesque *Renard* – *The Soldier's Tale* and the opera-oratorio *Oedipus Rex*.

Renard was composed in Switzerland 1915–16, and is as direct as Stravinsky's rough theatre gets:

> *Renard* is sheer, unadulterated Russian folk art as reimagined by an unwilling exile who had persuaded himself that the future of music, if not the world, depended on tapping down to the deepest roots of a culture which, as a matter of fact, he himself did not know at first hand and which perhaps had never even actually existed. Certainly no such vibrantly, ebulliently, richly uncouth musical idiom ever had.[16]

The work began, as Richard Taruskin shows us in detail, merely as a 'compost of children's songs and nonsense jingles',[17] Stravinsky initially setting songs from 'The Cat, the Cock and the Fox' out of Afanasyev's collection of Russian tales, and only later deciding to work with the whole story. The result, subtitled 'a merry performance', is a kind of pantomime and calls for

> clowns, dancers or acrobats, preferably on a trestle stage with the orchestra placed behind it . . . The players remain all the time on the stage . . . The roles are dumb. The singers (two tenors and two basses) are in the orchestra.[18]

The orchestra is a sort of peasant band of largely solo woodwind, brass and strings plus percussion and a cimbalom, the latter instrument imitating the *gusli*, a 'kind of fine, metal-stringed balalaika'. Stravinsky uses it to represent the goat: 'Part of the fun in *Renard* is that this extremely nimble-fingered instrument should be played by the cloven-hooved goat.'[19] The *gusli*'s origins lie with ancient Russian troupes of *skomorokhi* who performed mocking or satirical plays in public squares. Or, at least, it is possible that they did: Taruskin argues that Stravinsky drew and adapted from a variety of folkloristic sources to produce 'a putative picture of life in pre-Petrine Russia that is "realer than the real"'[20] (compare with Walsh's reference above to a 'reimagined' art that had perhaps never actually existed). Real or invented, its 'rough' credentials are nonetheless clear for all to appreciate: 'an imaginary quasi-improvised performance by strolling players'.[21]

The stage characters only mime or dance. The four singers are not specifically identified with any one of the four characters and are seated with the band. (Compare this with *Les Noces*, where, for example, the Bridegroom is represented by different voices on different occasions.) But they speak or sing in a stylised way on behalf of the animals on the stage, making their noises, engaging in witty dialogue. Because they are distanced from the characters, they can also occasionally take on a 'chorus' function, commenting on the action. This a highly effective narrative device that has the effect of stylising the theatre – or, rather, it means that the audience is alienated, is constantly made aware that what it is watching is merely a tale, nothing but a piece of theatre. This is affirmed at the very end when the singers announce the conclusion of the play to the audience ('Et si l'histoir' vous a plu, / Payez-moi c'qui m'est dû!' – 'Now the story is done, / You must pay for your fun!') as well as by the musical framing device of the rough March that serves the function of getting the performers in and out of the acting space.

The relationship between music and text in this work is fascinating and complex. Taruskin explores the forging of the text and how it relates to the music in exhaustive detail, concluding that in *Renard* Stravinsky succeeded

'in making the words of his "merry performance" literally and indispens-
ably a part of the music'.[22] The extraordinary exuberance and vitality of
this piece springs primarily from the accentual and metrical character of
the texts; in Stravinsky's setting, the accented syllables, musical metre and
ostinatos interact in vibrant ways, resulting in a music of engaging immediacy. Taruskin – for once – is prepared to confirm one of Stravinsky's own
observations: 'The music of *Renard* begins in the verse'.[23]

Renard's 'companion piece' is *The Soldier's Tale*, which was also composed in Switzerland in 1918. The French text was written by C. F. Ramuz,
with whom Stravinsky had first worked on the French translation of *Renard*,
and later as the translator into French of Russian folksong texts as well as
Les Noces. The origins of the tale lie again in Afanasyev; wartime economies
and the fact that both artists were cut off from their principal sources of in-
come resulted in what Stravinsky described as a '*théâtre ambulant*', a small-
scale work that could in theory be performed in any location, indoor or
outdoor. *The Soldier's Tale* shares other rough characteristics with *Renard*:
a small ensemble (three pairs of high and low woodwind, brass and strings
plus a percussionist, representing a stylised version of a jazz band); role-
play where a specific character is associated with a musical instrument (the
violin with the soldier, representing the soldier's soul, though Taruskin in-
terprets it instead as 'a kind of liberating and health-giving *élan vital* that
is in the end perverted and made the instrument of enslavement'[24]); the
fact that the seven instrumentalists, the three speakers and the dancer are
present and visible all of the time; and the tale's subject-matter of an ordinary soldier points – in theory at least – to the work's rough credentials,
removed from the ideals of bourgeois theatre. According to Brook, rough
theatre 'deals with men's actions, . . . it is down to earth and direct . . . [and,
unlike the Holy Theatre] it admits wickedness and laughter'.[25] This is clearly
appropriate to *The Soldier's Tale*. It should be noted, however, that for many
commentators those 'rough' aspects of this piece of theatre are less convincing than *Renard*'s. Walsh quotes Hermann Scherchen (the conductor of,
among other things, Pirandello's production of *The Soldier's Tale* in Rome in
Stravinsky's presence in 1926), who referred to Ramuz's 'symbolic-dramatic
romantic-yearning',[26] while Taruskin describes Ramuz's text as 'a trite and
schoolmasterly Everyman spiel, for the purposes of which a number of very
dull contemporary allusions and genteel grotesqueries are introduced'. 'It is
the music alone', he concludes, 'that rewards close examination'.[27]

But there is one key 'rough' device employed in this work and that is
the central role given to the narrator, 'adopted to satisfy the need for a
two-way go-between: that is, for someone who is an illusionist interpreter
between the characters themselves, as well as a commentator between the
stage and the audience'.[28] The narrator thus fulfils a chorus-like role. His

most important function is one of distancing the audience from the tale. As a member of the audience at a performance of *The Soldier's Tale*, you are involved with the theatre from the start because you share the performing space, you witness the costume changes, you can see the musicians at work – you respond as much, as Stravinsky wanted, to 'the scrape of the violin and the punctuation of the drums'[29] as to the music itself. Though a narrative is presented, the very presence of the alienating narrator allows for the disruption and fragmentation of that narrative: hence, the appropriateness of Stravinsky's musical 'collage'. In theatre works where there is no attempt at presenting a linear narrative, the result is a heightened sense of ritual (as in *Les Noces*). In such cases, rough merges with holy.

The eclectic musical materials in *The Soldier's Tale* include a reworking of ragtime alongside a mix of dances (a tango and a waltz), a Royal March that alludes to nineteenth-century opera, and two pseudo-Lutheran chorales. In many senses, it offers as much a critique of the chosen musical 'objects' as Stravinsky was to present two years later in *Pulcinella*. Just as he appears to distance himself from the jazz elements he uses (he 'reinvents' ragtime in the same way he was, in subsequent neoclassical works, to 'reinvent the past'), so the audience is made to distance itself from the subject-matter. The very presence of popular and folk musics helps reinforce the work's roughness, its 'street' character.

The paradigm of Stravinsky's 'holy' theatre, I suggest, is his opera-oratorio *Oedipus Rex*. He had been looking for a universal plot, and eventually settled on Sophocles's telling of the Oedipus myth: 'I wished to leave the play, as play, behind, thinking by this to distil the dramatic essence and to free myself for a greater degree of focus on a purely musical dramatization.'[30] One way in which this is achieved is by the fact that the chorus and the protagonists sing Jean Cocteau's text in Latin. As Stravinsky imagined it, a statuesque chorus of tenors and basses, masked and in costume, would be ranked in full view at the front of the stage, commenting on the action. Another distancing element is Cocteau's introduction of the Speaker, detached from the drama and introducing the work's events in the language of the audience: he 'expresses himself like a conferencier, presenting the story with a detached voice'. Wearing evening dress and standing in front of the proscenium, he appears both as one of the audience and as an intermediary between auditorium and stage, just like the narrator in *The Soldier's Tale*, or a chorus figure in a Greek tragedy. Other aspects of production specified in the preface to the score serve to reinforce the work's stylisation: bold, rough and two-dimensional décor; the use of masks; a stylised acting style where only arms and heads move. The conflict between the Speaker and the actors and singers, which disrupts narrative continuity and naturalistic representation, is matched by the music which, in a more extreme way than in

The Soldier's Tale, is a self-confessed '*Merzbild*' (collage). Even though individual moments, such as Jocasta's Act 2 aria in the nineteenth-century Italian operatic manner, might seem to invite narrative interpretation, they are not connected with other moments in the work, each of which is individually characterised, so that the musical as a whole takes on a 'monumental' static aspect. Just as the structure of the plot is overtly signalled by the Speaker, so through various devices of repetition, the music signals its own functions as structural punctuation and frame (in an almost baroque way). Music here *is* ritual; this is what defines it as 'holy'.

Aside from his opera-oratorio, Stravinsky only designated two works 'opera': the one-act opera buffa *Mavra* and the three-act opera *The Rake's Progress*.[31] Beyond the surface allusions to other operatic traditions (old Russian opera and Italian bel canto in *Mavra*; Mozart, principally, in *The Rake*), both achieve a distancing, an anti-naturalism, by adopting a number structure of arias, duets, recitatives, choruses and other familiar set pieces. What interested Stravinsky in opera, then, was not so much its dramatic-expressive possibilities (he was resolutely anti-Wagnerian) as its formalism. *The Rake* is framed by a Monteverdian Prelude ('*on va commencer*') and a Mozartian-cum-vaudeville Epilogue. The graveyard scene in Act 3 of *The Rake* – the work's dramatic turning-point where Tom Rakewell and Nick Shadow confront each other – is a masterpiece of invention where Stravinsky adopts the rhetoric (the framework) of – for example – recitative but invests it with a new musical and dramatic power all its own.

The completion of *The Rake's Progress* saw Stravinsky abandon neoclassicism and begin to explore the serial method. While he developed his serial thinking in one important stage work, the ballet *Agon* (discussed below), the only fully serial piece of theatre to emerge from Stravinsky's last years was the musical play *The Flood*. Its heterogeneity and concomitant stylisation were a result of the fact that it was written specially for television, a medium which, unlike the conventional stage, allowed instantaneous cutting from one scene to another. Its text was fashioned by Robert Craft from sources explicitly both rough and holy: the York Miracle Plays *The Creation and Fall of Lucifer* and *The Fall of Man*, and the Chester Miracle Play *Noah's Flood*, along with brief quotations from Genesis.

Stravinsky's compositional techniques may be new in this work, but they are put to theatrical ends similar to many of his other pieces. The drama is framed at start and finish by a mixed chorus singing in Latin the opening verses of the *Te Deum* (the text is in a kind of reverse order – or retrograde – at the end). These are the only times the chorus is heard: it stands outside the drama. Again, Latin reinforces this distancing, while a ritual mode is established through the chorus's chanting – Stravinsky himself described it as 'Byzantine'.[32] The other framing device is a purely musical one:

a twelve-note chord heard at the very start of the Prelude, the 'Represen-tation of Chaos',[33] an unexpectedly symmetrical formation, out of which emerge two versions of the basic twelve-note row of the work, a rising figure Stravinsky described as a 'musical Jacob's Ladder'.[34] This passage is repeated exactly, just before the end, ominously prefacing the words of Satan, who has also survived the flood ('The forbidden act will forever disobey . . .'). 'Jacob's Ladder' closes the work, as the words of the *Te Deum* fade away. As always in Stravinsky, musical and dramatic structures are intimately intertwined.

There are long purely instrumental moments in *The Flood* ('The Build-ing of the Ark' and 'The Flood') which are danced, and which Stravinsky himself originally planned carefully with his long-time collaborator George Balanchine. There is also a spoken narrator who comments, links events and recites the only extended Biblical passage in the piece. In fact, there is throughout a clear division between the characters who speak and those who sing ('the celestials should sing while the terrestrials should merely talk'[35]): all solo parts except for God (two basses) and Lucifer/Satan (a tenor) are spoken, for the most part delivered in a highly stylised man-ner. The stylisation of the role of God is underlined by the fact that it is sung *simultaneously* by two basses. God is unchanging: always slow, always 'other-worldly', and also always presenting together two forms of the row in rhythmic unison.

The other key stage work from Stravinsky's serial period is *Agon*. It was his last ballet score, and it is a summation of his work in the ballet since *Pulcinella*. A commission from Lincoln Kirstein and Balanchine for the New York City Ballet, it had a long gestation period. It was begun in December 1953, interrupted for the composition of *In memoriam Dylan Thomas* and the *Canticum Sacrum*, and not completed until April 1957. It involved a close collaboration between Stravinsky and Balanchine and demonstrates fascinating connections between the structures of music and dance.

Agon's audacity, its geometric precision, virtuosity and energy, suggest that Stravinsky had in later life found a new musical direction, a new, much more rarefied kind of neoclassicism, an even more refined stylisa-tion of past forms and traditions. Furthermore, its adoption of aspects of serial technique indicates an accommodation between what had for-merly been perceived as irreconcilable poles: Stravinskian neoclassicism and Schoenbergian/Webernian dodecaphony. But what is particularly fas-cinating about this work is the way in which the 'twelveness' of the pitch structure is also built into the patterning of the dances. There are twelve dances arranged into interlocking cycles and twelve dancers arranged in various combinations of one, two, three and four. The result is a kind of abstract Greek drama in keeping with the work's title (literally, a 'contest' or 'game'). The *pas de quatre* and coda form the dramatic frame, the sequence of French seventeenth-century dances (*pas de trois*) resembles a series of 'episodes', while everything turns on the central *pas de deux*.

Stravinsky's models came, in part, from two sources that Kirstein brought to his attention: de Lauze's dance manual, *Apologie de la danse* (1623), and Mersenne's *Harmonie universelle* (1636). But these ancient dances were transformed into something uniquely Stravinskian. In the 'Gailliarde', for example, French Baroque scoring is refracted through Stravinsky's sonic imagination. In Michael Oliver's words, we 'seem to be hearing a consort of lutes, viols and recorders, but from a great distance':[36] a canon between harp and mandolin (plus low flute) is accompanied by viola and three cellos, two flutes and two double basses in harmonics. In the 'Bransle Gay', the characteristic dance patterns are rhythmically reworked: the castanets maintain a 3/8 ostinato throughout, while the rest of the music is mainly in bars of 7/16 and 5/16. By such means, Stravinsky was able to achieve the reinvention of an archaic past in a music with a time*less* quality. And this distancing was reinforced in the original production by dressing the dancers in rehearsal costume only: a drama with no narrative, an abstract painting, or, as Stravinsky himself described it, a Mondrian composition.[37] Just as *The Rake's Progress* might be understood to be an opera about opera, so *Agon* might be understood to be, in essence, a dance about dance.

Balanchine first worked with Stravinsky on a production of *The Song of the Nightingale* in Paris in 1925. He later wrote that 'Stravinsky's effect on my own work has been always in the direction of control, of simplification and quietness.'[38] The first work on which they genuinely collaborated was the European premiere[39] by the Ballets Russes in 1928 of *Apollon musagète*. For Balanchine, *Apollon* was a revelation, the epitome of Stravinsky's neo-classical aesthetic: '*Apollon* I look back on as the turning-point of my life. In its discipline and restraint, in its sustained oneness of tone and feeling the score was a revelation. It seemed to tell me that I could dare not to use everything, that I, too, could eliminate.'[40] Stravinsky himself considered it a '*ballet blanc*', one of his most 'pure' and unified scores. It attempts to eschew contrast (as discussed later in the *Poetics*) by such means as the paring down of the scoring to strings only and the employment of an almost exclusively diatonic harmony. Walsh sees it as the companion to the statuesque *Oedipus*: 'a paradox of immobility rendered mobile'.[41] This highly stylised ballet score (in some senses pointing forward to *Agon*) was matched by Balanchine's 'abstract, non-anecdotal'[42] choreography; once again, the audience is distanced from the 'plot' as music and dance work in tandem to produce a work of measured 'holiness'. '*Apollon* is sometimes criticized for not being "of the theatre". It's true there is no violent plot . . . But the technique is that of classical ballet which is in every way theatrical and it is here used to project sound directly into visible movement.'[43] Music and dance in this work are equal partners.

Other collaborations between Stravinsky and Balanchine included the premieres of *Jeu de cartes* (New York, 1937) and *Orpheus* (New York, 1948), as well as the first American production of *The Fairy's Kiss* (New York, 1937). *Jeu de cartes* is an exuberant score that alludes to a wealth of other music (*Merzbild* would again seem to be an appropriate label); the music's playfulness is literally present in the dance sequences where the characters are the chief cards in a game of poker. The scenario is divided into three 'deals', the repetition of the introduction to each deal providing the music with a frame. *Orpheus* was the first piece into which Balanchine had direct input: he worked very closely with Stravinsky throughout and, Craft tells us, he even influenced its shape by inducing the composer 'to extend the return of the F major string music in the *pas de deux*'.[44] Like *Apollon musagète*, *Orpheus* tells a classical story in a stylised manner through a sequence of closed forms – dances, airs and interludes. Like *Apollon*, too, the music achieves a 'pure', hieratic character through its sense of control and through the use of such devices as fugue.

One other mid-period theatre work based on classical subject-matter should be mentioned here: *Perséphone*, a 'melodrama in three scenes' to a text by André Gide. In the *Dialogues*, Stravinsky called it 'a masque or dance-pantomime co-ordinated with a sung and spoken text'.[45] In this respect, it can usefully be compared with *Oedipus*. The part of Perséphone is shared by two performers (mime and speaker) and Stravinsky's account of his own ideal production emphasises, once again, his desire to achieve a kind of alienation through stylisation:

> The speaker Perséphone should stand at a fixed point antipodal to Eumolpus, and an illusion of motion should be established between them. The chorus should stand apart from and remain outside the action. The resulting separation of text and movement would mean that the staging could be worked out entirely in choreographic terms.[46]

Stravinsky's friend, the French poet Paul Valéry, certainly felt he had achieved this. Following the premiere, he wrote to Stravinsky: 'the divine detachment of your work touched me ... The point is, to attain purity through the will.' Valéry clearly recognised that in *Perséphone* Stravinsky had created a 'holy' theatre.

I conclude by looking back to the 'roughness' of Stravinsky's earliest theatre pieces, all of which have their origins in folk story and mythology. *The Nightingale* (a lyric tale based on 'The Emperor and the Nightingale' by Hans Christian Andersen), *The Firebird* (his first ballet for Diaghilev, based on a Russian folk tale) and *Petrushka* (a burlesque derived from the Russian version of the *commedia dell'arte* tradition) share certain narrative similarities. *The Nightingale* concerns itself with the rivalry between a real and a mechanical bird; *The Firebird* tells of both natural and supernatural creatures; Petrushka is half puppet, half human. In all three cases, taking his cue from his teacher Rimsky-Korsakov (most particularly from his last opera, *The Golden Cockerel*), Stravinsky composes these dramatic oppositions into the score. Human characters are cast – in general terms – in a diatonic world; supernatural characters occupy an altogether more chromatic or octatonic realm.[47] Sometimes the two worlds come together, musically and symbolically, as in the famous 'Petrushka motif', or in the more advanced musical language of *The Rite of Spring*, whose synthesising of the diatonic and chromatic reflects the mysterious and ritualistic dimension of the human characters. This musico-dramatic fusion was recognised even at the time of the works' premieres: Walsh writes of the initial Parisian reception of *The Firebird*, which acknowledged 'the integration of music, dance, and design, into what Henri Ghéo, writing in the *Nouvelle Revue française*, called "the most exquisite marvel of equilibrium that we have ever imagined between sounds, movements, and forms", a "danced symphony"'.[48] Daniel Albright has suggested that the opposition of natural and mechanical in *The Nightingale* lies symbolically at the heart of Stravinsky's aesthetic as a whole:

> This, I think, is what Stravinsky's music is 'about': the deep equivalence
> of the natural and the artificial. At the center of his dramatic
> imagination is the desire to juxtapose in a single work two competing
> systems – one which seems natural, tasteful, approved alike by man and
> God, the other of which seems artificial, abhorrent, devilish – and to
> subvert these distinctions as best he can.[49]

Given such an interpretation, it does seem extraordinary that Stravinsky should have worked so hard in later years to promote his early ballet scores as concert works when their very origins were in and of the theatre.

From *The Nightingale* to *The Flood*, from *The Firebird* to *Agon*, Stravinsky demonstrated an unerring sense of what kinds of music were right for the theatre, and what kinds of theatre were appropriate to his music. His ideas of how the two should work together were original and persuasive. He generally eschewed nineteenth-century narrative forms for new kinds of formalised, stylised theatres articulated through his own non-narrative, often ritualised musical structures. Formal, objectified, often simple in essence, his works nonetheless carry an enormous expressive weight, representing something primitive, powerful, immutable. Whether through the elemental directness of *The Rite of Spring* and *Les Noces*, the formal purity of *Apollon musagète* and *Agon*, or the self-conscious playfulness of *The Rake's Progress*, Stravinsky's work never fails to have an impact in the theatre.

8 Stravinsky the serialist

JOSEPH N. STRAUS

Introduction

By the spring of 1952, Stravinsky had reached the end of a compositional road he had travelled since *Pulcinella* in 1920. His brilliant Mozartian opera *The Rake's Progress* had been premiered the previous year to general acclaim. But, for Stravinsky, it marked not only a culmination of his musical neo-classicism, but a decisive turning-point as well. He had become aware of the low value placed on his music by outspoken members of the younger generation of avant-garde composers and had begun, for the first time, to acquaint himself with the music of Schoenberg and Webern, to whom younger composers were unfavourably comparing him. In the aftermath of those twin shocks, he turned in a new compositional direction.

Robert Craft, Stravinsky's amanuensis throughout his later years, describes the growing sense of strain, the crisis and its immediate consequences:

> *The Rake's Progress* was received by most critics as the work of a master but also a throwback, the last flowering of a genre. After the premiere, conducting concerts in Italy and Germany, Stravinsky found that he and Schoenberg were everywhere categorized as the reactionary and the progressive. What was worse, Stravinsky was acutely aware that the new generation was not interested in the *Rake*. While in Cologne, he heard tapes of Schoenberg's Violin Concerto . . . and of 'The Golden Calf' (from *Moses und Aron*); he listened attentively to both, but without any visible reaction . . . In contrast, a few days later, in Baden-Baden, when a recording of Webern's orchestra Variations was played for him, he asked to hear it three times in succession and showed more enthusiasm than I had ever seen from him about any contemporary music . . .
>
> . . . Then, on 24 February 1952 at the University of Southern California, I conducted a performance of Schoenberg's Septet-Suite (in a programme with Webern's Quartet, Opus 22), with Stravinsky present at all the rehearsals as well as the concert. This event was the turning-point in his later musical evolution.
>
> On March 8, he asked to go for a drive to Palmdale, at that time a small Mojave Desert town . . . On the way home he startled us, saying that he was afraid he could no longer compose and did not know what to do. For a moment, he broke down and actually wept . . . He referred

obliquely to the powerful impression that the Schoenberg piece [Septet-Suite] had made on him, and when he said that he wanted to learn more, I knew that the crisis was over; so far from being defeated, Stravinsky would emerge a new composer.[1]

Stravinsky himself described the episode several years later in more dispassionate terms:

> I have had to survive two crises as a composer, though as I continued to move from work to work I was not aware of either of them as such, or, indeed, of any momentous change. The first – the loss of Russia and its language of words as well as of music – affected every circumstance of my personal no less than my artistic life, which made recovery more difficult ... Crisis number two was brought on by the natural outgrowing of the special incubator in which I wrote *The Rake's Progress* (which is why I did not use Auden's beautiful *Delia* libretto; I could not continue in the same strain, could not compose a sequel to *The Rake*, as I would have had to do).[2]

The crisis led Stravinsky to a dramatic stylistic reorientation. From this point onwards, his music engaged, tentatively at first and then with growing individuality and confidence, the serial and twelve-note thinking of Schoenberg and Webern, which provided a starting-point for a remarkable voyage of artistic discovery. Far from merely imitating his Viennese predecessors, Stravinsky sought new ways of writing music in the serial idiom, and created a small body of astonishingly original and powerful serial music.

I can think of no other major composer, at a comparably advanced age and at the pinnacle of recognition and success, who so thoroughly altered his compositional approach, or whose late works differ so greatly from his earlier ones. While there is some truth in the cliché that Stravinsky always sounds like Stravinsky – and I will explore some of the links between early and late Stravinsky later in this chapter – none the less the late works differ radically from the earlier ones at every level, from their deep modes of musical formation to the rhythmic and intervallic details of the musical surface. Furthermore, Stravinsky's late works are not only radically different from the earlier ones, but are highly individuated from each other as well. There is no major work in this period in which Stravinsky did not try something new.

The result was an astonishing outpouring of music, remarkable for its sheer quantity as well as its ceaseless innovation, and all the more remarkable as the product of a man who was seventy years old at the time of the Cantata, the first of the late works, and eighty-five at the time of the *Requiem Canticles*, his last major work. And, while the quality is uneven in certain respects, the late works include some of the finest that Stravinsky ever wrote and thus some of the finest works ever written. *Agon, Movements* and *Requiem Canticles* are towering artistic achievements. *Abraham and Isaac* and *Introitus*, while less powerful, are nonetheless vivid and evocative. Even the comparably minor compositions of the period, such as the *Three Songs from William Shakespeare*, *In memoriam Dylan Thomas* and *Epitaphium*, are small gems.

Stravinsky's serial turn

Before discussing the music in detail, it is worth considering for a moment why Stravinsky took his serial turn. The central figure in the drama is Robert Craft, who lived with Stravinsky throughout the period, handled the complex logistics of his career, rehearsed orchestras in preparation for concerts and recordings, and increasingly acted as Stravinsky's artistic alter ego.[3] Craft's most important initial contribution, however, was to introduce Stravinsky to the music of Schoenberg and Webern. Until Craft arrived on the scene, Stravinsky had known virtually nothing of their music. Craft, however, was an important early exponent of the music of Schoenberg and Webern in the United States and, through him, Stravinsky experienced the shock of contact with music of extraordinary interest and power. The shock propelled him along the compositional path he followed for the rest of his life. In Craft's words:

> When I met Stravinsky in the spring of 1948, his fortunes were at a low ebb. Most of his music was not in print, he was not recording, and concert organizations wanted him to conduct only *Firebird* and *Petrushka*. More important, he was becoming increasingly isolated from the developments that extended from Arnold Schoenberg and had attracted the young generation. Stravinsky was aware of this despite the acclaim for *Orpheus*, his latest composition, and if he wanted to understand the other music, he did not know how to go about it. I say in all candor that I provided the path and that I do not believe Stravinsky would ever have taken the direction he did without me. The music that he would otherwise have written is impossible to imagine.[4]

Initially, Stravinsky may have been motivated in part by a desire to seem stylistically *au courant*, to do what the young people were doing and, if possible, to impress them in the process. But I think this aspect has been greatly exaggerated. A desire to impress Boulez, Stockhausen, Babbitt et al. may have been among the factors that sparked Stravinsky's initial interest but is wholly insufficient to account for his persistence in his new compositional approach, over a period of fifteen years and in the face of general indifference from the very composers whose favour he is presumed to have been cultivating. Long after Boulez, in particular, had lost all interest in Stravinsky's late music and relations between them had soured, Stravinsky continued along his serial path.[5] Evidently the serial approach meant a good deal more to him than simply a means of achieving social or artistic acceptance in avant-garde circles.

Throughout his career, Stravinsky sought various kinds of limitations on his field of activity, strictures and rules to give the enterprise shape and definition:

> The creator's function is to sift the elements he receives from [the imagination], for human activity must impose limits upon itself. The more art is controlled, limited, worked over, the more it is free ... My freedom consists in my moving about within the narrow frame that I have assigned myself for each one of my undertakings. I shall go even further: my freedom will be so much the greater and more meaningful the more narrowly I limit my field of action and the more I surround myself with obstacles. Whatever diminishes constraint, diminishes strength. The more constraints one imposes, the more one frees one's self of the chains that shackle the spirit.[6]

Stravinsky approached musical composition as a game, one which made sense only in obedience to explicit, strict rules. Unlike more familiar kinds of games, however, in this one the player is also the inventor of the rules. Indeed, devising appropriate constraints was, for Stravinsky, an integral part of the compositional or, more properly, pre-compositional process. Throughout his career, he imposed many different kinds of constraints, obstacles and limits upon his field of compositional action. I think the principal attraction of the serial enterprise for him was its well-articulated sense of necessary points of departure and ways of regulating the compositional flow. Stravinsky turned to serial composition not in spite of, but precisely because of, the strict discipline it promised.

Serialism was immediately attractive to Stravinsky as a way of organising the flow of notes and intervals. He had always composed with ostinatos and repeated groups of notes, and the series represented a kind of apotheosis of the ostinato. In addition, he had, in his own words, 'always composed with intervals', and the series embodied a selection of chosen intervals, which would be repeated and varied in predictable ways as the series was transformed.[7] Stravinsky quickly recognised that the series could provide him with a useful point of departure, a way of regulating the musical flow, a set of rules and constraints to accept, struggle with, or evade as he saw fit. It provided at least the beginning of a path into a new musical world.

Like his carefully chosen texts – most of the works in the late period are text settings – the serial idea permitted Stravinsky to contain and give shape to his creative impulses.

Schoenberg and Webern

It is important to understand what Stravinsky learned, and did not learn, from Schoenberg and Webern. Stravinsky began almost immediately to adopt the essential Schoenbergian principle of serial ordering. That is, in the absence of the traditional organising power of tonality (with its major and minor scales, its orientation towards a key, its commitment to resolution of dissonance) music can be organised instead with respect to a predetermined arrangement of notes, an arrangement that will differ from work to work. Works that draw their motivic, melodic and harmonic substance from a pre-composed ordering of notes (that is, a series) are serial works. When the series in question consists of all twelve notes, each represented only once, the work is a twelve-note serial work. Stravinsky's early serial works employ series that consist of either fewer than twelve notes (Cantata, Septet (first movement), 'Musick to heare' and 'Full fadom five' from *Three Songs from William Shakespeare*, *In memoriam Dylan Thomas*, *pas de quatre* from *Agon*) or more than twelve (the second and third movements of the Septet). Only in portions of *Canticum Sacrum* and *Agon*, and then in the entire vast expanse of *Threni* does Stravinsky begin to rely exclusively on twelve-note series.

Whatever the length of the series, Stravinsky also begins immediately to adopt another Schoenbergian principle: that the series, when presented in transposition, inversion, retrograde or retrograde inversion, retains its basic intervallic identity, and that series related by these transformations can be understood to constitute a homogeneous class. For Stravinsky, as for Schoenberg, the series class, or row class, provides the basic pitch material for a composition.

More specifically, Stravinsky accepted from the outset the Schoenbergian idea that four members of the series class, bound together by some particular musical relationship, might function as a referential norm, somewhat in the manner of a tonic region in a tonal composition. So not only the idea of a series, and a series class, but also the possibility of establishing a kind of tonic area within the series class, came directly from Schoenberg.

But while Stravinsky adopted Schoenberg's points of departure, he moved immediately in very different musical directions. In doing so, he developed his own highly original serial style and at the same time offered a strong, if implicit, critique of Schoenbergian serialism. From the outset, Stravinsky simultaneously invokes and satirises Schoenberg.

The Schoenbergian aggregate itself is the subject of Stravinsky's implicit critique. Schoenberg's twelve-note music treats the aggregate, the total collection of the twelve notes, as a basic structural unit. It creates aggregates within the series, between series forms and across wider musical spans. Stravinsky's early serial music and even his later twelve-note music, in contrast, are generally unconcerned with the aggregate. Indeed, Stravinsky employs a variety of compositional strategies to ensure intensive repetition of some notes and exclusion of others at all levels of structure.

Equally striking, Stravinsky persistently identifies his series with a theme – he gives it a distinctive melodic shape and keeps it in a single instrumental voice. Schoenberg, in contrast, makes use of sophisticated partitioning schemes in which the series is often divided up among the instrumental voices.[8] Stravinsky's approach represents a significant and deliberate simplification.

Despite his interest in Schoenberg's music, Stravinsky never warmed to what he considered its emotional bombast and self-indulgent excess.[9] It is this aesthetic distaste that motivates Stravinsky's transformation of Schoenberg. Stravinsky's early serial music engages with Schoenberg in direct and demonstrable ways. Schoenberg provided him with a vital challenge and stimulus, a starting-point and a useful framework for compositional inquiry. Later, as Stravinsky's style coalesced into what became a standard operating procedure for him, the sense of engagement with Schoenberg diminished to the vanishing point.

Stravinsky ultimately achieved the same artistic independence from Webern, although the stylistic affinities and structural debts are deeper.[10] Compared with Schoenberg, the shock of Stravinsky's initial contact with Webern was at least as profound – and its effects longer lasting.

> In the years between 1952 and 1955 no composer can have lived in closer contact with the music of Webern. Stravinsky was familiar with the sound of the Webern Cantatas and of the instrumental songs at a time when some of these works had not yet been performed in Europe. The challenge of Webern has been the strongest in his entire life. It has gradually brought him to the belief that serial technique is a possible means of musical composition.[11]

Comments about Webern, pro and con, but mostly pro, permeate Stravinsky's writings and interviews throughout the 1950s and 1960s.[12] The music obviously meant a great deal to him. Whereas Stravinsky basically rejected or ignored most of the stylistic and structural elements of Schoenberg's music, he overtly incorporates salient aspects of Webern's music. Webern's pointillistic textures are rarely duplicated in Stravinsky, but his spareness, his transparency, his relative contrapuntal simplicity often are. And three of the most characteristic features of Webern's musical structure find vivid, if distorted, reflections in Stravinsky's music. The first of these is canon. Like Webern, Stravinsky initially identified the series with a canonic subject, and its serial transformations (transposition, inversion, retrograde, retrograde inversion) as canonic imitations. Stravinsky's early serial music is usually contrapuntal/imitative in texture. Later, the canons go underground, absorbed into the special kind of arrays on which Stravinsky based his later twelve-note music.

A second shared feature is an interest in inversional balance and symmetry. In Webern's twelve-note music, a series and its inversion are often poised against each other. In Stravinsky's music an interest in inversional symmetry finds a variety of compositional expressions. A mutual focus on small motivic cells from which larger structures are generated by various compositional combinations is a third point of contact.

Stravinsky's musical critique of Webern is much less pointed than his critique of Schoenberg. His music evinces a deep and sincere engagement with Webern rather than the more distant, ironic treatment of Schoenberg. None the less, even in his early serial period, when Stravinsky borrowed most overtly and extensively from Webern, there is always a strong sense of transformation. Webern's materials are present, but recontextualised and filtered through Stravinsky's distinctive sensibility. Later, as his music became thoroughly twelve-note and abandoned entirely the persistent diatonic references of the early serial music, it paradoxically became less rather than more Webernian. As with the influence of Schoenberg, the principal impact of Webern was to shake Stravinsky free of many old compositional habits, and to suggest a new way of thinking about basic musical materials. Schoenberg and Webern provided a new framework for the compositional enterprise and new rules for the game, and had an immense initial impact. But as Stravinsky increasingly found his own way and created his own distinctive musical world, their presence gradually diminished and finally seemed to vanish almost entirely. Stravinsky had specific, concrete ideas of what kinds of sounds he wanted to write, and he appropriated, or invented, ways of doing so. Serialism presented itself to him as a set of musical possibilities, some well understood, some only partly understood, and some creatively misunderstood. He took what he wanted, and invented the rest.

Stravinsky, early and late

In recent Stravinsky scholarship, accounts of the late music have emphasised its connection with the earlier music.[13] One of the side effects has been to value the late music primarily for whatever qualities it shares with the earlier

Fig. 8.1 Five stylistic categories in Stravinsky's late music

Style category	Works
I Diatonicism (non-serial)	Cantata (1951–2), Septet (1952–3), *Canticum Sacrum* (1955), *Agon* (1953–7)
II Diatonic serialism	Cantata (1951–2), Septet (1952–3), *Three Songs from William Shakespeare* (1953), *Agon* (1953–7)
III Non-diatonic serialism	*Three Songs from William Shakespeare* (1953), *In memoriam Dylan Thomas* (1954), *Agon* (1953–7)
IV Twelve-note serialism	*Canticum Sacrum* (1955), *Agon* (1953–7), *Threni* (1957–8), *Epitaphium* (1959), *Double Canon* (1959), *Anthem* (1962), *Elegy for J. F. K.* (1964), *The Owl and the Pussycat* (1966), *Fanfare for a New Theatre* (1964)
V Twelve-note serialism based on rotational arrays	*Movements* (1958–9), *A Sermon, a Narrative, and a Prayer* (1960–1), *The Flood* (1961–2), *Abraham and Isaac* (1962–3), *Variations* (1963–4), *Introitus* (1965), *Requiem Canticles* (1965–6)

music, and thus to undervalue his late music for being insufficiently like his earlier music. From the opposite point of view, twelve-note scholarship has devalued Stravinsky's late music as insufficiently sophisticated: in short, insufficiently Schoenbergian. In this view Stravinsky was, at best, a weakly derivative imitator of his Viennese forebears.

I would like to counter both of these views by insisting on Stravinsky's independence from compositional models, including his own earlier music – an independence that was earned with a considerable struggle. The late music is neither a falling away from an earlier greatness nor a slavish capitulation to an alien power. Rather, it is a willed, adventurous voyage of compositional exploration.

Stravinsky's music in this late period can be roughly assigned to five stylistic categories, as shown in Fig. 8.1.

To some extent, these categories embody an evolutionary chronology, with the early serial works (diatonic and non-diatonic) giving way first to the twelve-note works and eventually to the twelve-note works based on rotational arrays. In practice, however, the categories overlap, even within individual works. *Agon*, for example, probably Stravinsky's most heterogeneous work, incorporates diatonic, serial and twelve-note elements, and these often co-exist as distinct layers in individual movements. Later, when Stravinsky adopted a consistent approach based on rotational arrays for his major works, he continued to use a more classical kind of twelve-note serialism for his smaller, minor works.

Diatonicism (non-serial)

Despite Stravinsky's description of a compositional 'crisis', his turn to serialism was gradual. At the outset, not only are the serial ideas themselves diatonic, but they often appear in company with diatonic non-serial music that would not have been out of place in earlier works. In the beginning of the first movement of the Septet, for example, a six-note series drawn from the notes of an A major or A minor scale is elaborated amid non-serial diatonic lines (see Ex. 8.1). The series, A–E–D–C/C♯–B–A, is presented in the clarinet and, simultaneously, in rhythmic augmentation in the bassoon, and, in inversion and rhythmic augmentation, in the horn. The series and this particular inversion, A–D–E–F♯–G♯–A, share the same first three notes. Stravinsky's desire to maintain centric focus amid serial elaboration is thus present from the outset, and remains in force throughout his later serial music as well. At the end of the passage the series is heard in stretto, leading to a cadence on A. Throughout the passage the series is treated as a theme, a line of pitches rather than pitch classes, with its contour preserved (or exactly reversed). The remaining instrumental parts thicken the contrapuntal texture and reinforce a sense of A-centred diatonicism, but are not themselves serial. In this way, Stravinsky's serialism emerges within a prevailing diatonic frame.

Diatonic serialism

In his earliest serial works, Stravinsky often uses series that are entirely diatonic, or nearly so. In 'Full fadom five', the second of the *Three Songs from William Shakespeare*, for example, his first compositional sketch was a simple E♭ minor scale (see Ex. 8.2a).[14] The scale establishes a concrete starting point, providing material to be shaped into a series. The second sketch (Ex. 8.2b) takes the seven notes of the scale and arranges them into an eight-note melody (the D♭ occurs twice) to set the first line of text, 'Full fadom five thy Father lies'.[15] The widely spaced melody, with its exclusive use of perfect fourths, perfect fifths and minor sevenths, is designed to evoke the tolling of funeral bells referred to at the end of the text.[16] In the third sketch (Ex. 8.2c), Stravinsky takes the seven notes of the E♭ minor scale and presents them in a different ordering to set the second line of text, 'Of his bones are Corrall made'. This seven-note melody functions as the seven-note series on which most of the rest of the song is based. The sketch reveals Stravinsky's intention to set the third line of text with the retrograde of the series (which Stravinsky calls 'canon'), the fourth line of text with the inversion (which Stravinsky calls 'inverse'), and the fifth line of text with the inversion of the retrograde (or the 'inverse' of the 'canon').[17]

The series E♭–D♭–G♭–F–B♭–C♭–A♭ is arranged symmetrically around A♭ and is designed as a wedge to converge on A♭. As a result, the 'inverse of the canon' (i.e. the IR form), which begins on A♭, wedges symmetrically outwards from that note and contains exactly the same seven notes as the original series, namely the notes of the E♭ minor scale. In this way Stravinsky

Ex. 8.1 Septet, movement I, bars 1–7

Ex. 8.1 (*cont.*)

Ex. 8.2 Compositional sketches for 'Full fadom five' from *Three Shakespeare Songs*, bars 1–11
a initial compositional sketch, an E♭ minor scale

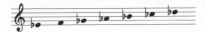

b ordered as a melody for the first line of text

Full fa - dom five thy Fa - ther lies,

c reordered as a series

reveals his understanding of the inversional symmetry of any diatonic scale
and his commitment to inversional symmetry as a basic compositional
resource in his serial music. Ex. 8.3 shows the score for the first thirteen bars
of the song. The melodic line follows the compositional sketches closely.

Ex. 8.3 'Full fadom five' from *Three Shakespeare Songs*, bars 1–13, with analytical markings

In fact, Stravinsky composed the vocal melody in its entirety before adding accompanying parts. This suggests his essentially contrapuntal conception of music in this period of his compositional life. The lines of a polyphonic fabric are understood as integral, self-sufficient and musically comprehensible in themselves. Each line has its own serial and musical justification. The combination of lines into a polyphonic whole is a separate issue, one that is addressed later in the compositional process. Stravinsky still imagines his series as a theme, but now one that is susceptible to octave displacements. Within the vocal line, contour is usually preserved, but in the accompanying parts the series is increasingly understood as a line of pitch classes rather than simply a line of pitches.

To his melody, Stravinsky adds other members of the row class as imitative counterpoints. There are a few notes that do not participate in any complete row statement; generally, these either duplicate the pitch-class content of the melody, or differ from it only slightly. In bars 2–3, for example, the original series in the melody is accompanied by its imitation at the octave in the viola and by IR in the clarinet. All three of these series have the same content, namely the seven notes of the E♭ minor scale. That scale thus comprises both a source of serial ordering and a distinctive harmonic area, a point of departure for 'modulations' to other diatonic scales. The music is a dense, intricate contrapuntal web that leaves a diatonic, or nearly diatonic, wash in its wake.

Non-diatonic serialism

Over the course of the early and mid 1950s, Stravinsky's serial music became more chromatic, less obviously based on diatonic scales. *In memoriam Dylan Thomas* is based on the five-note series E♮–E♭–C♮–C♯–D, which Stravinsky labels 'theme' in the first bar of the score (see Ex. 8.4). Like the series for 'Full fadom five', the series for *In memoriam Dylan Thomas* is constructed as a wedge, with the initial descending semitone, E–E♭, balanced by the ascending semitone, C–C♯, both pointing to the concluding D, around which the wedge balances. The first four notes, E♮–E♭–C♮–C♯, describe a familiar tetrachord type from Stravinsky's earlier music. The D fills the gap and asserts the entirely chromatic nature of the series.

In the passage that begins the work, a quartet of trombones deploys melodic lines based on series forms stitched together. The series are identified by Stravinsky on the score. This kind of serial self-analysis is characteristic of Stravinsky's music throughout the period, though usually the labels are erased before the manuscript is sent to the printer. As Stravinsky moves through a musical world that is new to him, he wants to know where he is, and study of the compositional sketches reveals that the more complicated the serial derivations, the more intense the self-analysis becomes.

Ex. 8.4 *In memoriam Dylan Thomas,* Prelude ('Dirge-canons'), bars 1–5

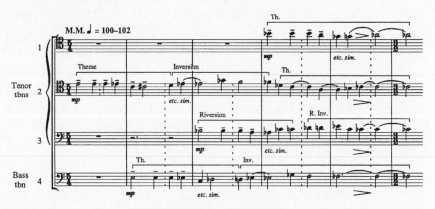

Ex. 8.5 *In memoriam Dylan Thomas,* first compositional sketch

The music is polyphonic and imitative, and often canonic. The leading voice, in tenor trombone II, begins with the 'theme', the last note of which becomes the first note of an 'inversion' (this kind of series overlap is typical throughout the period). An additional, transposed statement of the theme is adjoined at the end. Trombone IV follows in canon at the octave and trombone I at the tritone. Trombone III contributes a 'riversion' (retrograde) and a retrograde inversion. The series retains its contour (in the closest possible spacing) throughout this passage, but in the song to which this passage is part of a prelude, the series is treated freely, as a line of pitch classes with frequent octave displacements. Amid the dense contrapuntal weave, the vertical harmonies are probably best understood as mere by-products. The cadence of the passage, however, on an E major triad (spelled F♭ major) was part of Stravinsky's conscious design from the outset (see Ex. 8.5).[18]

In the bass Stravinsky presents a five-note idea, E–F–F♯–E♭–D, followed by its retrograde.[19] The bass line thus begins and ends on E. The two upper voices consist only of approaches to E from a semitone above and below. Stravinsky apparently wanted a cadence on E and planned to work out later which series forms would end appropriately, with either D♯–E or F–E. The central idea, then, is a serial passage that centres and cadences on E, and the cadence on an E major chord in the final, published version of the passage represents an elaboration of this initial impulse. A desire to maintain a clear sense of pitch focus thus remains intact in this chromatic serial work, as throughout Stravinsky's last compositional period.

Twelve-note serialism

Stravinsky's first completely twelve-note movement was 'Surge, aquilo', the setting of a passage from the biblical Song of Solomon, in *Canticum Sacrum*. The final bars are reprinted as Ex. 8.6b.

The series ends C–B–A, creating a sense of arrival on A that Stravinsky exploits at many points in the movement, including its final cadence. It moves primarily by small intervals and contains a number of intervallic and motivic repetitions. Of these the most important involve transposition by T_8 (eight semitones), as indicated.

The concluding passage begins with bell-like chords in the harp and double basses. These present a statement of the series in which its three tetrachords are verticalised. Stravinsky rarely writes chords during this period, because he has not yet discovered a satisfactory way of doing so with a convincing serial motivation. For the most part, the harmonies of his early serial music are best understood as by-products of the contrapuntal activity, except at cadences, where some real compositional control is often exerted. These verticalised series segments are a striking but rare occurrence in Stravinsky's serial music.

There follows immediately a three-voice canon in rhythmic augmentation. The voice leads with T_1I; the flute follows at the transposition of T_8 (the series is T_9I) in rhythmic values twice as long; and the harp follows T_8 away from the flute (the series is T_5I), again doubling the rhythmic values. These T_8 transpositional levels fully exploit the internal resources of the series and produce a large number of invariant segments. That is, many melodic fragments are shared among the three canonic lines, as shown in Ex. 8.6c. As a general rule, Stravinsky's serial music encourages repetition and duplication of pitch, giving shape and focus to the flow of the twelve notes.

The last and slowest of the three canonic voices, in the harp, concludes with its tenth note, A. That permits a strong final cadence on the perfect fifth, A–E. Even in Stravinsky's twelve-note music, the perfect fifth retains its cadential force.

Twelve-note serialism based on rotational arrays

Beginning with *Movements*, Stravinsky based all of his remaining large-scale works (*A Sermon, a Narrative, and a Prayer, The Flood, Abraham and Isaac,*

Ex. 8.6 *Canticum Sacrum,* 'Surge, aquilo'

a series

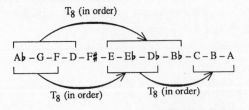

b bars 84–93

c three-voice canon

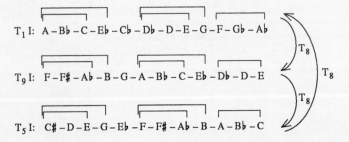

Ex. 8.7 Writing a rotational array

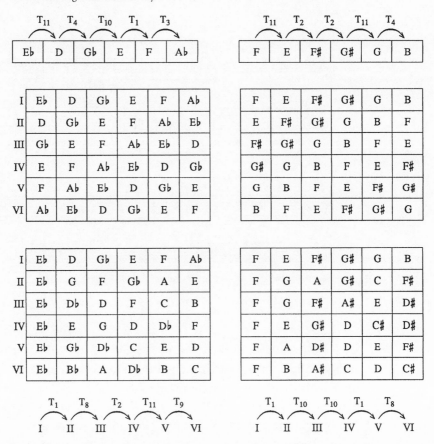

Variations, Introitus, Requiem Canticles) on a special kind of twelve-note construction known as a 'rotational array'.[20] During this period, Stravinsky restricts himself to what he considered the four basic forms of the series: an original, or prime, form (P), its inversion starting on the same note (I), its retrograde (R) and the inversion of the retrograde (IR).[21] With a few isolated exceptions these basic forms are not transposed. In this way, Stravinsky turns his back on the approach of Schoenberg and Webern, which depends on wide-ranging exploration of the entire row class. These four basic forms are sometimes heard in their entirety. More commonly, however, each is divided into its two hexachords, and each of the resulting eight hexachords is used to generate a rotational array. Ex. 8.7 shows how these arrays are created.

Stravinsky begins with a hexachord (Ex. 8.7 illustrates this, using hexachords from *A Sermon, a Narrative, and a Prayer* and *Abraham and Isaac*). Each hexachord has a distinctive intervallic profile. The hexachord is then rotated systematically to create an array of six rows, all of which contain the

Ex. 8.8 *A Sermon, a Narrative, and a Prayer,* bars 227–38, alto and tenor solo only: two sweeps through a rotational array

same six notes, beginning in turn on each of them.[22] At this stage the arrays embody a kind of six-voice canon at the unison, with each row beginning its canonic statement one note ahead of the row above it and one note later than the row below it. Finally, the rows of the array are transposed so that all begin on the first note of the first row. Stravinsky constructs arrays like these at a very early stage in the compositional process for all of his works from *Movements* onwards.

The six-voice canon is still preserved, but it is no longer at the unison. Now the intervals of canonic imitation are the same as the complements of the intervals of the hexachord itself, as shown at the bottom of Ex. 8.7. In this way the array can be understood as a large-scale expression of the intervals of the hexachord that generates it. The rows of the array are no longer identical in content, but there are potentially lots of repetitions of notes from row to row. Most obviously, all of the rows have the same first note, but they have lots of other notes in common as well.

The rows of these rotational arrays are the source of most of Stravinsky's melodies in his later music, and when he writes melodies derived from these arrays he thoroughly exploits the properties of canonic transposition and common-note repetitions. Exx. 8.8 and 8.9 give two reasonably typical examples, based on the arrays from Ex. 8.7. In Ex. 8.8 the tenor is the leading voice in a kind of two-part canon. It traverses the first rotational array in Ex. 8.7 from top to bottom, beginning with the second row of the array (the notes of each row may be stated in order either from first to last or from last

Ex. 8.9 *Abraham and Isaac*, bars 73–9: one sweep through a rotational array

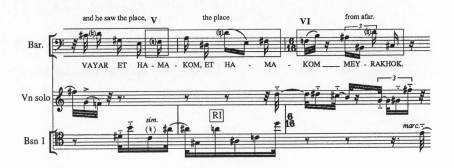

to first). The alto follows by traversing the same array, beginning on the first row. Many notes are shared in common by the hexachords, most obviously the Eb with which each of them begins or ends, but other notes as well, emphasised by occasional unisons between the parts. The melody in Ex. 8.9 is organised in a similar way, as a pass through a rotational array from top to bottom (the instrumental accompaniment is based on complete series statements). Stravinsky's melodies are not always as systematic as this, but they generally involve purposeful motions among the rows of his arrays.

Within both passages, all of the hexachords contain the same intervals and are related by transposition. Furthermore, the intervals within each hexachord are reflected in the intervals of transposition that connect them. And the relationships among the hexachords are further intensified by their shared notes. This is twelve-note music in a deep sense, but it shows no concern whatsoever with creating aggregates of all twelve notes. On the contrary, the melodies are organised to maximise repetitions of interval and pitch. The melodies give the feeling almost of ostinatos, based as they are on recurring cells of notes and intervals, and in that sense relate more closely to Stravinsky's own earlier music than to the twelve-note music of Schoenberg or Webern.

Ex. 8.10 *The Flood*, bars 180–90

Serial harmony

His rotational arrays also provided Stravinsky with a way of writing serial harmonies, particularly in chordal or chorale textures. His serial and twelve-note music was generally contrapuntal in conception, with series-forms or rows of the arrays layered against each other melodically. But

Ex. 8.10 (*cont.*)

| P | G# G A Bb D E F D# F# C B C# |

| I | G# A G F# D C B C# Bb E F D# |

rotational array from first hexachord of P

1	2	3	4	5	6
G#	G	A	A#	D	E
G#	A#	B	D#	F	A
G#	A	C#	D#	G	F#
G#	C	D	F#	F	G
G#	A#	D	C#	D#	E
G#	C	B	C#	D	F#

Stravinsky also wanted to be able to write true serial harmonies that were more than mere by-products of the counterpoint. His principal, and theoretically most impressive, response to this need involved the use of columns or 'verticals' of his rotational arrays (see Ex. 8.10). In this passage from *The Flood*, the voice of God is represented by a duet of bass soloists, one of whom (doubled by piano) sings the P-form of the series and the other (doubled by harp) the I-form. These two forms are related by inversion around G#, their mutual first note, and the symmetrical balance they create together may suggest here a divine attribute.

Some of the same sense of inversional symmetry around G# also shapes the accompanying chords, which move systematically through the rotational array generated from the first hexachord of the P-form. Arrays of this kind have many interesting properties. The first vertical always contains six instances of a single note, and that note will occur nowhere else in the array. Stravinsky often emphasises this note as a kind of pitch centre in passages based on these arrays. No other vertical is as redundant as that one, but usually many will contain at least some doubling of notes. Stravinsky often reflects this doubling in his instrumental settings, as in the chords of Ex. 8.10. Here, as in other aspects of his serial approach, Stravinsky welcomes the possibility of stressing some notes as a way of shaping the musical flow.

The array verticals also have an inversionally symmetrical arrangement created by the rotational-transpositional structure of the array, and

Ex. 8.11 *Requiem Canticles*, 'Exaudi', bars 71–80

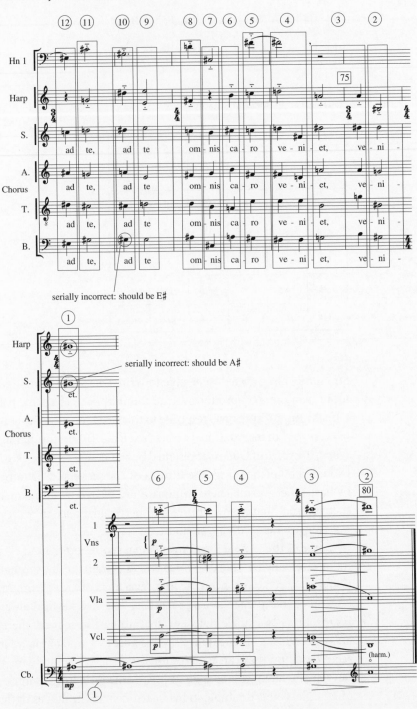

serially incorrect: should be E♯

serially incorrect: should be A♯

Ex. 8.11 (*cont.*)

four-part array

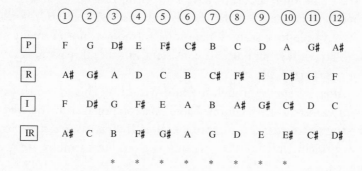

R^A (= first hexachord of Retrograde)

independent of the particular generating hexachord. The note in the first vertical defines an axis of symmetry for the array as a whole. Around that axis, vertical 2 balances vertical 6, vertical 3 balances vertical 5, and vertical 4 balances itself. The chords thus express, in a subtle way, the same sense of inversional balance around G♯ that exists in the melodies.

In addition to the rotational arrays, Stravinsky uses what are called 'four-part arrays' to create serial harmony, particularly in chordal passages. In arrays of this kind he lines up his four basic series forms – a prime, its inversion beginning on the same note, its retrograde and the inversion of the retrograde, beginning on the same note – and extracts twelve four-note chords as vertical slices through the array.

The passage in Ex. 8.11 begins with twelve chords, which simply work through the four-part array from last to first. Like the rotational arrays, the four-part arrays have many interesting properties.[23] They consist of two pairs of inversionally related forms: P and I, related by inversion around their shared first note (in this case F), and R and IR, related by inversion around their shared first note (in this case A♯). There is thus a kind of skewed inversional symmetry embodied in these arrays, as in the rotational arrays. The four-part arrays have a surprising propensity to generate whole-tone harmonies: all of the chords indicated with an asterisk are subsets of the whole-tone scale. Whole-tone harmony is not normally associated with Stravinsky, but it occurs consistently in chorale passages derived from four-part arrays like this one.

After sweeping through the four-part array, this movement concludes with an instrumental chorale based on a rotational array (derived from the first hexachord of the R-form of the series). In this passage, then, Stravinsky's two principal methods for writing twelve-note harmony are gently conjoined.

Expression

In much of the foregoing discussion I have emphasised the technical aspects of Stravinsky's late music. And, indeed, those aspects are remarkable in themselves. The rotational and the four-part arrays are theoretically powerful and original constructions. More generally, Stravinsky's serial music as a whole bespeaks an impressive degree of technical innovation and integration. In the final years of his compositional life, Stravinsky forged a distinctive and original compositional language, one that was new for him, and new also for the musical world.

At the same time, the late music is not only structurally rich but movingly expressive as well. Stravinsky abhorred what he considered to be the self-indulgent bombast of heightened Romantic self-expression, but his music, particularly his late music, is replete with static symbolic representations. Musical symbols are built up by an extensive network of cross-references, both to traditional musical models and to his own works. Stravinsky's music, taken as a whole, deploys a reasonably consistent gestural language, one which he uses to give expressive shape both to his dramatic or narrative works and to his instrumental works. In fact, Stravinsky's music vividly represents a wide range of human emotions and experiences.

Agon, for example, although it is an abstract ballet with no definite plot, employs many of the expressive devices that give meaning to Stravinsky's explicitly dramatic works. It was written over a period of several years during which Stravinsky's style was evolving rapidly. Its opening scene is essentially diatonic, but it quickly becomes more chromatic, then intermittently serial, and finally twelve-note serial. It comes as a stunning shock, then, when at the end of the ballet, the twelve-note discourse is suddenly interrupted by a recapitulation of the opening diatonic music.

The dramatic impact of this moment draws part of its power from its invocation of a familiar contrast in Stravinsky's music between the diatonic and the chromatic (or octatonic). In his earliest music, this dichotomy is a way of differentiating between the human and the fantastic worlds by associating the human with the diatonic and the fantastic with the chromatic, and often with the octatonic. In *The Firebird*, for example, this opposition is maintained in the contrast between the fantastic world of Kastchei and the firebird, and the human world of Ivan and the princesses. In *The Rake's Progress*, some forty years later, the same contrast is seen between the dark, painful reality of Tom Rakewell's 'progress' and the bright illusions of his dreams and his madness.[24] Of course, the interaction between diatonic and chromatic (often octatonic) elements is a central feature of the music of Stravinsky's first and second periods, one that is scarcely reducible to a simple mapping of diatonic onto human and chromatic onto fantastic. None the less, it remains a significant dramatic resource.

Like life, *Agon* ends with a bright blankness. At the end of *Agon*, the bright, clear, hard diatonicism emerges as a sharp shock of clarification from a dark, twisting, permeable chromaticism. The sudden shift from the serial to the diatonic seems to connote a movement from a dark, intricate dream of life to an awakening into death. As in *The Rake's Progress*, the moment of final clarification, of definitive diatonic emergence, is also the moment of death.

The Postlude of the *Requiem Canticles* bears some of the same expressive impact, but in a more intense, concentrated way. This was Stravinsky's last major work, written when he was eighty-five years old and in failing health, in full consciousness of the imminence of his own death. The movement consists mainly of solemn four-voice chorales punctuated before, between and after by five widely spaced chords that are sometimes referred to as 'chords of death'. The chorales – which are derived from four-part arrays – are scored for celeste, tubular bells and vibraphone. The evocation of funeral bells is unmistakable and creates a solemn, devotional atmosphere.

The 'chords of death', derived from the verticals of the rotational arrays, describe a progression that leads to a surprising diatonic conclusion.[25] The first four chords are large, complex and chromatic, with five, six, seven or eight different notes. The final chord is a diatonic tetrachord: B♭–C–D♭–F. This progression, like the large-scale motion in *Agon*, is thus one of sudden simplification and clarification, of emerging from a darkly rich chromatic night into a bright diatonic day. It comes as an awakening from a rich, complex dream of life into the hard reality of death.

Conclusion

Once Stravinsky embarked on his serial course, he persisted in it with extraordinary fidelity and intensity for the remainder of his compositional life. He was deeply committed to the pre-compositional serial designs he created for each of his works. From the time of *Threni*, his first entirely twelve-note work, every note has an explicit and demonstrable serial explanation. There are no 'free passages' or 'free notes'. Rather, everything falls within the constraints that Stravinsky has chosen to impose upon himself. The pre-compositional designs are themselves the product of inspiring creativity and originality and provided Stravinsky with a welcome and essential framework for compositional play. They rejuvenated him, liberated him and enabled him to produce, in the last decades of his long life, a succession of works of unsurpassed vitality, expressive power, structural richness and youthful energy.

PART III

Reception

9 Stravinsky conducts Stravinsky

NICHOLAS COOK

All truly modern musical performance (and of course that includes the authenticist variety) treats the music performed as if it were composed – or at least performed – by Stravinsky. TARUSKIN[1]

The years 1928–9, when Stravinsky first recorded his Russian ballets, have not yet passed beyond living memory.[2] And yet, when it comes to the history of performance (and especially of orchestral performance, since recording so large a group of musicians became possible only with the development of electrical recording around 1925), this is a remote and only just recoverable past. It is true that the pianola versions of *The Firebird*, *Petrushka* and *The Rite of Spring* push the horizon back to the early 1920s, but the ballets' premieres, from the last years before the First World War, lie altogether within the long, silent, initial phase of music history. Stravinsky recorded each of them on a number of occasions (he recorded *The Rite*, for instance, in 1929, 1940 and 1960), and in this way the history of these works unfolded, as Peter Hill puts it, 'exactly in tandem with the emerging record industry'.[3] Successive developments in recording technology represent one of the reasons why Stravinsky recorded many of his works several times: the 78 gave way to the LP in 1948 and to the stereo LP in 1957. ('Last year's record is as *démodé* as last year's motor car,' Stravinsky wryly observed.[4]) But there were further reasons. One was Stravinsky's financial dependence on recording and more generally on conducting, as a result of the drying up of his Russian royalties following the 1917 Revolution; there is a terrible irony in the fact that Stravinsky's career as neoclassical and serial composer was bankrolled by nearly a thousand performances of *The Firebird*.[5] The other reason takes longer to explain, for it opens up the whole issue of Stravinsky's intentions as a recording artist.

Stravinsky's attutide towards recording was formed largely by his experience with the pianola or player-piano.[6] He first encountered the instrument in 1914,[7] and composed an Étude for it in 1917. But it was only in the 1920s, when he held successive contracts with Pleyel (1921–4) and Aeolian (1924–9), that he created arrangements of his Russian ballets: 'created' rather than 'recorded', because many of them, including that of *The Rite*, were not taken from live performance but rather cut into the roll by hand, under the composer's more or less close direction. Stravinsky stressed that this made the pianola versions just that: *versions* of the music rather than 'recordings' in any normal sense. In 1925 he referred to them as 'Not a "photograph of my playing", as Paderewski has made of his...but rather a "lithograph", a full and permanent record of tone combinations that are beyond my ten poor fingers to perform';[8] three years later he explained in an interview that he saw the pianola as 'not an instrument to *reproduce* my works but one that could *reconstitute* them'.[9] Such statements – along with Stravinsky's later claim that the pianola's metronomic quality, its 'absence of tempo nuances', influenced his compositional style in the 1920s[10] – must make problematic any claim that the pianola versions provide a direct guide to the original performance practice of the Diaghilev ballets.

Stravinsky carried this thinking over into sound recording. In the same 1928 interview, he said that 'the gramophone produces the image of an image and not simply a transferral', and stressed the non-naturalistic circumstances under which early, non-editable recordings took place ('one's weariness accumulates, and when nerves are about to snap, the violinists' arms to succumb, and the mind to go blank with the monotony of the task, that is the moment when one must be perfect for the "take" which is to be recorded.') Paradoxically, however, he saw the introduction of editing technology in the 1950s as only furthering the separation between live and recorded performance: 'Natural balance, natural dynamics, natural echo, natural colour, natural human error', he told *Seventeen* magazine, 'have been replaced by added echo and reverberation, by a neutralizing dynamic range, by filtered sound, by an engineered balance...The resulting record is a super-glossy, chem-fab music-substitute never heard on sea or land, or even in Philadelphia.'[11] Add to all this 'the carelessness, the tension, and incompetence which usually pervade recording enterprises', as a jaundiced Claudio Spies put it,[12] and it is hard to know how far Stravinsky's recordings can be taken as a guide to his conception of the music, or even to the reality of contemporary concert performance. An early recording is not a kind of fly on the wall or historical surveillance technology. It is a historical document, presenting as many difficulties of interpretation (though different ones) as any other kind of documentary evidence.

The first recording Stravinsky ever made was a private one (intended presumably for his own study purposes), now lost: it was of his Octet, and was made in Paris in 1923, shortly after he premiered the work at one of Koussevitsky's Symphony Concerts. This was the first time Stravinsky had ever premiered one of his works as a conductor,[13] and it was in an article entitled 'Some ideas about my *Octuor*'[14] that he first set out the philosophy of performance which he reiterated and elaborated in his *Autobiography* and *Poetics of Music*,[15] as well as in some of the conversation books with Robert Craft. Central to this philosophy was his distrust of conductors and 'their notorious liberty,... which prevents the public from obtaining a correct idea of the author's intentions';[16] this, he said, is what drove him first to the pianola and then to the gramophone. (Age did not soften his opinion of conductors: even at the end of his life, in 'On conductors and conducting', he described them as 'a tremendous obstacle to music-making'.[17]) Such views were not, of course, exactly unique: Schoenberg was hardly less cutting ('Does not the author, too, have a claim to make clear his opinion about the realization of his work, even though no conductor of genius will neglect to override the author's opinion when the performance comes?'[18]), while Ravel's maxim, 'I do not ask for my music to be interpreted, but only for it to be played', sounds almost more Stravinskian than Stravinsky.[19] But there are three ways in which Stravinsky went beyond a merely conventional expression of this chronic composer's complaint.

First, in the Octet essay, but more systematically in the *Poetics*,[20] Stravinsky rationalised his distrust in terms of a distinction between 'execution' and 'interpretation': the former (corresponding to Ravel's 'playing') was to be understood as a strict and faithful realisation of the music itself and hence a characteristically modernist sweeping away of the Romantic indulgences of the latter. (The ethically charged vocabulary is an integral part of the message: interpretation 'is at the root of all the errors, all the sins, all the misunderstandings that interpose themselves between the musical work and the listener and prevent a faithful transmission of its message'.[21]) Second, Stravinsky translated his distrust of interpreters into action by performing his music himself. His conducting career took off rapidly after the Octet premiere, while his serious pianistic career as an exponent of his own music (which lasted about fifteen years) began after Koussevitsky suggested that he take the solo part in his Concerto in 1924; in his *Autobiography* Stravinsky commented that 'the prospect of creating my work for myself, and thus establishing the manner in which I wished it to be played, greatly attracted me'.[22] But third, and perhaps most intriguingly, he made a conscious attempt to build his distrust of performers into his music by making it, in effect, interpretation-proof. This meant more than simply transcribing rubato passages into strict rhythmic notation, so that a literal performance would produce a flexible effect, though Stravinsky did on occasion do this.[23] Traditionally, he explained in the Octet essay, it is the nuance which forms the 'emotive basis' of music,[24] and because of the difficulty of specifying nuance in the score such music is open to deformation (that is, 'interpretation'). By contrast, he says, the emotive content of the Octet has been built into the play of the musical materials, into the 'musical architecture'[25]: it has been drawn out of the performance and into the work itself. The music is, so to speak, pre-interpreted.

The performer's contribution, then, is already determined by the music itself: 'to the executant', Stravinsky continued in the Octet essay,[26] 'belongs the presentation of [the] composition in the way designated to him by its own form', while in the *Poetics* he was even more emphatic, referring to 'the great principle of submission' and explaining that 'The secret of perfection lies above all in [the performer's] consciousness of the law imposed on him by the work he is performing.'[27] This is not exactly to say that there is only one way in which a given work may be legitimately performed, but it limits the scope of performance variance to essentially technical issues of presentation: creative revelations of new and perhaps unforeseen aspects of the music are apparently precluded. (Here there is an unlikely but close parallel with Schenker's contemporaneous theory on performance,[28] which could quite reasonably be seen as another product of the 'new objectivity' that pervades the Octet essay.) And once performance is seen as bound in this intimate manner to composition, it follows that recordings can be no less definitive of the musical work than scores. Stravinsky reiterated this principle over a period of more than thirty years:

> 1928: 'the phonograph is currently the best instrument through which the masters of modern music can transmit their thoughts.'[29]
>
> 1935 (of his Columbia recordings from 1928): 'far better than with piano rolls, I was able to express all my intentions with real exactitude. Consequently these records...have the importance of documents which can serve as guides to all executants of my music... [E]veryone who listens to my records hears my music free from any distortions of my thought, at least in its essential elements.'[30]
>
> 1954: 'When I conduct, the music is presented pretty nearly the way I want it. That is why I've been conducting recording sessions of most of my music. In the future there will be no doubt as to how it should be played.'[31]
>
> 1959: 'I regard my recordings as indispensable supplements to the printed music.'[32]

In short, Stravinsky saw his recordings as establishing an authoritative performance tradition and in this sense as an extension of the compositional process. As usual, his aesthetics masked commercial acumen, for this represented the perfect sales pitch for a relatively inexperienced conductor competing with the likes of Monteux (the original conductor of *The Rite*, whose own recording was apparently made just a few weeks after Stravinsky's[33]) and Stokowski (whose recording appeared in 1930). And by emphasising the authority which only he could bring to the performance of his own music, Stravinsky succeeded in establishing the framework within which his concerts and recordings were received throughout his lifetime; hence the 'Stravinsky conducts Stravinsky' slogan which CBS employed to publicise their exclusive contractual relationship with the composer, which lasted from 1951 to the end of Stravinsky's life, and which included not only new recordings of the earlier works but more or less timely issues of new compositions. (In the early 1970s it emerged that some of these recordings should in fact have been labelled 'Craft conducts Stravinsky',[34] and Sony now market the recordings under the more discreet title 'Igor Stravinsky Edition'.)

Indeed, something like a standard Stravinsky record-review format emerged. First, you summarised the nature, historical significance, and/or aesthetic premise of the music. Then you acknowledged Stravinsky's technical shortcomings as a conductor, optionally contrasting his performances with those of other conductors, but turning this round into a recognition of the composer's special authority. ('Stravinsky is not a great conductor', wrote a reviewer of the 1940 *Rite*, 'but he manages to get results.'[35] By 1960 this has turned into 'At least we can be sure that when a composer conducts his own music the essentials are right, even if the inessentials give him trouble; as a result we get a directness of impact that we may look for in vain from more polished but less understanding performances.'[36]) A few complimentary comments on the quality and character of Stravinsky's performance follow ('The rhythms are sharp and savage still,' Edward Greenfield wrote of the 1960 *Rite*, 'enough to make this as much a physical experience as ever, but more satisfying in purely musical terms';[37] there is a general assumption of both technological and interpretative progress). And finally you reiterate the indispensable nature of Stravinsky's own recordings: 'Traditions do not live by scores alone,' proclaimed the *Gramophone* reviewer, 'and every scrap of evidence about how the greatest composer of our day wants his music to sound is invaluable.'[38]

All this assured a remarkably favourable critical response; a summary, published in *Notes*, of fourteen reviews of the 1960 double issue of *The Rite* and *Petrushka* reveals that thirteen rated it as excellent, one as adequate, and none as inadequate.[39] But the account of Stravinsky's conducting which most strikingly evokes the spirit in which his performances were received comes from the pianist Leo Smit,[40] referring to a 1960 concert performance of *Les Noces* in which Smit took part:

> Stravinsky started conducting with great energy and confidence.
> Gradually, imperceptibly the pace began to slacken and his interest
> seemed to shift from the players and singers to the score itself. By the
> time the basso had finished his concluding solo and the final
> piano-bell-cymbal chords were reverberating through space, Stravinsky's
> bent head was hovering just above the open pages, his motionless arms
> outstretched like some prehistoric bird mantling its helpless prey.[41] We
> held the last clang for a very long time while Stravinsky seemed lost in an
> ancient dream. The hall had been completely silent for what felt like
> minutes, when someone, far away, applauded, breaking the spell.
> Stravinsky looked up as though surprised to find himself in public . . .

The resonances with Beethovenian mythology, and with the subjectivity central to the Romantic construction of genius, are unmistakable and revealing. Smit's account vividly conveys the manner in which the reception of Stravinsky was moulded by the judgement which the *Gramophone* reviewer makes of him in the manner of a simple statement of fact: 'the greatest composer of our time'.

If Stravinsky's claim that his recordings 'express all my intentions with real exactitude' was in this way a highly effective rhetorical ploy, then it goes without saying that it invoked a thoroughly problematic concept: the concept of compositional intentionality falls to pieces as soon as there is any variance in its expression. (If Stravinsky plays *The Rite* one way and then another, which expresses his 'real' intentions? If we cannot answer that question, what does the concept of 'intention' add to a simple statement that he played it one way and then another?[42]) However, Robert Fink gives the argument an interesting twist when he demonstrates how many of the most characteristic features of *The Rite* emerged over a period of years, sometimes through a process of negotiation between Stravinsky and Monteux. An example of the former is the repeated downbows at the beginning of 'The augurs of spring', which first appear as a pencil marking in Stravinsky's copy of the 1922 full score, and of the latter the interaction between the ways Stravinsky and Monteux parsed the rhythms of the 'Sacrifical dance', the outcome of which was the 'revised first edition' of 1929 (itself revised in 1943[43]). As Fink puts it, it was only the experience of the music under Monteux's baton, and from 1926 his own,[44] that showed Stravinsky what 'he "had always wanted"',[45] which is a way of saying that he had not always wanted it at all. That is, he wanted it played one way, and then another.

Fink's demonstration forms part of a larger project, the purpose of which was to attack the assumption that *The Rite* was always associated with the metronomic strictness, the absence of 'interpretation' in Stravinsky's pejorative sense, that generally characterises present-day performances of it (and to a greater or lesser degree everything else). From around 1920, Stravinsky went to extraordinary lengths to rewrite the history of *The Rite*, claiming at one time or another that Nijinsky's choreography was a travesty, that the dances were in any case no more than a 'pretext' for the music, that his original conception of the work had been a purely musical one, and that apart from the opening bassoon solo there was no folk material in it. All these claims controvert Stravinsky's earlier statements, or the known facts, or both:[46] their purpose was to legitimise *The Rite* in the context of the aesthetic of autonomous music to which Stravinsky pinned his colours in the 1920s, for example in the Octet essay ('My Octuor is a musical object . . . I consider that music is only able to solve musical problems; and nothing else, neither the literary nor the picturesque, can be in music of any real interest'[47]). To these revisions of history we can now add, as a result of

Fink's researches, Stravinsky's invocation of *The Rite* as a prime example of music that requires only execution, not interpretation: 'the *chef d'orchestre* is hardly more than a mechanical agent, a time-beater who fires a pistol at the beginning of each section but lets the music run by itself'.[48]

Through an exhaustive study not only of the early recordings but also of the documentary evidence that predates them, Fink shows how early performances of *The Rite* involved the kind of large-scale tempo modification that we nowadays associate with Romantic interpretative traditions. This is a matter not just of local nuance (audible, for example, in the coupled crescendos and accelerandi of Stravinsky's 1929 performance of the opening bars of the 'Spring rounds'[49]), but of what might be termed structural nuance, or the differentiating of structural sections in accordance with their rhythmic or melodic nature: Monteux's 1929 interpretation [*sic*] of the 'Sacrifical dance', generally assumed to be the closest we can get to what the 1913 audience heard, begins at a vertiginous $\downarrow = 160$ but is full of unnotated tempo changes,[50] and their traces are also to be heard in Stravinsky's and Stokowski's earliest recordings. The 'metronomic strictness, no *rubato*' and 'mechanical regularity' which Stravinsky[51] himself saw as fundamental characteristics of his music were not, then, always there in *The Rite*: they were created over a period of years and retrospectively imputed to it as part of Stravinsky's 'back to basics' ideology. And so the subsequent performance history of *The Rite* unfolds, as illustrated by Stravinsky's later performances and by those of virtually all other conductors, involving what Hill calls an increasingly 'monolithic' approach to the 'Sacrificial dance',[52] with steadily maintained tempos adapted to the clear rendition of orchestral detail. In this way, 'now, finally', as Fink puts it, 'Stravinsky sounds like Stravinsky'.[53]

The danger in all this is of replacing one myth by another. Certainly Stravinsky became an influential exponent of a 'strict' performance style, to borrow his own word, applying it not only to his own music but also to mainstream repertoire, on the relatively rare occasions when he performed it. And certainly a comparison of Stravinsky's 1928 and 1960 performances of *Petrushka* reveals an increasingly monolithic conception, with the abrupt generic shifts of the earlier recording (for instance between the 'real' and the 'mechanical' music) being replaced by the continuity and orchestral sheen of the later one, in which the piece is well on the way to acquiring its present status as a benchmark for the latest hi-fi gear.[54] But the real picture is more complicated, and in particular Stravinsky's views on performance tempos were more complex than a cursory reading of the polemics of the 1920s and 1930s might suggest. (A more careful reading might, for example, ponder the significance of Stravinsky's statement in his *Autobiography* that recording 'enabled me to determine for the future the relationships of the movement (*tempos*) and the nuances in accordance with my wishes',[55] given that this is the composer who supposedly shunned nuance.)

The key text in this context is a section called 'The performance of music' from the *Conversations*[56] in which, instead of simply saying that music should be executed and not interpreted (and, as in the *Poetics*, that interpretation is inherently sinful), Stravinsky draws a distinction between two musical traditions. On the one hand, there is the Romantic tradition represented by Berg, which 'depends strongly on mood or interpretation. Unless mood dominates the whole, the parts do not relate, the form is not achieved, detail is not suffused, and the music fails to say what it has to say.'[57] Accordingly, the aim should be not a 'strict or correct' performance, but an 'inspired' one, and this means that 'considerable fluctuations in tempo are possible in a "romantic" piece ... "freedom" itself must be conveyed by the performer'. On the other hand, there is the 'classic' tradition, which 'eliminates the conductor',[58] which requires execution instead of interpretation – and, Stravinsky adds, 'I am speaking of my music', as if it were not already obvious. The complaint, then, is not that interpreters interpret as such, but that they interpret music that should not be interpreted, such as Stravinsky's, or for that matter Mozart's. ('Isn't this', Stravinsky asks rhetorically, 'why Mozart concertos are still played as though they were Tchaikovsky concertos?'[59])

What the Stravinsky of 1959 is doing here is rehabilitating the idea, which his own polemics of the 1920s and 30s had done more than anything to undermine, that different music should be played in different ways. Rubato is no longer a sin: it is a technique appropriate to certain genres or styles (including opera, which Stravinsky described as 'the field of the elastic beat'[60]), but not others. Similarly the mainstream (Germanic) conducting style represented by 'the silver-haired Karajan'[61] represents not so much the work of the devil as an approach inappropriate to Stravinsky's music: 'I doubt whether *The Rite* can be satisfactorily performed in terms of Herr von Karajan's traditions ... I do not mean to imply that he is out of his depths, however, but rather that he is in my shallows ... There are simply no regions for soul-searching in *The Rite of Spring*.'[62] And what would be the principle of a performance style that eschews soul-searching? Stravinsky spelled out the answer when, with immediate reference to *Pulcinella*, he said that

> eighteenth-century music is, in one sense, *all* dance music. Performance tradition ignores this. For example, in the famous recording of an eminent conductor rehearsing the *Linz* Symphony, he is continually heard inviting the orchestra to 'sing', while he never reminds it to 'dance'. The result of this is that the music's simple melodic content is burdened with a thick-throated late-nineteenth-century sentiment that it cannot bear, while the rhythmic movement remains turgid.[63]

In this way the distinction between the tradition of Tchaikovsky and Berg, on the one hand, and that of Mozart and Stravinsky, on the other, becomes one of subjectivity and sentiment versus objectivity and physicality.

Or, to go back to the terms of the Octet essay, whereas in Romantic music the expression has to be brought out through an exercise of subjectivity, Mozart and Stravinsky compose the expression into the music itself, thereby rendering it interpretation-proof.

This conjunction of Mozart's and Stravinsky's names might be seen as a further example of the latter's astute image management, but there is also a theoretical point behind the distinction Stravinsky is making. It would be hard to think of a conductor whose aesthetics and performance style were more different from Stravinsky's than Mahler (though we should remember that the youthful Stravinsky heard Mahler in St Petersburg, and described him as 'the conductor that impressed me the most'[64]). One of Mahler's contemporaries, Natalie Bauer-Lechner, quotes him as calling for 'a continual elimination of the bar . . . so that it retreats behind the melodic and rhythmic content' of the music.[65] One could translate this into the terminology of another of his contemporaries, Heinrich Schenker, and say that nuance – especially what I called structural nuance – comes from the middleground. (That is, one might think of it as a means whereby the musical surface is interpreted in the light of the middleground.) And what Robert Philip describes as the 'evening out of traditional expressive nuances'[66] that became more or less general in orchestral conducting after the 1930s is the correlate in performance of what Schenker attacked as the foreground (read: shallow) nature of Stravinsky's compositional style.

Rather than invoke Schenker's elaborate, and not entirely relevant, argument at this point, I shall quote another attack on Stravinsky's music, this time by Cecil Gray, who wrote in 1927 that

> The *Sacre du Printemps*, so far from being the triumphant apotheosis of rhythm, the act of restoration to its rightful supremacy of the most important and essential element of musical expression, is the very negation and denial of rhythm . . . Strip the music [of the 'Sacrificial dance'] of the bar-lines and time-signatures, which are only a loincloth concealing its shameful nudity, and it will at once be seen that there is no rhythm at all. Rhythm implies life, some kind of movement or progression at least, but this music stands quite still, in a quite frightening immobility.[67]

Many writers have commented on the way in which Stravinsky's music is built up from the combination and juxtaposition of single beats: that is the source of its rhythmic vitality.[68] But Gray does not hear the rhythmic vitality of the music's surface: he tries to hear *through* the surface to a rhythmic vitality that lies behind it and, being unable to do so, assumes that there is none. And this provides a context in which we can understand Stravinsky's apparently strange remark about Karajan being not out of his depths, but in Stravinsky's shallows.

It should follow from all this that Stravinsky conducted in a Stravinskian manner, so to speak, only music of the 'classic' tradition (including his own). What is the evidence of his recordings of Romantic music? There is an obvious problem here: he conducted little music by others (generally, as he explained, concertos for soloists with whom he was working, though the first two symphonies of Tchaikovsky were also in his repertoire), and recorded none.[69] There is a commercially released extract from a 1963 rehearsal of Tchaikovsky's *Sleeping Beauty*, in which he can be heard lovingly crafting the minutiae of articulation and texture.[70] More to the point, however, are the extensive passages of Tchaikovsky's music (sometimes unalloyed but generally reminted) in *The Fairy's Kiss*: in particular the 'Scène', based on Tchaikovsky's song 'Ah! qui brûla d'amour', incorporates phrase-based rhythmic patterns co-ordinated with harmonic and cadential structure and building to a fully Romantic climax. Stravinsky's 1965 recording[71] perfectly embodies the Romantic tradition of structural nuance: he takes the whole of the introduction at a flexible tempo centring on $\bullet = 50$, way below the notated $\bullet = 76$, making a drastic but unnotated change to around the notated tempo at rehearsal number 207. He then uses tempo to shape the successive phrases, developing the notated caesuras into arch-shaped tempo profiles but at the same time highlighting the sequential organisation around rehearsal number 208. And he gives the sudden undercutting of the climax at rehearsal number 211 a positively Mahlerian interpretation, the effect being magnified by the registrally exposed counterpoint and high solo horn of the following bars. Are we meant to hear this 'straight', as conveying a degree of identification with the Romantic tradition that dangerously reduces the critical distance between Stravinsky and Tchaikovsky? Or is the intention to parody the Romantic performance style along with the music itself? It is difficult to see how the question could be decided one way or the other.

If there is a particular musical style that forms a bridge between the *fin-de-siècle* Russian Romanticism of Stravinsky's earliest works and the foundation works of twentieth-century modernism, it is the 'changing background' variation technique. 'The princesses' *khorovod* (round dance)' of *The Firebird*, which corresponds to the 'Rondo (*khorovod*)' of the 1945 Suite, is unmistakably in the tradition of Glinka's *Karaminskaya*; it is even structured the same way, around two contrasting folk melodies, each of which has its own tempo. The resulting notated tempo changes are shown by the squares in Fig. 9.1 ($\bullet = 72$ and 92 for the respective tunes, and 58 for the coda).

The graphs superimpose on this the tempos of three of Stravinsky's recordings, from 1929, 1961 and 1967,[72] and should lay to rest once and for all any misconception that Stravinsky only knew how to conduct metronomically. Particularly striking is the overall similarity of the profiles (the major difference is the anticipation of the slower tempo of the coda in the

Fig. 9.1 Tempos in the 'Princesses' round dance'.

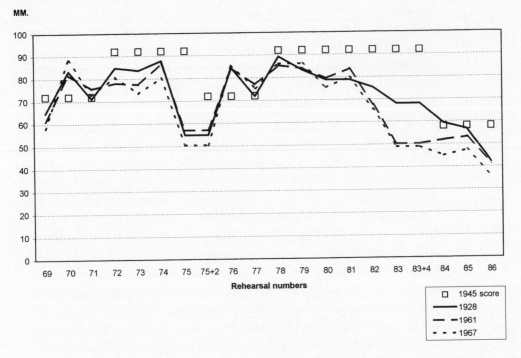

two later versions), while the tempo modifications are always co-ordinated with the phrase and sectional structure. All three performances, in other words, embody similar interpretations; on the basis of Fig. 9.1, it would be hard to argue for any consistent chronological evolution in the manner in which Stravinsky performed this music.

Rather than the 'Spring *khorovod* (round dance)' of *The Rite* (now usually abbreviated to 'Spring rounds'), it is the Introduction to Part Two, leading into the 'Mystic circles', that most clearly represents Stravinsky's modernist updating of the changing background technique: there are again contrasted folkloristic ideas which recur against different textures, though they are more fragmentary and the patterns of repetition less regular, and the cross-cutting form is underlined by alternations between $\quarternote = 48$ and 60. How might this interpolation of a Romantic compositional technique within a modernist ('classic') context be reflected in terms of performance style? In many respects, performance practice in *The Rite* seems to have converged by the time of the early sound recordings; in the Introduction to Part One, for instance, there is a considerable degree of consistency in conception and even sonority between the first recordings of Stravinsky, Monteux and Stokowski (and the same goes for the somewhat bowdlerised recording that Stokowski made for Disney's *Fantasia* at the end of the 1930s). But the

Table 9.1. Stravinsky, 'Sacrificial dance': comparison of tempos in score and recording

Rehearsal no.	1929 score	1960 recording
79	Tº 1 (48)	Tº 1 (50)
86		Tº 2 (62)
89	Tº 2 (60)	Tº 3 (82)
90	Tº 1	Tº 2
91	Tº 2	Tº 3
93	Tº 3 (80)	Tº 4 (110)

same cannot be said of the Introduction to Part Two, where Monteux starts at ♩ = 42, way below the 48 of the 1921 and subsequent published scores, whereas Stravinsky takes off at something approaching ♩ = 80. This fast tempo, though wildly inconsistent with the score, allows for a streamlined and relatively unnuanced (in this sense literal) performance.

The 1960 recording, by contrast, begins at ♩ = 50, close to the notated tempo, but anyone expecting a literal execution out of the ageing composer is in for a rude shock. Already at the end of the second bar there is a marked though unnotated *Luftpause* in the best Romantic tradition, and Stravinsky underlines the phrase junctions at rehearsal numbers 80, 81 and 82 in the same way. The same effect reappears on a larger scale with a ritardando down to about ♩ = 45 in the bars up to the flute and violin solo at rehearsal number 83. And while the kind of structural tempo change Fink notes in early recordings of the 'Sacrifical dance' is effectively composed into the Introduction to Part Two, Table 9.1 shows how Stravinsky's performance at once contradicts his own score and further develops the tempo-change principle embodied in it: at the trumpet duet (two bars before number 85), instead of continuing at the opening tempo, Stravinsky shifts gears to ♩ = 62, returning to this tempo instead of the notated 'Tempo I' at 90. The faster tempos of the 1921 score – ♩ = 60 at 89, and 80 at 93 – are also shifted up a notch, resulting in an interpretation (no other word will do) that adheres to the original constructive values but realises them in terms of four rather than three distinct tempos.

Luftpausen, structural tempo changes and disregard of the score: Stravinsky's 1960 performance of the Introduction to Part Two goes a long way towards rehabilitating Romantic performance traditions and, in so doing, rendering audible the very continuity between *The Rite* and the traditions of Russian Romanticism that, perversely, he was to deny just two years later, when he claimed that 'very little immediate tradition lies behind *Le Sacre du printemps*'.[73] It is equally hard to square this passage, at least, with Fink's description of the 1960 recording as 'grimly geometric',[74] and this illustrates the danger to which I referred of replacing an old myth by a new

Fig. 9.2 Tempos in *The Rite of Spring*

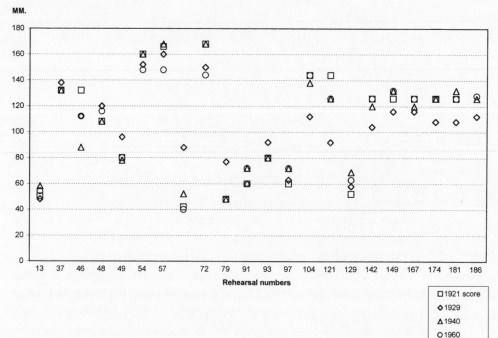

one: Fink recounts the story of how Stravinsky came to sound like Stravinsky, but here we have an example of a Stravinsky who no longer sounds like Stravinsky at all. And, in truth, trying to create any grand narrative out of Stravinsky's successive recordings is a recipe for frustration. After discussing Stravinsky's 1929 recording of *The Rite* at some length and charting the discrepancies between it and the 1921 piano roll, Hill concludes that Monteux's 1929 recording is a safer bet as a 'guide to Stravinsky's earliest intentions'.[75] Add Stravinsky's 1940 and 1960 recordings, he continues with mounting exasperation, and the picture

> becomes not clarified but more confused. Attempt a comparison of all the Stravinsky sources – his own recordings, the various editions of the score . . . and Stravinsky's written views on how the work should be performed – and one finds that all frequently contradict one another. Moreover, it is often on matters on which Stravinsky is most insistent that he differs most in his own recordings.

Certainly a tabulation of the tempos for each of Stravinsky's three performances (Fig. 9.2[76]) proves a poor basis for any kind of generalisation. (As in the case of Fig. 9.1, the squares represent notated metronome markings.) It is a general principle in the history of twentieth-century performance that the range of tempo both within and between movements is smaller in the second than in the first half of the century, and that the effect is more marked in the case of fast tempos, in line with the modern practice of setting tempos so as to allow clear articulation of the shortest note values.[77] It follows that in general one should expect a lower average tempo and a higher degree of tempo convergence in more recent performances. But it is difficult to see any respect in which Stravinsky's successive recordings of *The Rite* conform to this picture: on average, the fastest tempos are found in 1940, and the slowest in 1929 (largely as a result of the cautious tempo of the 'Sacrifical dance'). Even more tellingly, it is the 1929 recording that has the lowest standard deviation between its tempos: the history of Stravinsky's recordings of *The Rite* is one of divergence, not convergence. The conclusion to be drawn, perhaps, is that overall trends in the history of performance represent the sum of an indefinite number of micro-histories: individual works and even individual movements may have their own, largely independent, historical trajectories.

As Hill suggests, the discrepancies between Stravinsky's scores, recordings and pronouncements about performance are notorious, and it is easy to make fun of them. In the course of the series of 'reviews' of *The Rite* that he published in the two final conversation books,[78] for example, Stravinsky criticised Boulez's 1963 performance of 'The sage'[79] as 'more than twice too fast', and adds rhetorically, 'if there were an Olympic Games for speedy conductors...'. He might have finished the sentence, 'then he would have come in third', for Boulez's $\int = 52$, a mere ten metronome points above the notated 42, trails well behind Stravinsky's 1929 recording.[80] Then again, Karajan is criticised for performing the 'Ritual action' at the notated $\int = 52$ (unlike Stravinsky, who successively recorded it at $\int = 58, 69$ and 63), though here Stravinsky at least evinces a trace of embarrassment: 'Whether or not metronomically correct, this *tempo di hoochie-koochie* is definitely too slow... duller than Disney's dying dinosaurs'. What this goes to show, of course, is the limited value of measuring tempo when divorced from the other, generally non-notatable factors involved in performance: rhythmic articulation, sonority and the acoustic properties of the hall, for example. But then, where does that leave Stravinsky's insistence that, in performing *The Rite*, he was 'particularly anxious to give the bars their true metric value, and to have them played exactly as they were written'?[81] Or where does it leave his claim that 'any musical composition must necessarily possess its unique tempo... the variety of tempi comes from performers who often are not very familiar with the composition they perform or feel a personal interest in interpreting it'?[82]

Stravinsky appears to have found such questions unanswerable, for in the last decade or so of his life he began to dismantle the certainties of his pre-war philosophy of performance. One has the impression that the process was not an easy one.[83] A page after the statement I have just quoted, he is already qualifying it: 'a tempo can be metronomically wrong but right in spirit, though obviously the metronomic margin cannot be very great'.[84] And later, on the same page, there is a further slippage. He repeats that his music requires execution, not interpretation, and continues, 'But you will protest, stylistic questions in my music are not conclusively indicated by the notation; my style requires interpretation. That is true...But that isn't the kind of "interpretation" my critics mean.' He goes on to explain that the sort of interpretation they mean is whether or not a particular passage signifies 'laughter'. But this kind of hermeneutic commentary has nothing to do with the issue of interpretation versus execution that Stravinsky started out talking about, and so the statement about performance interpretation remains unchallenged. It is as if Stravinsky felt the need to backtrack on the whole issue of execution, but having done so, wanted to cover his tracks.

Nine years later, the retrenchment has become quite explicit, and he no longer ascribes to metronome markings the same absolute value that he once did:

> If the speeds of everything in the world and in ourselves have changed, our tempo feelings cannot remain unaffected. The metronome marks one wrote forty years ago were contemporary forty years ago. Time is not alone in affecting tempo – circumstances do too, and every performer is a different equation of them. I would be surprised if any of my own recent recordings follows the metronome markings.[85]

And by the time of the final conversation book he confesses that

> I have changed my mind...about the advantages of embalming a performance in tape. The disadvantages, which are that one performance presents only one set of circumstances, and that mistakes and misunderstandings are cemented into traditions as quickly and canonically as truths, now seem to me too great a price to pay. The Recording Angel I am concerned with is not CBS, in any case, but the One with the Big Book.[86]

'One performance represents only one set of circumstances': at last, it seems, Stravinsky recognises the indispensability as well as the inevitability of difference between one performance and another, and hence the necessity of performance interpretation. It hardly comes as a surprise when, towards the end of the book, we find him mocking the very principle on which he had insisted for half a century: speaking of Koussevitsky's conducting, he refers to 'execution – firing-squad sense'.[87]

If Stravinsky did not in the end conform to his own prescriptions about performance, then he was at least conforming to an established pattern of composers who say one thing and do another; among his contemporaries, Elgar and Rachmaninov are illustrious examples. Maybe there is a basic incommensurability between saying and doing, such that you talk most about what you are least sure how to do: that would explain why, as Hill complained, it is just where he is most insistent that Stravinsky's recordings differ the most.

But what is perhaps surprising is the extent to which, though Stravinsky did not do what he said, others did. Whatever reservations one may have about premature grand narratives in performance history, it is clear that after the 1920s and 1930s there was in orchestral performance as a whole a progressive 'evening out of traditional expressive nuances', to repeat Philip's phrase, a pursuit of clarity in rhythmic detail and strictness in execution – in short, a move towards making *everything* sound like Stravinsky (or 'Stravinsky', as we should perhaps say, to distinguish the critical construction from the man who died in 1971). And here there is a paradox. Richard Taruskin has persuasively demonstrated the affinities between Stravinsky's concept of 'execution' and what he calls 'authenticist performance':[88] early-music spokesmen such as Norrington and Hogwood appropriated Stravinsky's values and rhetoric in opposition to what they saw as the one-size-fits-all philosophy of mainstream performance. Yet that mainstream was largely moulded by the same rhetoric and values and, as I previously suggested, it was Stravinsky's polemics of the 1920s and 1930s that crucially undermined the idea that different music should be played in different ways, and so created the idea of a 'mainstream' in the first place. The recent history of performance, then, can be seen as revolving around the collision of two successive waves of Stravinskian modernism.

And this reflection prompts another. If Stravinsky's rhetorical question of 1959 could now be rephrased, 'Isn't this why Mozart concertos are still played as though they were Stravinsky concertos?', then we may need to re-think the composer's importance for twentieth-century music. 'Stravinsky's performance style gained an enormous prestige among progressive musicians in the 1920s and 30s', writes Taruskin.[89] But perhaps even more influential was the series of writings, beginning in 1920s Paris and culminating in the Charles Eliot Norton lectures at Harvard, through which Stravinsky disseminated a fashionable philosophy of music that encapsulated the 'new objectivity' of the inter-war years – but that formulated it in absolute terms and so gave a quality of self-evidence and permanence to an aesthetic that in other arts rapidly became as *démodé* as last year's recording. (The records changed, that is to say, but the philosophy endured.) In which case, maybe Stravinsky's most effective legacy was not the modernist scores through which he adumbrated a new musical future, nor the neoclassical scores with their incorporation of old styles into new contexts, but his fusion of the power of the baton and the word (even the ghost-written word) to create, through performance, a new musical past.

10 Stravinsky as devil: Adorno's three critiques

MAX PADDISON

Introduction

Adorno's *Philosophie der neuen Musik* was published in 1949,[1] at a decisive turning-point for music in the mid-twentieth century. In this highly influential book, Adorno put forward a dialectical reading of the New Music in the form of a critique of its two most extreme representatives, Schoenberg and Stravinsky. The effects were dramatic, providing a rallying cry for the generation of new composers emerging in the immediate post-war years, and who were to become associated both with the rejection of neoclassicism and with the espousal of the multiple serialism of the Darmstadt School. The reception of Adorno's critique by the two protagonists themselves was in some respects contrary to expectations. Schoenberg, who disliked Adorno, saw it primarily as an attack on himself, thus going directly against the general view, which regarded Adorno as the great advocate of the Second Viennese School. But at the same time Schoenberg also sprang to Stravinsky's defence, annoyed by Adorno's treatment of his old adversary.[2] Stravinsky, on the other hand, remained silent – in public, at least – thus making it difficult to gauge the extent to which Adorno's critique of his music may have played any determining role in the composer's own spectacular change of direction in the early 1950s, when he himself abandoned neoclassicism and turned to serialism. This has, naturally enough, prompted speculation. Célestin Deliège, for instance, has argued:

> Publicly, Stravinsky would make no mention of T.W. Adorno's criticism, but it is highly improbable that it could have left him indifferent, even if he was conscious of the weak points in the argument and disagreed with a philosophical approach whose materialistic tendencies could only disturb him . . . It has often been remarked that Stravinsky was very open to influence – at least, until he stepped into his study – and could not remain indifferent to a well-formulated argument. The acuity of his judgement warned him when the alarm bell really sounded.[3]

Apart from Robert Craft's dismissive and not very comprehending article 'A bell for Adorno',[4] there was little response from Stravinsky's immediate circle. Adorno himself, however, was perfectly clear as to his own influence on the larger course of events, when he later wrote that 'my discussion of

Stravinsky [in *Philosophy of New Music*] is commonly deemed to have played its part in causing the demise of neo-classicism'.[5]

It is understandable that most critical attention concerning Adorno's interpretation of Stravinsky's music has been directed at *Philosophy of New Music*, precisely because it was a book which, without trying, coincided so exactly with the historical moment it had anticipated. Some commentators, such as Carl Dahlhaus[6] and Peter Bürger,[7] have criticised its claims through seeing them in relation to Adorno's later reading of Stravinsky from the early 1960s, the essay 'Stravinsky: a dialectical portrait' (1962). To these two readings I add another: Adorno's early view of Stravinsky dating from the late 1920s and early 1930s. I shall consider some recurring themes from each of these three Stravinsky critiques in turn, using a cluster of key concepts taken from Adorno's philosophy of music history, and with particular emphasis on the concept of irony. It seems to me that, out of the contradictions, changing judgements, but also continuities of these three critiques, a convergence emerges which helps make sense of the immensely difficult and much misunderstood hermeneutic task Adorno had set himself.

A commonly held view has been that Adorno simply sanctified Schoenberg and demonised Stravinsky. This is certainly a crude simplification. What he did do was to put forward a philosophical evaluation of the truth or untruth of their music in terms of the interaction of subjectivity and objectivity and of their alienation within the musical work: a problematical and contentious project criticised by, among others, Jean-François Lyotard in his essay 'Adorno as the devil', on the grounds that the concept of the 'subject' itself remains unquestioned, and is easily equated with the 'expression' theory of art.[8] Schoenberg himself was not fooled by Adorno's apparently positive reading of his work, clearly recognising a criticism of his serial music when he saw it. As for Stravinsky, nothing is quite what it seems when it comes to the devil. An underlying theme of this essay is therefore Adorno's presentation of Stravinsky as devil, particularly in his repeated references to *The Soldier's Tale*. It needs to be remembered that Adorno's writing comes from a long German literary tradition of using the extremes and the rhetoric of exaggeration, irony and the grotesque, as strategies for revealing underlying truths. It goes back to E. T. A. Hoffmann, finds its greatest exponent in Nietzsche, and its most accomplished twentieth-century master in Thomas Mann (Adorno's own cameo appearance as the devil in intellectual guise in Mann's *Doctor Faustus*, delivering whole passages lifted straight out of an early draft of *Philosophy of New Music*, neatly reinforces the point).[9] Stravinsky's diabolical aspect needs therefore to be seen as a necessary part of Adorno's scheme, and the 'inauthenticity' of his music as an aspect of its truth.

The first critique: Stravinsky, stabilisation and the social situation of music

The first of Adorno's Stravinsky critiques is to be seen in two main sources, dating from 1928 and 1932, neither of which is exclusively on Stravinsky. First, in an article called 'Die stabilisierte Musik' from 1928 (although only published posthumously),[10] Adorno argued that by the late 1920s music had become 'stabilised', in the sense that there had already been a retreat from the advanced position reached by the musical avant garde before 1914 (i.e. as represented by the Second Viennese School). He identifies two dominant tendencies – neoclassicism and folklorism – which are characterised by stabilisation. However, although he identifies Stravinsky with both neoclassicism and folklorism, and argues that those composers within the category of 'stabilised music' are reactionary, he does not at this stage see Stravinsky entirely in these terms. While *Oedipus Rex* is regarded as the most representative work of neoclassicism to that point – a work which takes the use of masks and the return to forms and styles of the past to extremes, and which is also striking in its absence of irony – he also singles out for special mention *Renard* and *The Soldier's Tale* as 'authentic' works.

These themes are continued in the second of these articles, the important essay 'Zur gesellschaftlichen Lage der Musik' of 1932.[11] While the concept of 'stabilised music' itself is dropped, probably because of its crudity as a means of categorising the main tendencies in the music of the period, its place is taken by a more sophisticated set of dialectical concepts. Adorno now talks of the opposed categories of 'commodity music' and 'avant-garde music'. Historically music has become autonomous, in the process losing its historically associated social functions and acquiring instead a new function, that of the commodity. This leads to the alienation and fetishisation of art music, and drives it in one of two directions: either towards assimilation by market forces, to the point where all that music does is to affirm its commodity character; or towards critical self-reflection, where music becomes aware of itself as a form of cognition in relation to its handed-down materials, and of critical negation of its commodity character. 'Assimilated' music accepts its function as commodity, conceals alienation, and becomes entertainment, embracing market forces; 'critical' music rejects its commodity character, does not conceal alienation, and is considered by Adorno to be 'authentic' and 'true' in its relations to its material. As I have outlined elsewhere,[12] Adorno identifies four distinct types of music within this second category, that of critical, 'authentic' music. As we shall see, Adorno includes Stravinsky within two of these four types of 'authentic music'. The first type, however, is distinctly non-Stravinskian. It refers to a music that crystallises the contradictions of society immanently, within its own structure, and purely in terms of its relation to handed-down material. Furthermore, it does so without being necessarily conscious of the social and political context within which it finds itself. It is represented for Adorno by Schoenberg.

The second type recognises alienation, but does so through trying to deal with it by turning to styles and formal types of the past, in the belief that these can reconstitute a lost sense of harmony, totality and community. Adorno labels this 'objectivism', and returns to his 1928 article on stabilised music, maintaining that in capitalist societies neoclassicism constitutes 'objectivism', while in the largely pre-capitalist, agrarian societies of south-eastern Europe, as well as in those countries under fascist regimes, it is folk music which provides its material.[13] For Adorno, Stravinsky represents this type in both its forms. Likewise, the third type: this Adorno calls 'surrealist' music. He maintains that this type is socially conscious, and draws on the material of both art music and consumer/popular music as fragments, clichés and cultural residues, and employs montage techniques which both serve to emphasise the fragmentary character of musical material today as well as pointing to social fragmentation. Stravinsky, particularly of the period of *The Soldier's Tale*, also represents this type, as does Weill in the music he wrote in collaboration with Brecht.

Finally, the fourth type: this is a type which recognises social alienation, but tries to do something about it directly through intervention and engagement, but in the process, Adorno argues, sacrifices the integrity of its form. While critical of this music as 'utility music' (*Gebrauchsmusik*), which he argues simply ends up serving the market, Adorno sees some virtue in its *Gemeinschaftsmusik* version, which developed out of neoclassicism, and is represented for him by Eisler and to some extent Hindemith. Stravinsky is not included under this type.

We can see, therefore, that in his first critique, Adorno is relatively positive towards Stravinsky's music, at least towards certain works, which are included in his category of 'authentic music'. Stravinsky is seen, however, as part of a typology. It is hardly a dialectical critique as such, although it does identify elements that are taken up later. What is clear, however, is that the theoretical approach at this stage allows for a diversity of musics under the category of 'authentic music'. This is very much also in keeping with the diversity and tolerance of the experimental cultural and political milieu of Weimar Germany at this point, something which Adorno's typology seems to reflect, even though it remains distinctly weighted in favour of Schoenberg's music.

In seeing Stravinsky as a 'surrealist' composer, Adorno reads his use of montage, the juxtaposition of fragments (which also include elements of popular music), as an example of the Brechtian *Verfremdungseffekt avant la lettre* (it is certainly true that Weill was influenced by *The Soldier's Tale*). He also focuses here on one of the important themes of his writings from the 1920s: *irony*. In this way, *The Soldier's Tale* is seen as a landmark work of the early twentieth century. Adorno's complaint with the recently composed *Oedipus Rex*, however, is that the work is dominated by the use of stylistic montage in the absence of irony. For Adorno at this stage, therefore, the concept of irony in works of art may serve to fulfil the requirement for the necessary level of critical self-reflection in the structure of the work. Irony – saying the opposite of what is really intended – stands for an absent or distanced subjectivity. The seeming capitulation to 'objectivity', the 'way things are', is only apparent. Irony thus indicates the survival of the subject through marking the place where the subject *should* be.

The second critique: Stravinsky, Schoenberg and the *Philosophy of New Music*

Adorno's second Stravinsky critique – that of *Philosophy of New Music* of 1949 – differs fundamentally from the first, in that it sets out to use Schoenberg and Stravinsky antagonistically, as extremes, employing the dialectical method Adorno had derived from Walter Benjamin,[14] although, unlike Benjamin's, his approach is highly polemical in character. The key themes are the regression to myth and archaism, and the disintegration of the bourgeois principle of individuation, as regression to a pre-bourgeois, pre-modern condition. The sacrifice of the individual, as subject, and the identification with the collectivity, the apparent 'objectivity' of 'that which is', is what characterises Stravinsky's music for Adorno. His music fixes a state of fragmentation as the norm, the reification of a state of shock and alienation as the essentially static repetition and permutation of that which is too painful to be experienced by subjectivity. As Adorno puts it: 'In its own material, his music registers the disintegration of life and, simultaneously, the alienated state of the consciousness of the subject.'[15] Adorno's approach in *Philosophy of New Music* also draws heavily on psychoanalytical terminology (in particular Otto Fenichel's *The Psychoanalytic Theory of Neurosis*, New York, 1945), arguing that the concern of Stravinsky's music is 'to dominate schizophrenic traits through the aesthetic consciousness'.[16]

Adorno maintains that Stravinsky's music is characterised by the grotesque and meaningless sacrifice of the subject: the sacrificial victim in *The Rite of Spring* submits passively as an offering to the interests of the tribe. Stravinsky's delight in the grotesque, the suspension of individual identity, the assumption of roles and the recourse to masks – all of which contribute towards the suppression of expression and subjectivity – brings us to a consideration of the significance Adorno attaches to the figure of the tragic clown, in the contrasting forms of Stravinsky's *Petrushka* and Schoenberg's *Pierrot lunaire*. Adorno suggests that, with *Pierrot*, 'everything is based upon that lonely subjectivity which withdraws into itself',[17] and reflects upon itself. He points out that the entire last part of *Pierrot lunaire* is a return journey, a voyage home, and that the whole work is in effect a voyage of self-discovery. The subject transcends itself and achieves a kind of liberation. Pierrot, through anticipating anxieties and sufferings while at the same time retaining his capacity as subject to reflect upon and experience them, transcends them, and is transformed in the rarefied atmosphere of 'O alter Duft aus Märchenzeit' at the end of the work. In Stravinsky's ballet *Petrushka*, however, even though the central character, Petrushka himself, also shows certain subjective traits, the process and its outcome are quite different. Whereas in *Pierrot lunaire* the music itself is the suffering, conflict and final transcendence of Pierrot, in Stravinsky's piece, Adorno argues, the music takes instead the part of those who torment and ridicule Petrushka. The subject is sacrificed, while the music itself does not identify with the victim but rather with those who destroy him. The music is either indifferent to the sufferings of the subject – who after all is only a puppet – or cruelly parodies him. It plays the part of the crowd, regarding everything as entertainment, a distraction from its own emptiness.[18] Adorno remarks that the whole orchestra in the ballet is made to sound like a gigantic fairground organ – rather like one who submerges himself in the tumult to rid himself of his own psyche. Even the 'immortality' of Petrushka at the end is in the nature of a tormented spirit condemned to return and haunt its tormentors. Stravinsky's music, as revealed through Adorno's analysis, takes the part of the object, the collectivity that grinds the subject pitilessly within its machinery; Stravinsky's subject exhibits only the most pathetic tatters of humanity, expressed through a mocking sentimentality. 'Authenticity' in Stravinsky's sense could therefore be seen as reflecting a pitiless reality without hope of redemption, where the only way out is to evade suffering by repression and a soulless mimesis of the mechanics of suffering in the absence of a subject able to suffer. 'Authenticity is gained surreptitiously through the denial of the subjective pole,'[19] Adorno claims; only the object is left.

It is instructive to pick up here again the concept of irony, so important in Adorno's first Stravinsky critique. In *Philosophy of New Music* the concept of irony can be seen to be replaced largely by the concept of the *grotesque*. In his commentary on *Petrushka*, for instance, Adorno argues that 'the element of individuation appeared under the form of the grotesque and was condemned by it'.[20] He suggests that the use of the grotesque in modern art serves to make it acceptable to society: the bourgeois wishes to become involved with modern art if, 'by means of its form', it 'assures him it is not meant to be taken seriously'.[21] By the 1940s, and certainly by the closing years of the Second World War, Adorno came to see the liquidation of the individual not only as something enciphered within the monadic, closed world of the work of art; it was now a reality in the world after Auschwitz. For him at this stage, such extremes of horror mean not only the end of lyric poetry, as that most intensely individual form of expression, but also the demise of irony, humour and the grotesque as possible means of psychological defence against the shocks of the real world.

I have reduced Adorno's interpretation of Stravinsky as it occurs in *Philosophy of New Music* to the core of his argument regarding the fate of the subject, as Adorno himself considered this to be central to his critique. In drawing the extremes so sharply, and making his value judgements so explicit and condemnatory, Adorno employs the dialectic in such a way that the extremes appear to become fixed, and no further interaction occurs between them. This has something of the polemics of a political pamphlet, designed rhetorically to sway us, in this case, from authoritarianism towards autonomy and freedom. The fact that Adorno began the Schoenberg essay in 1941, in the dark days of the Second World War, himself the victim of political intolerance, is significant. The Stravinsky essay came later, and was not part of the original conception, which was to be a 'dialectical image' of Schoenberg. He was undoubtedly aware of Stravinsky's flirtations with Italian fascism in the late 1920s and early 1930s, and this meant that, in spite of his later refutation of the *ad hominem* accusation, Stravinsky is to a considerable extent pressed into service as representing the regression to myth and archaism and the rejection of historical responsibility which were so much a feature of the fascists' psychotic reaction to the complexities and ambiguities of the modern world.

The third critique: Stravinsky – a dialectical image

In his third critique, that in the essay 'Stravinsky: a dialectical portrait' of 1961, Adorno begins by fielding criticisms of his earlier critique in *Philosophy of New Music*. Having dismissed his critics for misunderstanding his philosophical interpretation, he proceeds to offer his own self-critique:

> My critics make me want to begin by giving them a helping hand. Even a straightforward text-based criticism might have found more damaging objections to my Stravinsky chapter. If it is true that his music represents an objectively false consciousness, ideology, then conscientious readers might argue that his music was more than simply identical with reified consciousness. They might insist that his music went beyond it, by contemplating it wordlessly, silently allowing it to speak for itself.

> The spirit of the age is deeply inscribed in Stravinsky's art with its
> dominant gesture of 'This is how it is'. A higher criticism would have to
> consider whether this gesture does not give it a greater share in the truth
> than music which aims to give shape to an implicit truth which the spirit
> of the age denies and which history has rendered dubious in itself.[22]

In this significant passage Adorno is not only telling his critics what they
could have identified quite justifiably as lacking in his earlier Stravinsky critique; he is, in effect, laying out the programme for his third critique. He also
goes on to acknowledge that his previous reading of Stravinsky's essentially
static, non-developmental temporality against the yardstick of Schoenberg's
organic-developmental model was inappropriate and misleading:

> By opposing the static ideal of Stravinsky's music, its immanent
> timelessness, and by confronting it with a dynamic, emphatically
> temporal, intrinsically developing music, I arbitrarily applied to him an
> external norm, a norm which he rejected. In short, I violated my own
> most cherished principle of criticism.[23]

Thus, in his third Stravinsky critique, via such deflecting self-criticism,
Adorno returns to some of the features of the first critique, and avoids
the polemical character of the second. Bürger, in particular, sees the two
readings – *Philosophy of New Music* and 'Stravinsky: a dialectical portrait' –
as incompatible, and considers the latter to be the superior one, arguing
that:

> Whereas the polemical interpretation proceeds in a globalizing fashion,
> understanding neo-classicism as a unitary movement, the [later]
> interpretation seeks differentiation. It leaves open at least the possibility
> of seeing more in neo-classical works than a sheer relapse into a
> reactionary thinking of order.[24]

But Adorno still insists that there is, as he puts it, 'quelque chose qui ne
va pas' with Stravinsky's music. This remains, in spite of his self-criticisms
concerning inappropriate values applied in his second critique, the problem of non-developmental temporal succession in Stravinsky. He writes:
'As a temporal art, music is bound to the fact of succession and is hence
as irreversible as time itself. By starting, it commits itself to carrying on, to
becoming something new, to developing.'[25] In this way, music points beyond itself, and protests against the eternal repetition of myth. Stravinsky's
repetitions and permutations negate the temporality and progression of
musical events. They constitute a kind of 'marking time', and this has implications, of course, for the identity of the subject. It was precisely this
aspect of Adorno's Stravinsky critique that had so irritated Dahlhaus, who
had complained of Adorno's dogmatism in considering the only valid mode

of temporal progression to be developmental.[26] Jonathan Cross also takes this view, arguing:

> The corollary of Adorno's position – that any music which does not display the developmental characteristic of 'becoming' is dangerous because, like the products of the culture industry, it serves to subjugate the freedom of the individual subject, to bring about the dissolution of individual identity – would now seem, from our present perspective, generally untenable.[27]

Cross considers that, in denying him his modernist credentials in relation to temporal succession and the disintegration of the subject, Adorno has, in effect, 'turned Stravinsky into a *postmodernist*'.[28] But in his first critique, as we have seen, Adorno places Stravinsky firmly in the modernist category, as 'authentic' music which opposes and negates music's commodity character and the effects of the culture industry. Stravinsky's music is typified as 'objectivist' and, in certain works which Adorno clearly considers both typical and highly significant (in particular *The Soldier's Tale*, but also other works like *Ragtime* and *Renard*), as 'surrealist'. I argue that, while Adorno does not deviate from this assessment of Stravinsky as an 'authentic modernist' (all appearances to the contrary!), he recognises both the radical character of 'objectivism' and 'surrealism', and also their problematical character. That is to say, while the denial of subjectivity and of expression, the ironic play with the displaced fragments of 'second-hand' material, the rejection of developmental progression and temporal continuity in favour of the juxtaposition of montage structures, are all defining features of important tendencies within modernism, they at the same time carry with them the attendant perils of becoming identical to the world from which they are drawn. They risk losing their critical edge in their regression either to a mythic past through distancing from the real world, or to a cartoon-like mimicking of an unacceptable reality as protection from it. This, it seems to me, is the difficult task Adorno sets himself in his second critique, *Philosophy of New Music*: to explore the philosophical implications of this knife-edge balancing act. Thus, the question posed by Adorno becomes the criterion of 'authenticity' in Stravinsky's music: to what extent does Stravinsky hold fast to his insight into ultimate emptiness and lack of meaning? The judgement in the second critique – by now distinctly existentialist, and having certain affinities with Adorno's later critique of Heidegger in *Jargon of Authenticity* – is that Stravinsky's music recoils from this recognition, and regresses into archaism and myth 'as image[s] of eternity, of salvation from death', through the barbaric suppression of subjectivity and as a defence mechanism against fear.[29]

In this context, it is again instructive to return to the theme of irony. In Adorno's third critique of Stravinsky it is not irony as the place-holder for an absent self-reflecting subjectivity, but instead the concept of *clowning* (which we have also noted in *Philosophy of New Music*). In 'Stravinsky: a dialectical portrait', Adorno writes: 'This is the element of mimicry, of clowning – of constantly busying himself with something important that turns out to be nothing at all, strenuously working at something without any result.'[30] But this was, of course, also the nub of Adorno's criticism of Stravinsky in his second critique. What constitutes a significant shift in Adorno's position on Stravinsky in the third critique lies precisely in his changed interpretation of this aspect of clowning. It is seen to have an ironic relationship to an absent subjectivity, the lack of meaning to an absent meaning, but with the added dimensions now of an implied infinite regress, as an intolerable ambiguity: perhaps the ultimate irony is that there is no subject left to suffer, there is no meaning, nor was there ever any meaning in the absence of illusion and myth. The key to understanding this shift in interpretation is to be found, I suggest, in the fact that between his second and third critiques of Stravinsky Adorno had discovered the work of Samuel Beckett.

Stravinsky, Schoenberg, Beckett: convergence in Adorno's late critique

Adorno's interest in Beckett dates from the mid 1950s, and in the plays and novels Adorno came to see the ultimate *reductio ad absurdum* of the human condition, Walter Benjamin's 'dialectics at a standstill'. He admired Beckett's work greatly, and also came to know him personally, discussing his work with him, particularly in the autumn of 1958 in Paris.[31] From this came the substantial essay on Beckett, 'Trying to understand *Endgame*', which Adorno published in 1961 – the year before his third Stravinsky critique. The similarities between the two essays are striking, and the revised assessment of Stravinsky from 1962 is clearly the result of his reading of Beckett. Indeed, it is through his Beckett interpretation that Adorno comes to see a kind of reconciliation of Stravinsky and Schoenberg, as opposed to the polemics of *Philosophy of New Music*. Concerning Beckett he writes: 'Not the least of the ways in which Beckett converges with the most contemporary trends in music is that he, a Western man, amalgamates features of Stravinsky's radical past, the oppressive stasis of a continuity that has disintegrated, with advanced expressive and constructive techniques from the Schoenberg school.'[32] The influence of Beckett on his third critique is particularly clear in his further interpretation of *The Soldier's Tale*, where the account of the work at times could easily be transferred to Beckett's *Endgame*. He describes the work now as 'music built out of ruins in which nothing survives of the individual subject but his truncated stumps and the tormented awareness that it will never end.'[33] That is to say, he now concedes that something of the subject seems to survive, however bleakly. And conversely, what he writes of *Endgame* could equally be applied to Stravinsky's music: 'Understanding it can mean only understanding its unintelligibility, concretely reconstructing the meaning of the fact that it has no meaning.'[34] But the full import of this thought, which pervades his writing throughout the 1960s and underlies much of his last work, the unfinished *Aesthetic Theory* (which he had intended dedicating to Beckett), is easy to miss. I can perhaps give it added emphasis by restating it another way: 'meaninglessness' – and indeed the resistance to interpretation – becomes itself a structuring principle of the avant-garde work, presenting itself as a formal problem which demands interpretation and understanding, but which at the same time refuses to allow the contradictions presented by its form to be reconciled.[35] This principle, which Adorno had previously applied to Schoenberg, he now applies to Stravinsky. However, having recognised the possibility that Stravinsky can also be understood in this way, as a kind of 'positive negativity', reservations regarding the composer's consistency in realising it in practice remain.

Adorno's final verdict on Stravinsky's music is that, in its identification with the object and in its negation of subjectivity, Stravinsky compels absolute negativity 'to appear as if it were the truth'.[36] The triumph of taste and technical accomplishment convinces us of its validity, and distracts us, as if by a sleight of hand. But as the soldier realises in *The Soldier's Tale*, 'if the devil did not lie, he would cease to be himself'.[37] For Adorno, the false consciousness of Stravinsky's music *is* its truth, in that it tells us how the world is, while at the same time urbanely convincing us that this is the only way it can be. It is, of course, only when he lies that the devil tells the truth – something that could be seen to apply as well to Adorno as to Stravinsky. For as Adorno said of psychoanalysis, 'nothing is true except the exaggerations'.[38]

11 Stravinsky in analysis: the anglophone traditions

CRAIG AYREY

I

When *Chroniques de ma vie* was published in 1935, Stravinsky sanctioned what has become his most famous remark: 'Music is powerless to *express* anything at all.'[1] Even if he capitulated to the ventriloquism of his ghost writer Walter Nouvel on that occasion, Stravinsky's faith in the precept of objectivity, 'perhaps the overriding feature of Stravinsky's modernism',[2] pervades his aesthetic manifesto, *Poetics of Music* (1942), to the extent that his 'explanation of music as I conceive it' is egoistically declared not to be 'any the less objective for being the fruit of my own experience and my personal observations'.[3] Objectivity, and its ascendance over what he called 'the subjective prism', was, or became, Stravinsky's distinctive habit of mind, an aesthetic and compositional position maintained in relation to any musical material, including his own free inventions. 'What is important for the lucid ordering of the work – for its crystallisation –', he wrote in *Poetics*, 'is that all the Dionysian elements which set the imagination of the artist in motion and make the life-sap rise must be properly subjugated before they intoxicate us, and must finally submit to the law: Apollo demands it.'[4] Stravinsky's identification with the Apollonian – order, selection, construction, logic and unity – exemplifies the rationalising tendency within modernism and dominates, but does not expel, the Dionysian – freedom, fantasy, emotion, expressivity and irrationality. Yet although this ostensibly black-and-white personification of the relation of objective and subjective as Apollo/Dionysus often seems all too neatly to map onto the oppositions mind/body and thought/emotion in *Poetics*, the Apollonian in Stravinsky essentially describes a process of expressive refinement aiming at the transcendence of such conflicts. As he explained later, in conversation with Robert Craft:

> music is suprapersonal and superreal and as such beyond verbal
> meanings and verbal descriptions... A composer's work *is* the
> embodiment of his feelings and, of course, it may be considered as
> expressing or symbolizing them... More important is the fact that the
> composition is something entirely new *beyond* what can be called the
> composer's feelings... A new piece of music *is* a new reality.[5]

Too late, perhaps. By 1962, when these second thoughts were published, the stark image forged in his pre-1945 writings of Stravinsky as a formalist composer and thinker committed to the (neo)classical values of autonomy, universality and 'the music itself' was already fixed as a given in reception history and even in his self-reflection. Richard Taruskin argues that Stravinsky's adoption, as early as the 1920s, of the ideology of the 'purely musical' was 'a creative swerve that colored all the rest of his career',[6] evidenced by his revisions of the history and genre of *The Rite of Spring*: claiming (in 1920) a musical rather than mythological inspiration for *The Rite* and reinventing (in 1962) the work as a concert piece, Stravinsky intended to conceal its 'prehuman or sub-human reality' and emphasised the dimension of 'civilized consciousness [that] cloaks but does not replace' the subhuman.[7] The composer's revisionary acts of decontextualisation are, according to Taruskin, signs of his collusion with the modernist myth of 'the music itself', a phrase and ideology picked up by Stravinsky in the United States[8] – that is to say, from an anglophone, formalist and positivist intellectual environment sustained by a professional, technical and academic discursive climate. Taruskin's association of these critical conditions with Stravinsky's aesthetic attitudes (as defensive reactions to the descent from humanism to 'biologism' – to the politics of nationalism and modern primitivism foreshadowed by *The Rite* in its first incarnation) is an argument for the complicity of the American Stravinsky with the dominant style of post-war music analysis and theory. This is undeniable, and cuts both ways: Stravinsky's sanction of musical autonomy in *Poetics of Music* (a concise, accessible, decisive aesthetic statement by a major composer) can hardly have failed to stimulate and validate rationalist, non-contextual, abstract modes of criticism.[9]

Authentically Stravinskian effects of *Poetics* first appeared in three essays from the 1960s that decisively established the formalist mode of Stravinsky analysis. Cone's theory of form (1962), Berger's theory of pitch structure (1963) and the English translation of Boulez's analysis of rhythm (1968)[10] addressed Stravinsky's Apollonian complexity parametrically, a characteristically formalist tactic highly appropriate to Stravinsky's containment of pitch, rhythm and form in autonomous, interactive schemes. These studies provided the seminal technical analyses of formal discontinuity, pitch centricity and octatonic pitch structure that underpin Stravinsky's distinctive types of harmonic conflict, integration and structural cohesion, and they consolidated the cornerstones of the formalist Stravinsky canon: *Petrushka* (often reduced critically to the structure and structural effects of the C/F♯ major tritone relation in the 'Petrushka chord'), *The Rite of Spring* (as a treatise on rhythm) and the *Symphonies of Wind Instruments* (as the paradigmatic work of formal discontinuity). Although Stravinsky's foregrounding of rhythm, the parameter popularly considered to be the main site of his

revolutionary procedures, is sometimes acknowledged by the American theorists, their focus on pitch structure in the composer's 'new realities' sustains
the classically modernist privileging of pitch, as evident in Schoenberg's
theoretical writings as in the symptomatically cursory treatment of rhythm
in *Poetics*. Boulez's revelation of an apparently independent and systematic rhythmic structure in *The Rite* springs clearly from the neo-modernist
concerns crucial to Boulez in the early 1950s – the aesthetic death of
Schoenberg,[11] the desire to find a precursor in the systematic organisation of
rhythm to match Webern's pre-eminence as the seer of genuinely new possibilities of twelve-note serialism and the extension of serial principles to non-
pitch parameters in integral serialism – but they are also given a personal
configuration in the non-Viennese procedures of Stravinsky's serial music
that demanded technical explication and received it in exemplary formalist
engagements with contemporary music of the time, the analyses by Milton
Babbitt (1964) and Claudio Spies (1965–7) of three products of Stravinsky's
serial maturity (*Threni, Abraham and Isaac* and the *Variations*).[12]

II

Some major discoveries in these theoretical enquiries are confirmed by
Taruskin's monumental, recontextualising restoration of Stravinsky to his
Russian origins.[13] Berger's identification and designation of the octatonic
scale (previously classified in non-Russian theory as Messiaen's second
'mode of limited transposition')[14] was instigated by the formalist imperative to uncover unity in Stravinsky's chromatically transformed diatonicism, a unity resisting explanation in terms other than local hybrid scales
or non-functional bitonal combinations that often fail to support contextually defined pitch foci. Analysing some extended passages of *Les Noces*,
Berger refers their total pitch content to 'a single referential collection of
eight pitch classes with a few exceptions so marginal as to scarcely require
mention (some dozen tones, mainly ornamental . . .)',[15] now firmly demonstrated by Taruskin to be the 'tone-semitone scale' that Stravinsky imbibed
from Rimsky-Korsakov's theory and practice.[16] Ascending by alternating
semitones and tones (or descending by alternating tones and semitones),
the three non-identical transpositions of the octatonic scale (beginning, for
instance, on C♯, D♮ and E♭) have an alchemical capacity for interaction with
many diatonic and chromatic constituents of tonality (major and minor
triads, diminished and 'dominant' seventh chords, 'French' augmented
sixths) and with the whole-tone scale (four pitch classes are held in common with the octatonic).[17] Where Rimsky-Korsakov exploited the scale
as a means of creating harmonic consistency for various types of tonally

controlled chromatic progression, both Berger and Pieter van den Toorn (the most thorough-going analyst of Stravinsky before Taruskin) demonstrate the function of Stravinsky's octatonicism as a harmonic ground that, bounded by the extremities of tonality and serialism, can be oriented toward the diatonic or the chromatic.[18]

One such tonal-octatonic intersection is Stravinsky's trademark major-minor tetrachord (for example, C–E♭–E♮–G), which informs the harmonic structure of a large number of Stravinsky's middle-period works as a referential 'neoclassical' collection; it also has a constant presence in all Stravinsky's 'styles' via the 'major-minor third emphasis' of its trichord subsets (for example, C–E♭–E♮; or E♭–E♮–G).[19] Like all symmetrical scales, though, the octatonic lacks inherent pitch functions,[20] a condition that disposes of arguments (intrinsically weak in any context) for structural unity according to a 'referential scale' alone. Extrapolating from Berger, van den Toorn's strategy is to emphasise, according to style, either the structural effects of the distinctive properties of the ascending and descending forms ('Models A and B') and the three transpositions ('Collections I–III') or residual tonal functions (the 'dominant–tonic relation' and dominant seventh progressions) in order to produce complete analyses of pitch coherence in small- or medium-range spans. Although he does not seriously question the assumption of unity in any work, the type of Stravinskian coherence demonstrated by van den Toorn is local rather than global. 'Coherence' alone does not satisfy all the requirements of large-scale unity: van den Toorn's approach (and Taruskin's after him) suggests that unity must take the form of a complex, multi-centered amalgamation of structural forces not susceptible to totalitarian explanations. This view of Stravinsky's music as a partially demonstrable synthetic balance of tensions, variably weighted according to style, is reflected in the procedures of conservatively modernist composition and also persists as a received critical consensus that prefers to accept a dimension of failure in the formalist enterprise and (wary of a single-minded response to Stravinsky's belief that 'the One precedes the Many')[21] to close the apparently intractable issue of global unity. Such scepticism underlies the stormy reception history of Allen Forte's monograph (1978) on *The Rite*, an analysis that attempts a global account of harmonic organisation while deliberately excluding 'tonality, large-scale linear connections, register and orchestration'.[22] Taruskin's attacks on Forte's approach to this work appear to equate lack of comprehensiveness with a failure of comprehension, as if a theory of global unity could only arise from an analytical synthesis of parameters;[23] but Forte's strategically restricted investigation of 'underlying harmonic units, ... unordered pc sets, considered quite apart from the attributes of specific occurrences' is comprehensive in a deeper and wider sense, showing a hyper-formalist faith in universals that allows him to risk suggesting that, in its sub-surface harmonic consistency, *The Rite* 'resembles the extraordinary early atonal works of Schoenberg and his students ... and has more in common with those works than with the later works of its composer'.[24] Although Forte's modernist impulse to scrutinise sub-intentional, or pre-conscious, harmonic consistency through the objective prism of abstract theory might indeed seem designed to invite an anti-formalist's rejection, the analysis yields results compatible with van den Toorn's (generally approved of by Taruskin). The major-minor tetrachord (Forte's set 4-17 [0, 3, 4, 7]),[25] for example, emerges as a significant harmony that 'plays a supportive, secondary role'[26] indicated by its presence in all the networks ('set complexes') available to it and by the wide representation of its trichord subsets within the twelve-note chromatic pitch universe. And while no set theorist would be surprised that these functions foreshadow van den Toorn's similar description of the role of this tetrachord in the more exclusive octatonic pitch fields,[27] the interpretative neutrality in Forte's associative classification of harmonic relations (among sets that are frequently octatonic) promotes the forensic discovery of a depth of non-functional consistency that is foreclosed by van den Toorn's pre-selection of significant collections in the service of an intentionally directed, more overtly functional outcome.

Interpretations of specifically Stravinskian, rather than pan-modernist, large-scale structure are facilitated when global unity is located in the control of multiple oppositions by repetitive schemata. Cone's formal triad for the *Symphonies of Wind Instruments* – stratification–interlock–synthesis – proposes that formal discontinuity inheres in blocks of similar material separated by the interruption of different (often opposed) material, progresses to the interlocking of the similar blocks ('the delayed satisfaction' of the suspended 'resumption and completion' of each one), and then to unification by reduction, transformation or assimilation.[28] The appropriately non-teleological type of closure dependent on radical simplification described in this process is a formal manifestation of Taruskin's stylistic triad gleaned from the Russian critical tradition: a complex of intersecting stylistic features and states, *drobnost'* (splinteredness, formal disunification, sum-of-parts), *nepodvizhnost'* (immobility, stasis, non-developmental form) and *uproshcheniye* (simplification)[29] overlap and intersect with Cone's theory sufficiently to suggest that Cone both captures and demonstrates their formal, processive function. Subsequent developments of Cone, primarily Jonathan Kramer's durable theory of 'moment form' and proportion in the *Symphonies*,[30] leave aside Stravinsky the Russian in order to assimilate him into the central traditions of modernism (originating in the 'non-linear' temporal structure of Beethoven's late music) and their post-war continuation. Stravinsky finds himself in company with composers for whom Time is a 'multi-directional' compositional variable – Stockhausen (inventor of the concept of moment form) and *Kontakte* (1960), the modernist Debussy

(*Jeux*), and Messiaen (*Chronochromie*) – and who could be said to show the influence of his oppositionally configured 'block forms'.[31] 'Discontinuity', the process of formal disunity inherent in the as yet unrecognised *drobnost'*, becomes the cardinal structural principle of Stravinsky analysis, valued both as surface shock (it can therefore be 'a profound musical experience') and as the generator of new, proportional modes of 'global coherence':[32] time shaped in proportionally related blocks presents a cohesion that can bind discontinuous material into a higher unity with no need of harmonic or other teleology (though these are not axiomatically obstructed) and facilitates formal processes based on principles of recurrence, circularity and rotation. The burden of large-scale structure is therefore carried by perceived associations in temporal succession, a process Stravinsky located in 'ontological time' (the 'normal flow' of 'real time'), which activates similarity rather than contrast, unity rather than variety,[33] and opposed to 'psychological time', the developmental–teleological conception of music. This distinction in the *Poetics* serves to draw a line in the sand of aesthetic ideology (primarily, Stravinsky against Schoenberg, for whom 'repetition alone often gives rise to *monotony*. Monotony can only be overcome by *variation*');[34] but its rather glib metaphysics also exemplifies Stravinsky's 'third-hand Bergsonian' ideas,[35] received here from Pierre Souvtchinsky (another ghost writer). 'Ontological' and 'psychological' time clearly misread and recast Bergson's concepts of *temps espace* (measured or 'clock' time) and *temps durée* (time as experiential duration), pervasively influential in early modernist aesthetics.[36] Bergsonian *temps espace*, 'a fourth dimension of space, ... homogeneous time',[37] is 'real' only in the sense that it can be divided and measured using spatial descriptions (number, division, 'blocks') and therefore cannot host similarity or unity (musical or otherwise) without the intervention of perception and psychological experience; but what can be retrieved from Stravinsky's self-alignment with 'ontological' time is precisely that essentially Stravinskian illusion of objective reality in which identity and difference within temporal process are grasped by spatial metaphors.[38]

III

Rotation, one such metaphor, has a claim to be Stravinsky's transcendent principle. Its structural and historical manifestations are transparently evident in *Requiem Canticles*, his final large work, particularly in the 'Lacrimosa', where three interdependent contexts of rotation – formal, serial and harmonic – are constructed as an organisational technique for the succession of blocks of material. Formally, there is a rotation of four distinct timbral groups – A (voice), B (piccolo, flutes, harp, double bass), C (strings),

Table 11.1 'Lacrimosa' text and timbral groups

phrases			timbral groups
1, 2	Lacrimosa dies illa,	Tearful that day,	A/B C D, A/B C D
3	Qua resurget ex favilla	When will arise from the dust	A/B C D
4	Judicandus homo reus.	To be judged guilty man;	A/B C D
5	Huic ergo parce, Deus:	Therefore O God, spare him:	A/B C D
6	Pie Jesu Domine,	Kind Lord Jesus,	A/B/C
6	Dona eis requiem.	Grant them rest.	A/C/B
7	Amen.	Amen.	A/C/B D

D (trombones) – in which groups A and B always occur simultaneously, followed by C and D. The distribution of the rotation is unequal in relation to the text (there are two rotations in the first line, 'Lacrimosa dies illa', forming discrete musical phrases), and in the second 'stanza' ('Pie Jesu') the rotation is transformed by the elision of groups A, B and C, resulting in a delay of D for cadential purposes (see Table 11.1).

Rotational transformation therefore installs a formal marker between the 'Lacrimosa' section and the 'Pie Jesu' (often a separate movement in extended settings of the Requiem), but is otherwise only partially determined by the form of the text: while the end of both 'Lacrimosa' phrases (and the 'Amen') is marked by the statement of group D, the content of groups B, C and D is rotated largely independently of the voice-group A. This structural isolation of the voice is implicit both in the absence of any rotation or features of recurrence in the text (except for the end-rhyme pairs in lines 1–4) and in its discursive progression towards the plea for eternal rest ('requiem'). Rotational structures are anti-discursive: but when in 'Pie Jesu' the instrumental scheme is broken, a sense of evolution and discursive progression arises to complement the voice's lapidary declamation of discrete blocks of text in a heightened style of hieratic chant. A rapprochement of the discursive and repetition occurs in this exchange of properties: the discursive nature of the linguistic is made discrete while the instrumental rotations are turned away from recurrence towards the linearly progressive.

Where Taruskin hears the echo of *Zvezdolikiy* in the texture and harmonic organisation of the first phrase of the 'Lacrimosa' (one of the multiple signs of Stravinsky's 'Russian manner' in *Requiem Canticles*),[39] I also hear a Verdian presence in the style and timbre of the vocal line – not the *Requiem*, probably consulted during the composition of Stravinsky's *Requiem*,[40] but Azucena's music in *Il Trovatore* (particularly the ballad, 'Stride la vampa'). Non-direct stylistic allusion, though subjectively intertextual, is consistent with Stravinsky's constant habit of 'stylistic' rotation (which applies equally within his own music) and in this case adds to his allusive pantheon of popular composers of late nineteenth-century stage music (if Rimsky-Korsakov in *The Firebird* and Tchaikovsky in *The Fairy's Kiss*, why not Verdi?).[41] Such stylistic refashioning exemplifies rotational thinking as transformative historical recurrence ('remaking the past' in Joseph Straus's phrase).[42]

Stravinsky's way with pre-formed stylistic material, however, remains his own. In the neoclassical music, primarily, the harmonic techniques of the common-practice period are detoured from functional progression towards the repetition of mildly dissonant collections (often with free contrapuntal elaboration). To persuade an autonomous, theoretically ramified system to come into the orbit of a Franco-Russian technical personality is a trick repeated in his appropriation of serial technique, in which the principle of rotation transforms the pre-formalised system into a mechanism for generating both a consistent rotation of sets among the row forms and an array of harmonically related chords.

The 'Lacrimosa' uses series 1 of *Requiem Canticles* divided into two hexachords.[43] In the IR forms, which are given priority in the movement, hexachords are generated by beginning IR1a-5a with pcs 2–6 of the first hexachord (IR0a) transposed to A♯, the first note of IR0a, and displaying in order the subsequent pcs at the new transposition level. Once the same principle is applied to IR0b, twelve hexachords are produced, six beginning on A♯ (IRa), six on G (IRb) (Table 11.2).

Each hexachord belongs to set class 6-2,[44] and within this hexachordal frame six pentachords, eight tetrachords and nine trichords rotate symmetrically through IRa and b (Table 11.3). These set rotations are presented contiguously in the vocal line (group A), which is constituted of all 12 hexachords in a 'spiral' rotation (Table 11.4), determined partly by the desire to connect vocal phrases or row forms by the common pitch classes G and A♯, as shown in Ex. 11.1 below (see group A). The trichord content of the series is structurally activated in harmonic configuration of the Ia hexachords in group D (trombones: see Ex. 11.1), and although internal serial ordering is maintained, whenever G appears it is placed as the final bass note of each statement, consolidating the limited priority, as inaugural or cadential pitch, of the vocal line's Gs. This correspondence points to the interaction of IR (group A) and Ia forms (group D) that has a clear formal function in the first four phrases of the movement (bars 229–49): as summarised in Table 11.5, the pc-identical pairs IR5b/I1a, I0a/IR3b and IRb/I2a respectively frame, connect and cadence these phrases, a formal consistency that seems to have determined group D's order of Ia rotation (I1a-0a, 3a-2a, 5a-4a). Similarly, in groups B and C, the non-systematic choice of normal or retrograde order in the sequential progression of the Ra forms from Ra0 seems determined by the requirement to complete the total chromatic collection in all phrases except the 'Huic ergo' and 'Amen'.[45] The rotation of instrumental groups A–D therefore conforms to the essential serial rotation of all twelve pcs, with the proviso that repetitions promote the typically Stravinskian focus on referential pitches.

Table 11.2. 'Lacrimosa' series (from Claudio Spies, 'Some notes on Stravinsky's Requiem settings', p. 236, Ex. 11)

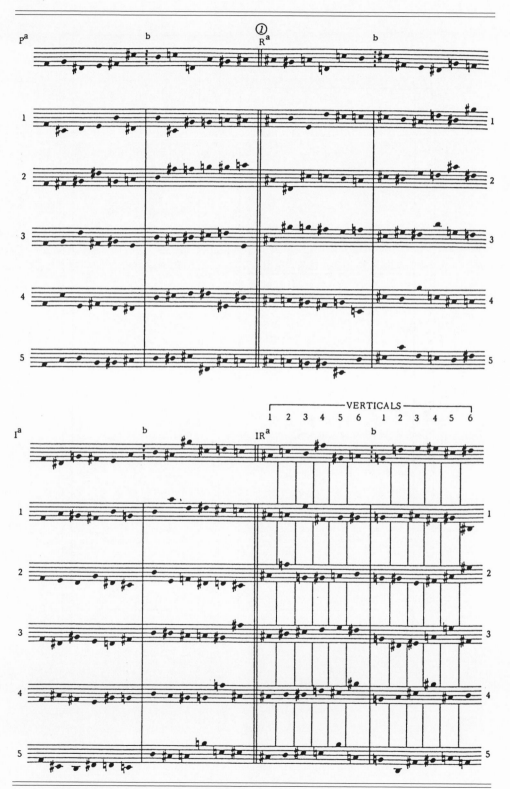

Table 11.3. Set rotations in the IR hexachords

	6-2	5-9	5-10	5-2	5-8	5-1	5-4	5-9	4-5	4-Z15	4-10	4-2	4-1	4-5	4-Z15	3-1	3-5	3-7	3-2	3-1	3-2	3-5	3-7
IR0a	•	•	•								•	•				•	•	•	•	•			
IR1a	•	•	•								•	•	•			•	•	•	•	•			
IR2a			•	•	•				•	•	•	•	•			•	•	•	•	•			
IR3a	•			•	•								•	•	•				•	•			
IR4a						•	•	•						•	•					•	•		
IR5a	•					•	•	•						•	•					•		•	•

	6-2	5-10	5-1	5-8	5-9	5-4	5-2	5-10	4-10	4-3	4-2	4-21	4-5	4-4	4-10	4-3	3-7	3-2	3-3	3-6	3-8	3-4	3-7	3-2	3-3
IR0b	•	•	•						•	•	•						•	•	•	•					
IR1b	•	•	•								•	•					•	•	•	•					
IR2b	•			•	•							•	•				•	•	•	•					
IR3b	•					•	•						•	•						•	•	•			
IR4b	•					•	•							•	•					•	•	•	•		
IR5b	•							•							•	•						•	•	•	•

Note: (1) Read from left to right.
(2) Each hexachord contains two pentachords, three tetrachords and four trichords.
(3) These subsets are obtained by segmenting each hexachord as follows: for pentachords, beginning at the first and second pcs (i.e., 1–5, 2–6); for trichords, beginning at the first, second and third pcs; for tetrachords, beginning at the first, second, third and fourth pcs.
(4) The rotation of subsets shows recurrences within each set type (pentachords, tetrachords, trichords): like the rotation itself, these recurrences are distinctive to Stravinsky's serial technique and are not a feature of traditional serialism.

Table 11.4. 'Spiral' rotation of hexachords in the vocal line

The content of the rotational scheme contains a clear dimension of be-coming, redolent of the evolutionary and memorial transformations of perception (inherent in both Bergson's *temps durée* and Souvtchinsky's 'psychological time'). Each group contains similar pitch material differently configured and each rotation transforms its predecessor: as the temporal distance from the source rotation ('Lacrimosa') increases, the transforma-tion of the later rotations is correspondingly distant in content (as if in memory), preserving only the normative G cadences of group D and the high-register woodwind chords of group B. These chords form a second level of rotation formed pre-compositionally (and therefore abstractly) from the progression through twelve verticals derived from the stack of the IR forms of the 'Lacrimosa' series (see Table 11.2). Ex. 11.2 shows the verticals in their 'Lacrimosa' ordering (Vb2–6, 1; Va2–6, 1 omitted),[46] in which the content of the woodwind chords (treble clef) are identical to the pitch-class content of the abstract derivations in Table 11.2; pitch classes provided by group C instruments (bass clef) create larger sets.

Important features of Stravinsky's distinctive modes of pitch structure are exemplified in this array of chords (Stravinsky in 1959: 'I compose

Ex. 11.1 'Lacrimosa', synoptic analysis

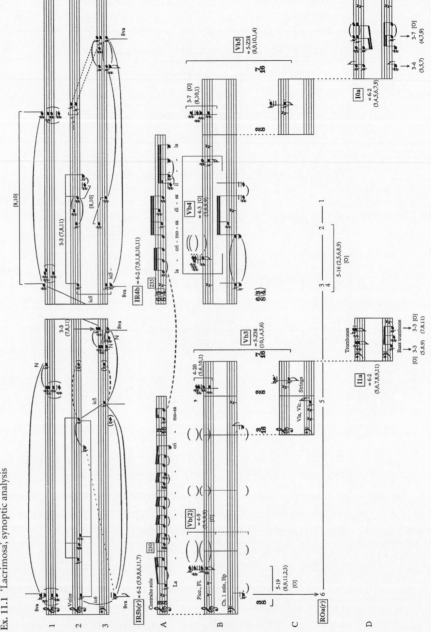

Ex. 11.1 (cont.)

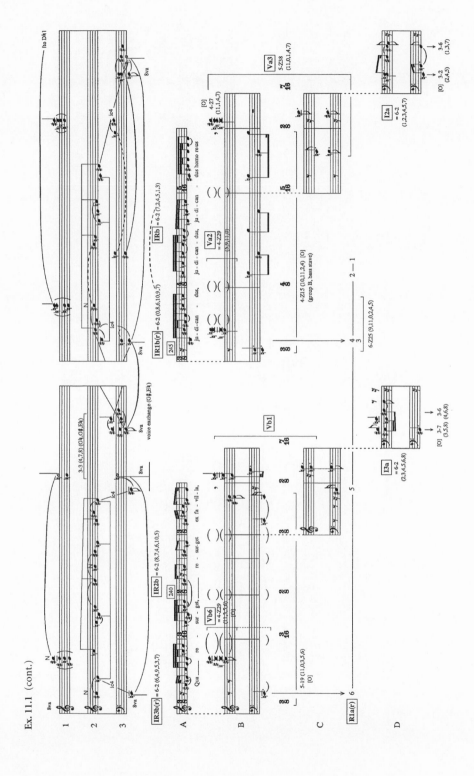

Ex. 11.1 (cont.)

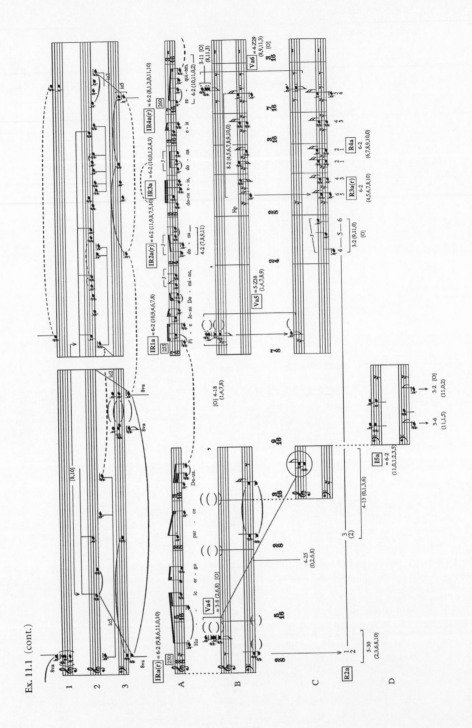

Ex. 11.1 (cont.)

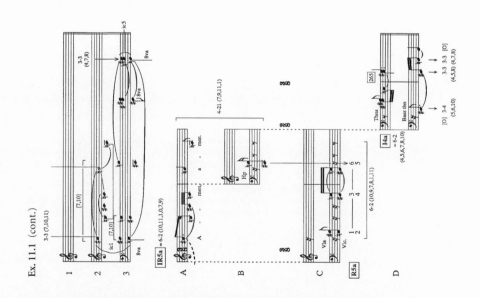

Table 11.5. 'Lacrimosa', synopsis of series, verticals and sets

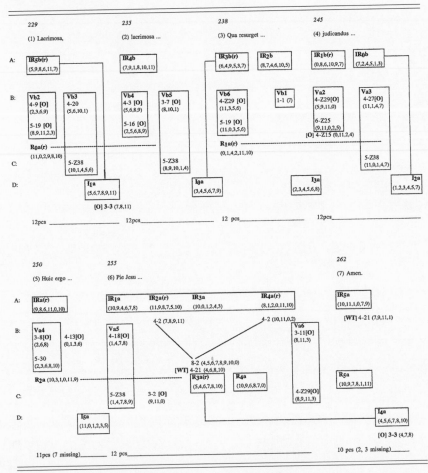

Note: (1) Set names identify collections that have similar interval content (although their pc content may be transposed or inverted). Non-tonal harmonic consistency depends on this type of abstract similarity.

(2) Each IR, R and I hexachord expresses set class 6-2; pcs are shown in order of appearance.

(3) The pc content of all other sets is shown in normal order and is included here to reveal repetitions of pcs within set classes and between dissimilar sets (for example, phrase 4, 5-Z38 and I$_{2a}$ [6-2], both of which contain [1, 4, 7]).

(4) [O] = octatonic set; [WT] = whole-tone set.

(5) In phrase 6, set class 4-2 is the transposed complement of set 8-2 (i.e., each 4-2 contains the four pcs, in transposition, required by 8-2 to complete the total chromatic).

vertically and that is, in one sense at least, to compose tonally' – 'one sense' can be taken to mean to compose harmonically[47]), most obviously harmonic consistency, opposition and an additional definition of pitch centricity. Eleven of the twelve verticals extracted from the serial stack are used: Va1 (unison A♯) is discarded, thus isolating the remaining unison G as the harmonic exception, a singularity heightened by the removal of G from the systematic rotation of the verticals and relocating it centrally (bar 243); these pre-compositional manipulations already indicate the centric role envisaged

Table 11.6. Verticals in group B (woodwind)

Vb:	2	3	4	5	6	Va:	2	3	4		5	6
	O	d/c	O	O	O		O	O	WT	(O)	O	O

O = octatonic
d/c = diatonic/chromatic
WT = whole tone

Table 11.7. Chords, groups B and C

Vb:	2	3	4	5	6	Va:	2	3	4	5	6
	O	d/c	O	d/c	O		d/c	d/c	d/c	d/c	O
	5-19	5-Z38	5-16	5-Z38	5-19		6-Z25	5-Z38	5-30	5-Z38	4-Z29

O = octatonic
d/c = diatonic/chromatic

Ex. 11.2 'Lacrimosa', set content of the verticals

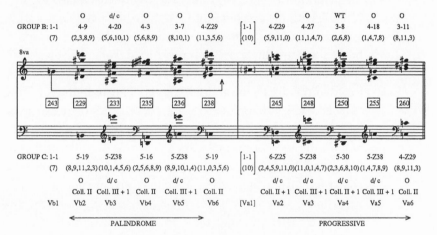

		O	d/c	O	O	O			O	O	WT	O	O
GROUP B: 1-1		4-9	4-20	4-3	3-7	4-Z29	[1-1]		4-Z29	4-27	3-8	4-18	3-11
	(7)	(2,3,8,9)	(5,6,10,1)	(5,6,8,9)	(8,10,1)	(11,3,5,6)	[(10)]		(5,9,11,0)	(11,1,4,7)	(2,6,8)	(1,4,7,8)	(8,11,3)

| | 243 | 229 | 233 | 235 | 236 | 238 | | 245 | 248 | 250 | 255 | 260 |

| GROUP C: 1-1 | | 5-19 | 5-Z38 | 5-16 | 5-Z38 | 5-19 | [1-1] | | 6-Z25 | 5-Z38 | 5-30 | 5-Z38 | 4-Z29 |
| | (7) | (8,9,11,2,3) | (10,1,4,5,6) | (2,5,6,8,9) | (8,9,10,1,4) | (11,0,3,5,6) | [(10)] | | (2,4,5,9,11,0) | (11,0,1,4,7) | (2,3,6,8,10) | (1,4,7,8,9) | (8,9,11,3) |

		O	d/c	O	d/c	O			d/c	d/c	d/c	d/c	O
		Coll. II	Coll. III + 1	Coll. II	Coll. III + 1	Coll. II			Coll. II + 1	Coll. III + 1	Coll. II + 1	Coll. III + 1	Coll. II
	Vb1	Vb2	Vb3	Vb4	Vb5	Vb6	[Va1]		Va2	Va3	Va4	Va5	Va6

←——— PALINDROME ———→   ←——— PROGRESSIVE ———→

for G (see below). Shaping the twelve verticals in this way produces two five-chord arrays (Vb2–6, Va2–6) with obvious potential for systematic organisation according to set type (informally, according to different scales).[48] The chords in group B exhibit an organisation dominated by the octatonic character of four chords in each array (Table 11.6):

Although the whole-tone chord (Va4, the anomaly in array Va) is centrally placed,[49] this is not the case in array Vb (the diatonic/chromatic Vb3 is left of centre), an asymmetry that was corrected in Stravinsky's configuration of these chords in the score, where a more developed, systematic function is elaborated for this raw serial product. When the pitch classes of group B (bass clef) and group C are combined with the raw verticals, the array of set types in Vb is made palindromic: Va, on the other hand, extends the diatonic/chromatic and returns to the octatonic set 4-Z29 in Va6 (see Ex. 11.2 and Table 11.7).

The opposition of set types within this palindromic rotation reveals several types of harmonic consistency. In Vb the first and last chords belong to the same set class (5-19), while the non-octatonic chords always express set class 5-Z38, the location of which remains constant in array Va. Comparison with the raw verticals (Ex. 11.2, group B) illustrates that 5-Z38 is often formed by adding a pc to an octatonic tetrachord (formally, O+1); since each 5-Z38 in Table 11.7 contains one tetrachord of octatonic collection III (3,4,6,7,8,9,10, 0,1),[50] this diatonic-chromatic set is significantly infused with octatonic content. Va2 (6-Z25) and Va4 (5-30) contain subsets of octatonic collection II (2,3,5,6,8,9,11,0), thus relating them closely (as O+1) to the octatonic sets of collection II (5-16, 5-19 and 4-Z29) which acts as the harmonic ground of the composition. This collection is activated structurally in the first rotation ('Lacrimosa', bars 229–34) where the octatonicism of the first raw vertical (set 4-9) is projected at first harmonically in the pentachord 5-19 (Vb2) then laterally to encompass the whole of bars 229–32, with the exception of C (double bass) and G (voice),[51] the latter again isolated in the immediate harmonic context. Octatonic consistency is both inherent in the series and constructed from it. Each form of the series contains at least one octatonic tetrachord or pentachord, a property projected by the strictly linear display of serial forms in the vocal line, but only two of the four octatonic sets (4-3, 4-10, 4-Z15, 5-10) are structurally active harmonically. One of these, set 4-Z15, completes the octatonic organisation of the 'judicandus' (group B, bars 245–7, bass clef); the other, set 4-3, is the only linear set also generated as a raw vertical (Vb4). All other verticals are constructed from intersecting hexachords and are not simply products of a single linear series, guided (firmly in phrases 1–3, more loosely in phrases 4–7) by the octatonic imperative that seems to have determined both the choice of the retrograde forms in the lower instruments of groups B (double bass, harp) and C (strings) and the precise disposition of the R-forms' pitch classes.

IV

Such constant presence of the octatonic realises Stravinsky's invocation of 'the logic of the ear' in a statement (contemporaneous with the composition of *Requiem Canticles*) that catches him in death-defying mode: 'I continue to believe in my taste buds and to follow the logic of my ear, quaint expressions which will seem even quainter when I add that I require as much hearing at the piano as I ever did before; and this, I am certain, is not because of age, is not a sign of dotage.'[52] The full context indicates that the 'logic of the ear' was for Stravinsky an *a priori* subsisting beneath his existential dislocations as the guarantor of structural coherence and stylistic continuity. Rhetorically, the figure is an Apollonian bid for permanence – in retrospect, as the constant that makes consistent sense of the past, in prospect, as the projection of that constancy into the future in works made into monumental artefacts through the consistency of their aural logic. Taruskin's contextualisation of *Requiem Canticles* in the Russian traditions 'revisited' relies heavily on the persistence of the octatonic in Stravinsky's ear, on the harmonic logic that endures intermittently in the progression of stylistic and structural determinants – Russian/chromatic, neoclassical/triadic, serial – in Stravinsky's music. This aural logic is not only conservative: Babbitt asserts, positivistically and also transcendentally, the absolute necessity of the 'logic of the ear' as the organ of construction in Stravinsky's 'new serial combinations' that extracts music from abstract serial relations:

> as for those who seize upon ['the logic of the ear'] to intimate that the music is less 'out of ear' than 'out of mind', let them – instead – contemplate Stravinsky's mode of affirming that the 'ear' is at least as theory laden as the eye and mind, and that only the mind's ear and the ear's mind can provide the now so necessary sorting, selecting and censoring.[53]

If serial technique heightens the importance of the ('now so necessary') selection and rejection of possibilities present in the pre-compositional material, the 'theory-laden ear' must discern new structural forms in the tensional space between its residual burden of theory and the potential suggested by the material for new types of logic. Although octatonicism is one of the potentialities exploited in the 'Lacrimosa', its limited capacity for projection as a structural principle means that it remains only a standard of consistency, subject to constructive forces activated from elsewhere. Prior to seeking a relational logic of diverse harmonies in the 'Lacrimosa', Stravinsky's pursuit of the aural logic of consistency and similarity crystallises in other types of structural singularity, primarily pitch centres. He has much to say in the *Poetics* about 'the eternal necessity of affirming the axis of our music and to recognise the existence of certain poles of attraction'.[54] Composition, defined even pre-serially as an act of selection and ordering, entails 'a search for a centre upon which the series of sounds in my undertaking should converge':

> if a centre is given, I shall have to find a combination that converges upon it. If, on the other hand, an as yet unoriented combination has been found, I shall have to determine the centre towards which it should lead. The discovery of this centre suggests to me the solution of my problem.[55]

To the teleological ear, Stravinsky's 'centres' may often appear as minimal manifestations of non-teleological singularity, the type of stasis scornfully rejected by Adorno as 'hypostatisation', ungenerated by structural processes and extruded from the musical material as the outcome of a precompositional quest for pivotal, unifying features. But what, for Adorno, is the sign of the absence of intention and a non-reflective absolutisation of the event[56] is, for Stravinsky, the definition of the intentional will to consistency: the 'logic of the ear' is a poietic rationale for the integrity and rightness of singular events that, in opposition to Schenkerian teleological logic or Schoenbergian developmental logic of form and structure, supports the extended structural immobility of *nepodvizhnost'* and may at once underpin and undermine structural unity.

These harmonic and formal ambiguities were sensed in the first, Schenker-inspired analyses of Stravinsky's tonal procedures – by Adele Katz (1947), Felix Salzer (1952) and Allen Forte (1955)[57] – an issue newly invigorated by the neoclassical works of 1920–40 (which these writers did not always assume uncritically to be masterpieces). In an attempt to discover a consistent theoretical basis for extended tonality – a conservative and ideologically (if not theoretically) Schoenbergian enterprise perpetuating the nineteenth-century belief in the progressive and radical functions of tradition – the coherence of Stravinsky's music was assimilated in the continuation of contrapuntally based tonal practice (together with that of Debussy, Bartók, Hindemith and Schoenberg's early atonal works) and implicated in a modernist revision of Schenker's aggressively anti-modernist theoretical concepts. That this assimilation could only be achieved by recognising various dimensions of rupture is illustrated by Salzer's analysis of the *Symphony in Three Movements* in which prolongation on the surface levels is abandoned in favour of static 'chord blocks' established by 'repeating and circling around a chord in lieu of thematic development and chord prolongation'.[58] Salzer's intuition of the structurally radical nature of pitch centricity, however, is immediately compensated by a perception of goal-directed motions in the deeper levels, asserting teleology (the primary function of prolongation in Schenker) as hierarchically fundamental and rescuing the prolongationally deprived foreground from structural immobility. Driving teleology into the structural depths of Stravinsky's music, Salzer intends to demonstrate both the persistent stylistic vitality of tonality and its capacity for original renewal as manifested in Stravinsky's innovatory surface configurations. This results in a dilution of the concept of contrapuntal hierarchy to one of relatively independent strata lacking the binding connections of the Schenkerian system of grounds, the issue addressed by Schenker himself in his notorious analytical critique of Stravinsky's 'inability to create tension by means of appropriate linear progressions' in the Piano Concerto in which dissonances 'substitute for [contrapuntal] content and cohesion'.[59] Salzer's analysis of intra-parametrical dissociation in the *Symphony*'s pitch structure therefore treads a critical high-wire: at the same time, it partly accepts the terms of Schenker's critique, conforms to the classically modernist position (articulated most cogently by Schoenberg and Adorno) in which the modern is rooted in, advances and transforms tradition, and pinpoints crucial antagonisms between linear conceptions of structure and Stravinsky's harmonic syntheses.

Identifying as tonic 'a polytonal chord on G with D♭ as a secondary chord of fusion' in the *Symphony*,[60] Salzer defines a synthetic referential dissonance (G, B, D♭, F, A♭) that 'in no way implies two tonalities which would be contradictory to the unity-creating essence of tonality, regardless of style',[61] and is composed out by projecting the elements of the D♭ triad in the upper voices and G/B in the lower ones (he ignores the significant interference of B♭ as a goal in the upper voice that also creates the conditions for the tonicity of the G major-minor triad). In the analysis of the opening section (bars 1–38), 'fusion' in fact occurs rarely – at the beginning (bars 1–3) and at the approach to the dominant (bars 22, 25) when the triadic elements coincide as simultaneities: otherwise, the analysis demonstrates a projected co-existence of G and D♭ held in a horizontal polarity,[62] the disunifying bifurcation Salzer hoped to avoid. This tonic sonority exemplifies the importance of Arnold Whittall's subtle (and determinedly Stravinskian) concept of 'focused dissonance', a fusion of traditional consonant and dissonant elements that forces a re-evaluation of the nature and function of this essential tonal polarity. In *The Rite*, focused dissonances may 'override (but do not eliminate) their absorbed tonal and triadic segments, [and] drive the music into a peculiarly intense state of explosive energy'.[63] Salzer's G/D♭ tonic (an insecure fusion of consonances creating a dissonant sonority) has such energising potential, but in contrast to the procedures of the earlier work, it deflects intensity, regularly expelling its dissonant elements (to expose purely diatonic elements or a unison G) or transferring them to other sonorities in which their role is less triadically disruptive (for example, the synthetic D/A dominant (bar 38) – D, F♯, A, C♯, E – in which the D♭ of the tonic sonority is held invariant, as C♯). Furthermore, prolongation of the *Symphony*'s synthetic G/D♭ tonic is achieved only by loosening the rules of contrapuntal writing so that structural counterpoint may progress freely as 'dissonant voice leading', a category of 'greater freedom and elasticity'[64] in which linear motions both unfold dissonantly and connect dissonant sonorities. A compensation for the severe reduction in the capacity for linear cohesion that this loosening entails appears in Roy Travis's analysis of the Introduction to *The Rite* where the 'dissonant tonic sonority' (A♭, D♭, C) is prolonged by saturating the texture;[65] as Whittall and others have realised, this amounts to little more than a definition of harmonic consistency (the same chord or set repeated in transposition), a necessary but insufficient condition for grounding linear processes congruent with non-tonal chromatic verticals.[66] The demise of a common theoretical practice condemns the tonicity of a dissonant sonority to be defined and prolonged contextually, and therefore uniquely, most often by repetition or the recursively static neighbouring-note structure. Katz's earlier willingness to reserve judgement on the structural implications of Stravinsky's 'new techniques' ('bitonality' and 'polytonality'), rather than to yoke the issue of dissonant prolongation to the perpetuation of tradition,[67] now seems more sensitive structurally than Salzer's conviction that linear processes in a dissonant context are directed (at least on the higher levels of structure). But even when Katz defends the dissonant linearity of imitative 'linear counterpoint' in the Octet (in which 'the integrity of the melodic line is not sacrificed to harmonic considerations'[68] and the horizontal takes precedence over the vertical), the devices of structural stability remain unintegrated or stubbornly static: imitation (horizontalising the principle of repetition), a high degree of harmonic immobility and repeated pitch centres.[69]

Recent voice-leading theory, less enthralled by teleological thinking (and, to that degree, less narrowly formalist than the earlier prolongation theorists) has accepted that the various images of tonal stasis in Stravinsky radically transform or petrify prolongational models, and has explored the ramifications of 'attraction to' rather than 'prolongation of' Stravinsky's centres.[70] To return to our example, we know that Stravinsky 'discovered' G as a potential centrum[71] for the 'Lacrimosa' in the first pc of each IR form of the series and in the isolation of this pc in the array of verticals. Naturally, then, G is prominent in the composition – in the vocal line from the end of the opening phrase ('lacrimosa', bar 232) to the mid-point (bar 243), after which it is emphasised durationally in bar 254 ('dona') and bar 263 ('Amen'), and as the final pitch class of four of the six cadential segments (group D, trombones) ending each phrase, including the last (bars 264–5). Is G a tonic? Like the *Symphony in Three Movements*, the 'Lacrimosa' gives priority to G but now elaborates it with distinct splinteredness. Its regular cadential location obviously defines a minimal centricity as a pitch that provides a structural focus and serves the formal function of tonicity (without, in this serial context, engaging the harmonic or contrapuntal processes of common-practice tonality). But when Stravinsky fixes the harmonic centrality of G natural by stating it in four octaves at the durational centre of the movement (bar 234), he performs a modernist act opposed to the normative beginning–end locations of pre-modernist tonics that has far-reaching consequences for the status of the cadential Gs. As the only structural downbeat in the movement, the centrum both focuses and destablises the material that precedes and follows it, weakening the cadential function of the other Gs (which sound perfunctorily formal) while at the same time activating their pitch priority – a process that epitomises the centrum's function as a 'pole of attraction'.

Ex. 11.3 'Lacrimosa', summary of linear structure (see also Ex. 11.1)

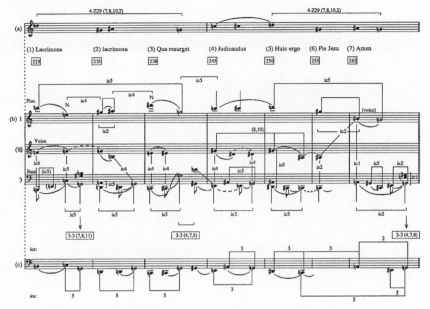

An interpretation of the ways in which G attracts different pcs is presented in the voice-leading analysis of the 'Lacrimosa' in Ex. 11.1 and summarised in Ex. 11.3, where the centrum orients the serial surface and creates small-scale spans of prolongation that can be associated in larger constellations. My method incorporates Joseph Straus's theory of associative voice-leading in Stravinsky, based on the principle that the middleground relation of sonorities or individual pcs replicates similar associative complexes in the foreground without achieving the large-scale linear cohesion essential to prolongation.[72] Two versions of set class 3-3, a simple focused dissonance, end the first phrase (bar 234) as [7, 8, 11], the third (bars 243–4) and the last (bar 265) as [4, 7, 8] and function as a tonic sonority extending the vertical range of the centrum (Ex. 11.3, stratum b3). These G-focused octatonic trichords are inversionally (and therefore symmetrically) related in that they hold the dyad G–G♯ invariant with the third pc at ic3 above or below (Ex. 11.4). They also sum to set 4-17 [4, 7, 8, 11], the definitive major-minor tetrachord, which functions here as a referential set splintered into the trichord expressions of the tonic sonority. Furthermore, the first trichord (bar 234) is approached from the C at the fourth above (ic5+); having attracted this pc, the bass G projects ic5 symmetrically – in phrase 2, D–G (ic5–), and phrase 3, C–G (ic5–) – after which the interval contracts in phrase 4, E–G (ic3+), phrase 5, D♯–C natural (ic3–), and phrase 7, A–G (ic2–). (See Ex. 11.3, strata b and c). Phrase 6 sustains C below the final G (phrase 7) in a larger-scale expression of ic5– paired with a top-voice symmetry (see below). This process – symmetries followed by and (in phrases

Ex. 11.4 'Lacrimosa', symmetrical formations of set class 3–3

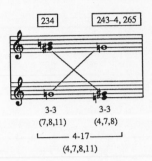

6 and 7) encapsulating contractions to ic2 – is elaborated by various sub-sidiary chromatic pcs: but its essential feature is G's attraction of a limited number of diatonic pcs (C, D, E, A), thus producing discrete blocks of succession emptied of the goal-directed functions of tonal progressions, even when their resemblances remain.

The top voice (carried by the piccolo in phrases 1–6, then in the voice in phrase 7) engages some of the bass voice's pcs and intervals, but is distinguished from the processes of that voice (Ex. 11.3, stratum b1). Repeating a large-scale linear projection of the octatonic set 4-Z29 [7, 8, 10, 2], the top voice both defines a formal boundary (phrases 1–3, and phrases 5–7) and connects the content of the linear process to the penultimate cadential function of 4-Z29, the set class of Va6 which ends the 'Pie Jesu'. Since 4-Z29 is also a (transposed) subset of four of the other nine verticals (those belonging to set classes 6-Z25, 5-16 and 5-19),[73] it is the only set that can be said with theoretical certainty to be projected through the structure.[74] First projected linearly in phrases 1–3, the set displays a new version of the ic5 relation, D (bar 229) above G (bar 243) (ic5+), providing the symmetrical inversion pairing the cadential ic5– (C–G) in the bass voice (bars 255–65) – that is to say, balancing the fifths above and below G. The same linear structure, shorn of elaboration, is repeated in phrases 5–7 (with a closing registral descent of A♯ and G) preceded by the only goal-directed motion in the piece, C–C♯–D (phrase 4), which re-establishes the structural role of D, first and provisionally suggested by its inaugural position (bar 229). The two projections therefore polarise the G centrum within the octatonic tetrachord. However, the top-voice D and G (elaborated in the first statement of 4-Z29 by the neighbouring notes E and F♯) are separated by the pc pair G♯–A♯ ([8, 10], phrases 2, 6–7) widely disseminated in the voice-leading detail of each section (see Ex. 11.1) as the constant chromatic interference with the G centrum, an interference that refers to the G♯ of the tonic sonority (set 3-3). The prominent role of G♯ in the top voice implies no specific or functional connection with G♯s elsewhere in the structure: connection, and therefore priority, inheres not in the (mere) repetition of G♯ (a technique reserved for the centrum) but in the constant presence of G♯ in various configurations within the voice-leading strata.

These instrumental processes operate largely independently of the pitch structure of the vocal line, which unfolds a two-part linear motion converging on the final pc of phrases 1–3; subsequently, separation becomes the norm, culminating in the non-integration of the motions A♮–G and B–A in the final phrase 7 necessitated structurally by the non-participation of the instrumental music in the closure of the top-voice structure. The extremities of each vocal phrase, however, may condition a partial integration of vocal and instrumental structure if the vocal pcs and the bass are related in a progression of vertical interval classes (Ex. 11.3, strata b2–3): beginning with ic5, F/B (bar 229), the two strata proceed, a little irregularly, through contracting interval classes until ic1 is reached in bar 262, soon repeated in the final trombone chord as G♯/G♮.[75] The relative independence of the voice (reflecting its distinct textural, rhythmic and verbal character) confirms the non-organic, stratified and non-hierarchical nature of the linear organisation, a structurally disruptive effect intensified in the serial context by the strong tonal implications of vertical intervals of phrases 1–3 (see Ex. 11.1). Phrase 1's opening tritone, F/B, may be heard to imply a resolution to the major third C/E present in split form when the bass progresses to C (bar 232) and the strings arrive on E (bar 233); this potential reference to C major is confirmed by the vocal G (bar 232). While such a tonal hearing is strongly contradicted by the tetrachord 4-20 (bar 233) and by the G♯–F♯ repetition in the voice (bar 230), the latter figure also raises the ghost of E-based harmony, represented in the linear analysis (Ex. 11.1, stratum 3, and Ex. 11.3, stratum b3) by the implied E in the bass, so that an ambiguous and disorienting tonal ambience shrouds the whole of the first phrase. The possibility of more direct aural privileging of tonal forms occurs in phrase 3, bar 239 (bass C, voice E) and bar 241 (bass C♯, voice E♯), but in so far as tonal implications weaken in force approaching the G centrum (after which the G-based trombone cadences take priority), one strategy of Stravinsky's compositional intention may be to neutralise them. If the tonal intervals are not heard as octatonic dyads (or if we do not learn to hear them this way), they can only disrupt the dissonant consistency of atonality, allusively turning it toward the tonal without producing a tonal existence: even though local connections could be proposed, these triadic forms resist systematic explanation and cannot be heard, at least by the ear attuned to Stravinsky's octatonic logic, as functionally connected.[76]

V

Beneath the various types of recurrence – rotations, repetitions and pitch centricity – the 'Lacrimosa' can be heard to sustain a dynamic process formed from the differences within the repetitions, animating formal stasis and proceeding non-teleologically towards a unit of completion (the final major-minor tetrachord subset 3–3). This sense of an ending for the block-articulated linear process is articulated by the group D music (trombones), the only material with a specifically rhythmic character: the six segments present a series of composite durational patterns (Ex. 11.5) delineating a process of statement and transformation in which, from the second half of the sequence (bar 249), long values gradually predominate.

Repetition in the first three segments, followed by processive transformation, replicates the design of the pitch processes of the movement (in particular the structure of the verticals in Ex. 11.2) and is similarly marked by the three statements of set 3-3 (bars 234, 244, 265) the formal function of which is now clearly evident. The subtle non-insistence of these pitch processes makes them seem almost accidental, as givens emanating from the pre-compositional manipulation of the series accepted into the structure and gently brought to life by the group D rhythmic pulsations.

Objectivity, already the product of Apollonian refinement, is further purged here as 'the objectification of all anxiety'.[77] Such transcendental objectivity arrests time and distances subjective, 'psychological' temporality, but the installation of an essentially spatial conception within time cannot avoid setting in motion the potential for becoming inherent in general temporality. Adorno's view, in paraphrase, that Stravinsky composed against the temporal nature of music entails that Stravinsky's music resists temporality but does not escape from it. For all Stravinsky's efforts to constrain the listener's or interpreter's experience, his music (the late music in particular) – conflicted and splintered by its projection of rational order into temporal becoming – is unusually vulnerable to the listener's subjectivity (as the work of Marianne Kielian-Gilbert demonstrates),[78] and is particularly receptive to diverse theoretical representations, not least because the music revels in the potential of various types of contradiction, narrating the process of contrast–dispersal–synthesis in a spatialised presentation of units that seem strongly impelled to unification in our perception of their temporal succession. The analyst who, like the prolongation theorists, hears unification as a process may respond too readily to the temporal element in which Stravinsky's constructions are placed and remain deaf to the spatially transformed time that, in *Poetics*, masquerades as the (mis)conception of 'real' time. Schenker's judgement, handed down from teleological formalism, that Stravinsky is 'unmusical' is therefore as apposite as the focus on Stravinsky's music in the theoretical systems of Cone, Berger, Forte

Ex. 11.5 'Lacrimosa', rhythmic organisation of group D

and van den Toorn, informed as they are by spatial and abstract conceptions of musical structure – networks, centres, collections, strata, sets: his music and ideas were actively implicated, as partial instigation and testing ground, in the concretisation of such spatial metaphors that (with the exception of Chandler Carter's analysis of *The Rake's Progress*,[79] and the later work of Kielian-Gilbert) have all but lost their figurative power in their reification as the constitutive concepts of modern music theory.

There are, then, signs of theoretical renovation in Stravinsky studies. But having so conscientiously prolonged the formalist moment in musical culture so that it achieved a Stravinskian dynamic stasis, Stravinsky has had a compositional rather than conceptual after-life in theory, as traced in Kramer's alignment of Stravinsky with 'new temporalities' (time split by the reversible and multiple referentiality of musical material), in Cross's examination of the 'Stravinsky legacy' eliding him with the second, post-Second World War phase of modernism, and in Andriessen and Schönberger's proto-postmodern Stravinsky: in compositional practice, they write, 'the true influence of Stravinsky has only just begun. It is an influence that can do without Stravinskianisms.'[80] This recommendation might also sustain the nascent liberation of analytical Stravinsky interpretation from its all-too-appropriate Stravinskian ideology.

12 Stravinsky and the critics

STUART CAMPBELL

Introduction

R.C.: What do you mean when you say that critics are incompetent?

I.S.: I mean that they are not even equipped to judge one's grammar.
They do not see how a musical phrase is constructed, do not know
how music is written; they are incompetent in the technique of the
contemporary musical language. Critics misinform the public and
delay comprehension. Because of critics many valuable things
come too late.[1]

In this exchange with Robert Craft, Stravinsky testified to the generic hostility felt by composers toward critics. As we shall see, however, this attitude on
the part of this composer concealed a much more complicated relationship
with the supposed enemy.

For the purposes of this chapter, 'critic' is broadly defined. The tasks of the
critic include discriminating between good and bad – with all the interme-
diate gradations – in composition and performance; discerning continuities
and discontinuities between new and older work (again, in both composition and performance), whether of the recent or the more remote past;
informing the readership about current issues in the world of the arts. A
critic in practice serves as an intermediary between consumer and creator
(that is, between listener and composer, or listener and performer), helping
both sides by creating an intellectual environment where the former un-
derstands better the work of the latter. Critics' activities are informed by
the work of historians and analysts, though the character of their output
is different. Criticism may take any form from brief newspaper reviews to
book-length studies; in some cases humble journalistic endeavour facilitates
the development of ideas that later find full expression in a monograph. But
both are species of criticism.

Besides giving a taste of the reception that Stravinsky's music has met
at different times, this chapter aims to tease out ideas about it which have
been at the centre of debate. How Stravinsky's compositions fitted into
the general musical picture, and which composers he was compared and
contrasted with, are also incorporated in the remit.

Stravinsky presented critics with several distinctive challenges. The
length of his creative life was not unique, but his successive immersion

in several different cultures is unusual among front-rank composers. After copying the compositional practice of a St Petersburg guild, Stravinsky later gave free rein to his imagination, at first within the guild's framework and later beyond it, before several times turning in other directions – first in France and later in the USA. Critics seeking to do justice to all the composer's work must ideally be attuned to Russian music of the Silver Age, the French musical world of the 1920s and 30s, and the German–American currents flowing strongly in the Craft-influenced American years. Whilst Stravinsky certainly traversed a broad territory of compositional styles, his music also covers a long distance as regards aesthetic character. Ballet, opera and hybrid theatrical genres, Russian folklore and literature, Greek myth, Orthodox and Catholic ritual – these must all be within the range of the ideal critic. Some of the most revealing insights into Stravinsky's music come from colleagues who, like him, belonged to 'Russia abroad' (*russkoye zarubezh'ye*) – Russians who emigrated from their homeland during its troubled twentieth century (Lourié, Nabokov, Schloezer, Souvtchinsky).

Composer and critic commonly clash when the composer's attention is concentrated on his most recent composition, while the critic is struggling with the one before. It is not always possible to hear works in chronological order. Nikolay Myaskovsky understood the evolution of Stravinsky's harmonic language between *The Firebird* and *The Rite of Spring* only when he looked into the intervening works, the songs and the cantata *Zvezdolikiy*.[2] Later, too, shorter pieces illuminated the path between the more substantial ones. *Les Noces* is a particular problem because its abnormally long gestation period made it seem atypical when it finally emerged from the womb. There can be difficulties also when an early composition establishes itself so securely in the repertory (as with *The Firebird*, Rachmaninov's C♯ minor Prelude or Schoenberg's *Verklärte Nacht* or *Pierrot lunaire*) as to entrench a particular view of its creator. All subsequent works have to contend with this view, and at first are usually adjudged to fall short of the earlier achievement. This problem afflicted Stravinsky's music several times, with *Petrushka* and *The Rite*, like *The Firebird*, winning recognition and impeding response to subsequent works. Those who had accommodated their thinking to (say) the *Symphony of Psalms* were confounded by *Canticum Sacrum*. Part of the critic's task is to convey to his readership that a composer's activities are a dynamic process demanding a shift of focus from one work to another, rather than a production line where every unit resembles its neighbours as closely as possible.

At some stage Stravinsky himself concluded that his music would speak more clearly if he helped it by giving interviews and publishing open letters, articles and entire books, even if some were ghost-written. One motivation was probably simple self-promotion: he saw the advantages of his work being discussed in influential publications. Another motivation was to create a climate more congenial for new compositions, in particular to change the criteria by which his music was judged – to escape being typecast as a composer of Russian ballets. It probably did not matter greatly to him whether the words were actually written by himself or formulated by a critic using his ideas. But a critic could not always be trusted to preserve the purity of the composer's thought, any more than a conductor could be kept from developing the composer's wishes in accordance with his own creative will – hence the ups and downs in relationships between Stravinsky and individual critics and conductors.

Scott Messing describes the first half of the 1920s, with Ansermet, Edwin Evans, Roland-Manuel and Schloezer:

> A symbiotic relationship seems to have been reached between Stravinsky and several sympathetic critics; advocates could enjoy an intimacy with a musician of vast creative and intellectual gifts while he could rely on their conveying his thoughts and keeping his name in the vanguard of contemporary art.[3]

By Stravinsky's time, it was rather the norm than the exception for composers to write about music for publication. For that reason, several composer-authors are mentioned in this chapter (Auric, Poulenc, Boulez). The professional critic is supposed to be detached from what he is writing about, though it is a moot point whether the detached critic is any more of a reality than the dispassionate historian. The major professional composer-turned-critic will be read for any light he sheds on his own music. If Stravinsky's aim as pianist and conductor was to establish a performance tradition free of the distortions allegedly caused by the interposing of the personalities of professional pianists and conductors, then his aim in writing was also to impose his own intellectual interpretation of his works upon readers who might otherwise fall victim to misunderstandings wrought by ill-informed or uncomprehending interpreters.

Stravinsky was not simply developing his musical language from one work to the next – he tried at several stages to show himself in a light which comprehensively misrepresented his thinking when he had composed earlier works. This is most obvious in the *Chronicle of my Life* (1936) and *Poetics of Music* (lectures delivered in 1939–40), where he sought to make out that his opinions in the mid 1930s coincided with his earlier ones. A critic's work is not made easier by propaganda barrages from interested parties.

Stravinsky and critics in Russia

The first Russian critics to comment on Stravinsky's music in the press, such as Yuly Engel' (Joel Engel), Vyacheslav Karatïgin and Nikolay Myaskovsky,

had a thorough grounding in music. They knew the music of Stravinsky's
teacher Rimsky-Korsakov and his Belyayev circle, and could divine the developing relationship between the compositions of the mentors and their dis-
ciple. They were also conscious of newer European styles propagated by the
Evenings of Contemporary Music, where Stravinsky found further friends
and associates. That group included many of the art connoisseurs (and
Diaghilev associates) who as librettists, designers and musicians bridged
Stravinsky's St Petersburg and Paris years. These critics felt musical currents
from outside their homeland, and Karatïgin in particular pinpointed what
the young Stravinsky had learned from his French near-contemporaries,
particularly Debussy. A frequent motive in early Russian Stravinsky reception was admiration for the 'invigorating' character of his music. The
technical accomplishment of his orchestral conceptions was also praised
('extraordinary gorgeousness of orchestral hues',[4] for example), though
there were sometimes hints that this aspect acquired a disproportionate
virtuosity of its own. While noting the historic importance of *The Rite
of Spring* ('a monument to the impressionist phase in Russian music'),
Karatïgin's extended review of its Russian premiere conducted by Koussevitzky in 1914 concludes that the work itself contains too many superficially
clever tricks repeated excessively without further invention; the same applies to its harmonic asperity.[5] As Stravinsky advanced beyond the principles
of the Belyayev group, his membership in it lapsed, personal relationships
with old friends in the wider Rimsky-Korsakov family soured, and their
sympathy changed to antipathy. Artistic divergence turning into jealousy
and suspicion is voiced by Leonid Sabaneyeff:

> Stravinski's fame is based not only on his musical gifts ... but chiefly on
> his virtuosity in making full use of musical conditions and taking full
> accounts of fashions and fads ... It depends least of all on the magnitude
> of endowments, but more on the composer's technical and even
> 'commercial experience'.[6]

Stravinsky is nevertheless 'the recognised master of minds and the supreme
leader in the field of musical creative art, only Richard Strauss and
Schoenberg, perhaps, sharing this hegemony with him'.[7]

One of the most perceptive accounts of Stravinsky's music was written
and published in Russia, even if it had to wait for over fifty years to be
translated into English. Boris Asaf'yev's *Book about Stravinsky*,[8] published
in 1929, is the work of the most influential music theorist and historian
of Soviet Russia. It kept Russian readers abreast of the glittering career
unfolding abroad and introduced works such as *Oedipus Rex* and *Apollon
musagète*. To the non-Russian reader, Asaf'yev presents a Stravinsky who
belongs, on the one hand and in certain compositions, to the tradition
of Russian music exemplified by the Mighty Handful and their heirs and,

on the other hand, in different pieces, to the line which includes Glinka, Varlamov, Dargomïzhsky and Tchaikovsky. The discussion of *Mavra* is particularly enlightening. The book is informed by the ideas that Asaf'yev was developing concurrently, which are set out in his *Muzïkal'naya forma kak protsess* (Musical form as a process), published in two volumes in 1930 and 1947.

During much of the Soviet period, Stravinsky's music was little discussed in public and less heard in Russia. As one who had opted out of his country's historic destiny as the test bed for Marxism, and had advertised his strong disapproval of what took place there, any influence over his compatriots could only have been reckoned harmful by the increasingly controlling authorities. From about 1930 until Stalin's death in 1953, little that was worthy of the name criticism appeared there. During the Khrushchev era, the climate softened sufficiently for Stravinsky to visit his homeland in 1962, and for his music to be removed from the proscribed list. In itself, this did not lead to any great rush of performances – partly because in the minds of concert organisers a policy newly relaxed could always be tightened again, and, partly because his most recent work attracted hostility on stylistic grounds. The most interesting subsequent study of Stravinsky's work as a whole to be published in Russia was that of Mikhail Druskin;[9] this appeared in 1974. Druskin was an eminent St Petersburg Conservatoire professor who in the 1920s and 30s had had his finger on the musical pulse, and his book helped restore Russians' links with their own past. Viktor Varunts has recently done invaluable work by assembling the Russian documents (criticism included) of Stravinsky's past.[10]

Stravinsky's years in France

The French musical community was, in general, well disposed towards Russian music in the period before the First World War. This benevolence was part of a wider sympathy that had political and financial as well as cultural resonances. Against the background of Parisians' introduction to works by Balakirev, Borodin, Musorgsky and Rimsky-Korsakov, beginning substantially in 1878 and climaxing in the seasons of concerts, ballet and opera that Diaghilev began offering in 1906, Stravinsky seemed a natural extension of the school. *The Firebird* established this perception convincingly in 1910, and for some listeners the process continued through the following two ballets. But French perceptions did not necessarily coincide with Russian ones. As Schloezer wrote later,

> What [Westerners] look for first and foremost in Russian art is precisely
> that which is different from theirs; it is a certain 'barbaric' aspect –

rough, untutored and, in a word, Asiatic. This Asiatic face of Russia, they think, is Russia's true face.[11]

Writing after *The Rite of Spring*, Pierre Lalo pronounced Stravinsky 'the spiritual son of Rimsky-Korsakov, and the sole true heir of the generation of composers represented by the Five'.[12] To Florent Schmitt, that score marked the 'climactic point not just of [Diaghilev's] Russian Season [of 1913] but also of Russian music' (and added ' – and perhaps of music *tout court*');[13] much later Pierre Souvtchinsky, whose connections with Stravinsky lasted longer than anyone else's, beginning in Russia and continuing until the composer's death, observed that Stravinsky had raised Russian music to 'universal rank'.[14] The rhythmic dislocations and the dissonance of *The Rite*'s harmony were cited by early critics as defining its status as a landmark in music history. It was repeatedly said (by Schmitt, Lalo, Karatïgin and Jean Marnold[15]) that Stravinsky's harmony went further even than that of Richard Strauss. Writing in August 1913, Jacques Rivière made a bold claim for *The Rite*: 'It marks a significant date not only in the history of dance and music but also in that of all the arts.'[16] To him it represented a work 'which changes everything, which alters the very source of all our aesthetic judgments, and which must at once be counted among the very greatest'.[17] In November he claimed historical primacy for it as the first masterpiece which could be set against those of Impressionism;[18] as Adorno put it in 1948, 'ever since *Sacre* [Stravinsky] had been proclaimed as the anti-pope to Impressionism'.[19]

It is legitimate to wonder how much the first-night audience were able to concentrate on the music. For one thing, Nijinsky's choreography drew the attention. For another, the *scandale* at the premiere made hearing the music at all difficult, and assessing it all but impossible – at least for those without access to a score. Describing what he called this 'Massacre du printemps', Léon Vallas observed that the usual Parisian ballet audience showed better judgement when using its eyes than when using its ears, and was inherently incapable of accepting such a challenging score.[20]

Pierre Lalo observed that the music emerged in greatly altered perspective when Pierre Monteux conducted a concert performance in April 1914. Where the reviews from the theatre had emphasised primitivism, rhythmic complexity and harmonic audacity, Lalo could now hear that much of the score was gentle and not in the least barbarous or ugly.[21] We cannot be certain, of course, that other things were equal: Lalo's ears may in the interim have become better attuned, or the orchestra's performance in the concert hall may have been significantly better. At any rate, Louis Laloy agreed with his colleague when he reported that the injustice done to *The Rite* in spring 1913 had been made good by a triumph the following year.[22]

Fault lines opened up rapidly. Senior English critics found Stravinsky's work problematic. For Ernest Newman, writing in 1921, *Petrushka* appeared to be the summit of Stravinsky's work, with the talking-up of *The Rite of Spring* by unnamed diehard supporters 'the most farcical imposture in the music of our time'.[23] E. J. Dent, more sympathetic to contemporary music than Newman, was none the less unable to accept what he thought the 'silliness' contained in some of Stravinsky's works after *The Rite*:

> Possibly their jokes are intelligible to people who have been brought up
> in a Russian nursery or have frequented certain social circles in Paris. If
> that is the point of view which the listener is expected to take, it seems
> rather inappropriate – to use no harsher word – to perform them in
> London.[24]

The view that Stravinsky's music was a fashion accessory for some in-crowd was expressed by several critics. For some, the peak of Diaghilev's creative success, the moment when the ideal match of sound, picture and movement was achieved, coincided with the period of the three great Stravinsky ballets; thereafter, it was downhill for both impresario and composer. In 1926 Schloezer was lamenting the loss by the Ballets Russes of 'that spirit of invention, that free imagination, that taste for risk and adventure, that continual renunciation [of what they had done before]' which had characterised their work earlier.[25]

Whatever music Stravinsky was writing, he came to hold an influential position among the younger generation of French composers. Jacques Rivière noted this in 1920:

> The extraordinary freedom, of which our young composers of today avail
> themselves with taste, talent and discretion, they owe ... to Stravinsky, to
> that frail Samson who, making an easy gesture and behaving as if very
> drowsy, has moved back the walls of music's temple from all quarters.[26]

The young composers of Les Six, with Erik Satie as mascot and Jean Cocteau as herald, joined Stravinsky in rejecting Romanticism with its predominantly German heritage and in seeking something new. They shared the light-hearted tone, sense of parody of established musical styles and small-scale operation of, for example, *Renard* or *The Soldier's Tale* – even before the notion of 'neoclassicism' shortened the distance between Stravinsky and these admirers.

Certain of Stravinsky's works found readier press championship from these younger French composers than among professional critics. Some of Les Six spoke out vociferously in support of works of the late 1910s and early 1920s. *Pulcinella* played an important role in this development, as Paul Collaer pointed out:

> It is not surprising that it should have been *Pulcinella* which allowed Stravinsky's influence to hold sway over the younger generations. The specific character of *The Rite* or *Les Noces* did not permit any 'follow-up'. The universality of *Pulcinella*'s language allowed it to be assimilated by other composers. *Pulcinella* lent impetus to a large part of young French music.[27]

To Schaeffner, on the other hand, 'the young musicians attached an importance to *Pulcinella* which overstated that which the ballet actually had in Stravinsky's art';[28] perhaps the composer himself was guilty of this error (see the discussion of 'neoclassicism' below).

Francis Poulenc and Georges Auric lavished praise in particular on *Mavra*, the work most beloved by its composer and least understood by people outside his immediate entourage. Auric wrote of:

> a work that, after Satie, bearing the precious imprint of the young music of France, conveys to our hearts and minds its unforgettable pages, bound together like a bouquet whose fragrance will grow from day to day, far from all scholastic prejudice, esthetic argument, false bravado, or the cant of base disciples.[29]

Jean Cocteau expressed part of Stravinsky's problem at this stage:

> What could be more admirable than the spectacle of this hard man being begged by an amorous public to be brutal to them and deal still more blows – and then offering them lace. So graceful a gift perplexes them. They understood the blows better.[30]

This remark demonstrates how the generality of French opinion lost enthusiasm for Stravinsky once his music had parted company with their ideas of what was 'Russian'.

'Neoclassicism' was a central term in musicography of the interwar period, and Scott Messing has recounted the origins and development of the term. While its use did not originate in descriptions of Stravinsky's works, it became indissolubly associated with them, and they to be viewed as classic representatives of the phenomenon. It was regarded as embodying Latin cultural values (especially French and Italian) in opposition to Teutonic culture.

The first to apply the term to Stravinsky was Boris de Schloezer in 1923, though in reviewing *The Rite* in 1914 Karatïgin had discerned 'a gravitation towards classical clarity and elegance', a striving for simplicity in opposition to the previous dominant trend of impressionism.[31] In his article of 1923 Schloezer observed of the *Symphonies of Wind Instruments* that:

> This genial work is only a system of sounds, which follow one another and group themselves according to purely musical affinities; the thought of the artist places itself only in the musical plan without ever setting foot in the domain of psychology. Emotions, feelings, desires, aspirations – this is the terrain from which he has pushed his work. The art of Stravinsky is nevertheless strongly expressive; he moves us profoundly and his perception is never formularized; but there is one specific emotion, a musical emotion. This art does not pursue feeling or emotion; but it attains grace infallibly by its force and by its perfection.[32]

Schloezer also expounded what was becoming the standard view – that Stravinsky was in most respects the antithesis of such 'German' composers as Schoenberg, whose music continued within a framework laid down by Wagner.

Arthur Lourié was from 1924 to 1931 'one of the two or three most important associates in Stravinsky's life'.[33] He wrote a number of articles that closely reflect the composer's opinions by anticipating ideas that Stravinsky was to express in *Chronicle of my Life* or *Poetics of Music*. In *Neogothic and Neoclassic* Lourié asserted that in 'the esthetic approach of artists...neoromantic emotionalism is giving way to classical intellectualism'.[34] Neogothic is equivalent to neoromantic, the present-day continuation of which is represented by Expressionism, identified with Schoenberg. 'To make a generalization, one may locate the contemporary musical camps as to their relative positions in the following way: at the extreme left, the expressionists; at the extreme right, the neoclassicists; with the adherents of impressionism in the center.'[35]

Stravinsky frequently uttered words with connotations of the right wing in politics (order, discipline) and often gave vent to his detestation of Bolshevism, an extreme form of left-wing politics. This was coupled with a claim to detest modernism in art. While such attitudes resonated favourably in influential quarters during the 1920s and 1930s, by the end of the 1940s they were increasingly a liability, as a new generation of European artistic modernists influenced by the political left occupied the musical stage.

To Lourié also fell the honour of introducing the Stravinskian idea of the *forme-type* 'which results from primary general conceptions';[36] the idea reappears in Schloezer, who refers to a series of *oeuvres-types* beginning with *The Soldier's Tale*.[37] This is linked with the notion that classical means typical.[38] In 1928, as if on Stravinsky's behalf, Lourié set aside any idea that music could be a surrogate for religion,[39] or that any part of its purpose involved sexual arousal.[40]

Two works have contended for the position of the first Stravinskian demonstration of 'neoclassicism': *Pulcinella* and the *Symphonies of Wind Instruments*. Whatever the experimental gains made through the ballet, it is the *Symphonies* which have the stronger claim as the earliest convincing demonstration of radical thought. The composer himself, however, in hindsight, wrote about the role of *Pulcinella* in his creative evolution:

> *Pulcinella* was my discovery of the past, the epiphany through which the whole of my late work became possible. It was a backward look, of course – the first of many love affairs in that direction – but it was a look in the mirror, too.[41]

A related, though different, view of *Pulcinella* was expressed by Boulez, reflecting post-Adornian opinions, in 1971:

> Stravinsky's way of 'discovering' history or tradition was initially by means of anecdote. His handling of Pergolesi [Boulez refers to *Pulcinella*] suggests a chance visit to a museum by a wandering visitor, quite unprepared for what he finds ... This chance visit whetted his appetite and he soon began to vary his itineraries, exploring other museums that aroused his curiosity but without any serious purpose.[42]

Stravinsky would surely have agreed with Schloezer when he wrote in 1928:

> Music has broken its last ties with reality; it remains no less disturbing, capable of upsetting the listener to the extent of tears; but this emotion is something quite particular, of absolute purity, unable to be reduced to our daily psychological experience, however profound or subtle it might be. And that is precisely the quality of the music of *Apollon musagète* which contains not even an ounce of the real![43]

As early as 1913, in the context of *The Rite*, Rivière had argued that 'Stravinsky upheld clarity, simplicity, precision, and above all he sought the elimination of all superfluous and gratuitous elements in his expression'.[44] These sentiments accorded with the wish of Rivière, who was first and foremost a *littérateur*, to see the same qualities – part of the later stock-in-trade of 'neoclassicism', supposedly traditional in French art – restored in new literature: Stravinsky's music served as welcome additional support.

Rivière's successor as music critic of the *Nouvelle Revue française* was Boris de Schloezer. As a consequence of his Russian birth, his residence in the Russian capitals between 1903 and 1918 and his Franco-Belgian education, Schloezer was in an almost uniquely favourable position to understand Stravinsky's compositions. He earned the composer's disapproval with his notice about *Mavra*, of which he wrote: 'the subject is too thin, too fragile, and the Italo-Russian and black-American styles do not mix'.[45] A monograph published in 1929 couples a portrayal of Stravinsky as a cultural phenomenon with some technical discussion of his music. It is unusual in aiming 'not to consider the development of these works in time but rather to examine the different aspects and characteristic features which this art offers us, as it presents itself to us as a whole today'.[46] It is divided into chapters entitled 'The Russian and the European', 'Technique', 'The problem of style' and 'A classical art'. After an extensive exposition of the idea that Russian art is European art with additional features rather than some primitive antithesis of it, Schloezer argues that Stravinsky's art develops not progressively but by means of discontinuity, with the relationship between parameters moving in a zigzag pattern rather than a straight line.[47] Schloezer singles out certain works, finding *Petrushka* especially impressive, not least as the first work to challenge Wagnerian harmonic thought.[48] *The Rite of Spring* is important, but it is atypical of its composer.[49] *Pulcinella*, on the other hand, 'marks an important date in Stravinsky's production – I'd say in the history of modern music itself', as a turning-point in the composer's style; until then his role among composers of the younger generation had been to help in cleansing their palates (and, indeed, their palettes), but now 'the composer acquired a profound and fruitful [positive] influence upon them'.[50] Schloezer's opinion of Stravinsky's latest work is evident from his book review:

> Reading [Stravinsky's] *Chroniques* is somewhat like listening to one of his recent compositions: clean, precise, dry ... with emotion scattered here and there but in carefully rationed terms.[51]

From 1912 to 1938 Louis Laloy was a faithful champion and friend of the composer, while on occasion expressing reservations about specific works. The following passage from 1934 shows a critic eventually able to grasp Stravinsky's changes of direction:

> Monsieur Stravinsky attains in this work [*Perséphone*] a simplicity which can be called Classical although it does not recall – or rather because it does not in any way recall – the procedures consecrated before his time by the practice of the masters to achieve that effect. He has been striving towards it for a long time, restraining at all costs the dazzling ardour which so seduced us in *L'Oiseau de feu*, *Petrouchka* and *Le Sacre du printemps*. We were able to admire unreservedly certain works in this second manner, like *Le Rossignol* and *Histoire du soldat*, in which the reform had not yet been carried to its furthest point and so left him his freedom of movement, and his richness of colour. But other works betrayed a voluntary abstention and from time to time donned borrowed forms. He continued, however, deaf to our cries of alarm, digging in stony ground, plunging into the night, and he was certainly right, for he is now coming out of the tunnel into the light, into another land where his wishes are fulfilled.[52]

In 1930 Paul Collaer, who had helped arrange Stravinsky's Belgian concerts, brought out a study generously illustrated with music examples. Some of the key Stravinskian terms and ideas of this period occur ('objectivisme',[53] 'objectivité intégrale',[54] and 'classicisme'[55]), and the author incorporates an article by Ernest Ansermet on *The Soldier's Tale*.[56] On the other hand, while *Oedipus Rex*, the Octuor, and the Serenade are recognised as the equals of *Mavra* (the most recent work considered at length),

> [t]he *Concerto for Piano* . . . makes us think too much of Bach. The balance between the old elements and Stravinsky's personal contribution, so agreeable in *Mavra* or *Oedipus Rex*, is here disrupted in favour of Bach and to the detriment of Stravinsky.[57]

The idea of the grand division between the musical cultures of Germany, on the one hand, and France and Russia on the other[58] is also explored here; this was not incompatible, however, with learning from the music of J. S. Bach, for 'German' music meant principally that of Wagner and Strauss.

André Schaeffner's book-length study of the composer published in 1931 considers Stravinsky's compositions in the context of contemporary French music. It was written with the objective of 'reproducing as exactly as possible the course to date of the life and work of Igor Stravinsky' at a time when 'a good many legends about Stravinsky are already spreading'.[59] (Stravinsky himself complained that 'in numerous interviews I have given, my thoughts, my words, and even facts have often been disfigured to the extent of becoming absolutely unrecognizable'.[60]) The writer acknowledges the 'spontaneous help' given to him by the composer, and uses the composer's words – but only when corroboration was available. In spite of the likelihood, given this framework, of promulgating the composer's views as they were at the beginning of the 1930s rather than at the specific periods when earlier works were composed, Schaeffner offers some interesting *aperçus* – for instance, when he notes a peculiarly Parisian practice of surrounding events in the theatre with a huge *scandale* (mentioning the premiere of Victor Hugo's play *Hernani* in 1830).[61] While noting Stravinsky's penchant for appropriating the styles of other composers,[62] he concludes by pointing to the progress of 'one and the same art of which eventually, probably, the unity, manifold and wandering, will be underlined'.[63] Stravinsky wrote of this book on 2 July 1931 to one of his publishers that 'Schaeffner's documentation is precise . . . .'[64]

Stravinsky reception in European countries other than France was to a degree dependent on performances by the Ballets Russes. In countries that they visited – notably Britain, Spain and Italy – there was some awareness of Stravinsky's music; these tended to be countries where there was some political sympathy with Russia before 1914. Switzerland was, of course, exposed to some of Stravinsky's works during wartime, but this meant that, on the whole, the pieces written then became known in Switzerland before their larger-scale predecessors. The same was true of Germany and Austria. There is little evidence of performances before 1914, and still less, for obvious reasons, between 1914 and 1918. Even after the end of the war, it was some time before musical life was restored. And for such a period the shorter, small-scale compositions of Stravinsky's Swiss years were ideal. A decisive moment was the ISCM concert in Berlin on 19 November 1922, when Ansermet gave *The Rite of Spring* its German premiere. Just as Paris and London took the young Stravinsky as an unmistakably Russian figure, so did Berlin – except that for Germans of that generation Russia meant a somewhat menacing nearby power still identified with aspects of barbarism. This is evident in Adolf Weissmann's reaction to the work:

> Stravinsky is a product of his race and of our time . . . Stravinsky is
> certainly not a musician of culture. An element of barbarism still throbs
> within him and he does not shy away from declaring it openly. In that
> respect he is absolutely Russian.[65]

This view is symptomatic of an attitude to Russian music still sometimes encountered among countrymen of Bach, Beethoven and Wagner, whose understandable devotion to their own tradition deafens them to their neighbours' music. A variant of this view, intensified by the strong emotions left by the humiliating Versailles treaty, was voiced by Alfred Heuss in 1923, after the Gewandhaus's *Rite* premiere:

> Should Stravinsky, that Russian torturer, be performed in Germany?
> Even now, everyone does as he wants. We have gradually sunk so low
> that particularly musicians who set the tone approach what they
> perform thinking only about whether it will create a great sensation.
> Foxtrots, Negro songs [*Niggersongs*], Russian peasant hideosities and
> other such things.[66]

The first German book on Stravinsky appeared in 1931, by which time Klemperer, Scherchen and other conductors had introduced the composer's newer music to Weimar Republic audiences. The author was the otherwise unknown Herbert Fleischer, but the publisher was one that was important to the composer: Edition russe de musique, founded by Serge Koussevitzky, operating from its Berlin office as Russischer Musikverlag. The aim was to see Stravinsky 'as representative of the culture of his era, as the leader of a generation, as a person of our time'.[67] Surprisingly, the book does not seem strongly influenced by the composer in major matters, though there is one good anecdote where Stravinsky claims that a bell-ringer's limited room for rhythmic or expressive manoeuvre in performance makes him the prototype of an ideal conductor.[68] Among the book's noteworthy features are the detailed discussion, in descriptive vein, of a small number of large-scale works (*Petrushka, The Rite of Spring, Les Noces, Oedipus Rex* and the *Symphony of Psalms*), accompanied by 194 music examples. It is also the first text which, while showing awareness of the composer's Russian and French background, considers his work in the light of musical developments in the German-speaking world. Thus Schoenberg, Hindemith and Weill are mentioned, and in one place also Mahler (the Third and Tenth Symphonies and *Das Lied von der Erde*). The most extended comparison (though it is not pursued far) is between Stravinsky and Schoenberg.

> What a difference between Schoenberg's pure, abstract constructivism and Stravinsky's most natural music-making using earth soaked in blood! Stravinsky proves that the *most stringent, almost mathematical construction and the most natural idea are not mutually exclusive opposites*: at least, not for the creative artist of our time.[69]

During the pre-war Hitler years, it was not certain whether Stravinsky was to be regarded officially as a link in a sinister chain joining Bolshevik and Jewish conspiracies or as a right-thinking, safe composer. It is a sign of how much the German marketplace meant to Stravinsky that he gave Willy Strecker (of the music publisher Schott) so much evidence (through an exchange of letters) establishing that his music did not belong in a 'Degenerate Art' exhibition and that he was not of Semitic descent.[70]

Stravinsky's American years

One of the most influential critiques of Stravinsky's work is that of Theodor Adorno. His interpretation is generally understood to place Stravinsky and Schoenberg as the opposite poles in twentieth-century music.[71] His *Philosophie der neuen Musik*, first published in 1949 (and, as *Philosophy of Modern Music*, in 1973) was, however, neither the first nor the last to propound this view. He was, in fact, teasing out in his own way a strand that had run through criticism for a long time. In 1914 Myaskovsky had discerned much in common between the harmonic thinking of Schoenberg and that of Stravinsky, with similar results achieved by composers proceeding by two different routes: Schoenberg from Wagner by way of Mahler, and Stravinsky from Rimsky-Korsakov via Skryabin and certain French composers.[72] Schloezer, teeth gritted on behalf of the patriotic readership of the *Nouvelle Revue française*, recognised that by 1924 European musical leadership was in the hands of those two composers.[73] The point was repeated in Vienna (by Julius Korngold[74] and Paul Stefan[75]) when *The Rite of Spring* arrived there in 1925; if this was those critics' first encounter with *The*

Rite, we cannot be sure what they knew of developments in Schoenberg's aesthetics and language since 1913.

Adorno's critique – just like all the rest, of course – is a product of its author's time and milieu. The present-day reader perceives that, for the Adorno of the 1940s, there was something inevitable about the Second Viennese School's work. For all Adorno's insights into Stravinsky, however, the Russo-French composer stood for something rather outside his range. The greater space is devoted to Schoenberg, who is considered first, thus prompting the reader to regard his work as somehow normative, whereas Stravinsky's is not.

This reading enjoyed a deep resonance among the western European avant garde in its heyday in the 1950s. Boulez, Stockhausen and their Darmstadt followers recognised a kindred spirit in the Viennese composer who composed with manifest rigour, disdaining popular success and therefore avoiding any danger of consequent commercialisation. Stravinsky's work, by contrast, represented the musical establishment, when they were looking for fresh excitement from newer sources. They sought a 'renewed modernism', as G. W. Hopkins called it (in the 'Boulez' entry in the *New Grove*[76]), whereas Stravinsky was accepted at his own pre-war valuation as an anti-modernist.

Boulez held certain works, especially *The Rite of Spring*, in great respect; his 1953 essay 'Strawinsky demeure' is devoted to an examination of its rhythm, and elsewhere Boulez made clear that he most prized the older composer as an innovator in rhythm.[77] As a conductor, Boulez included Stravinsky selectively among the twentieth-century composers he championed. Yet the ideals of Boulez as composer admitted only certain works:

> it is impossible to avoid asking questions with a degree of anguish about the Stravinsky 'case'. How can one explain the speeded-up exhaustion which shows itself, after *Les Noces*, in a sclerosis in all spheres – in harmony and melody, where one ends up with a faked academicism, and even rhythmically, where one sees a painful atrophy appearing?[78]

It was, then, the 'neoclassical' works that Boulez found impossible to accept, with their 'reworkings' of fragments drawn from previous music (see Boulez on *Pulcinella* above). The later Boulez knew the works of Stravinsky's final period, when Schoenberg and Webern were added to the Russian composer's armoury.

In his final phase, Stravinsky presented perhaps his greatest challenge to listeners and critics. In the words of Massimo Mila, writing in 1956:

> between the wars Stravinsky was the personification of neo-classicism; in him it achieved a depth and a splendour not found in any of its other exponents. Now that the age of neo-classicism is over . . .

> Stravinsky . . . has edged closer and closer to the opposite extreme of
> contemporary musical sensibility of which he was for so long the
> antithesis.[79]

A number of old friends and admirers failed to follow him in his embrace
of twelve-note serialism, so great did the change of direction appear. Yet a
few years later, and with the experience of works from *Threni* to the *Requiem
Canticles*, the perspective had changed:

> It becomes clearer every day that figures like Debussy, Stravinsky,
> Schoenberg, Berg and Webern, far from being mutually exclusive, were
> needed in their different ways to forge what we see today as the new
> universal language of music in its various dimensions and its varied
> aspects. The seemingly inevitable division and segregation into
> watertight compartments of the different outlooks and movements
> which appeared as if they were leading twentieth-century music along
> different paths is at present disappearing; indeed, in retrospect the
> apparent antagonism seems like a figment of the imagination rather than
> concrete fact.[80]

Stravinsky took a dim view of many critics who worked in his final
homeland, considering Virgil Thomson and Olin Downes in particular as
long-term foes. Nicolas Nabokov wrote on 13 October 1943 to ask Stravinsky
to send him 'any particularly stupid reviews that you may happen to have,
Downes's for example'.[81] Stravinsky's resentment against some critics is
evident in the following observation from 1962:

> As for Brother Criticus, I do not wish to spoil my temper, and my book,
> by speaking of *him* here.

A footnote follows:

> The open-door policy to new music in England in the last few years was
> made possible to a great extent by the accession of an intelligent younger
> generation in the musical press. In consequence, London has become a
> great capital of contemporary music. New York could and should be
> such a capital, too, for it boasts a greater number of fine instrumentalists
> than any city in the world. But New York must clean its journalistic
> house first.[82]

Some composers and performers make it a point of honour not to dispute
with critics who they think have done them down. This attitude allows them
to occupy higher ground than the lowly hacks. Posterity, they reckon, will see
matters in their true light, and right the wrongs of the detestable present.
This approach is taken by Ernst Krenek in writing to Stravinsky on 21
January 1962:

Naturally, your angry refutation of [Albert] Goldberg's misstatements [in a review of *The Rake's Progress* in the *Los Angeles Times*] is entirely justified, and so is your exasperation with his general attitude toward new music. Unfortunately, the vagueness of the subject matter and the standards prevailing in our society make it very difficult for the artist to take exception to unfair criticism because the critic can always claim that his judgment was based on subjective opinion (which Mr. Goldberg predictably has done immediately). That, again unfortunately, reduces the controversy in the public eye to a conflict of disadvantage because the artist is suspected of having an axe to grind, while the critic is basking in the light of the (however unwarranted) assumption that he is unbiased. Thus it is usually a thankless task for the artist to reply to his critics. Perhaps silent contempt is the best punishment, although one's patience frequently is taxed to the breaking point.[83]

Stravinsky's reply of 7 February indicates that he too subscribed to the principle but offers an explanation for behaving differently in this case:

Your letter gave me much satisfaction. I share your attitude towards the critics and if I did not keep silence this time it is because I wanted to help the young generation to act. I have nothing to lose with the Goldbergs of the world: too old for that.[84]

A feeling of moral superiority warms the heart, but a dash of controversy is better for the box office (not to mention the royalties).

Stravinsky's replies to several notices in the *Los Angeles Times* (in 1962 and 1970[85]) and the *New York Times* (in 1965, 1970 and 1971[86]) illustrate his intense interest in how his work was viewed. (Correspondence with M. D. Calvocoressi from London provides evidence of this interest much earlier, in 1913.[87]) Stravinsky protested about various statements made by Albert Goldberg and Martin Bernheimer in the west-coast newspaper, and Harold Schonberg and Clive Barnes in the east-coast one. The virtuosity in using the English language suggests Robert Craft's hand, but the zest – flowing, presumably from the composer himself – was equal to that evident when squibs were launched earlier in Stravinsky's career.

Recent critics have tended to find common ground where their predecessors saw only sharp antagonisms. Thus wrote Charles Rosen in 1975:

Neoclassicism and serialism (or twelve-tone music) are often considered polar opposites. The enmity between Vienna and Paris, between the school of Schoenberg and the school of Stravinsky, is a fact of history . . . This opposition has long since broken down: not only have the two 'schools' drawn closer together, but their differences – even at the height of the crossfire in the late 1920s – no longer seem significant.[88]

A sense of the fundamentally Stravinskian quality of Stravinsky's music, of its basic unity in spite of the many evident differences, is now frequently expressed.

Conclusion

Audiences in the present like their picture of contemporary art to be limned in vivid colours, with heroes and villains embodying opposing parties. It is in the interest of composers too, as they forge ahead of colleagues less musically gifted (or simply less publicity-conscious) to claim their work as more new, radical and challenging than that of predecessors or coevals. Many of these claims will be couched in simple phrases that try to encapsulate much larger ideas. Milton Babbitt wrote in 1971 about what he considered a slick, meaningless catchphrase:

> To Stravinsky, 'back to Bach' was just that, an alliteratively catchy slogan, which had no pertinence to professional activity or professional discourse. It was there, permitted to be concocted, like 'neoclassicism', to be talked about by those who could not and should not talk about the music, who didn't even bother to hear the music, but who, when they bandied about the catch words, were 'talking about Stravinsky'.[89]

One of the functions critics perform, in the guise of sifting good from less good, is to present the views of one composer or another, one camp or another, to the musical community. They thereby help spread awareness of the issues involved. The work of a great composer will not lend itself to crude pigeon-holing, but will take a route that is unpredictable and (in the strict sense) peculiar because prompted by the composer's genius. Critics' attempts to connect specific works with specific models or assign them to particular traditions will be hampered by a great composer's idiosyncratic selection of his own methods and style. As Jonathan Cross has put it:

> Whereas Adorno tried to evaluate Stravinsky in an Austro-German context, for Taruskin the enormity of Stravinsky's achievement and, indeed, the very root of his modernity are a result of his willingness... to be an out-and-out Russian composer.[90]

The attempt to identify conjunctions and affiliations is none the less valid, and whether composers like or dislike the results, the process is established and probably ineradicable. Though Stravinsky thought that critics gave him a hard time, he would have had a harder time without them.

13 Composing with Stravinsky

LOUIS ANDRIESSEN AND JONATHAN CROSS

The true influence of Stravinsky has only just begun.   ANDRIESSEN AND
SCHÖNBERGER, 1989[1]

Stravinsky into the twenty-first century

JONATHAN CROSS

There was a time when the course of twentieth-century music was charted
almost exclusively in terms of Austro-German modernism.[2] While certain
key non-Teutonic early-modern works were recognised for their revolutionary status – among them, Debussy's *Prélude à l'après-midi d'un faune*, Ives's
'Concord' Sonata, Bartók's *Miraculous Mandarin* and, of course, Stravinsky's
The Rite of Spring – the development of the avant garde was constructed in
general in relation to a line starting with Schoenberg and his two most
famous pupils, and projecting itself through its Darmstadt manifestations
(Boulez, Stockhausen) into the future. And this is precisely how Schoenberg
himself imagined history would turn out when, on developing his twelve-
note method of composition, he declared: 'Today I have discovered something that will ensure the supremacy of German music for the next hundred
years.'[3] In 1951, Pierre Boulez attempted to perpetuate Schoenberg's myth
by proclaiming that 'since the discoveries of the Viennese School, all non-
serial composers are *useless*'[4] (not a view he would necessarily hold today).
Led in the 1940s by Theodor Adorno (most notably in *Philosophie der
neuen Musik*) – a highly influential figure at Darmstadt – Schoenberg and
Stravinsky were pitted against each other as polar opposites: Schoenberg
the Progressive, Stravinsky the Regressive. It became fashionable to dismiss
Stravinsky as a mere neoclassicist (as if Schoenberg, too, were not guilty of
such a charge). It was only when, following the death of Schoenberg in 1951,
Stravinsky himself turned towards serialism, that he was seen to have joined
the 'mainstream' (Adorno expressed his 'pleasure' in 'Stravinsky's departure from the reactionary camp'[5]). In fact, what happened to Stravinsky in
the 1950s is an extraordinary and virtually unprecedented phenomenon:
having inspired a younger generation of composers early in the century,
he was later in life to be influenced himself by those younger generations.
It seems Stravinsky was fascinated by the goings-on at Darmstadt and was
present at – among other things – the premiere of Boulez's *Structures*, as

well as being deeply affected by Robert Craft's American performances of Webern.

> Of course, it requires greater effort to learn from one's juniors... But when you are seventy-five and your generation has overlapped with four younger ones, it behoves you not to decide in advance 'how far composers can go', but to try to discover whatever new thing it is makes the new generation new.[6]

Stravinsky's own *Movements* for piano and orchestra of 1958–9 is a clear response to the Webern-inspired experiments of his younger colleagues. Yet Stravinsky went on to develop his own brand of (not necessarily dodecaphonic) serialism that anticipated the re-evaluation of the twelve-note method that took place in the last few decades of the twentieth century. In this regard, the slightly earlier *Agon* is fascinating. Cited by figures as diverse as Birtwistle, Boulez, Carter and Tavener, its influence on younger composers has proved to be as much a result of its formal structure, its acutely heard orchestration, and its balancing of diatonic, chromatic and twelve-note materials, as of its serial organisation *per se*.

But – to introduce a theme explored by Louis Andriessen in the conversation that follows – how is Stravinsky still a revolutionary figure for the twenty-first century? We can certainly say that Stravinsky's legacy to the whole of the twentieth century has been enormous. This has only gradually become clear as Stravinsky emerged from Schoenberg's dominant shadow, as the history of modernism has been rewritten to take account of a far wider network of influences. There have, of course, been composers who have directly imitated aspects of Stravinsky's musical language, from contemporaries such as Varèse and Antheil, through Poulenc, Orff and Copland (the 'Brooklyn' Stravinsky), to countless contemporary film composers (listen to John Williams's music for Steven Spielberg's *Jaws* and you will hear *The Rite of Spring* at almost every turn). But Stravinsky's influence has also been far more subtle and far-reaching than these examples might at first suggest.

Take just one work: *The Rite*. It has certainly had its imitators. But the power of its rhythmic and metric innovations, its block structures and simultaneous layering of musical ideas, its phenomenal orchestration, its sheer elemental energy – all these radical features have ensured that *The Rite* has cast a strong shadow over the entire century. Varèse's *Amériques*, Messiaen's *Turangalîla-symphonie*, Xenakis's *Metastasis*, Carter's Double Concerto for piano and harpsichord (which Stravinsky himself described as a 'masterpiece'), and Birtwistle's *Earth Dances* are all modelled in fascinating ways on aspects of *The Rite of Spring*.

Other works by Stravinsky have proved to be equally influential. The unrelenting rhythmic energy of *Les Noces* is, if anything, even more powerful than that of *The Rite*, and certainly more sustained – a feature that was picked up and pushed to extremes in Antheil's extraordinary *Ballet mécanique*. And its ritualised concluding bells ring right across the twentieth century into the spiritual rituals of, for example, Arvo Pärt.

In purely structural terms, Stravinsky's most influential work has undoubtedly been the *Symphonies of Wind Instruments*.[7] Its aesthetic is described by Taruskin using the Russian word *drobnost'*, which he defines as '"splinteredness"; the quality of being formally disunified, a sum-of-parts'.[8] This can be related to the cut-and-paste techniques of film production. In the *Symphonies* this manifests itself as a mosaic-like organisation whose consequences can be heard echoed in the 'episodic' organisation of music as diverse as Messiaen's *Cantéyodjayâ* and *Couleurs de la cité céleste*, Tippett's Piano Sonata no. 2 and his opera *King Priam*, Stockhausen's *Momente*, Andriessen's *De Staat*, everywhere in Birtwistle and Xenakis, even – in places – in Ferneyhough. This is not to say that block structures are not found elsewhere in Stravinsky (they are certainly also clearly present in *Petrushka* and *The Rite*), and indeed in the music of other composers such as Debussy (most notably in *Jeux*). But the *Symphonies* is the boldest expression of *drobnost'*: its confident anti-organic stance sets it in stark opposition to contemporary through-composed German music, and it remains – even almost a hundred years on – one of the freshest and most imaginative works of the twentieth century.

One of the defining features of Stravinsky's music that distinguishes it most clearly from other strands of modernism is its sense of ritual. It was to this dimension of his music, among other things, that Stravinsky was referring when he famously wrote in his *Autobiography* that music is powerless to express anything at all. It is not that this music is without emotion: rather, it is concerned with an expression of communal, collective experiences; it is symbolic and stylised rather than representational; it taps into ancient, timeless ceremonies and acts of worship. This is variously evident in such stage works as *The Rite*, *Oedipus Rex* and *The Flood*, and also in the almost Brechtian 'alienation' achieved in such works as *Renard*, *The Soldier's Tale* and *The Rake's Progress*. But it is evident in so many of his concert works too: the ritualised final chorale of the *Symphonies of Wind Instruments*, the folk rituals of *Les Noces*, the religious rituals of the *Symphony of Psalms* and *Requiem Canticles*, the instrument role-play of the *Three Pieces for String Quartet*. While it is true that many playwrights were also exploring ritualised, non-narrative theatres at the same time, Stravinsky's brand of musical ritual has proved a fruitful model for composers as diverse as Berio and Reich, Maxwell Davies and Henze.

Finally, Stravinsky has become increasingly important to us because of the ways in which he anticipates so many of the concerns of our postmodern age. The breaking down of the barriers between so-called 'high' and 'low' art by means of his free use of popular musical materials (*Ragtime*, the *Ebony Concerto*, even aspects of the *Symphony in Three Movements*) pre-echoes the thinking of many of today's 'crossover' artists. The boundaries between 'classical', 'experimental', 'rock', 'pop' and 'jazz' have been infinitely stretched, as demonstrated by (in the Netherlands) Andriessen and his work with De Volharding, or (in the USA) Michael Gordon, or (in the UK) Steve Martland and Michael Nyman. And where would so many minimal and post-minimal composers be without Stravinsky (Reich, Adams, Torke, Fitkin, etc.)? Not only their attitudes to the materials that they use, not only the rhythmic vitality of their music, but their very sound-world is deeply indebted to Stravinsky. (Just compare the opening of Adams's frequently performed *Short Ride in a Fast Machine* with the opening of *Petrushka*.) Stravinsky was never a postmodernist; he was 'essentially a pre-postmodern composer'.[9] But by placing past music and contemporary popular musics in new contexts he enabled us to see them in new ways, he suggested rich compositional possibilities. The past becomes a part of the present. This is why *The Rake's Progress* is such an important work, because it can be understood on so many different levels, from pastiche Mozart to a powerful critique of the whole of operatic history. If Schoenberg's legacy to the century was his method, then Stravinsky's legacy was his attitude.[10]

Arnold Schoenberg dominated the first half of the twentieth century. It could be said that John Cage dominated the second half. But increasingly it is being acknowledged that, in so many different ways, the twentieth century was Stravinsky's century. And it is only in recent decades that composers of so many persuasions have felt able wholeheartedly to acknowledge their indebtedness to Stravinsky. While it might be argued that the possibilities suggested by serialism and aleatoricism have been exhausted, composers today are still freely working with the ideas and even the materials bestowed by Stravinsky. At the beginning of a new century, it will be fascinating to see how far Andriessen's assertion holds up: the true influence of Stravinsky has only just begun.

Composing with Stravinsky

LOUIS ANDRIESSEN IN CONVERSATION
WITH JONATHAN CROSS[11]

Jonathan Cross *You have often said that you believe the music of Stravinsky to be important for the twenty-first century as well as for the twentieth. Further, you wrote in your book that the 'true influence of Stravinsky keeps* *beginning all over again*.[12] *Do you still stand by these statements? In what ways do you think they are still true today?*

Louis Andriessen There was a great deal of wishful thinking in those statements! I hope that they're still true and I don't have any strong reason to feel that the situation has changed very much. In the first place, it has to do not with Stravinsky's attitude to musical material, which is a philosophical subject, but more with the social element in his music, its social character. By this I mean Stravinsky's idea of the anti-hierarchical nature of musical sources and materials. I think that was Stravinsky's most important step forward compared with what Schoenberg did, who had tried to democratise only the pitches. It looks as if I might be right: with the advent of what is called postmodernism, modernism (complex chromatic music) seems no longer to be the future of music but more like the final dead-end of German Romanticism.

I already had my doubts about it in the late 1950s/early 1960s, and many more people are on my side now. I do think that young composers – America is a good example – have turned away from what they call Eurocentric thinking. They have started to understand that there are all kinds of other musics that can be very important to study and to use in the development of their musical languages. Of course, there is also a neo-colonial side to American culture which I hate, which they call 'world music'. That is all disgusting.

JC *This is not democratic at all, then?*

LA On the contrary. It is a kind of capitalist colonialism. But there is this other side. Steve Reich is probably an elegant example. Precedents for such thinking can be found in Stravinsky's music, even in the early works. That is what I meant by Stravinsky's influence.

JC *Do you think, in that case, that Schoenberg and Webern have had their day, that their influence has run its course?*

LA Well, the problem is that history is not one line. But I think it's true: certainly for Schoenberg it's true. But since Schoenberg created late Webern, we get into difficulty, because late Webern has something to do with a non-developmental form which is very traditional and classical, not Romantic at all, and which is much closer to Josquin. From there we get back to Stravinsky. And probably also Morton Feldman, whom I regard as a very important composer. So with geniuses like Anton Webern – and Schoenberg – it's very difficult to pin them down historically. And it's the same when you talk more generally about serialism. Of course, there is an enormous amount of very stupid and muddy music written in the style, but there are also the masterpieces of Stockhausen and Boulez, who are very important composers. They were historically necessary. On the other hand, serial thinking itself, when you abstract it from the acute twelve-note works, is extremely strong, a very important way out of all the silly optimistic music which was written before and after the Second World War. All those Sinfoniettas for String Orchestra, all the Carl Orff stuff, and all that second-hand music.

JC *So, serial thought remains important, even though the influence of Schoenberg himself has declined?*

LA The funny thing is that when Boulez and Stockhausen did what they did in the late 1940s, they didn't think for one minute that it had anything to do with German Romanticism. They had no idea. Stockhausen worked in studios. He was busy finding completely new sounds and (he thought) new musical ideas. I remember a conference on electronic music in Venice in 1958. Nono was there, Berio, Germans also: I met a lot of impressive people. And then Holland showed up with a little octatonic, optimistic piece for violin and electronics by Henk Badings. The music really offended people like Nono who believed you should not combine old musical material with new media. The new medium meant, for them, new musical thinking.

JC *Boulez, it seems to me, is a very interesting figure because, on the one hand, we immediately think of him as part of that Darmstadt generation of the late 1940s who reinterpreted Webern, but, on the other hand, he's a very Stravinskian composer.*

LA Yes, he would admit that.

JC *Not just as a result of his famous analysis of* The Rite of Spring *but because of the kind of compositional attitude he has: an interest in ritual, in building large structures out of relatively limited material, constantly reviewing ideas rather than their being developed in a Schoenbergian sense.*

LA He's not a Romantic or an Expressionist composer at all. In the best French tradition, he's an *artisanat* composer. He would not have read Maritain much, but on the philosophical level he's much more a Stravinskian than a Schoenbergian. In fact, he was one of the first to say that Schoenberg was dead.

JC *Can you remember the first piece of Stravinsky you ever heard?*

LA No! What I remember very strongly were the 78 rpm records we had of *The Rite of Spring*. It was a very good recording (I think it was Telefunken: Eduard van Beinem with the Concertgebouw Orchestra) which was one of the few records we had in the house in the early 1950s. We also played a lot of piano for four hands as a family. I suppose I must have heard other Stravinsky before that, but this is my strongest, longest love. There was a score in the house too, though not a piano four hands version.

JC *So was Stravinsky – and* The Rite *in particular – important to your father as a composer?*

LA In 1950 – I was ten years old then – we moved from Utrecht to Den Haag. I remember the score of *Oedipus Rex* was in the house, and the *Symphony of Psalms*. There was also a recording of the *Symphony of Psalms*. My father always talked of it with much admiration. His only criticism was that he found the choral writing too stiff, too square. It was a recurrent theme of his: as a Catholic composer, he was deeply rooted in brilliant choral writing (all those Masses in the French or Italian style).

JC *You have also said of* The Rite *that it is a key work for the twenty-first century. Clearly it was an influential work in its day and you can easily see the shadow that* The Rite *has cast on the twentieth century. But what leads you to say that even for the twenty-first century it's a revolutionary work?*

LA I think it still makes sense to say this. What we and the next age have to learn from *The Rite* is not, in the first place, the development of rhythm, but the magical combination of diatonic melodic material and chromatic harmonic material. That's a key point that Stravinsky never talked about. It's very clear. It's the crux of the piece, much more than the 'oompa-oompa-oompa'. I think the strange combination of very simple melodies with very refined harmony is still a secret. We all try to find how it works and nobody will ever find the answer: that's the magic of *The Rite*, I suppose. I think that's the idea of crossing the borders of highbrow and lowbrow music.

JC *In what way, precisely – the high and the low working together?*

LA Well, the melodies are just little pop songs, basically! But the harmonies are linked much more closely to what happened at that time in the most advanced music of Skryabin, Ravel – that is, the people he was really influenced by.

JC *And Rimsky-Korsakov, of course.*

LA Yes. Always Rimsky.

JC *I find that very interesting. We know all those pieces from the 1920s and 1930s that imitate the most obvious rhythmic features of Stravinsky (you mentioned Carl Orff). One tires of it so quickly. But what is so exciting to me about a work like* Les Noces *is precisely that its harmonic complexity is virtually impossible to imitate.*

LA And the combination [of harmony and rhythm]. The harmonies were already used in part by Ravel and Debussy. But then it's still only the harmonies. Stravinsky seems to be different.

JC *In what sense have you worked consciously with Stravinsky? What have you as a composer drawn from Stravinsky?*

LA I would probably now say different things from what I said in *The Apollonian Clockwork*. Basically, a lot of that book is about what I did. It's my homage to composing. But the way I think of it now is that what I call an 'attitude towards material' is by far the most important thing. I also find this same attitude in other arts and I make connections with them. Nabokov is a very good example in literature; Picasso in the visual arts. We give some examples of composers in the book. It has to do with what I call alienation. You start at a distance. Distance is necessary to protect your vulnerability as a composer. Irony has to do with protecting your sentiments. And then you are freed for composing. I don't mean irony in the sense of saying the opposite of what you mean. It is a very profound form of philosophy in art. I discovered in recent years that the word irony was used by German philosophers around the time of Hegel. Schlegel spoke of dramatic irony. This was the start of Romanticism. This early Romantic period is also very interesting in music, I think: Berlioz, Mendelssohn, Chopin are very important. Later there is no irony; they fall into sentimentality. There's a big difference.

JC *Do you think that was what Stravinsky was getting at in his much misquoted and misunderstood statement about music being powerless to express anything at all? Some take this simply as a credo of art for art's sake, but could it in fact have something to do with this ironic distancing?*

LA I think ultimately it has to do with his love for early or non-Romantic music. You should realise that, at that time, Romantic music was all you heard. That was musical life in Europe. There was no new practice, no Baroque practice, there was no contemporary music. That was what Stravinsky criticised: an angry young man railing against this bourgeois practice. However, it is a little bit more precise and profound than that: you see in his Harvard lectures that he must have discussed the whole *artisanat* philosophy with Roland-Manuel . . .

JC *Yes. But it is a problem that much of* Poetics of Music *wasn't actually written by Stravinsky.*

LA But they [Stravinsky, Alexis Roland-Manuel and Pierre Souvtchinsky] must have had discussions. Stravinsky said what he wanted to say.

JC *And he kept on saying it, and it became more and more rigidified. You are very engaged politically as a musician, not just in the music you write but in the way you wish your music to be understood, the context within which it is to be played. How do you relate to that aspect of Stravinsky who – at least on the surface – seemed totally disengaged politically? Is that problematic for you?*

LA No. The person has very little to do with his work. As I said in the heat of political struggle in the 1960s and 70s, a good communist is not necessarily a good composer, and vice versa. Stravinsky's music crosses social and geographical borders. Stravinsky opposed the class-based society in Europe of the early twentieth century.

JC *Could we talk a little more about the specifics of Stravinsky's music? The Stravinsky 'sound' is something I hear in your music: an acute attention to the way in which voices move, how they're placed, and so on...*

LA It certainly has something to do with voice leading. There's what we call in the book the 'unison as utopia'. There's a kind of voice leading which is completely 'wrong' from one voice to another, all the time. And this 'wrongness' in his music after 1920 he stole from Bach. In the book we talk about playing the 'Brandenburg' Concertos for four hands – there you see how Bach has very funny voice leading all the time. In Stravinsky it's completely different: in every bar there's one note out of place, completely wrong. But it sounds *almost* right; that's so funny. That's very typical for Stravinsky, I think. His instrumentation is ultimately of lesser importance. And there are a lot of other things, like his harmonic rhythm, which is very strange.

I gave a lesson today to a young composer who works with Ligeti-like development of little musical 'quarks'. Today I criticised the fact that he likes to write in 4/4; he changes the tempo, but 4/4 is easy for him to do. And then I told him of the possibility of a dialectical situation with the bass seeming to be rhythmical but which is sometimes on and sometimes off the beat. Stravinsky achieves this with time-signature changes. Why does he do that? The melody is extremely important for him but he makes the bass sometimes syncopated, sometimes not. It becomes very light: that's what he wants. You show this to your pupils to make them looser or more flexible. But they should not imitate.

JC *What fascinates me is Stravinsky's theatre and the different kinds of theatres he's built. We've talked about alienation, but ritual is also important and, it seems to me, it's an important part of what you do in your theatre pieces too. Is the Stravinskian idea of theatre something you keep coming back to?*

LA I think theatre is absolutely essential. Diaghilev must have had an incredible influence on Stravinsky. Boulez once asked what would have happened had Stravinsky and Brecht worked together.

JC *But Brecht always wanted his audience to remain disengaged from the action, which I'm not convinced Stravinsky did.*

LA But that is later, much later. In the 1920s I think what he wanted to do with *Oedipus Rex* was very Brechtian. Brecht was one of the first to study non-Western theatre: he knew everything about Noh theatre; he studied Chinese things. It's the same attitude, I think.

JC *Do you think about Brecht when you're making your theatre pieces?*

LA I had a lot of experience working for a theatre group in the 1970s –
Baal it was called, which is also the title of Brecht's first play. They were
completely crazy! The little operas we did (with a lot of spoken
dialogue) made me the theatre man I became. Before that I had already
done film and theatre music, I worked with dance people; I had even
done puppet theatre music by the time I was fifteen. Yes, I feel very
much that Brecht is there.

JC *What about film? This was a medium Stravinsky didn't really work in at
all. One would imagine that the kind of music he wrote would have worked
very well with film.*

LA At that time, film was only a commercial attraction. It had nothing
really to do with any art form at all, with a few exceptions. There was
some avant-garde film-making in the 1920s in Europe, and of course
there was Buñuel. Nobody knew this work in the 20s. Hollywood meant
only third-rate art . . . and money. Sometimes Stravinsky tried it, and he
got a commission [for *Jane Eyre*, with Orson Welles as Rochester]. Of
course, they thought it crazy music. They couldn't use it and they asked
somebody else [Bernard Herrmann]. But they paid him. Nowadays,
with video, it's different. You can do crazy things. But in Stravinsky's
time the medium was not interesting; theatre was much more advanced.

JC *How do you view the current situation of new music in the Netherlands,
both through your own pupils and other composers around you? It's often
said anecdotally that Stravinsky has always been very important for
post-Second World War Dutch composers. Would you say this is still true?*

LA I still believe it's true. I suppose the fact that we were liberated by
Canadians and Americans means that the influence of American culture
in general – both positively and negatively – has been much stronger in
Holland than even in England and certainly than in Germany and
France. I think the influence of American film culture and American
jazz was extremely strong. That's why the musical scene here since the
1960s has been different – in general more Stravinsky- or Varèse-
oriented . . . American-oriented, I would say. Stravinsky could almost
have been considered an American composer by then.

Perhaps it's also because we don't have mountains: the land is flat, the
light is sharp. People say it has to do with Calvinism. There's a lot of
very strong reformed Protestantism in Holland and many composers
like to be very rigid . . . like Mondrian, as an example in art. But I think
it's amazing how many things are possible here, and I think this is why
Stravinsky is supposedly very important.

It has also to do with jazz music, improvisational music, which is very
strong in Holland. This is also close to American culture. Thinking of
Schoenberg or Webern and jazz is totally impossible. The big advantage

[of the presence of strong jazz departments in all the major Dutch conservatoires] for what I'm doing, and for the future, is the emancipation of so-called lowbrow instruments like guitar or saxophone or percussion. Nowadays, Dutch saxophone players can play everything. They can improvise fantastically, they play all the bebop changes; but they can also play all my music. I need that kind of saxophone player, not the French-style elegance. The guitar's the same. When I wrote the very difficult bass guitar part in *De Staat* in 1976 there was one brilliant guy who could do a reasonably good job. Nowadays several players can do it.

But there is this Dutch sound. Cornelis de Bondt, for instance, is very Dutch: his is a really new approach to Stravinsky. Totally new.

JC *You've spent a fair amount of time in America where your music is very popular. What do you see there? Is it possible to generalise about what young composers in America are doing now?*

LA In general, you should not generalise.

JC *But are there certain trends you observe?*

LA I think that, in general, composers in America are less historically aware; in Europe we have much more the feeling that there is this profound support from history. I suppose Americans like me because my music shows both aspects. It's very Americanised – at least my music from the 1970s and early 80s is.

In university teaching of composition in America there were some fortresses of modernism – let's say Columbia, Yale, Princeton. But those things have changed completely now. In almost all good universities there are teachers who know everything about, say, Charlie Parker.

JC *How do you see other European countries ... Germany? Britain?*

LA I think in other European countries contemporary music often consists only of playing complex twelve-note stuff, and only fifty well-dressed bourgeois people come to hear it. It's always the same people: a totally closed circle. In Holland, and specifically in Amsterdam, it's different. One of my German composer friends, Heiner Goebbels, has the same attitude as me: he writes a kind of music that is quite intelligent and sharp but not *too* much like Brian Ferneyhough. Berlin seems to be very active and we hope that there will be some crossovers there.

Britain I cannot judge. I suppose it's somewhat closer to Holland than it is to France and Germany. However, the diversity in England is also very clear. You have your elegant [George] Benjamin kind of composers. And the Finnissy kind. There is not one line: nowadays that's probably true only for very small countries. And then I think there's a kind of optimistic Stravinskian writing which I find also in some Irish composers such as Gerald Barry. Colin Matthews, Julian Anderson I like, many neo-Stravinskian composers. There are several thirty-five-year-olds like them. And don't underestimate a composer like Harry Birtwistle. He's not simply a Schoenbergian or a Stravinskian (though he's more Stravinskian than Schoenbergian). He's a very good composer.

JC *What are you working on at the moment?*

LA I finished my second opera with Peter Greenaway [*Writing to Vermeer*, 1999], which was a completely different kind of music for me. Ravel was the person I thought of when I wrote the music. But that's not so far away from Stravinsky. Now what I'm very interested in is the combination of sound and image, so I work a lot with visual artists. Of course, I have been incredibly spoilt with Greenaway: he's a genius. Now I work with another film maker in New York, Hal Hartley, whom I like very much. We did one little video [*The New Math(s)*, 2001], and we will do another one I hope. And we will probably do a live theatre work in 2003. But at the moment I'm writing a kind of double concerto.

JC *Are you aware, even now, of the shadow of Stravinsky falling over you when you're sitting at your desk composing?*

LA Well, above my grand piano, on the right-hand side is a little picture of my wife, and on the left-hand side is the incredible picture of Balanchine looking over Stravinsky's shoulder. It's an amazing photo.

I don't know. He's like a friend. My father is, of course, closer just because he was my father. [*Pointing to his bookcases*] This is all the Stravinsky literature for the book – there's even languages I cannot read like Finnish and Russian. There are all the scores and the piano scores. I discussed with Craft the possibility of writing an orchestral suite from *The Rake's Progress*, but I think I will not do it, because I need trombones. When you take out the voices you need some more instruments, and I find that too difficult because there are no trombones in the original orchestra. I can't do it. I'm probably too puritanical to do that.

14 Stravinsky and us

RICHARD TARUSKIN

When, at the dawn of the third millennium, we use the word 'Stravinsky', we no longer merely name a person. We mean a collection of ideas – ideas embodied in, or rather construed out of, a certain body of highly valued musical and literary texts that acquired enormous authority in twentieth-century musical culture. That authority and its consequences are what have been preoccupying my thoughts about Stravinsky since completing *Stravinsky and the Russian Traditions*, which, though published in 1996, was not as recent a study as it seemed. It had spent almost seven years in press, during which time my thinking about the bundle of notions called 'Stravinsky' underwent considerable change.

In keeping with the scholarly tradition in which I was trained, my book was almost wholly concerned with the production of those texts, and with determining their place within the historical context contemporaneous with them. My thinking since has been more concerned with the relationship between those texts, and the ideas construed from them, and the contexts in which they have existed since the time of their production, up to their present contexts, including this book. Just as in *Stravinsky and the Russian Traditions* I considered the reciprocal manner in which Stravinsky received influences from his surroundings and influenced those surroundings in turn, so I continue to be interested in that reciprocity of influence in the period since his death.

As I hope to demonstrate, Stravinskian ideas have been so influential that one could almost say that twentieth-century European and Euro-American musical culture has been created in the image of Stravinsky. But at the same time, as Stravinsky reminded us over and over again, an influence is (or can be) something we choose to submit to. And we can be very choosy indeed about what we value and make our own in what is offered to us. So one could say with equal justice that we have created Stravinsky in our image.

This text is a speech, not a book chapter, although in its slightly modified printed form it has been provided with references. It was commissioned by Nicholas Kenyon for the BBC and delivered at the Royal College of Music in August 1996 as the inaugural BBC Proms Lecture. Thereafter it served for five years as its author's lecture-platform Bucephalus, at venues ranging from The Hague to Melbourne. Its last oral delivery took place as the Faculty Research Lecture at the University of California at Berkeley in April 2001. I am grateful to my many audiences for points raised at question time, often leading to improvements.

This reciprocity is what I have taken for my theme: the mutually defining relationship, Stravinsky and us.

The meanings and values arising out of that relationship fundamentally structured our beliefs and our behaviour as twentieth-century musicians, music lovers and human beings. Some of them, I believe, are overdue for re-examination now that we have become inhabitants of the twenty-first century.

In 1966, which turned out to be the last year of Igor Stravinsky's active creative life, his musical and literary assistant Robert Craft summed up the composer's position in the history of twentieth-century music by observing that 'he is one of the representative spokesmen of 1966 as he was of '06, '16, '26, and so on'.[1] Indeed he was far more than that. By 1966 he did not merely represent the history of twentieth-century music; he practically constituted it. The story of his career had been generalised into the story of twentieth-century music. But in the process of that generalisation it had been turned into a myth – or rather, into a congeries of myths, some of them of Stravinsky's own devising, others myths to which he had willingly submitted, still others myths to which his work had been assimilated without his direct participation.

The first work of Stravinsky's to achieve mythical status was, of course, *The Rite of Spring*, the ballet first performed under the title *Le Sacre du printemps*. Stravinsky conceived the work (as 'The Great Sacrifice') in 1910; began composing it in 1911; endured the riotous fiasco of the May 1913 premiere; experienced through it, shortly before his thirty-second birthday the next year, the triumph of his career ('such as *composers* rarely enjoy', as he bragged in old age[2]); and spent the rest of his long life telling lies about it.

In 1920 he told a reporter that the ballet had been originally conceived as a piece of pure, plotless instrumental music ('une oeuvre architectonique et non anecdotique').[3] In 1931 he told his first authorised biographer that the opening bassoon melody was the only quoted folk song in the score.[4] In 1960 he asserted through Craft that the work was wholly without tradition, the product of intuition alone. 'I heard and I wrote what I heard', he declared. 'I am the vessel through which *Le Sacre* passed.'[5] These allegations and famous words have long since passed into the enduring folklore of twentieth-century music.

Now we know that the ballet's scenario is a highly detailed and (but for the culminating human sacrifice) an ethnographically accurate pair of 'Scenes of Pagan Russia', as the ballet's oft-suppressed subtitle proclaims. It was planned in painstaking detail, by the composer in collaboration with the painter and archaeologist Nicholas Roerich, before a note was written.

The score contains nine identifiable folk songs, all of them selected with the same eye towards ethnographic authenticity as governed the assembling of the scenario. And finally, in its technique of composition, the music magnificently embodied and extended a very specific immediate and local tradition – a repertoire of harmonic devices based on an 'artificial' scale of alternating whole tones and semitones, which Stravinsky's teacher Rimsky-Korsakov had educed from the music of Liszt and passed along to all his pupils.[6]

So the myth of *The Rite of Spring* incorporated at least two big truths at variance with the ascertainable facts: first, that the music was 'pure', abstract, unbeholden to any specific time and place for its inspiration; and second, that it represented a violent stylistic rupture with the past, when all the while it was conceived as an exuberantly maximalistic celebration of two pasts – the remote past of its subject and the more recent past of its style.

And yet myths are not merely lies. They are explanatory fictions, higher truths – enabling or empowering narratives that take us *a realibus ad realiora*, 'from the real to the more real', to quote Vyacheslav Ivanov, the symbolist poet who was counting on the artists of the early twentieth century, and the musicians above all, to usher in a new mythological age.[7] Stravinsky gave tacit acknowledgement of Ivanov's idea when, in conversation with Robert Craft, he tried to improve upon his famous fighting words of the 1930s – that music 'is incapable of *expressing* anything at all' – by remarking that 'music is supra-personal and super-real and as such beyond verbal meanings and verbal descriptions', and that instead of depicting ordinary reality, 'a new piece of music *is* a new reality'.[8] This mythographic or mythopoetic sense of music is one of the essential Stravinskian truths.

In the first instance, the myth or 'new reality' of *The Rite of Spring* empowered Stravinsky. Having first made his name, courtesy of Sergey Diaghilev and the Ballets Russes, as the protagonist and beneficiary of the greatest craze for Russian music ever to possess the West (as a result of which it was widely, if briefly, acknowledged that Russia had inherited the musical leadership of Europe), but having renounced Russia in the wake of the 1917 revolution and the ensuing Bolshevik *coup d'état*, Stravinsky wished frantically not only to attach himself to the Western – or 'panromanogermanic' – musical mainstream, as nationalistic émigrés like him understood it,[9] but to keep up his status as its leader. He rejected the parochial lore of his birthright and embraced an aggressively cosmopolitan ideology of absolute music – music without a passport, without a past, without 'extramusical' content of any kind.

At the same time this myth of *The Rite* was a powerful enabler for others as well. Detached from their national background and their motivating subject-matter, the neo-primitivist musical innovations in *The Rite* – its fragmentedness, its 'staticness', its radical structural simplifications – provided its legions of imitators with a quick, very necessary bath in the river Lethe at a time when the European tradition seemed over. That is why there *were* so many imitators.

And that, by the way, is what 'neoclassicism', at least at first, was all about. It had nothing to do, at first, with stylistic retrospectivism or revivalism, with 'returning to Bach' or with vicarious imperial restorations. It had everything to do with a '*style dépouillé*', a stripped-down, denuded style, and with the same neo-primitivist, anti-humanistic ideals that had already motivated *The Rite* and the other masterworks of Stravinsky's late 'Russian period', especially *Svadebka* (*The Wedding*, first performed as *Les Noces*).

This much we may read in the very first journalistic essay to attach the N-word to Stravinsky – the very first essay, in fact, to apply the word without irony to modern music. It was written in 1923, the year in which Stravinsky's Octet for wind instruments (the first 'back to Bach' piece) was performed, but several months earlier. The man who wrote it was Boris de Schloezer, like Stravinsky a Russian émigré, who is best known for his writings on Skryabin, his brother-in-(common)-law.

The most revealing aspect of Schloezer's early exposition of Stravinsky's neoclassicism is the work that inspired it: not *Pulcinella*, not the Octet, but the *Symphonies d'instruments à vent*, a work we now tend to look upon (and that Stravinsky surely looked upon then) as the composer's valedictory to his 'Russian period'. Nothing could be more critical than this unexpected circumstance to our understanding of Stravinsky's neoclassicism.

What made the *Symphonies* 'neoclassical' for Schloezer, thence for many others, was the assumption that it was

> only a system of sounds, which follow one another and group themselves
> according to purely musical affinities; the thought of the artist places
> itself only in the musical plan without ever setting foot in the domain of
> psychology. Emotions, feelings, desires, aspirations – this is the terrain
> from which he has pushed his work.[10]

These words might seem quite irrelevant to the poetic conception underlying the *Symphonies* (a memorial for Debussy that is actually cast in the form of an Orthodox funeral service),[11] but Stravinsky lost no time in appropriating Schloezer's view. As early as the next year, he was looking back on the *Symphonies* as the first of his 'so-called classical works'.[12] Schloezer had, in effect, revealed to the composer the underlying, indeed profound relationship between his earlier rejection of personal 'emotions, feelings, desires and aspirations' in ritualistic works such as *The Rite* and *The Wedding*, and the new aesthetic of abstraction that attracted not only Stravinsky but any number of modernist artists to the postwar 'call to order' (Cocteau's

famous phrase)[13] – a call they heeded in the name of a resurgent, reformu-
lated 'classicism'.

From this perspective the *Symphonies* was indeed a turning-point – or
could be one if its 'extramusical' content were purged. And so, in a programme note that accompanied performances of the *Symphonies* in the
late 1920s and 1930s, Stravinsky went one better than Schloezer, describing
the work as entirely formalist and transcendent: an arrangement of 'tonal
masses ... sculptured in marble ... to be regarded objectively by the ear'.[14]
The Bachian resonances that we now associate with 'neoclassicism' came
later, as a metaphor for that transcendence and that objectivity. They have
about as much to do with the historical Johann Sebastian Bach as the new
line about *The Rite of Spring* had to do with the historical Igor Fyodorovich
Stravinsky and his original expressive aims.

But no matter! We are dealing here not with facts but with myths, not
with *realia* but with *realiora*, not with the real but with the realer, and the
fundamental formalist commitment is the great Stravinsky myth, the great
Stravinsky idea, the great Stravinsky truth – the precept or edict (shall we call
it the ukase?) that has been regulating the behaviour of twentieth-century
(and now twenty-first-century) musicians ever since. Ever since the 1920s,
in other words, a commitment to formalist aesthetics has been the great
distinguishing feature of panromanogermanic classical music.

The purity and absoluteness of Stravinsky's music remains an article of
faith to many. I have become quite inured over the years to hearing from colleagues and reviewers that the investigations I have made into the sources and
backgrounds of Stravinsky's Russian-period work are interesting enough but
quite irrelevant aesthetically. And it is certainly true, as Pieter van den Toorn
says on the very first page of his important book, *Stravinsky and 'The Rite of
Spring'*, that 'for the greater part of this century our knowledge and appreciation of *The Rite of Spring* have come from the concert hall and recordings'.[15]
To that extent, the myth of *The Rite* has come true, for the music has become
quite happily detached from its original scenario and mise-en-scène. For
many, if not for most spectators, visual exposure to the work as a ballet comes
after years of tremendous stagings before the mind's eye under the stimulus
of the powerful noises that it makes, and seeing it is often disappointing. Even
Nicholas Roerich, the original designer and co-scenarist, admitted that 'we
cannot consider "Sacre" as Russian, nor even Slavic – it is more ancient and
pan-human'.[16] To insist that *The Rite* still means what it originally meant –
that it is nothing more and nothing less than a pair of 'scenes of pagan
Russia' – would surely limit and diminish its full human significance, and I
for one would never wish my findings about the ballet to diminish it so.

But it may still be worth asking whether that full human significance
is well or adequately described by the phrase 'architectonique et non

anecdotique'. The phrase still sounds like a Pandora's box, and one has
to wonder what is being locked up within, just as I still wonder why, despite
his ample and detailed knowledge of the historical circumstances in which
Stravinsky developed his ostensibly radical musical style (knowledge he does
not hesitate in the least to share with his reader), van den Toorn nevertheless subtitled his book 'The *Beginnings* of a Musical Language' (emphasis
added). This willed amnesia, I would suggest, is an example of behaviour
regulated by the Stravinsky myth.

Is there any harm in that? Van den Toorn says not, in no uncertain terms.
He sees nothing but gain. Propositional knowledge, especially historical
knowledge, can only interfere, in his view, with aesthetic bonding. He quotes
(or rather, slightly paraphrases) a remark from one of Stravinsky's books of
'conversations' with Craft:

> The composer works through a perceptual, not a conceptual process. He
> perceives, he selects, he combines, and is not in the least aware at what
> point meanings of a different sort and significance grow into his works.
> All he knows or cares about is the apprehension of the contours of form,
> for form is everything.[17]

There you have it: *form is everything*. You could not get more categorical
than that in declaring formalist principles. Van den Toorn's move, unantici-
pated by Stravinsky, perhaps, but clearly regulated by his principles, is to
apply the composer's description of composerly behaviour to the listener.
'One need only substitute listener for composer in the above quotation',
he writes, 'and the reasoning becomes impregnable'.[18] We need not dwell
on distinctions here: what van den Toorn calls reasoning is pretty clearly a
tautology, I think, but what of that? Its purpose and effect are what count
for Stravinsky and for van den Toorn, not its logical status. The purpose,
simply, is pleasure, aesthetic rapture. 'The source of the attraction', van den
Toorn writes,

> the source of our conscious intellectual concerns, is the passionate
> nature of the relationship that is struck. But this relationship is given
> immediately in experience and is not open to the inquiry that it inspires.
> Moments of esthetic rapport, of self-forgetting at-oneness with music,
> are immediate. The mind, losing itself in contemplation, becomes
> immersed in the musical object, becomes one with that object.[19]

The trouble is that, as Stravinsky actually concedes, 'meanings of a different sort and significance grow into his works', whether or not he knows or
cares about them. The aesthetic rapture van den Toorn seeks demands, once
again, a willed ignorance, a willed blindness. Directing attention resolutely
away from content and focusing entirely on form is hardly an 'immediate'
response to art. It is no one's first response. (Why else, after all, is a taste for

'absolute music' the most notoriously 'cultivated' of all artistic tastes?) It is a learned response – learned from Stravinsky. It has its costs.

To explore these costs, I want to focus the rest of this discussion on one of Stravinsky's best known and surely most written-about late works, the Cantata. One reason I want to focus on it is because it is one work about which I have some new research findings, albeit modest ones, to report. But that research was not, I confess, 'disinterested'. What interested me about the Cantata was the way it problematised the congeries of ideas we call 'Stravinsky'.

The Cantata was the first composition to follow *The Rake's Progress*, Stravinsky's longest work. At first, it was to have followed *The Rake* quite directly and unproblematically. It was, in effect, a second collaboration between Stravinsky and W. H. Auden, the *Rake* co-librettist, who had just published, with Norman Holmes Pearson, a five-volume school anthology, *Poets of the English Language* (New York: Viking Press, 1950), and made Stravinsky a present of it. From a letter from Auden to Robert Craft one gathers that Stravinsky was planning a song cycle for mezzo soprano and small instrumental ensemble on texts from the anthology.[20] In the end, not only the Cantata, but Stravinsky's next vocal composition as well, *Three Songs from William Shakespeare*, were mined from the contents of Auden's collection. (One can tell that this was Stravinsky's Shakespeare source because he retained all of the quaint spellings that most editors remove but that Auden and his co-editor lovingly restored.)

The first item from *Poets of the English Language* to be set, in July 1951, was 'The maidens came', one of six poems grouped under the rubric 'Anonymous Lyrics and Songs' in Vol. I (Fig. 14.1). The setting is in a sort of period style, both as regards prosody and as regards texture. Stravinsky had been hearing a great quantity of renaissance and baroque music at the so-called Evenings on the Roof Concerts in Los Angeles, at which Craft had become a frequent conductor. At the first such concert he attended, in 1944 (four years Before Craft), he heard Elizabethan virginals music and some keyboard works of Purcell, both for the first time.[21] Later he heard Dowland lute songs and Elizabethan madrigals and much more. 'The maidens came' is full of the Lombard or 'Scotch snap' rhythms characteristic of Purcellian text declamation. They must have struck Stravinsky's ear as especially fresh, even though he did not grasp – or characteristically chose to ignore – the distinctive relationship of the Lombard pattern to the English short stress. The setting is also full of short stretches of canonic writing, often by inversion, such as one finds in early keyboard and consort fantasias.

In his letter of September 1951, Auden sent Craft a rather long list of additional suggestions from his anthology for inclusion in the cycle, mainly

Fig. 14.1 *Poets of the English Language*

Elizabethans like Sidney, Jonson and Campion, but also Pope, Blake, Burns, even Christina Rossetti. By the time Stravinsky returned to the composition, however, in February 1952, he had decided to cast the work for a more complex medium including a small women's chorus and two solo singers, the original mezzo and also a tenor, each of whom sings solos, now called 'ricercars', and who then combine for a duet. And, possibly because he wanted to maintain the archaic period flavour of the original setting, he decided to confine the texts to the little group of anonymous lyrics from which he had taken 'The maidens came', setting the group to music practically *in toto* (omitting only the second and third

Ex. 14.1 Cantata, 'Tomorrow shall be my dancing day', derivation of subject

items as listed), as many readers will already have noticed after glancing at Fig. 14.1. He gave the Cantata an elegant overall shape by using one of the longer items, 'A lyke-wake dirge', as a kind of choral refrain, its successive verses intercalated around and between the solo items.

The longest item in the group, the carol 'Tomorrow shall be my dancing day', was set as a tenor solo to form the Cantata's centrepiece. Now 'Tomorrow shall be my dancing day' is not only the longest and most elaborately composed piece in the Cantata; it is also one of the most revered items in the later Stravinsky catalogue, owing to the circumstances of its creation, which entail an important creative crisis. No biography of the composer or critical study of his work fails to cite it, usually with at least one music example.

On the face of it, the setting does not seem very different from 'The maidens came'. Like its predecessor, it uses canonic textures of a rather archaic sort, admitting cancrizans writing alongside inversion to its repertoire of contrapuntal devices. Unlike 'The maidens came', however, and especially in view of its length, the composition is severely limited in its melodic material. The eleven-note canonic subject on which the entire piece is based is a complex derivation from a phrase, seemingly selected at random, from 'The maidens came' (see Ex. 14.1).

As Craft has testified, immediately on fashioning this little theme, Stravinsky drew a chart on the back of a sheet of stationery from 'La boutique', his wife's art gallery on La Cienega Boulevard in Los Angeles (Ex. 14.2), which shows, as Craft put it, 'the four orders – original, retrograde, inverted, retrograde inverted – of his eleven-note "series"'.[22] As can be seen from Ex. 14.2, the cancrizans is so arranged as to produce a harmonic closure on its starting point – a traditional pendular (there-and-back) motion with an implied tonic–dominant/dominant–tonic harmony, the old 'binary form' we have all studied at school. The inversion is contrived so as to produce the same progression. Its pitch level is chosen so that its opening pair of notes reproduces the pitches of the original phrase with exchanged positions. In formal terms this would be described as a transposition down a major third (in more formal terms, transposition by eight semitones, or – in still

Ex. 14.2 Cantata, 'Tomorrow shall be my dancing day', sketch

(a)

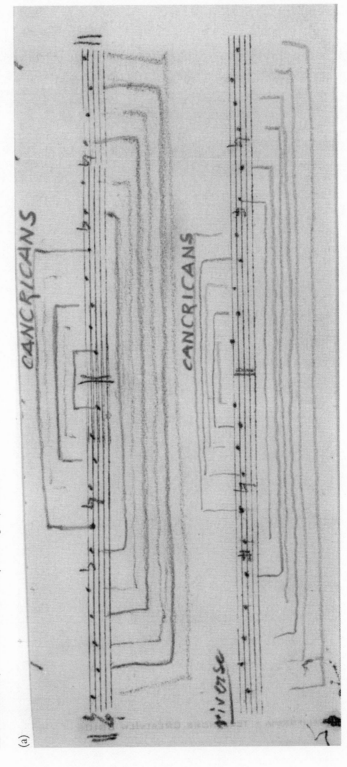

Ex. 14.2 (cont.)

(b)

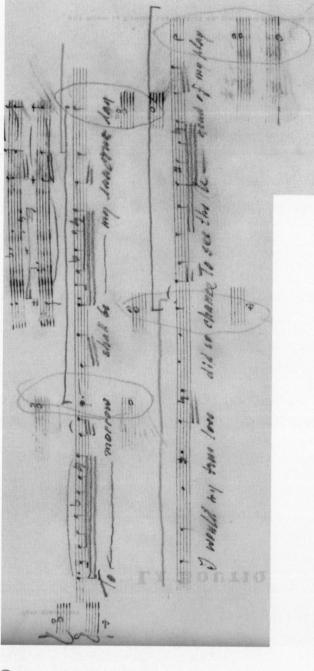

more formal terms, those of the theory journals – 't$_8$'), but I am sure that Stravinsky did not think of it as a transposition at all – quite the opposite, in fact. He must have thought of it not in purely pitch or intervallic terms, but in harmonic terms, according to which the inversion changes as little as possible.

Now, although the material in the second Ricercar, and its handling, might well seem just as archaistic as in the first ('The maidens came'), the second Ricercar is radically separated in the historical, biographical, analytical and critical literatures from the rest of the Cantata and attached to a different story altogether. Craft put it very succinctly when he wrote that the second Ricercar in the Cantata 'marks the first effect on Stravinsky of Schoenberg's serial principle', and most of the succeeding literature on the piece has been more or less a gloss on that little sentence.[23]

Realising that the internal evidence for such an assertion is slim, Craft elaborated with some historical reportage of a kind that he, not only a witness but an actual participant on the scene, was uniquely qualified to give: 'Although cancrizans of the kind found in this Ricercar were [*sic*] employed centuries before', he wrote, 'Stravinsky came to them there by way of his contemporary' – his recently deceased contemporary and neighbour, one should add, Schoenberg having died in Los Angeles the year before, as it happened, while Stravinsky was hard at work on 'The maidens came' – and Craft added as further corroboration that Stravinsky 'heard some of the Viennese master's music, as well as much discussion about it, in Europe in the autumn of 1951' when he returned to the old world for the first time after the war to conduct the *Rake* premiere.

Craft went on to record the fact that while working on the second Ricercar, Stravinsky attended several rehearsals of a performance Craft was then preparing at UCLA of Schoenberg's Septet-Suite, Op. 29, and was full of questions about Schoenberg's technique. Once one knows this, it makes some sense to relate the manipulations of the eleven-note motive in the second Ricercar to the so-called twelve-note technique, since like a tone row the motive is treated as an entirely abstract ordered succession of pitches – or rather, pitch classes, as Milton Babbitt would christen them a few years later. Unlike the canons in 'The maidens came', the ones in the second Ricercar are entirely free as to rhythm and octave register.

Evidence of another sort comes from a touching entry in Craft's diary, describing an occurrence Craft first made public in a centennial lecture published in the *Atlantic Monthly*, and, in characteristic fashion, retold subsequently with a great deal of exasperating variation in the details.[24] I quote it here in its latest, and in some ways most plausible (because least sensational) incarnation, from the revised *Chronicle of a Friendship* (pp. 72–3). The date is 8 March 1952, four days after the second Ricercar had been completed:

We drive to Palmdale for lunch, spareribs in a cowboy-style restaurant, Bordeaux from I.S.'s thermos. A powdering of snow is in the air, and, at higher altitudes, on the ground: Angelenos stop their cars and go out to touch it. During the return, I.S. startles us, saying he fears he can no longer compose; for a moment he actually seems ready to weep. V. gently, expertly, assures him that whatever the difficulties, they will soon pass. He refers obliquely to the Schoenberg Septet and the powerful impression it has made on him. After 40 years of dismissing Schoenberg as 'experimental,' 'theoretical,' '*démodé*,' he is suffering the shock of recognition that Schoenberg's music is richer in substance than his own.

Craft's interpretation here is a little different from those he has offered elsewhere, which have centred on the perhaps more telling fact that Stravinsky was becoming aware that younger musicians, especially in Europe, were more interested just then in Schoenberg than in himself. At any rate, it is clear that Stravinsky was suffering a crisis of confidence, one brought on, as far as I can read the circumstances, precisely because he realised that, as the second Ricercar demonstrated, even when emulating Schoenberg's serial procedures, he found himself still tied willy-nilly to his older harmonic thinking, his deeply ingrained habits of the ear. He was evidently afraid that he himself might be becoming 'démodé'. It was a frightening thought indeed to one who had become so used to the role of defining, at times fairly dictatorially, what would be 'à la mode'.

More evidence of Stravinsky's crisis mentality can be found in the printed documents surrounding the Cantata – namely, the published score, and a programme note that Stravinsky wrote (or at least signed) for the premiere performance in Los Angeles in November 1952. I quote a little of the latter. First, he notes the general circumstances of the composition: 'After finishing *The Rake's Progress* I was persuaded by a strong desire to compose another work in which the problems of setting English words to music would reappear, but this time in a purer, non-dramatic form.' Following a description of the Dirge and the first Ricercar, he comes to 'Tomorrow shall be my dancing day'. It is, he says,

> also a Ricercar in the sense that it is a canonic composition. Its structure is more elaborate than that of 'The Maidens Came'. The piece begins with a one-bar introduction by the flutes and cello, the statement of the canonic subject which is the subject of the whole piece. This subject is repeated by the tenor, over a recitative style accompaniment of oboes and cello, in original form, retrograde (or cancrizans, which means that its notes are heard in reverse order – in this case, in a different rhythm), inverted form, and finally, in retrograde inversion.

Then comes a music example, showing the voice part of the opening stanza with the four forms, taken as if exactly from Ex. 14.2, marked off

Ex. 14.3 Cantata, 'Tomorrow shall be my dancing day',

with brackets (Ex. 14.3). What is truly surprising is that the published score incorporates these brackets, not only in the opening or expository section Stravinsky quoted in the note, but throughout the piece, showing every single permutation of the eleven-note motive, as Stravinsky cumbersomely attempted to describe them in prose, as the note continues:

> The fourth and sixth canons are nine bars long, the others are twelve bars long. The instrumentation of all the canons is two oboes and cello. In the first canon, the second oboe proposes the original subject and the first oboe takes it up at the minor third above, while the tenor sings it in inverted form. The second canon begins with the voice singing the Cantus in cancrizans form, a minor third below; the cello is in original form a fourth below. The third canon is identical with the first. In the fourth canon the first oboe follows the second at the interval of a second while the voice transposes the Cantus in inverted form down a minor third to A. In the three last bars, the cello, which has been accompanying with a new rhythmic figure, plays the Cantus in F, original form, while the voice and first oboe play it in A, original form. The fifth canon is identical with the first. The sixth begins with the Cantus in the voice in original form . . .[25]

And so on – and on and on. And what makes this programme note particularly noteworthy, over and above what I believe it is fair to call its obsession with technical detail, is the fact that this was only the second time in his career that Stravinsky ever offered a technical analysis of any of his compositions. (The other, very brief, concerned *The Firebird*, composed forty-two years earlier.)[26] One begins to get a feel for what Craft described in his memoir as the 'substance' that Stravinsky had begun to envy in Schoenberg, and the way it jibed with the older versions of the Stravinsky myth.

A more explicit indication of this tie-in, and of its relationship to the Cold War artistic temper, came in an interview Stravinsky gave a Paris reporter on 28 April 1952, about seven weeks after that tense moment in the car that Craft so hauntingly described. Craft's description of this occasion is very droll.[27] Stravinsky was returning to Europe for the first time since *The Rake*, and was touching down in Paris, his home for almost twenty years, for the first time since before the war. It was just a touching-down: Stravinsky was actually on his way to Geneva, and the plane was refuelling. His friend Nicolas Nabokov, the newly-appointed Secretary-General of the Congress for Cultural Freedom, was waiting with a gaggle of paparazzi, whom he hustled into the waiting-room for what we would now call a 'photo opportunity'. Here is what Stravinsky told the reporter from the Congress's own organ, *Preuves*, during that hectic stopover, in response to what was by then an inevitable question:

> The twelve-tone system? Personally I have enough to do with seven tones. But the twelve-tone composers are the only ones who have a discipline I respect. Whatever else it may be, twelve-tone music is certainly pure music.[28]

Of course he was describing his second Ricercar, which appropriated the twelve-note discipline and applied it to seven (well, eight) notes. The discipline was what he wished to claim, and relate to his old notions of 'pure' music – something that Schoenberg never did, because he never had that notion. Quite the contrary: Schoenberg always refused to offer technical descriptions of his music, and claimed to despise them. To Rudolf Kolisch, his brother-in-law, who had worked out an exemplary formalistic analysis of Schoenberg's Third Quartet very much on the order of Stravinsky's analysis of his Cantata, Schoenberg addressed one of his most famous missives: 'I can't utter too many warnings against overrating these analyses, since after all they only lead to what I have always been dead set against: seeing how it is *done*; whereas I have always helped people to see: what it *is*!'[29]

Stravinsky, on the contrary, seemed only to be interested in showing how it was done. And so have been almost all the later commentators on the Cantata, of whom there have been so many. Meanwhile, he embarked on the task of expanding from seven to twelve. He did it the way countless other students were doing it at the time. He got hold of *Studies in Counterpoint* (1940) by Ernst Krenek, one of his California neighbours, only the second practical primer in twelve-note composition ever published, and began working his way through the exercises in it. You can see some of them right on the surface of *Threni*, Stravinsky's first completely dodecaphonic construction, composed in 1957–8. On the way to that piece there had been several others that used rows containing more or less than twelve notes, and a couple of larger works that were intermittently twelve-note (*Canticum Sacrum*, *Agon*). The trajectory by which Stravinsky zeroed in on the new discipline is one of the most orderly and trackable processes of its kind in the history of music, and so, of course, it has been traced very frequently in the literature, especially after Milton Babbitt's seminal exposition, 'Remarks on the recent Stravinsky', first given as 'a lecture under the auspices of the Santa Fe Opera as part of its Festival in honour of Igor Stravinsky's 80th birthday', that is, in 1962, and published two years later in *Perspectives of New Music*.

Babbitt set the tone for these surveys by looking back on Stravinsky's quest from the perspective of its completion, thus comparing Stravinsky's serial practice at every stage with the fully elaborated twelve-note technique he finally embraced – which made for some very tortuous descriptions. Here is how the analysis of the second Ricercar from the Cantata begins:

> The serial unit here consists of eleven ordered pitch elements, but only six different pitch elements. Since there are, then, non-immediate repetitions of pitch elements within the unit, the serial characterization, in terms of the relation of temporal precedence among pitches, requires that each occurrence of a pitch element which occurs multiply be differentiated ordinally; more concisely, if it is agreed to represent a pitch element of a serial unit by an ordered pair signifying the element's order number and pitch number, then the collection of such ordered pairs associated with the twelve-tone set necessarily defines a biunique, one-to-one function, while that of a serial order with repetitions cannot. This latter collection defines a function, but not a biunique one, and the inverse, therefore, is not a single-valued function.[30]

And here is another pertinent excerpt:

> Whereas the operations in the twelve-tone system necessarily result in permutations of the elements of the set, in a non twelve-tone serial unit, they do not. Indeed, if the serial unit is not inversionally symmetrical, as it is not in the Cantata, the effect of inversion can never be to permute, but rather to adjoin pitches which are not present in the original unit. So, whereas an inversion of a twelve-tone set can be so identified only by virtue of order, in the case of such a serial structure as that of the Cantata, it can be identified by pitch content alone. Here, then, is combinational rather than permutational serialism, since each form of the serial unit represents a selection from the twelve pitch classes rather than a particular ordering of these classes.[31]

I said that these were pertinent excerpts, and I meant it, but what are they pertinent to? Not the Cantata, because Babbitt is saying only what Stravinsky did not do in composing that piece, and sheds no light at all on what he did do. Why then, despite that impertinence and despite its extreme tortuousness, has Babbitt's telling of this tale become so influential? It has been influential because it effectively turns the story of Stravinsky's late career into a teleology, a quest narrative, and in so doing it assimilates the story to yet another myth, one of the great myths of the twentieth century, that of the general teleology according to which the structure of music, and the compositional practices that produce that structure, have been said to evolve by stages, and inevitably, from tonal to atonal, finally to serial.

Because Stravinsky underwent this evolution late, presumably, he was allowed to bypass the middle term and evolve directly from tonal to serial. But this discrepancy does not prevent his career from assuming a kind of paradigmatic status, by which his ontogeny recapitulates the phylogeny of twentieth-century music. By doing so, Stravinsky's career can be subsumed into a progress narrative, progress being the most potent form that myth has taken in the nineteenth and twentieth centuries. So we end up with an assimilation of one powerful myth, the Stravinskian myth of purity, to an even more powerful myth, the positivistic myth of progress. Like any myth, but doubly so, this double myth has functioned as a regulator of belief and behaviour. It has immense authority, an authority that has only recently, with great difficulty, and against strong resistance, begun to be challenged.

What has been the chief regulation? I have already hinted at it: the resolute deflection of musical consciousness from 'what it is', as Schoenberg would say, to 'how it's done'. Often, and very misleadingly, it is expressed as an exclusion of 'extramusical' ideas from consideration of 'the music itself'. And this taboo, to reiterate, has cost us very dear.

To return to the second Ricercar: it can hardly have escaped notice that Stravinsky's description, to say nothing of Babbitt's, has entirely avoided any mention of what the piece *is*. At its most basic level, it is a setting of a carol that narrates the life of Christ. How is it that this fact is thought to be irrelevant to a description of the piece, especially as we know Stravinsky to have been, or at any rate to have professed being, a religious believer? Could the subject really have played no part in the selection of the text? Was it only 'problems of setting English words' that mattered to Stravinsky, not the words he set?

Let us look closely at a part of the piece, the last part for which I quoted Stravinsky's description above, namely the fourth canon (Ex. 14.4). We may see all the things to which Stravinsky called attention, underscored by his use of brackets, to which I have added identifications of the serial forms employed using the standard music-theory representational mode. First there is the beautifully worked out canon in the voice and the two oboes in which three different transpositions of the inverted form of the theme are combined. Then the voice shifts over to the original form of the 'riverso cancrizans', as Stravinsky called it on his chart (Ex. 14.2), or the retrograde inversion as it is called in standard terminology. Finally, as Stravinsky pointed out, the original eleven-note 'serial unit', as Babbitt puts it, is enunciated

Ex. 14.4 Cantata, 'Tomorrow shall be my dancing day', fourth canon

by the voice and first oboe in A major, while the cello plays it in F major. All of this is worked out ingeniously and beautifully. Contemplating the musical construction one can indeed experience, with van den Toorn, a 'moment of esthetic rapport, of self-forgetting at-oneness with music', in which 'the mind, losing itself in contemplation, becomes immersed in the musical object, becomes one with that object'.

But there is something else in Ex. 14.4 besides what Stravinsky, Babbitt or van den Toorn would recognise as the 'musical object'. There is something 'extramusical' as well – something never alluded to by Stravinsky, by Babbitt, by van den Toorn, by Colin Mason, by Heinrich Lindlar, by Henry Cowell, by André Boucourechliev, by Robert Morgan, by Paul Griffiths, by Louis Andriessen and Elmer Schönberger, by Stephen Walsh, by Joseph Straus, or by any of the other musician-commentators who have offered detailed descriptions of the Cantata in print. There is also this, which you may not have noticed yet:

> The Jews on me they made great suit,
> And with me made great variance;
> Because they lov'd darkness rather than light.

Is it necessary to point out that this is a deplorable text, even if a venerable one, rehearsing as it does the old guilt-libel against the Jews as children of darkness and as deicides, a libel that has caused rivers of Jewish blood to be spilled? And does it surprise you that it could strike someone like me, your academic colleague, as incomprehensible that a great composer, whose prestige must inevitably lend it respectability, would choose such a text to set, seven years after Hitler?

But I want to emphasise at the outset, and as forcefully as I know how, that Stravinsky's motives in setting this text are not the issue I am addressing. His anti-Semitism is not my present subject, nor is anyone's. My subject is blindness to its presence, a blindness that innumerable performers and commentators have shared with Stravinsky, and that is the most urgent aspect of what I see as the issue of 'Stravinsky and us' – taking 'Stravinsky' now in the sense I originally announced, to mean a set of regulative ideas and premises, and taking 'us' to mean those whose beliefs and behaviours have been so regulated.

For purposes of the present discussion I am perfectly willing to grant that Stravinsky was blind – or, if you prefer, insensitive – to the import of the words he was setting. This for him was a longstanding habit. From his earliest modernist days he claimed to be interested in words only for their sounds, not their meaning. There is evidence that this was the case in the Cantata, both in his explicit remark that the verses he chose for it 'attracted me not only for their great beauty and their compelling syllabification, but for their construction which suggested musical construction',[32] and also in a hilarious entry in Craft's diary in which Auden, after the Cantata has been performed and is in the process of publication, finally explains to Craft and Stravinsky what the words of the 'Lyke-wake dirge' actually mean.[33] Stravinsky set them without knowing, probably without caring.

It was not the first time. More than one piece from the Russian period – *Svadebka* for one, or (for a particularly piquant instance) the *Zapevnaya* or 'counting game' from the *Quatre chants russes* of 1919 – contain Russian peasant words and phrases that even Pyotr Kireyevsky, the compiler of the anthology of folk verses on which Stravinsky relied, and a legendary connoisseur, found incomprehensible. He marked such texts in his anthology with little question marks and ellipses that seem to have attracted Stravinsky to them as honey attracts a bear.

More evidence of Stravinsky's lack of concern for the words in his second Ricercar is the fact that he was inattentive to the form of the poem even as he was setting it. As can be seen in the text that Auden printed (Fig. 14.2), the poem is a carol, and like all carols it has a burden, which Auden printed once in full and once abbreviated to show that it should follow every stanza. Stravinsky set the poem exactly as it was printed, not the way it should be performed. (He did not actually set the words 'Sing, oh! etc.', but he set the burden only the two times Auden printed it.) Yet more evidence of his unconcern: he gave an inscribed copy of the Cantata score to Otto Klemperer, a Hitler refugee, whom I cannot think he meant to insult.[34] So it was not that Stravinsky sought out a text to set libelling the Jews. It simply did not matter to him.

Other people's texts, however, did matter to him at times. About Schoenberg he once remarked, 'Nearly all of his texts are appallingly bad, some of them so bad as to discourage performance of the music.'[35] He no doubt had *Die glückliche Hand* in mind, or some other embarrassing expressionistic effusion like that. But all that this shows is that Stravinsky's artistic sensibilities were more acute than his moral ones. Here is another manifestation of the dichotomy. It is a letter from Stravinsky to Craft, or rather a passage from a letter from Stravinsky to Craft, dated 8 October 1948, that has been silently expunged from both purportedly complete documentary publications of the letter.[36] The subject of comment is a demonstration against Serge Lifar, Diaghilev's last *premier danseur*, on account of his wartime collaboration with the Germans in occupied Paris. Stravinsky writes:

> If there were some intelligent Jews picketing before Lifar not for his 'fascism' (or, later on, 'communism', about which they are silent of course), but for his quite obvious want of talent, I would gladly change my mind about Jews.

The expression here is gratuitously vulgar and malicious, and for that reason repellent on its face, but the actual sentiments expressed are not unrelated, I would argue, to the blindnesses and exclusions I have been describing, and that we all practise to some extent, even those of us who are trying to shed them. We all operate under pressure to put what we call

Fig. 14.2

To-morrow shall be my dancing day

To-morrow shall be my dancing day,
    I would my true love did so chance
To see the legend of my play,
    To call my true love to my dance.
Sing, oh! my love, oh! my love, my love, my love,
This have I done for my true love.

Then was I born of a Virgin pure,
    Of her I took fleshly substance;
Thus was I knit to man's nature,
    To call my true love to my dance.
Sing, oh! etc.

In a manger laid and wrapp'd I was,
    So very poor, this was my chance,
Betwixt an ox and a silly poor ass,
    To call my true love to my dance.

Then afterwards baptized I was,
    The Holy Ghost on me did glance,
My Father's voice heard from above,
    To call my true love to my dance.

Into the desert I was led,
    Where I fasted without substance;
The Devil bade me make stones my bread,
    To have me break my true love's dance.

The Jews on me they made great suit,
    And with me made great variance,
Because they lov'd darkness rather than light,
    To call my true love to my dance.

For thirty pence Judas me sold,
    His covetousness for to advance;
Mark whom I kiss, the same do hold,
    The same is he shall lead the dance.

Fig. 14.2 (*cont.*)

Before Pilate the Jews me brought,
    Where Barabbas had deliverance,
They scourg'd me and set me at nought,
    Judged me to die to lead the dance.

Then on the cross hanged I was,
    Where a spear to my heart did glance;
There issued forth both water and blood,
    To call my true love to my dance.

Then down to Hell I took my way
    For my true love's deliverance,
And rose again on the third day
    Up to my true love and the dance.

Then up to Heaven I did ascend,
    Where now I dwell in sure substance,
On the right hand of God, that man
    May come unto the general dance.

(*As printed in Sandys'* Christmas Carols, *London, 1833*)

'artistic' considerations front and centre in any discussion of art, and to resist – indeed, to disdain – considerations of any other kind.

Nowadays that pressure and that resistance are most easily seen, in the musical world, in the ongoing debate about Wagner. Not content to print one, the editors of the *Musical Times* recently printed two separate hostile critiques of a single book, Marc Weiner's *Richard Wagner and the Anti-Semitic Imagination*, in a single issue. The one that shocked and depressed me was the one that prefaced any consideration of the author's arguments with an elaborate ritual in which the reviewer crossed himself, spat in all directions, and calumniated in advance all who raise the very issue of 'Richard Wagner's racist and antisemitic theories' in the context of his art. Such people are pre-judged as 'careerist journalists and musicologists' who 'pander' to fashion and aim merely to present themselves as 'trendily anti-establishment'.[37]

In the critique that followed, much was made of the fact that Prof. Weiner and others who have tackled these problems are not professional musicians and are therefore unqualified to write about music. But of course it is inevitable that these 'extramusical' questions will be broached from the standpoint of disciplines that are not regulated by the Stravinsky myth.

And that, of course, is the reason why the only discussion I have ever seen of the anti-Semitic text in Stravinsky's Cantata appeared not in a musical or musicological publication, but in a Jewish-interest periodical called

Midstream. The author, a painter and literary anthologist named Jacob Drachler, described his persistent efforts to lodge an effective protest at Stravinsky's setting of lines so offensive to Jews, efforts that culminated in a letter to Robert Craft, posted on 15 April 1971 (the date was poorly chosen, being that of Stravinsky's funeral). The reply came not from Craft but from Lillian Libman, Stravinsky's personal manager:

> [Mr. Craft] says that Mr. Stravinsky, of course, was not thinking about 'the holocaust of modern European Jewry' when he set those lines of 15th century verse. In fact, he got quite a jolt from the lines himself when he first heard the piece, and he had changed the text, substituting, I think, 'my foes' or 'my enemies' (we can't remember exactly) – but in any case the words were definitely changed, and the music amended, but again we don't know exactly when.
>
> If and when a new edition of the score comes out, Mr. Craft will see to it personally that the change is made.[38]

It will probably not surprise you to learn that this was never done, and I think it is clear that Ms Libman's letter was just an offhand attempt to dispose of a nuisance.[39] But how should we deal with the question, if we agree that there is a problem? Ought moral sensibilities, as much as artistic ones, discourage performance of excellent music? Stravinsky's answer, I believe, has been sufficiently implied. What should ours be? The dichotomy normally invoked in such discussions, between 'the music itself' and 'the extramusical', can be easily unmasked in this particular case. For if the music itself – what van den Toorn calls 'the musical object' – is alone what engages 'esthetic rapport', and the extramusical is altogether to be excluded from a proper aesthetic response, then we should have no problem with the second Ricercar. We can perform and enjoy it as an instrumental solo, or a vocalise.

But of course this would not be an acceptable solution. Why? Because it would violate the integrity of the musical text as the composer left it. In more casual language, it would make the performance 'unauthentic'. The composer's intentions, as we normally construe them, would not be carried out, and that would breach the most fundamental ethical obligation of 'classical music' as practised in the twentieth century.

Of course, this too is an ethical constraint we owe in large part to the myth-making authority of Stravinsky, who inveighed constantly against the performer's right to any exercise of subjective judgement. The snooty 'neoclassical' sermon in the last of his Harvard lectures of 1939, published under the title *Poetics of Music*, transfers the objectivist aesthetic identified by Schloezer in Stravinsky's composerly attitudes to a performance practice, the most influential set of performerly precepts ever explicitly enunciated in the twentieth century. The insistence in that lecture on the distinction between *execution* – selfless submission to 'an explicit will that contains nothing beyond what it specifically commands' – and *interpretation* – which lies 'at the root of all the errors, all the sins, all the misunderstandings that interpose themselves between the musical work and the listener' – has been, much more than any earlier historical precedent, the driving force behind 'authentic' performance, manifested not only in 'Early Music', but in all performances that adhere to the ethic of scrupulous submission, which means just about all performances one will hear today.[40]

But how ethical are such ethics, if they cause us to value the integrity of works of art above humane concerns? How ethical is an ethic that obliges us, when the Cantata is on the programme, to lend our unprotesting presence to an execration of the Jews, and thus become complicit in it, and even more than that, to maintain a pretence that nothing of the sort is taking place? How ethical is an ethic implying that artistic excellence or beautiful form redeems ugly or objectionable content, as so many have argued of late in the case of T. S. Eliot? What is the difference between saying that and saying that artistic excellence excuses objectionable content of any kind? And if we allow this much, then what prevents art from becoming for all of us, as it undoubtedly is for some of us, a means for secretly gratifying our inner bigot?

How ethical, finally, is an ethic that holds artists and art lovers to be entitled by their artistic commitment to moral indifference, and that *the greater the artist, the greater the entitlement*? The truth of this last corollary, I think, can be confirmed by a thought experiment. As many readers surely know, Gustav Holst also made a setting, in his case for mixed chorus, of 'Tomorrow shall be my dancing day', the carol that furnished the text for Stravinsky's second Ricercar. It is an attractive piece. Unlike Stravinsky's setting, it was written long before the Holocaust, in 1916. I would wager, though, that performers would be far more likely to think twice before performing Holst's setting than they evidently are before performing Stravinsky's, and that audiences hearing Holst's setting would be far more likely to notice and protest about the meaning of the words. The only reason I can think of for the difference is the differing stature of the composers. It is Stravinsky, not Holst, who has been classified as an unassailable great. Hence the dispensation he is granted, and hence the distress my words may be causing some readers.[41]

But is great art ennobled by this attitude? Are we? Or are we not debased and diminished, both as artists and as human beings, by such a commitment to 'abstract' musical worth? And for a final disquieting thought, has that commitment got nothing to do with the catastrophic decline that the prestige of classical music – and of high art in general – has suffered in our time?

So what, you may finally wonder, do I think we should do about the Cantata? Certainly not suppress it; although I personally would not be opposed to instrumental performance of the second Ricercar or some modification of the text, especially if it is not done 'silently', à la Dr Bowdler, which evades the problem, but rather with an accompanying announcement or explanation that exposes and confronts it.[42] I hope and trust that it is clear to one and all that inviting performers to consider such a course is not the same as decreeing that they do, and that an appeal to discretion is a far cry from censorship.

But even without modification, exposure of the problem is very much to be encouraged, I believe; and that is what I have sought to make of my opportunity here. In an unfortunately acidulous exchange with me about the Cantata in the *New York Review of Books* some years ago, Robert Craft made the claim (later included in the expanded *Chronicle of a Friendship*) that in his own first Los Angeles performance he substituted 'my enemies' for 'the Jews on me' in the first line of the fourth canon, and that for this he was reproached by Auden.[43] '"By any definition *The Merchant of Venice* is anti-Semitic," [Auden] said, "but we can't change it".' Modifying a performance does not change the work; and in any case we are not called upon to change it. But we *are* called upon to face the issue and talk about it, I believe; and we had better. That is the very least we can do if we want to escape from the counterproductive complacency on which the Stravinsky myth insists, and keep high art kosher.

Chronological list of works

Tarantella, for piano (1898)

'Storm Cloud' ('Tucha'), for soprano and piano (Russian text: Alexander Pushkin) (1902)

Scherzo, for piano (1902)

Sonata in F♯ minor, for piano (1903–4)

Cantata (for Rimsky-Korsakov's sixtieth birthday), for mixed choir and piano (presumed lost) (1904)

'How the Mushrooms Prepared for War', song for bass and piano (text: trad. Russian) (1904)

Symphony in E♭, Op. 1, for orchestra (1905–7)

'Conductor and Tarantula', for voice and piano (text: Kosma Prutkov) (presumed lost) (1906)

The Faun and the Shepherdess (*Favn i pastushka, Faune et bergère*), Op. 2, suite for mezzo-soprano and orchestra (Russian text: Alexander Pushkin) (1906)

Pastorale, for soprano (without words) and piano (1907). Arr. for soprano and four wind instruments (1923) and for violin and piano, or violin and four wind instruments (1933)

Two Songs (*Romances*), Op. 6, for mezzo-soprano and piano (Russian text: Sergey Gorodetsky) (1907–8)

Scherzo fantastique, Op. 3, for orchestra (1907–8)

Chant funèbre (in memoriam Rimsky-Korsakov), Op. 5, for wind instruments (presumed lost) (1908)

Four Studies, Op. 7, for piano (1908)

Fireworks, Op. 4, for orchestra (1908)

Nocturne in A♭ and *Grande valse brillante* in E♭ (Chopin), orchestrated for the ballet *Les sylphides* (1909)

Song of the Flea (Beethoven and Musorgsky), arr. for bass and orchestra (text: Goethe in Russian translation) (1909)

The Firebird (*L'Oiseau de feu, Zhar-ptitsa*), 'fairy tale' ballet in two scenes for large orchestra (1909–10). Concert suites: (a) 1910; (b) 1919 (rev. for reduced orchestra); (c) 'ballet suite', 1945 (as 1919 but with additional music). Piano reduction by Stravinsky

Kobold (Grieg), arr. for orchestra for the ballet *Les orientales* (1910)

Two Poems of Verlaine, Op. 9, for baritone and piano (1910). Rev. for orchestra (1910); rev. for baritone and small orchestra (1951–2)

Petrushka, 'burlesque' in four scenes for large orchestra (1910–11; rev. 1946, published 1947). Piano reduction (four hands) by Stravinsky. Transcribed as *Three Movements* for piano (1921, see below)

Two Poems of Bal'mont, for high voice and piano (text in Russian) (1911). Rev. and transcribed for soprano and small orchestra (1954)

Zvezdolikiy (*The King of the Stars, Le Roi des étoiles*), for male chorus and large orchestra (Russian text: Konstantin Balmont) (1911–12)

The Rite of Spring (*Le Sacre du printemps*), 'scenes of pagan Russia', ballet in two parts for large orchestra (1911–13; rev. 1943). Reduction for piano (four hands) by Stravinsky

Three Japanese Lyrics, for soprano and piano or chamber orchestra (Japanese text: anon.) (1912–13)

Khovanshchina (Musorgsky), orchestration of Shaklovitïy's aria and completion of final scene from the opera (1913)

Three Little Songs ('Recollections of my Childhood'), for voice and piano (text: trad. Russian) (1913). Rev. and transcribed for voice and small orchestra (1929–30)

The Nightingale (*Solovey, Le Rossignol*), 'musical fairy tale' in three acts for soloists, chorus and orchestra (Russian text: Stravinsky and Stepan Mitusov, after Hans Christian Andersen) (1908–9, 1913–14)

Three Pieces for String Quartet (1914; rev. 1918). Transcribed for orchestra as nos. 1–3 of *Four Studies* (see below); arr. for piano duet

Pribaoutki (*Chansons plaisantes*), for medium voice and eight instruments (text: trad. Russian) (1914)

Valse des fleurs, for piano duet (1914)

Three Easy Pieces, for piano duet (1914–15)

March, arr. of *Three Easy Pieces*, no. 1, for twelve instruments (1915)

Souvenir d'une marche boche, for piano (1915)

Cat's Cradle Songs (*Berceuses du chat, Kolïbel'nïye*), for medium voice and three clarinets (text: trad. Russian) (1915)

Renard (*Baika*), 'burlesque in song and dance' for two tenors, two basses and fifteen instruments (text: Stravinsky, after Alexander Nikolayevich Afanasyev) (1915–16)

Trois histoires pour enfants (*Three Tales for Children*), for voice and piano (text: trad. Russian) (1916–17). No. 1 rev. and transcribed for voice and orchestra (1923), nos. 1 and 2 transcribed as nos. 3 and 4 of *Four Songs* (1954, see below)

Valse pour les enfants, for piano (1916 or 1917)

Five Easy Pieces, for piano duet (1917)

Song of the Nightingale (*Pesnyas Solov'ya, Chant du rossignol*), symphonic poem / ballet for orchestra, derived from parts of Acts 2 and 3 of *The Nightingale* (1917)

Song of the Volga Boatmen, arr. for wind and percussion (1917)

Four Russian Peasant Songs (*Podblyudnïye*: 'Saucers'), for female voices a cappella (text: trad. Russian) (1914–17). Rev. for equal voices and four horns (1954)

Les Noces (*Svadebka, The Wedding*), 'Russian choreographic scenes' in four tableaux for four soloists, SATB, four pianos and percussion (text: Stravinsky, after Alexander Afanasyev Pyotr Vasilyevich Kireyevsky) (begun 1914; short score completed 1917; final scoring completed 1922–3)

Canons for Two Horns (presumed lost) (1917)

Étude, for pianola (1917)

Berceuse, for voice and piano (Russian text: Stravinsky) (1917)

Lied ohne Name, for two bassoons (1917 or 1918)

Ragtime, for eleven instruments (1917–18). Transcribed for solo piano by Stravinsky

The Soldier's Tale (*L'Histoire du soldat*), 'to be read, played and danced', in two parts, for three actors, female dancer and seven instrumentalists (French text: C. F. Ramuz) (1918). Suites: (a) for original ensemble of seven players (1920), (b) for violin, clarinet and piano (1919)

Three Pieces, for clarinet solo (1918)

Boris Godunov (Musorgsky), arr. of a chorus from the Prologue for piano (1918)

Quatre chants russes (*Four Russian Songs*), for voice and piano (text: trad. Russian) (1918–19). Nos. 1 and 4 transcribed as nos. 1 and 2 of *Four Songs* (see below)

Piano-Rag-Music, for piano (1919)

La Marseillaise, transcribed for solo violin (1919)

Pulcinella, 'ballet with song' in one act, for soprano, tenor, bass and chamber orchestra (1919–20). Suites: (a) for chamber orchestra (1922), (b) for violin and piano (1925), (c) *Suite italienne* for cello and piano (1932), and (d) for violin and piano (c. 1933) (see below)

Concertino, for string quartet (1920). Transcribed for twelve players (1952, see below)

Symphonies of Wind Instruments (*Symphonies d'instruments à vent*), for twenty-four wind players (1920; rev. 1947 for twenty-three instruments)

Suite no. 2, for small orchestra, arr. of *Three Easy Pieces* and 'Galop' from *Five Easy Pieces* (1915–21)

Les cinq doigts, easy pieces for piano (1921)

Sleeping Beauty (Tchaikovsky), arr. of Aurora's variation and Act 2 Entr'acte for violin and orchestra (1921)

Three Movements from *Petrushka*, for piano (1921)

Mavra, 'opéra bouffe' in one act for four soloists and orchestra (Russian text: Boris Kochno, after Pushkin) (1921–2)

Octet (*Octuor*), for wind instruments (1922–3; rev. 1952)

Concerto, for piano, wind instruments, timpani and double basses (1923–4; rev. 1950)

Sonata, for piano (1924)

Serenade in A, for piano (1925)

Suite no. 1, for small orchestra, transcribed from the first four of the *Five Easy Pieces* (1917–25)

Otche nash, for SATB chorus a cappella (text in Slavonic) (1926). Rev. 1949 as *Pater Noster* with Latin text

Oedipus Rex, opera-oratorio in two acts for speaker, soloists, chorus and orchestra (text: Jean Cocteau, after Sophocles, trans. into Latin by Jean Daniélou, with narration in language of audience) (1926–7; rev. 1948)

Apollon musagète (*Apollo*), ballet in two scenes for string orchestra (1927–8; rev. 1947)

The Fairy's Kiss (*Le Baiser de la fée*), 'allegorical ballet' in four scenes for orchestra, after songs and piano pieces by Tchaikovsky (1928; rev. 1950). Suite: *Divertimento* (1934, see below). *Divertimento*, for violin and piano, transcribed by Stravinsky and Samuel Dushkin (1932)

Four Studies (*Quatre études*), arr. for orchestra of *Three Pieces for String Quartet* and the *Étude* for pianola (1928–9; rev. 1952)

Capriccio, for piano and orchestra (1928–9; rev. 1949)

Symphony of Psalms, for SATB chorus and orchestra (Latin text: Bible: Psalms 38, 39, 150) (1930; rev. 1948)

Concerto in D, for violin and orchestra (1931)

Duo concertant, for violin and piano (1932)

Suite italienne, transcribed from *Pulcinella* (a) by Stravinsky and Gregor Piatigorsky
  for cello and piano (1932); (b) by Stravinsky and Samuel Dushkin for violin and
  piano (1932)

Simvol verï, for SATB chorus a cappella (text in Slavonic) (1932). Rev. 1949 as *Credo*
  with Latin text.

Perséphone, melodrama in three scenes for female speaker, tenor, chorus and orchestra
  (French text: André Gide) (1933–4; rev. 1949)

Bogoroditse devo, for SATB chorus a cappella (text in Slavonic) (1934). Rev. 1949 as
  Ave Maria with Latin text

Divertimento, 'symphonic suite' for orchestra (from *The Fairy's Kiss*) (1934; rev.
  1949)

Concerto, for two solo pianos (1932, 1934–5)

Jeu de cartes, 'ballet in three deals' for orchestra (1936)

Praeludium, for jazz ensemble (1936–7; rev. 1953)

Petit Ramusianum harmonique, 'three quatrains' for solo voice (French text: Stravinsky
  and Charles-Albert Cingria) (1937)

Concerto in E♭, 'Dumbarton Oaks', for chamber orchestra (1937–8)

Symphony in C, for orchestra (1938–40)

Tango, for piano (1940). Transcribed for nineteen instruments (1953)

The Star-Spangled Banner (John Stafford Smith), transcribed for orchestra and mixed
  choir (1941)

Sleeping Beauty (Tchaikovsky), 'Bluebird' *pas de deux* transcribed for small orchestra
  (1941)

Danses concertantes, for chamber orchestra (1940–42)

Circus Polka (for a young elephant), for piano (1941–2). Transcribed by Avid Raksin
  for wind band (circus band) (1942). Version for symphony orchestra (1942)

Four Norwegian Moods, for orchestra (1942)

Ode, 'elegiac chant' in three parts for orchestra (1943)

Scherzo à la russe, for jazz band (1943–4). Transcribed for orchestra (1945)

Sonata, for two pianos (1943–4)

Babel, cantata for male chorus, male narrator and orchestra (English text: Bible:
  Genesis 11, 1–9) (1944)

Scènes de ballet, for orchestra (1944)

Elegy, for solo viola or violin (1944)

Symphony in Three Movements, for orchestra (1942–5)

Ebony Concerto, for clarinet and jazz band (1945)

Concerto in D, ' "Basle" Concerto', for string orchestra (1946; rev. 1947)

Petit Canon pour la fête de Nadia Boulanger, for two tenors (French text: Jean de
  Meung) (1947)

Orpheus, ballet in three scenes for orchestra (1947)

Mass, for SATB chorus and ten wind instruments (1944–8)

The Rake's Progress, opera in three acts for soloists, chorus and orchestra (English text:
  W. H. Auden and Chester Kallman) (1947–51)

Cantata, for soprano, tenor, female chorus and five instruments (text: anon. fifteenth-
and sixteenth-century English verse) (1951–2)

Septet, for clarinet, bassoon, horn, string trio and piano (1952–3)

Concertino, arr. of string quartet original for twelve instruments (1952)

Three Songs from William Shakespeare, for mezzo-soprano, flute, clarinet and viola
(1953)

Four Songs, for voice, flute, harp and guitar, transcribed from nos. 1 and 4 of *Four
Russian Songs* and nos. 1 and 2 of *Three Tales for Children* (1954)

In memoriam Dylan Thomas, 'dirge canons and song' for tenor, string quartet and
four trombones (text: Dylan Thomas) (1954)

Greeting Prelude, 'for the eightieth birthday of Pierre Monteux', arr. of 'Happy
Birthday to You', for orchestra (1955)

Canticum Sacrum ad honorem Sancti Marci nominis, for tenor, baritone, chorus and
orchestra (Latin text: Vulgate Bible) (1955)

Chorale Variations on 'Von Himmel hoch' (J. S. Bach), transcribed and arr. for chorus
and orchestra (text in German) (1955–6)

Agon, 'ballet for twelve dancers' for orchestra (1953–7)

Threni: id est Lamentationes Jeremiae prophetae, for six solo voices, chorus and orchestra (Latin text: Vulgate Bible) (1957–8)

Movements for piano and orchestra (1958–9)

Epitaphium (Für das Grabmal des Prinzen Max Egon zu Fürstenberg), for flute, clarinet
and harp (1959)

Double Canon (Raoul Dufy in memoriam), for string quartet (1959)

Tres sacrae cantiones (Gesualdo), completed for SATB chorus a cappella (1957–9)

Monumentum pro Gesualdo di Venosa (ad CD annum), three madrigals by Gesualdo,
recomposed for instruments (orchestra) (1960)

A Sermon, a Narrative and a Prayer, cantata for alto and tenor soloists, speaker, chorus and orchestra (English text: Bible: Romans, Hebrews and Acts; and Thomas
Dekker) (1960–61)

Eight Instrumental Miniatures, for fifteen players, transcribed and recomposed from
Les cinq doigts (1962)

The Flood, 'musical play' for soloists, speakers, chorus and orchestra (English text:
Robert Craft, after the Bible and the York and Chester mystery plays) (1961–2)

Anthem 'The dove descending breaks the air', for SATB chorus a cappella (text: T. S.
Eliot, *Little Gidding*) (1962)

Abraham and Isaac, 'sacred ballad' for baritone and chamber orchestra (Hebrew text:
Bible) (1962–3)

Canzonetta for strings (Sibelius), transcribed for eight instruments (1963)

Elegy for J. F. K., for medium voice and three clarinets (text: W. H. Auden) (1964)

Fanfare for a New Theatre, for two trumpets (1964)

Variations (Aldous Huxley in memoriam), for orchestra (1963–4)

Introitus (T. S. Eliot in memoriam), for male chorus and chamber ensemble (Latin text
from Requiem Mass) (1965)

Canon (on a Russian Popular Tune), 'Concert Introduction or Encore' (on a theme
from *The Firebird*) for orchestra (1965)

Requiem Canticles, for contralto and bass soloists, chorus and orchestra (Latin text from Requiem Mass) (1965–6)

The Owl and the Pussycat, for soprano and piano (text: Edward Lear) (1966)

Two Sacred Songs (Wolf), transcribed for mezzo-soprano and ten instruments (texts: anon. Spanish in German translation by Paul Heyse and Emmanuel Geibel) (1968)

Four Preludes and Fugues (from *Das wohltemperirte Clavier*) (J. S. Bach), transcribed for strings and woodwind (1969)

Notes

1 Stravinsky's Russian origins

1 Robert Craft, *Stravinsky: Chronicle of a Friendship, 1948–71* (London: Alfred A. Knopf, 1972), 295.

2 See, for example, his fifth Harvard lecture, 'The avatars of Russian music', in *Poetics of Music in the Form of Six Lessons*, trans. Arthur Knodel and Ingolf Dahl (Cambridge, MA: Harvard University Press, 1947).

3 Craft, *Chronicle of a Friendship*, 185, 183.

4 Both Stravinsky and Nabokov grew up in St Petersburg and emigrated after the 1917 Revolution, first to France and then to the United States. The works of both are renowned for their apparent stylistic independence.

5 Richard Taruskin, *Stravinsky and the Russian Traditions: a Biography of the Works Through Mavra* (Oxford: Oxford University Press, 1996); Stephen Walsh, *Stravinsky: a Creative Spring: Russia and France 1882–1934* (London: Jonathan Cape, 1999).

6 Craft, *Chronicle of a Friendship*, 195.

7 Mikhail Druskin, *Igor Stravinsky: his Personality, Works and Views*, trans. Martin Cooper (Cambridge: Cambridge University Press, 1983), 2.

8 See Appendix 3 in Rosamund Bartlett, *Wagner and Russia* (Cambridge: Cambridge University Press, 1995), 304–5, which shows the percentage of Russian works in the repertoire each season between 1890 and 1914.

9 Igor Stravinsky and Robert Craft, *Expositions and Developments* (London: Faber and Faber, 1962), 66.

10 See Walsh, *Stravinsky: a Creative Spring*, 53.

11 I. F. Stravinsky, *Perepiska s russkiimi korrespondentami: materialy k biografii*, ed. Viktor Varunts, 2 vols. (Moscow: Kompozitor, 1997, 2000), Vol. 1.

12 Stravinsky and Craft, *Expositions and Developments*, 66.

13 Walsh, *Stravinsky: a Creative Spring*, 65.

14 V. Kamensky (ed.), *The World of Art Movement in Early 20th-Century Russia* (Leningrad: Aurora, 1991), 20.

15 Taruskin, *Stravinsky and the Russian Traditions*, 375.

16 Ibid., 376, 377.

17 Walsh, *Stravinsky: a Creative Spring*, 108.

18 *Russkaya muzykal'naya gazeta*, 51/52 (1901), col. 1334; cited in Varunts, *Perepiska s russkiimi korrespondentami*, vol. 1, 110.

19 Walsh, *Stravinsky: a Creative Spring*, 74.

20 Taruskin, *Stravinsky and the Russian Traditions*, 376–7.

21 Ibid., 352.

22 John E. Malmstad and Nikolay Bogomolov, *Mikhail Kuzmin: a Life in Art* (Cambridge, MA: Harvard University Press, 1999), 126.

23 Taruskin, *Stravinsky and the Russian Traditions*, 355.

24 Walsh, *Stravinsky: a Creative Spring*, 543.

25 It is interesting that Stravinsky felt aristocratic taste, such as that of Tchaikovsky, was no less Russian than what was 'peasant-like'. See Taruskin, *Stravinsky and the Russian Traditions*, 1533.

26 For further details, see ibid., 524–5. See also Rosamund Bartlett, 'Diaghilev as musician and concert organizer', in Ann Kodicek (ed.), *Diaghilev, Creator of the Ballets Russes: Art, Music, Dance* (London: Barbican Art Gallery/Lund Humphries, 1996), 49–52.

27 Taruskin, *Stravinsky and the Russian Traditions*, 524–5.

28 Stravinsky and Craft, *Expositions and Developments*, 34–5.

29 Druskin, *Igor Stravinsky*, 15.

30 Stravinsky and Craft, *Memories and Commentaries* (London: Faber and Faber, 1962), 29.

31 L. Belyakaeva-Kazanskaya, 'Stepan Mitusov. 2: Khronika neomrachennoi druzhby: Stravinskii i Mitusov', in *Ekho serebryannogo veka* (St Petersburg: Kanon, 1998), 36.

32 L. Belyakaeva-Kazanskaya, 'Stepan Mitusov. 1: ryadom s Rerikhom', in *Ekho serebryannogo veka*, 24.

33 See Taruskin, *Stravinsky and the Russian Traditions*, vol. 1, 502–18; and Beverly Whitney Kean, *All the Empty Palaces: the Merchant Patrons of Pre-Revolutionary Russia* (London: Barrie & Jenkins, 1983), for a history of neo-nationalism in the Russian arts.

34 See Taruskin, *Stravinsky and the Russian Traditions*, 497–502, for a discussion of the process of denationalisation in Russian music.

35 Taruskin, *Stravinsky and the Russian Traditions*, 615.

36 See ibid., 692–3.

37 For an extended survey of the musical sources for *Petrushka*, see Taruskin, *Stravinsky and the Russian Traditions*, 695–737.

38 Cited in ibid., 764.

39 See ibid., 851–2.

40 See ibid., 849–966, for a comprehensive history of the work's composition.

41 Ibid., 18.

42 Ibid., 954.

43 Ibid., 1449–1502.

44 Ibid., 1133.

45 Richard Gustafson, *Leo Tolstoy, Resident and Stranger: a Study in Fiction and Theology*, (Princeton: Princeton University Press, 1986), xiii.

46 Druskin, *Igor Stravinsky*, chap. 10.

47 Ibid., 133.

48 B. A. Uspensky, *Semiotika ikona* (Tartu: Tartu University Press, 1971), cited in Druskin, *Igor Stravinsky*, 128 (no page reference given).

49 Pavel Florensky, 'Obratnaya perspektiva', *Trudy po znakovym sisteman* 3 (1967), 402; cited in Druskin, *Igor Stravinsky*, 128.

50 See Taruskin, *Stravinsky and the Russian Traditions*, 1126–34.

51 Walsh, *Stravinsky: a Creative Spring*, 329.

52 Ibid., 433.

53 Ibid., 434.

54 Taruskin, *Stravinsky and the Russian Traditions*, 13.

2 Stravinsky as modernist

1 See Richard Taruskin's monumental study of the Russian Stravinsky: *Stravinsky and the Russian Traditions: a Biography of the Works through* Mavra (Oxford: Oxford University Press, 1996). But I am primarily concerned here with the Parisian Stravinsky.

2 There are many other portraits of Stravinsky. See Glenn Watkins's account of portraits of Stravinsky from 1913–16 in his *Pyramids at the Louvre: Music, Culture, and Collage from Stravinsky to the Postmodernists* (Cambridge, MA: Belknap Press, 1994), 243ff.

3 See Igor Stravinsky and Robert Craft, *Memories and Commentaries* (London: Faber and Faber, 1960), 103ff. The quotation is from p. 122f.

4 Ibid., 73ff. Stravinsky had read M. Teste before 1914, and asked Valéry to comment on his *Poetics of Music*.

5 Taruskin, *Stravinsky and the Russian Traditions*, and Stephen Walsh, *Stravinsky: a Creative Spring: Russia and France 1882–1934* (London: Jonathan Cape, 1999).

6 *Stravinsky: Selected Correspondence*, ed. and with commentaries by Robert Craft, 3 vols (London: Faber and Faber, 1982–5), vol. 2, 189.

7 He grew up with a big library, read and spoke German and French, and in his early twenties read Wilde, Hoffmann and Maeterlinck, and saw Chekhov and Ostrovsky, Tolstoy, Gorky and Shakespeare. See Michael Oliver, *Igor Stravinsky* (London: Phaidon, 1995), 25.

8 *Stravinsky in Conversation with Robert Craft* (Harmondsworth: Penguin, 1962), 108.

9 Igor Stravinsky and Robert Craft, *Expositions and Developments* (London: Faber and Faber, 1962), 115.

10 Diaghilev was interested in performing Balla's *Macchina tipografica* (1914); he was impressed by Futurist events in London; he mooted an alliance with Marinetti in 1915; and with Stravinsky he planned a restaging of *Feux d'artifice* (which had previously been performed by Loïe Fuller) by Giacomo Balla, to be performed in Paris in 1917. But the first performance was a fiasco. Diaghilev dropped *Feux d'artifice* and cancelled plans for a Futurist version of *The Nightingale*. See the account in Gunter Berghaus, *Italian Futurist Theatre* (Oxford: Clarendon, 1998), 253ff.

11 See, for example, Lawrence Rainey, *Institutions of Modernism* (New Haven: Yale University Press, 1998).

12 W. H. Auden, 'On the circuit', in *Collected Poems*, ed. Edward Mendelson (London: Faber and Faber, 1976), 549.

13 Oliver, *Igor Stravinsky*, 35, echoing the general view.

14 Watkins, *Pyramids at the Louvre*, 321.

15 Walsh, *Stravinsky: a Creative Spring* (*passim*).

16 Oliver, *Igor Stravinsky*, 60.

17 *Stravinsky in Conversation*, 138ff.

18 For a brief account of this in the early period, see Christopher Butler, *Early Modernism* (Oxford: Clarendon, 1994), 106–23. See also William Rubin (ed.), *Primitivism in Twentieth Century Art: Affinity of the Tribal and the Modern* (New York: Museum of Modern Art, 1984), and Jill Lloyd, *German Expressionism: Primitivism and Modernity* (New Haven: Yale University Press, 1991).

19 Watkins, *Pyramids at the Louvre*, 255.

20 Ibid., 262.

21 Ibid., 231.

22 Ibid., 216.

23 John Berger, *Success and Failure of Picasso* (Harmondsworth: Penguin, 1965), 90ff.

24 See Nancy Perloff, *The Art of the Everyday: Popular Entertainment and the Circle of Erik Satie* (Oxford: Clarendon, 1991).

25 Stravinsky, *Chronicle of My Life* (London: Victor Gollancz, 1936), 130; Roman Vlad, *Stravinsky*, trans. Frederick and Ann Fuller, 2nd edn. (London: Oxford University Press, 1967), 56.

26 Theodor W. Adorno, *Philosophy of Modern Music*, trans. Anne G. Mitchell and Wesley V. Blomster (London: Sheed and Ward, 1973), 170, 171.

27 Constant Lambert, *Music Ho!* (London: Faber and Faber, 1934; repr. 1966), 74–6.

28 Stravinsky and Craft, *Expositions and Developments*, 113.

29 Stephen Walsh, *The Music of Stravinsky* (Oxford: Oxford University Press, 1993), 96.

30 This statement comes from an article published in New York in a journal called *The Arts*; cited in Walsh, *Stravinsky: a Creative Spring*, 24.

31 See Walsh, *Stravinsky: a Creative Spring*, 431ff, discussing the influence of Lourié and Maritain.

32 Oliver, *Igor Stravinsky*, 217, citing the *Chronicle*.

33 T. S. Eliot, 'Tradition and the individual talent', in *The Sacred Wood* (London: Methuen, 1920; repr. 1960), 48.

34 Ibid., 49.

35 T. E. Hulme, in Karen Csengeri (ed.), *The Collected Writings of T. E. Hulme* (Oxford: Clarendon, 1994), 61.

36 *Expositions and Developments*, 118.

37 Schoenberg, diary entry 1928, in *Style and Idea*, ed. Leonard Stein, trans. Leo Black (London: Faber and Faber, 1975), 482.

38 Stravinsky, *Poetics of Music in the Form of Six Lessons* (Cambridge, MA: Harvard University Press, 1947; repr. 1998), 80ff.

39 Dermée, 'Quand le symbolisme fut mort', a programmatic statement for his *North South*, cited in Peter Nicholls, *Modernisms* (Basingstoke: Macmillan, 1995), 243.

40 Cited in Nicholls, *Modernisms*, 245.

41 T. S. Eliot, 'Ulysses, order, and myth', *Dial*, 65/5 (November 1923), 483.

42 'Without the capacity for adaptation of a Picasso – who, having lost if temporarily his iconoclastic fervor, retreated into a highly productive self involvement – or the social utopianism of a Léger (or the Purists), most of the pre-war members of the Parisian avant garde had little to fall back on . . . the unqualified optimism of the pre-war period was an outmoded point of view. Henceforth a desperate effort to resuscitate a fading vision of a hegemonic "West" would compel attention in French cultural circles.' Kenneth E. Silver, *Esprit de Corps: the Art of the Parisian Avant Garde and the First World War, 1914–1935* (Princeton: Princeton University Press, 1989), 360. You had to be a classicist or a *constructeur*, and 'the world of the Parisian avant garde was left with a bankrupt social identity' (ibid., 361).

43 In its latest form in her *The Picasso Papers* (Cambridge, MA: MIT, 1999).

44 For a recent elegy from this point of view, see T. J. Clark, *Farewell to an Idea* (New Haven: Yale University Press, 1999). Clark comments on modernism – which 'had two great wishes', just as if it were one person – as 'tied to, and propelled by, one central process: the accumulation of capital' (7). He adds, 'if I cannot have the proletariat as my chosen people any longer, at least capitalism remains my Satan' (8). This orientation does not seem to prevent the brilliant interpretation of particular works in the rest of the book – but it does select them.

45 Walsh, *The Music of Igor Stravinsky*, 168–78.

46 Letter of 31 August 1953, in *Selected Correspondence*, vol. 1, 287.

47 Watkins, *Pyramids at the Louvre*, 365.

48 See Judith Mackrell, *Reading Dance* (London: Michael Joseph, 1997), 53ff.

3 Stravinsky in context

1 Richard Taruskin, *Stravinsky and the Russian Traditions: a Biography of the Works Through Mavra* (Oxford: Oxford University Press, 1996), 1675.

2 Ibid., 662.

3 Ibid., 1675.

4 Richard Taruskin, 'Stravinsky and the subhuman. A myth of the 20th century: *The Rite of Spring*, the tradition of the new, and "the music itself" ', in *Defining Russia Musically* (Princeton: Princeton University Press, 1997), especially 460–65. See also Taruskin's 'Stravinsky and us' in this volume.

5 See the arguments summarised in Marc A. Weiner, *Richard Wagner and the Anti-Semitic Imagination* (Lincoln, NE: University of Nebraska Press, 1995).

6 Stephen Walsh, *Stravinsky: a Creative Spring: Russia and France 1882–1934* (London: Jonathan Cape, 1999), 376.

7 Jonathan Cross, *The Stravinsky Legacy* (Cambridge: Cambridge University Press, 1998), 239.

8 Walsh, *Stravinsky: a Creative Spring*, 260.

9 Arnold Schoenberg, *Style and Idea*, ed. Leonard Stein, trans. Leo Black (London: Faber and Faber, 1975), 174.

10 This polarisation is at its most highly charged in Adorno's *Philosophy of Modern Music*: 'Schoenberg and progress', 'Stravinsky and restoration'. For a much more recent formulation of essential difference not predicated on the argument that Schoenberg is good, Stravinsky bad, see Pieter C. van den Toorn, 'Neoclassicism and its definitions', in James M. Baker, David W. Beach and Jonathan W. Bernard (eds.), *Music Theory in Concept and Practice*, (Rochester, NY: University of Rochester Press, 1997), 154–5.

11 Igor Stravinsky, *An Autobiography* (New York: Steuer, 1958), 100. (First published in French, two volumes, 1935–6.)

12 Walsh, *Stravinsky: a Creative Spring*, 260.

13 Igor Stravinsky, *Poetics of Music*, trans. Arthur Knodel and Ingolf Dahl (New York: Vintage, 1947), 14.

14 Igor Stravinsky and Robert Craft, *Dialogues* (London: Faber and Faber, 1982), p. 107. Arthur Lourié was an early proponent of the idea that 'Schönberg may be considered the *Thesis* and Stravinsky the *Antithesis*. Schönberg's thesis is an egocentric conception dominated by personal and esthetic elements which assume the significance of a fetish ... Stravinsky's whole aim, on the other hand, is to overcome the temptations of fetishism in art, as well as the individualistic conception of a self-imposed esthetic principle.' ('Neogothic and neoclassic', *Modern Music* 5 (1928), cited in Walsh, *Stravinsky: a Creative Spring*, 461.)

15 Stravinsky and Craft, *Dialogues*, 108.

16 See Taruskin, *Stravinsky and the Russian Traditions*, 1022.

17 Ibid.

18 Allen Forte, *The Harmonic Organization of 'The Rite of Spring'* (New Haven: Yale University Press, 1978). See also *Music Analysis* 5/2–3 (1986), 313–37.

19 Pierre Boulez, *Conversations with Célestin Deliège* (London: Eulenberg, 1976), 31.

20 See *The Boulez–Cage Correspondence*, ed. Jean-Jacques Nattiez, trans. Robert Samuels (Cambridge: Cambridge University Press, 1993).

21 Boulez, *Conversations*, 17.

22 Pierre Boulez, *Orientations*, ed. Jean-Jacques Nattiez, trans. Martin Cooper (London: Faber and Faber, 1986), 355.

23 See the critical discussion of this topic in Jonathan Kramer, *The Time of Music* (New York: Schirmer, 1988), and Alexander Rehding, 'Towards a "logic of discontinuity" in Stravinsky's *Symphonies of Wind Instruments*: Hasty, Kramer and Straus reconsidered', *Music Analysis* 17/1 (1998), 39–63.

24 In a brief note written towards the end of his life, Schoenberg referred to 'a turn – perhaps you would call it to the Apollonian side – in the Suite for Seven Instruments, Op. 29 [1925–6]'; *Style and Idea*, 110.

25 The reference is to the title of Eric Walter White's early study, *Stravinsky's Sacrifice to Apollo* (London: Hogarth Press, 1939).

26 Igor Stravinsky and Robert Craft, *Conversations with Igor Stravinsky* (London: Faber and Faber, 1959), 71–2.

27 Stravinsky and Craft, *Dialogues*, 124–5.

28 See Arnold Whittall, 'Berg and the twentieth century', in Anthony Pople (ed.), *The Cambridge Companion to Berg* (Cambridge: Cambridge University Press, 1997), 247–58.

29 Cross, *The Stravinsky Legacy*, 16.

30 See *Poetics*, 'The phenomenon of music' (Lecture 2).

31 *Poetics*, 43.

32 Walsh, *Stravinsky: a Creative Spring*, 249–50.

33 Stephen Walsh, *Stravinsky: Oedipus Rex* (Cambridge: Cambridge University Press, 1993), 65.

34 Ibid., 36, 39.

35 Ibid., 43, 45.

36 Ibid., 46.

37 Ibid., 61–3.

38 Stravinsky and Craft, *Dialogues*, 34.

39 See Arnold Whittall, 'Music analysis as human science? *Le Sacre du printemps* in theory and practice', *Music Analysis* 1/1 (1982), 33–53; Whittall, 'Defusing Dionysus? New perspectives on *The Rite of Spring*', *Music Analysis* 21/1 (2002), 87–103; Taruskin, *Defining Russia Musically*, 375–6.

40 Stephen Walsh, *The Music of Stravinsky* (Oxford: Oxford University Press, 1988), 275.

41 Ibid., 238.

42 Martha M. Hyde, 'Neoclassic and anachronistic impulses in twentieth-century music', *Music Theory Spectrum* 18 (1996), 214. The analytical example from the Octet that Hyde discusses is taken from Pieter C. van den Toorn, *The Music of Igor Stravinsky* (New Haven: Yale University Press, 1983), 334.

43 Chandler Carter, 'Stravinsky's "special sense": the rhetorical use of tonality in *The Rake's Progress*', *Music Theory Spectrum* 19 (1997), 77–8, 80.

44 Michael Cherlin, 'Memory and rhetorical trope in Schoenberg's String Trio', *Journal of the American Musicological Society* 51 (1998), 559.

45 Ibid., 563.

46 Ibid., 564.

47 Ibid., 573.

48 Ibid., 589.

49 See n. 23 above.

50 Cherlin, 'Memory and rhetorical trope', 595.

51 Michael Cherlin, 'Schoenberg and *Das Unheimliche*: spectres of tonality', *The Journal of Musicology* 11 (1993), 370.

52 Walsh, *The Music of Stravinsky*, 202; Daniel Albright, *Stravinsky: the Music Box and the Nightingale* (New York: Gordon and Breach, 1989), 41.

53 Walsh, *Stravinsky: a Creative Spring*, 376.

54 Stravinsky, *Autobiography*, 100.

55 Stravinsky, *Poetics*, 83, 34.

56 Walsh, *Stravinsky: a Creative Spring*, 376.

57 Boris Asaf'yev, *A Book About Stravinsky*, trans. Richard F. French (Ann Arbor: UMI Research Press, 1982), 278.

58 Letter of 9 July 1928, as translated in Walsh, *Stravinsky: a Creative Spring*, 455.

59 Walsh, *Stravinsky: a Creative Spring*, 500.

60 See ibid., 469, quoting Boris de Schloezer, 'Chronique musicale', *Nouvelle revue française* (1 July 1928), 104–8.

61 The dithyramb is 'an ancient Greek choric hymn, vehement and wild in character' (*Shorter Oxford Dictionary*). For some sense of the difficulties of interpreting the scant surviving evidence as to the content of these hymns to Dionysus, see A. Pickard-Cambridge, *Dithyramb, Tragedy and Comedy* (Oxford: Oxford University Press, 1962), and Andrew Barker, *Greek Musical Writings*, vol. 1 (Cambridge: Cambridge University Press, 1984).

62 Arnold Schoenberg, *Fundamentals of Musical Composition*, ed. Gerald Strang and Leonard Stein (London: Faber and Faber, 1967), 58–62. See also 'Reduction (ii)' in Ian Bent and William Drabkin, *The New Grove Handbooks in Music: Analysis* (London: Macmillan, 1987), 128–30.

63 See above, p. 39.

64 Most of this paragraph appears, in a different context, in my article 'Fulfilment or betrayal? Twentieth-century music in retrospect', *Musical Times* 140 (Winter 1999), 11–21.

65 Mikhail Druskin, *Igor Stravinsky: his Personality, Works and Views*, trans. Martin Cooper (Cambridge: Cambridge University Press, 1983), 122.

4 Early Stravinsky

1 Charles Rosen, *The Classical Style: Haydn, Mozart, Beethoven*, rev. edn (London: Faber and Faber, 1976), 19–23 and *passim*.

2 Igor Stravinsky and Robert Craft, *Expositions and Developments* (London: Faber and Faber, 1962), 43.

3 For a description of Stravinsky's family music-making from the mid 1890s to c.1901, see Richard Taruskin, *Stravinsky and the Russian Traditions: a Biography of the Works through Mavra* (Oxford: Oxford University Press, 1996), 94.

4 Brief passages of the *Tarantella* are given as music examples in Taruskin, *Stravinsky and the Russian Traditions*, 96.

5 Stravinsky, letter (13 March 1908) to G. H. Timofeyev, quoted in Vera Stravinsky and Robert Craft (eds.), *Stravinsky in Pictures and Documents* (London: Hutchinson, 1979), 21–2.

6 Taruskin, *Stravinsky and the Russian Traditions*, 99.

7 Stravinsky, letter (13 March 1908) to G. H. Timofeyev, quoted in *Stravinsky in Pictures and Documents*, 21–2.

8 *Expositions and Developments*, 43.

9 The manuscript is reproduced in Taruskin, *Stravinsky and the Russian Traditions*, 101.

10 See Igor Stravinsky and Robert Craft, *Memories and Commentaries* (London: Faber and Faber, 1960), 24, and Taruskin, *Stravinsky and the Russian Traditions*, 109–10.

11 Stravinsky, letter (13 March 1908) to G. H. Timofeyev, quoted in *Stravinsky in Pictures and Documents*, 21–2.

12 V. V. Yastrebtsev, *Reminiscences of Rimsky-Korsakov*, ed. and trans. F. Jonas (New York: Columbia University Press, 1985), 328.

13 See ibid., 340 and 523, n. 9.

14 The word 'conductor' in the title is to be understood in the sense of the conductor of a train or horse-drawn carriage, rather than an orchestra! Taruskin renders the Russian word *Konduktor* as 'driver' in his translation of the poem; *Stravinsky and the Russian Traditions*, 112–13.

15 Taruskin, *Stravinsky and the Russian Traditions*, 150–61.

16 Stravinsky, letter (13 March 1908) to G. H. Timofeyev, quoted in *Stravinsky in Pictures and Documents*, 21–2.

17 Direct parallels between Stravinsky's Sonata and works by Glazunov, Skryabin and Tchaikovsky are charted by Taruskin in *Stravinsky and the Russian Traditions*, 115–33.

18 Taruskin, *Stravinsky and the Russian Traditions*, 133.

19 *Memories and Commentaries*, 22, 28.

20 Taruskin, *Stravinsky and the Russian Traditions*, 116.

21 *Memories and Commentaries*, 20–22.

22 Taruskin, *Stravinsky and the Russian Traditions*, 171.

23 Stravinsky, *An Autobiography (1903–1934)* (London: Marion Boyars, 1975), 21; Yastrebtsev, *Reminiscences*, 344.

24 Taruskin, *Stravinsky and the Russian Traditions*, 172–3.

25 Stravinsky, *An Autobiography*, 20–24.

26 Taruskin, *Stravinsky and the Russian Traditions*, 175–222.

27 See ibid., 225–6.

28 *Memories and Commentaries*, 59.

29 Yastrebtsev, *Reminiscences*, 421.

30 Taruskin, *Stravinsky and the Russian Traditions*, 391–4.

31 As detailed in a letter from Rimsky-Korsakov to Alfred Bruneau, quoted and translated in ibid., 172.

32 From Glazunov's ballet *The Seasons* (1899). See ibid., 241–2.

33 For suggested correspondences between the Four Studies and particular passages in Skryabin's music, see ibid., 380. For details of the chronology, see p. 334.

34 Ibid., 365–8.

35 See Herbert Schneider's introduction to the 1990 Eulenburg edition.

36 In Igor Stravinsky and Robert Craft, *Conversations with Igor Stravinsky* (London: Faber and Faber, 1959), 40.

37 Taruskin, *Stravinsky and the Russian Traditions*, 318–23.

38 Strictly speaking, just as one of the tritones is a diminished fifth and the other an augmented fourth, so one of the 'major thirds' has to be spelled as a diminished fourth and one of the 'minor thirds' as an augmented second; the whole arrangement assumes enharmonic equivalence in these cases.

39 See Edward T. Cone's famous discussion of this technique: 'Stravinsky: the progress of a method', in Benjamin Boretz and Edward T. Cone (eds.), *Perspectives on Schoenberg and Stravinsky* (Princeton: Princeton University Press, 1968), 156–64.

40 The classic discussion of octatonicism in Stravinsky's music is Pieter C. van den Toorn, *The Music of Igor Stravinsky* (New Haven: Yale University Press, 1983).

41 *Conversations*, 41, n. 1.

42 See Taruskin, *Stravinsky and the Russian Traditions*, 400–401 (performance), 407–8 (reviews).

43 Ibid., 401–2.

44 Stravinsky, *An Autobiography*, 24.

45 *Memories and Commentaries*, 59.

46 According to Robert Craft, writing in *Stravinsky: Selected Correspondence*, 3 vols (New York: Knopf, 1982–5), vol. 2, 432; the first draft of the opera's scenario is given in English translation on pp. 433–5.

47 These sketches are described and reproduced in Taruskin, *Stravinsky and the Russian Traditions*, 469–73.

48 Ibid., 474–5.

49 Ibid., 450–62.

50 See Anthony Pople, *Skryabin and Stravinsky 1908–1914: Studies in Theory and Analysis* (New York: Garland, 1989). See also Stephen Walsh's comments on this musical correspondence in a review of this book in *Music Analysis* 9/3 (1990), 342.

51 Diaghilev later attended the premiere of *Fireworks*. See Taruskin, *Stravinsky and the Russian Traditions*, 418, n. 113.

52 Ibid., 574–5.

53 Ibid., 576–7.

54 Ibid., 579.

55 Ibid., 481–6.

56 See Stravinsky's letter of 29 March 1929 to C. G. Païchadze, quoted in V. Stravinsky and Craft, *Stravinsky in Pictures and Documents*, 58, and I. Stravinsky and Craft, *Conversations*, 96.

57 Recorded in 1961; reissued on CD in 1991 (Sony SM3K 46 291).

58 *Expositions and Developments*, 132.

59 Though there is no 'Op. 8', it seems likely that this designation was at one stage intended for *The Nightingale*.

60 Letter from Debussy to Stravinsky (18 August 1913), in *Conversations*, 51.

61 *Conversations*, 51, n. 1.

62 See also Simon Karlinsky, 'Igor Stravinsky and Russian preliterate theater', in Jann Pasler (ed.), *Confronting Stravinsky: Man, Musician, and Modernist* (Berkeley: University of California Press, 1986), 3–15.

63 Igor Stravinsky and Robert Craft, *Themes and Conclusions* (London: Faber and Faber, 1972), 198. Stravinsky identifies *Nightingale*-like traits in *Les Noces* on p. 199.

5 Russian rites: *Petrushka, The Rite of Spring* and *Les Noces*

1 This discussion of *Petrushka* is based on the revised 1947 version of the score.

2 Richard Taruskin, *Stravinsky and the Russian Traditions: a Biography of the Works Through Mavra* (Oxford: Oxford University Press, 1996), 662.

3 Stephen Walsh, *The Music of Stravinsky* (Oxford: Oxford University Press, 1993), 24.

4 Richard Taruskin, *Stravinsky and the Russian Traditions*, 695.

5 Nikolai Rimsky-Korsakov, *Sto russkikh naraodnïkh pesen* (St Petersburg: Bessel, 1877), no. 47. See Taruskin, *Stravinsky and the Russian Traditions*, 696.

6 See Taruskin, *Stravinsky and the Russian Traditions*, 737–59. For a concise definition of octatonicism, see Anthony Pople, 'Early Stravinsky', this volume, p. 66. Further discussions of octatonicism can be found in this volume in the chapters by Martha Hyde and Craig Ayrey.

7 Arthur Berger, 'Problems of pitch organisation in Stravinsky', in Benjamin Boretz and Edward T. Cone (eds), *Perspectives on Schoenberg and Stravinsky* (rev. edn New York: Norton, 1972), 123–54.

8 See Taruskin, *Stravinsky and the Russian Traditions*, 737–59, and Pieter C. van den Toorn, *The Music of Igor Stravinsky* (New Haven: Yale University Press, 1983), 31–3.

9 For an introduction to some of the theoretical problems involved in the concept of polytonality, see Jonathan Dunsby and Arnold Whittall, *Music Analysis in Theory and Practice* (London: Faber, 1988), 112–13.

10 Igor Stravinsky, *Poetics of Music*, trans. Arthur Knodel and Ingolf Dahl (Cambridge, MA: Harvard University Press, 1947), 36.

11 Taruskin, *Stravinsky and the Russian Traditions*, 746, Ex. 10.20.

12 Joseph Lanner, *Streyerische Tänze*, Op. 165, and *Die Schönbrunner*, Op. 200, in *Denkmäler der Tonkunst in Oesterreich*, vol. 65 (Vienna: Universal Edition, 1926), 78, 107.

13 Taruskin, *Stravinsky and the Russian Traditions*, 697.

14 Taruskin identifies this melody as 'Along the road to Piter' (*vdol' po piterskoy*), a.k.a. 'I was out at a party early last night' (*ya vechor mlada vo piru bila*) from P. I. Tchaikovsky, *50 naradnïkh russkikh pesen, obrabotka dlya fortep'yano v 4 ruki* (Moscow: Jurgenson, 1869); or Tertiy Filippov, *40 naradnïkh pesen s soprano-zhdeniyem fortepiano garmonizannikh N. Rimskim-Korsakovïm* (Moscow: Jurgenson, 1882); see Taruskin, *Stravinsky and the Russian Traditions*, 697. Sternfeld describes this melody as 'Dance song'; see Fredrick W. Sternfeld, 'Some Russian folk songs in Stravinsky's *Petrouchka*', in Charles Hamm (ed.), *Petrushka: an Authoritative Score of the Original Version* (New York: W. W. Norton, 1967), 211.

15 Van den Toorn, *The Music of Stravinsky*, 73–90.

16 See Craig Ayrey, 'Stravinsky in analysis', in this volume, n. 25, for a brief explanation of Forte's terminology.

17 This melody has been identified as no. 157 from Anton Juszkiewicz, *Melodie ludowe litewskie* (Cracow: Wydawn Akademji Umiejetno'sci, 1900). For commentary on this source see Lawrence Morton, 'Footnotes to Stravinsky studies: *Le Sacre du Printemps*', *Tempo* 128 (1978), 9–16; Richard Taruskin, 'Russian folk melodies in *The Rite of Spring*', *Journal of the American Musicological Society* 33 (1980), 501–43, and *Stravinsky and the Russian Traditions*, 891–923.

18 For a chronology of the compositional process see Pieter C. van den Toorn, *Stravinsky and 'The Rite of Spring': the Beginnings of a Musical Language* (Berkeley: University of California Press, 1987), 22–38. See also Robert Craft, 'Genesis of a masterpiece' and 'Commentary to the sketches', in Igor Stravinsky, *The Rite of Spring Sketches 1911–1913* (London: Boosey and Hawkes, 1969).

19 This introductory solo has received detailed commentary in the analytical literature. See Adele T. Katz, *Challenge to Musical Tradition* (London: Putnam, 1947), 321–2; Roy Travis, 'Towards a new concept of tonality', *Journal of Music Theory* 3 (1959), 262; Allen Forte, 'New approaches to the linear analysis of music', *Journal of the American Musicological Association* 41 (1988), 317–22; Anthony Pople, *Skryabin and Stravinsky 1908–1914: Studies in Theory and Analysis* (New York: Garland, 1989), 257–68.

20 Van den Toorn, *Stravinsky and 'The Rite of Spring'*, 141.

21 Taruskin, *Stravinsky and the Russian Traditions*, 939.

22 Ibid.

23 The term *Grundgestalt* is generally translated and understood as 'basic shape'. According to Walter Frisch, 'In his critical and theoretical writings Schoenberg often stresses that a motivic or thematic idea must have generative power – that all the events of a piece must be implicit in, or foreseen in, the basic shape, or *Grundgestalt*, presented at the opening.' Walter Frisch, *The Early Works of Arnold Schoenberg* (Berkeley: University of California Press, 1993), 206.

24 *Music Analysis* 5/2–3 (1986), 313–20 and 321–37.

25 Arnold Whittall, 'Music analysis as human science? Le Sacre du printemps in theory and practice', *Music Analysis* 1/1 (1982), 43–4. Clearly the use of the consonance/dissonance terminology is problematic, as it appropriates the language of common-practice tonality, a language which is some distance from that of the sound world of *The Rite of Spring*. Nevertheless, its use in this context provides a useful point of reference and helps retain a background of tradition/convention. However, the difference between the views held by Taruskin and those held by Forte indicate the problems involved in defining this work as either tonal or atonal. See *Music Analysis* 5/2–3.

26 Whittall, 'Music analysis as human science?', 45.

27 Igor Stravinsky and Robert Craft, *Expositions and Developments* (London, Faber and Faber, 1962), 147.

28 Whittall, 'Music analysis as human science?', 51.

29 Taruskin, *Stravinsky and the Russian Traditions*, 937.

30 For a summary of these sources see ibid., 1423–46.

31 Stravinsky and Craft, *Expositions and Developments*, 118.

32 Ibid., 115.

33 Walsh, *The Music of Stravinsky*, 78.

34 Van den Toorn, *The Music of Stravinsky*, 177.

6 Stravinsky's neoclassicism

1 Milan Kundera, *Testaments Betrayed*, trans. Linda Asher (New York: HarperCollins, 1995), 95–8.

2 Ibid., 97.

3 Igor Stravinsky and Robert Craft, *Memories and Commentaries* (New York: Doubleday, 1960), 104.

4 Scott Messing, *Neoclassicism in Music from the Genesis of the Concept through the Schoenberg/Stravinsky Polemic* (Ann Arbor: UMI Research Press, 1988); Stephen Hinton, *The Idea of Gebrauchsmusik: a Study of Musical Aesthetics in the Weimar Republic (1919–1933) with Particular Reference to the Works of Paul Hindemith* (New York: Garland, 1989); Joseph N. Straus, *Remaking the Past: Musical Modernism and the Influence of the Tonal Tradition* (Cambridge, MA: Harvard University Press, 1990); Richard Taruskin, 'Revising revision', *Journal of the American Musicological Society* 46 (1993), 114–38, and 'Back to whom? Neoclassicism as ideology', *19th-Century Music* 16 (1993), 286–302.

5 For a more detailed discussion of these issues, see my 'Neoclassic and anachronistic impulses in twentieth-century music', *Music Theory Spectrum* 18 (1996), 200–35. The following discussion borrows passages and summarises key arguments from this article.

6 T. S. Eliot, 'What is a classic?', in *On Poetry and Poets* (New York: Noonday Press, 1968), 52–74.

7 Frank Kermode, *The Classic* (Cambridge, MA: Harvard University Press, 1983), 40. Kermode defines the second mode, accommodation, somewhat differently: 'any method by which the old document may be induced to signify what it cannot be said to have expressly stated'. *The Classic* rewards close reading for those interested in the vagaries of musical 'classics'.

8 Thomas Greene offers a fuller account of anachronism and its use in literary texts in 'History and anachronism', in *The Vulnerable Text: Essays on Renaissance Literature* (New York: Columbia University Press, 1986), 218–35.

9 Ibid., 221.

10 Thomas Greene, *The Light in Troy: Imitation and Discovery in Renaissance Poetry* (New Haven: Yale University Press, 1982), 37–8.

11 Ex. 6.1 uses the first edition of *Piano-Rag-Music*, published in 1919. This early group of pieces based on contemporary popular dances, while more parodic than neoclassical, nonetheless provides excellent examples of stylistic features that become more fully developed in Stravinsky's later neoclassical works.

12 Greene, *The Light in Troy*, 28–53. In the following discussion, I draw upon Greene's work which, though focused on Renaissance poetry, develops several generally useful categories of imitation.

13 'Octatonic pitch structures' refers to any group of pitch classes that represents a subset of an octatonic collection. An octatonic collection contains eight pitch classes that can be arranged in an ascending scalar pattern of alternating semitones and whole tones. The octatonic scale is highly symmetrical and has only three distinct forms, which are referred to as Collections I, II and III.

14 Igor Stravinsky and Robert Craft, *Dialogues and a Diary* (New York: Doubleday, 1963), 11.

15 Greene, *The Light in Troy*, 39.

16 *Dialogues*, 71.

17 The analysis here follows Pieter C. van den Toorn's discussion of this passage in *The Music of Igor Stravinsky* (New Haven: Yale University Press, 1983), 333–6. This book provides many useful analyses of Stravinsky's neoclassical works.

18 While a precise definition of moment form remains allusive, Stockhausen's concept of the 'moment' is often cited in reference to Stravinsky's works. G. W. Hopkins gives the following definition: 'Each individually characterized passage in a work is regarded as an experiential unit, a "moment", which can potentially engage the listener's full attention and can do so in exactly the same measure as its neighbours. No single "moment" claims priority, even as a beginning or ending; hence the nature of such a work is essentially "unending" (and, indeed, "unbeginning"),' in Stanley Sadie (ed.), *The New Grove Dictionary of Music and Musicians* (London: Macmillan, 1980), s.v. 'Stockhausen, Karlheinz', vol. 18, 152. Many critics have drawn parallels between Stravinsky's moment forms and contemporary cubist painting, both of which

cultivate a concise pattern of repeating varied shapes that omit smooth transitions, emphasising instead abrupt movement from one shape to the next. In both, form is constructed by means of opposition, discontinuity and stratification.

19 The Russian Five, sometimes called the 'Mighty Five', were a group of nationalist composers made up of César Cui, Mily Balakirev, Alexander Borodin, Modest Musorgsky and Nikolai Rimsky-Korsakov. Richard Taruskin has powerfully explained why Stravinsky tried to distance himself from the Russian tradition that he so publicly embraced prior to World War I: '[L]ike so many other artists in the aftermath of the Great War, Stravinsky became outwardly conservative, allying himself volubly and vehemently with the elite culture of the Western past, seeking to defend its purity against all that threatened to defile it, including his own early work.' See Richard Taruskin, *Stravinsky and the Russian Traditions: a Biography of the Works Through* Mavra (Oxford: Oxford University Press, 1996), 1513.

20 Cited passages come from a letter by Stravinsky that appears in a programme book reproduced in Robert Craft (ed.), *Igor and Vera Stravinsky: a Photograph Album (1921–1971)* (London: Thames and Hudson, 1982), 54. For a detailed discussion of why Stravinsky switched historical allegiances after the First World War and the influence of politics, see Taruskin, *Stravinsky and the Russian Traditions*, 1507–38.

21 The piano reduction is by the composer; the verse libretto, originally in Russian and written by Boris Kochno, appears in an English translation.

22 Jonathan Cross, *The Stravinsky Legacy* (Cambridge: Cambridge University Press, 1998), 13.

23 Stephen Walsh, *The Music of Stravinsky* (Oxford: Oxford University Press, 1993), 119.

24 For a detailed discussion of how Stravinsky organises texture into highly differentiated and harmonically independent layers, see Lynne Rogers, 'Stravinsky's break with contrapuntal tradition: a sketch study', *Journal of Musicology* 13 (1955), 476–507.

25 Stravinsky borrowed music for *Pulcinella* from two of Pergolesi's *opere buffe*, *Il Flaminio* and *Lo frate' nnamorato*, together with a cantata and various instrumental sonatas that scholars no longer believe are by Pergolesi.

26 Igor Stravinsky, *Stravinsky: an Autobiography* (New York: Simon and Schuster, 1936), 229.

27 Taruskin, *Stravinsky and the Russian Traditions*, 1614.

28 Arthur-Vincent Lourié, 'Neogothic and neoclassic', *Modern Music* 5/3 (1928), 5; cited in Taruskin, *Stravinsky and the Russian Traditions*, 1610.

29 *Stravinsky and the Russian Traditions*, 1618.

30 For a similar evaluation, see Walsh, *The Music of Stravinsky*, 160–63.

31 For a more detailed discussion of heuristic imitation and its use by Bartók, see my 'Neoclassic and anachronistic impulses', 214–22.

32 For a more detailed discussion of this topic, see Walsh, *The Music of Stravinsky*, 170–79. There are several excellent analyses of the Symphony in C which reward close reading. See especially Edward T. Cone, 'The uses of convention: Stravinsky and his models', *Musical Quarterly* 48 (1962), 287–99; Paul Johnson, 'Cross-collectional techniques of structure in Stravinsky's centric music', and Joseph N. Straus, 'Sonata form in Stravinsky', in Ethan Haimo and Paul Johnson (eds), *Stravinsky Retrospectives* (Lincoln, NE: University of Nebraska Press, 1987), 55–75, 148–55; and Cross, *The Stravinsky Legacy*, 198–211.

33 Cross, *The Stravinsky Legacy*, 210.

34 Just as the progression from I to II lacks conviction in this large-scale I–II–V–I progression, so too does the progression from V to I (see bars 48–53).

35 Johnson, 'Cross-collectional techniques', 60.

36 For a more detailed discussion of the durational intricacies in Stravinsky's form, see Cone, 'The uses of convention', 287–95.

37 Here 'dialectical' is not used in the Hegelian sense of continuous unification of opposites, but in the Platonic sense of critically examining the truth of an opinion through discussion or debate or dialogue. This dialogue occurs between at least two voices or positions and involves their indirect or oblique comparison.

38 In preparing the libretto, Auden accepted assistance from Chester Kallman, without informing Stravinsky, an arrangement that Stravinsky at first accepted only reluctantly.

39 The programme note was written for a BBC television documentary on Auden (Hollywood, 5 November 1965), cited in Paul Griffiths, *Igor Stravinsky: The Rake's Progress* (Cambridge: Cambridge University Press, 1982), 2.

40 Ibid., 4.

41 Kerman's review appears in his *Opera as Drama* (New York: Random House, 1956), 234–49. This version, however, omits his

original suggestion to revise the ending. The original review appeared as 'Opera à la mode', *The Hudson Review* (Winter 1954), 560–77.

42 Geoffrey Chew, 'Pastoral and neoclassicism: a reinterpretation of Auden's and Stravinsky's *Rake's Progress*', *Cambridge Opera Journal* 5 (1993), 239–63.

43 Straus, *Remaking the Past*, 155–61.

44 For a more detailed account of the musical analysis that follows, see Chandler Carter, 'Progress and timelessness in *The Rake's Progress*', *The Opera Journal* 28 (1995), 15–25. I borrow here Carter's perceptive analysis of the transformation of the recurring Ballad theme (as well as some phrasing); his interpretation of its meaning, however, differs somewhat from my own.

45 W. H. Auden, 'Balaam and his ass', in *The Dyer's Hand and Other Essays* (New York: Random House, 1962), 107–45.

46 I have found two essays particularly helpful in summarising the principal themes and interpretative problems in Goethe's *Faust*: Walter Kaufmann's 'Introduction' to his translation of *Faust* (New York: Anchor Books, 1963), 3–56; and Fred J. Nichols, '*Faust*', in Michael Seidel and Edward Mendelson (eds.), *Homer to Brecht: the European Epic and Dramatic Traditions* (New Haven: Yale University Press, 1977), 292–316.

47 I have used the Louis MacNeice translation of *Faust* (New York: Oxford University Press, 1960).

48 Auden, 'Balaam and his ass', 115–16.

49 Igor Stravinsky and Robert Craft, *Memories and Commentaries* (London: Faber and Faber, 1960), 167–76.

7 Stravinsky's theatres

1 Jonathan Harvey, *In Quest of Spirit: Thoughts on Music* (Berkeley: University of California Press, 1999), 16. For a fuller discussion of *The Rake's Progress*, see Martha Hyde, 'Stravinsky's neoclassicism', in this volume.

2 Stravinsky on the American premiere of *The Rake's Progress*, quoted in Eric Walter White, *Stravinsky: the Composer and his Works*, 2nd edn. (London: Faber and Faber, 1979), 452.

3 Ibid., 18.

4 Stravinsky, in Igor Stravinsky and Robert Craft, *Dialogues* (London: Faber and Faber, 1982), 24.

5 Aristotle, 'On the art of poetry', in *Classical Literary Criticism*, trans. T. S. Dorsch (Harmondsworth: Penguin, 1965), 40.

6 Stephen Walsh, *Stravinsky: a Creative Spring: Russia and France 1882–1934* (London: Jonathan Cape, 1999), 10.

7 As reported by Valeriy Smirnov, quoted by Walsh in ibid., 28.

8 See Rosamund Bartlett, 'Stravinsky's Russian origins', in this volume, for a fuller account of Stravinsky's relationship with Rimsky-Korsakov.

9 See Glenn Watkins, *Pyramids at the Louvre: Music, Culture, and Collage from Stravinsky to the Postmodernists* (Cambridge, MA: Belknap Press, 1994), 256–64.

10 See Richard Taruskin, *Stravinsky and the Russian Traditions: a Biography of the Works Through* Mavra (Oxford: Oxford University Press, 1996), 1486–99.

11 Peter Brook, *The Empty Space* (London: Pelican, 1972). I discuss this at greater length in chap. 4 of *The Stravinsky Legacy* (Cambridge: Cambridge University Press, 1998).

12 For a fuller account of Stravinsky's familiarity with such theatrical thinking, see Watkins, *Pyramids at the Louvre*; parallels between Stravinsky and Meyerhold are explored in Stephen Walsh, *Stravinsky: Oedipus Rex* (Cambridge: Cambridge University Press, 1993), especially 11–22.

13 Brook, *The Empty Space*, 47–8.

14 Antonin Artaud, *The Theatre and its Double*, trans. Victor Corti (London: Calder, 1993), 42.

15 *The Empty Space*, 63.

16 Walsh, *Stravinsky: a Creative Spring*, 259.

17 *Stravinsky and the Russian Traditions*, 1247.

18 Stravinsky, quoted in Eric Walter White, *Stravinsky*, 240.

19 Igor Stravinsky and Robert Craft, *Expositions and Developments* (London: Faber and Faber, 1962), 119–20.

20 Taruskin, *Stravinsky and the Russian Traditions*, 1246.

21 Walsh, *Stravinsky: a Creative Spring*, 258.

22 Taruskin, *Stravinsky and the Russian Traditions*, 1292 (his emphasis).

23 *Expositions and Developments*, 120.

24 *Stravinsky and the Russian Traditions*, 1298.

25 *The Empty Space*, 80.

26 Walsh, *Stravinsky: a Creative Spring*, 413.

27 Taruskin, *Stravinsky and the Russian Traditions*, 1300, 1301.

28 *Expositions and Developments*, 91.

29 Ibid., 92.

30 Stravinsky and Craft, *Dialogues*, 22.

31 Both works are given substantial coverage by Martha Hyde in her chapter 'Stravinsky's neoclassicism' in this volume. *The Nightingale*, though to all intents and purposes an opera, is designated by Stravinsky a 'musical fairy tale'.

32 *Expositions and Developments*, 125.

33 Ibid., 124.

34 *Dialogues*, 72.

35 *Expositions and Developments*, 123.

36 Michael Oliver, *Igor Stravinsky* (London: Phaidon, 1995), 190.

37 See Eric Walter White, *Stravinsky*, 496.

38 George Balanchine, 'The dance element in Stravinsky's music', in Minna Lederman (ed.), *Stravinsky in the Theatre* (New York: Da Capo, 1949), 81.

39 Indeed, it was the 'real premiere', as Stravinsky had had nothing to do with the Washington production. See Walsh, *Stravinsky: a Creative Spring*, 455.

40 'The dance element in Stravinsky's music', 81.

41 Walsh, *Stravinsky: a Creative Spring*, 451.

42 Ibid., 467.

43 Balanchine, 'The dance element in Stravinsky's music', 82.

44 *Dialogues*, 78, n. 1.

45 Ibid., 36.

46 Ibid., 37.

47 See also Anthony Pople, 'Stravinsky's early music', in this volume.

48 Walsh, *Stravinsky: a Creative Spring*, 142–3.

49 Daniel Albright, *Stravinsky: the Music Box and the Nightingale* (New York: Gordon and Breach, 1989), 4.

8 Stravinsky the serialist

1 Robert Craft, 'Influence or assistance?', in *Present Perspectives* (New York: Knopf, 1984), 251–3; reprinted in *Stravinsky: Glimpses of a Life* (London: Lime Tree, 1992), 38–9. Craft gave a slightly different version of the story in 1994: see *Stravinsky: Chronicle of a Friendship, 1948–1971*, rev. and expanded edn (Nashville: Vanderbilt University Press, 1994). This alternative version, although it omits the actual shedding of tears, is even more emphatic than the earlier one in its assessment of the impact of Schoenberg's music.

2 Igor Stravinsky and Robert Craft, *Themes and Conclusions* (London: Faber and Faber, 1972), 23.

3 'We have been working together for twenty-three years ... [Craft] introduced me to almost all of the new music I have heard in the past two decades ... and not only to the new music but to the new everything else. The plain truth is that anyone who admires my *Agon*, my *Variations*, my *Requiem Canticles*, owes some gratitude to the man who has sustained my creative life these last years.' Letter to the Music Editor of the *Los Angeles Times* (23 June 1970); reprinted in *Themes and Conclusions*, 216.

4 Craft, 'A centenary view, plus ten', in *Stravinsky: Glimpses of a Life*, 16–17.

5 The history of the Boulez–Stravinsky relationship is detailed in Craft, 'Boulez in the lemon and limelight', in *Prejudices in Disguise* (New York: Knopf, 1974), 207–13.

6 Stravinsky, *Poetics of Music in the Form of Six Lessons*, trans. Arthur Knodel and Ingolf Dahl (Cambridge, MA: Harvard University Press, 1947), 63–5.

7 Personal communication from Stravinsky to Milton Babbitt. Cited in Babbitt, *Words about Music*, ed. Stephen Dembski and Joseph N. Straus (Madison, WI: University of Wisconsin Press, 1987), 20.

8 For a basic discussion of partitioning in Schoenberg's twelve-note music, see Ethan Haimo, *Schoenberg's Serial Odyssey: the Evolution of his Twelve-note Method, 1914–1928* (Oxford: Oxford University Press, 1990), 17–26.

9 'Schoenberg's work has too many inequalities for us to embrace it as a whole. For example, nearly all of his texts are appallingly bad, some of them so bad as to discourage performance of the music. Then too, his orchestrations of Bach, Handel, Monn, Loewe, Brahms differ from the type of commercial orchestration only in the superiority of craftsmanship: his intentions are no better ... His expressionism is of the naïvest sort ... his late tonal works are as dull as the Reger they resemble, or the César Franck'. Stravinsky and Craft, *Conversations with Igor Stravinsky* (London: Faber and Faber, 1959), 70–71.

10 The Stravinsky/Webern relationship has been extensively discussed. See, for example, Henri Pousseur, 'Stravinsky by way of Webern', *Perspectives of New Music* 10/2 (1972), 13–51 and 11/1 (1972), 112–45; Pieter C. van den Toorn, *The Music of Igor Stravinsky* (New Haven: Yale University Press, 1983); Susannah Tucker, 'Stravinsky and his sketches: the composing of *Agon* and other serial works of the 1950s', PhD diss., Oxford University, 1992.

11 Craft, 'A personal preface', *The Score* 20 (1957), 11–13.

12 The following comment is reasonably typical: '[Webern] is the discoverer of a new distance between the musical object and ourselves and, therefore, of a new measure of musical time; as such he is supremely important ... he is a perpetual Pentecost for all who believe in music.' Stravinsky and Robert Craft, *Memories and Commentaries* (London: Faber and Faber, 1960; repr. edn Berkeley: University of California Press, 1981), 103–5.

13 See, for example, van den Toorn, *The Music of Igor Stravinsky*, and Richard Taruskin, 'The traditions revisited: Stravinsky's *Requiem Canticles* as Russian music', in Christopher Hatch and David W. Bernstein (eds.), *Music Theory and the Exploration of the Past* (Chicago: University of Chicago Press, 1993), 525–50.

14 No. 114–0737. Throughout this chapter, sketch and manuscript materials will be identified by their microfilm numbers in the Paul Sacher Stiftung, Basel.

15 The text is a passage from Shakespeare's *The Tempest* in which Ariel claims (falsely) that Ferdinand's father has drowned.

16 Craft refers to this opening melody as the 'bells motive' (Craft, *Avec Stravinsky* (Monaco: Editions du Rocher, 1958), 149). In the final version of the song, this melody is accompanied by canons in the viola (in augmentation at the unison) and clarinet and viola (at the perfect fifth above). It is notable that Stravinsky composes the melody in its entirety first and adds accompanying parts later.

17 Stravinsky considered these four forms – which I shall normally refer to as P (prime), I (for its inversion beginning on the same note), R (retrograde) and IR (inversion of the retrograde) – as the basic forms of the series throughout the remainder of his compositional life.

18 109–0694.

19 The five-note idea in the sketch, E–E–F♯–E♭–D, is related by retrograde inversion to what later emerged as the series (Theme) for the piece, E–E♭–C–C♯–D. Both versions thus begin on E and end on D, and the same musical motion is composed-out over a large musical span in the relationship between the Prelude and the Postlude.

20 There is an extensive literature on these arrays, including Claudio Spies, 'Some notes on Stravinsky's *Abraham and Isaac*', *Perspectives of New Music* 3/2 (1965), 104–26; 'Some notes on Stravinsky's *Variations*', *Perspectives of New Music* 4/1 (1965), 62–74, and 'Some notes on Stravinsky's Requiem settings', *Perspectives of New Music* 5/2 (1967), 98–123; John Rogers, 'Some properties of non-duplicating rotational arrays', *Perspectives of New Music* 7/1 (1968), 80–102; Charles Wuorinen, *Simple Composition* (New York: Longman, 1979); Milton Babbitt, 'Order, symmetry, and centricity in late Stravinsky', in Jann Pasler (ed.), *Confronting Stravinsky: Man, Musician, and Modernist* (Berkeley: University of California Press, 1986), 247–61, and 'Stravinsky's verticals and Schoenberg's diagonals: a twist of fate', in Ethan Haimo and Paul Johnson (eds), *Stravinsky Retrospectives* (Lincoln, NE: University of Nebraska Press, 1987), 15–35; Robert Morris, 'Generalizing rotational arrays', *Journal of Music Theory* 32/1 (1988), 75–132.

21 He occasionally uses also the retrograde of the inversion (RI).

22 Stravinsky's source for rotational arrays was undoubtedly Ernst Krenek. See Catherine Hogan, '*Threni*: Stravinsky's debt to Krenek', *Tempo* 141 (1982), 22–9. Stravinsky's use of the arrays, however, differs greatly from Krenek's.

23 See Joseph N. Straus, 'Stravinsky's "construction of twelve verticals": an aspect of harmony in the serial music', *Music Theory Spectrum* 21/1 (1999), 231–71. For discussion of the apparent misprints in chords 10 and 1, see Joseph N. Straus, 'Stravinsky's serial "mistakes"', *Journal of Musicology* 19/1 (1977), 55–80.

24 On *The Firebird*, see Taruskin, *Stravinsky and the Russian Traditions*, 275. On *The Rake*, see Chandler Carter, 'Stravinsky's "special sense": the rhetorical use of tonality in *The Rake's Progress*', *Music Theory Spectrum* 19/1 (1977), 55–80.

25 The serial derivation of these chords is clarified in Karen Lesley Grylls, 'The aggregate re-ordered: a paradigm for Stravinsky's *Requiem Canticles*', PhD diss., University of Washington, 1993. The derivation offered in Richard Taruskin, 'The traditions revisited', 525–50, is incorrect.

9 Stravinsky conducts Stravinsky

1 Richard Taruskin, *Text and Act: Essays on Music and Performance* (New York: Oxford University Press, 1995), 114.

2 For the most comprehensive discography of Stravinsky's conducting, also including details of his many unpublished live recordings from 1930 on, see Philip Stuart, *Igor Stravinsky – The Composer in the Recording Studio: a Comprehensive Discography* (New York: Greenwood Press, 1991). By far the most accessible source of Stravinsky's recordings is 'The recorded legacy', first issued as a thirty-one-record set in 1982 to mark the centenary of Stravinsky's birth (for a list of contents see Stuart, pp. 62–4), and reissued with small changes by Sony Classical on 22 CDs (SX22K 46290). This set does not however include key early recordings, such as the 1928 *Petrushka* (no. 6 in Stuart, reissued on Pearl GEMM CD 9329) and the 1928 *Firebird* and 1929 *Rite* (nos 7 and 9 in Stuart, both reissued on Pearl GEMM CD 9334).

3 Peter Hill, *Stravinsky: the Rite of Spring* (Cambridge: Cambridge University Press, 2000), 118.

4 Igor Stravinsky and Robert Craft, *Expositions and Developments* (London: Faber and Faber, 1962), 110.

5 Ibid., 133.

6 The authoritative general introduction is Rex Lawson, 'Stravinsky and the pianola', in Jann Pasler (ed.), *Confronting Stravinsky: Man, Musician, and Modernist* (Berkeley: University of California Press, 1986), 284–301; expanded version published in *The Pianola Journal* 1 (1987), 15–26 and 2 (1989), 3–16.

7 Eric Walter White, *Stravinsky: the Composer and his Works*, 2nd rev. and expanded edn (London: Faber and Faber, 1979), 619.

8 Vera Stravinsky and Robert Craft (eds.), *Stravinsky in Pictures and Documents* (London: Hutchinson, 1979), 165.

9 Interview of Stravinsky by Florent Fels, *Les nouvelles littéraires*, 8 December 1928, quoted in V. Stravinsky and Craft, *Stravinsky in Pictures and Documents*, 164.

10 Stravinsky and Craft, *Expositions and Developments*, 70.

11 Interview with *Seventeen* magazine, in Igor Stravinsky, *Themes and Conclusions* (London: Faber and Faber, 1972), 87; see also Igor Stravinsky and Robert Craft, *Conversations with Igor Stravinsky* (London: Faber and Faber, 1959), 123.

12 Claudio Spies, 'Notes in his memory', *Perspectives of New Music* 9/2–10/1 (1971), 155.

13 As a pianist he premiered his *Four Studies for Piano* in 1908. In his *Autobiography*, Stravinsky records that his first attempt at conducting was a 'reading' of his Symphony in E♭ at one of Ansermet's rehearsals in 1914 (Igor Stravinsky, *An Autobiography (1903–1934)* (London: Victor Gollancz, 1936), 52; see also White, *Stravinsky*, 177), and refers to conducting, 'for the first time in public', selections from *Firebird* in Geneva and Paris in 1915 (*An Autobiography*, 59). Although this was followed by abortive discussions concerning a contract for Stravinsky to conduct his own works at the Metropolitan Opera House, New York, his conducting skills were clearly underdeveloped at the time; it was probably not long after this that Otto Luening (then a member of the Tonhalle Orchestra, Zurich) rehearsed *Fireworks* under him, noting that 'He was so nervous that he was not in control of the situation', while in *An Autobiography* Stravinsky admits that, at the time of the Octet premiere, 'I was only just beginning my career as a conductor, I had not yet got the necessary technique, which I acquired later only with practice' (Otto Luening, (untitled), *Perspectives of New Music* 9/2–10/1, 131; Stravinsky, *An Autobiography*, 109).

14 English version (from *The Arts* 6/1 (January 1924)) reprinted in White, *Stravinsky*, 574–7.

15 I shall not enter into the question of how far these books were the work of Stravinsky or of ghost-writers (respectively, Walter Nouvel and Roland-Manuel).

16 Stravinsky, *An Autobiography*, 101.

17 Stravinsky, *Themes and Conclusions*, 223.

18 Arnold Schoenberg, *Style and Idea*, rev. edn, ed. Leonard Stein, trans. Leo Black (London: Faber and Faber, 1984), 342 (but written in 1926).

19 Robert Philip, *Early Recordings and Musical Style: Changing Tastes in Instrumental Performance, 1900–1950* (Cambridge: Cambridge University Press, 1992), 11–12, citing Margaret Long, *Au piano avec Maurice Ravel* (Paris, 1971), 36.

20 Igor Stravinsky, *Poetics of Music in the Form of Six Lessons* (Cambridge MA: Harvard University Press, 1947), 122–3.

21 Ibid., 122.

22 Stravinsky, *An Autobiography*, 113.

23 See for example Richard Hudson's account (*Stolen Time: a History of Tempo Rubato* (Oxford: Clarendon Press, 1994), 387–8) of the successive notations of the Magician's motive from *Petrushka*. The section of Hudson's book devoted to Stravinsky (381–400) offers an exhaustive account of the surprisingly frequent indications of rubato, explicit or implicit, to be found in Stravinsky's scores of all periods, together with some comparisons from his recordings.

24 White, *Stravinsky*, 576.

25 Ibid., 575.

26 Ibid., 576.

27 Stravinsky, *Poetics*, 127.

28 Heinrich Schenker, *The Art of Performance*, ed. Heribert Esser, trans. Irene Schreier Scott (New York: Oxford University Press, 2000).

29 From the Florent Fels interview (see n. 9 above) as quoted in Robert Craft, *Igor and Vera Stravinsky: A Photograph Album (1921–1971)* (London: Thames and Hudson, 1982), 20.

30 Stravinsky, *An Autobiography*, 150, 152.

31 From the *Seattle Post-Intelligencer*, 5 March 1954 (quoted in Vera Stravinsky and Craft, *Stravinsky in Pictures and Documents*, 308).

32 Stravinsky and Craft, *Conversations*, 119

33 Hill, *The Rite*, 159, contradicting Robert Fink, ' "Rigoroso (♩ = 126)": *The Rite of Spring* and the forging of a modernist performing style', *Journal of the American Musicological Society* 52 (1999), 335; Hill quotes some of the competing promotional material issued by the respective record companies. Monteux's recording (reissued on Pearl GEMM CD 9329) outsold Stravinsky's – possibly because, though actually a few seconds longer than Stravinsky's (31'50" as against 31'18"), it was

squeezed on to four discs instead of five, and therefore cheaper; Stuart, *Igor Stravinsky*, 8.

34 Stuart discusses what he calls the 'Craft problem' at some length (*Igor Stravinsky*, 14–16); the scandal broke following Lillian Libman's revelation that CBS had included takes by Craft in recordings released under Stravinsky's sole name.

35 *American Music Lover* 7/2 (October 1940), 58.

36 *The Gramophone* 38 (1961), 533.

37 *Musical Times* 102 (1961), 369.

38 *The Gramophone* 38 (1961), 534.

39 'Index of record reviews with symbols indicating opinions of reviewers, compiled by Kurtz Myers and Donald L. Leavitt', *Notes* 18 (1960–61), 625. The first issue of the volume summarises two other recordings of *The Rite*, with less favourable outcomes: Dorati scores two as excellent, four as adequate and two as inadequate, while Goossens scores three, one and one respectively (p. 118). The following volume, 19 (1961–2), 666–7, summarises reviews of four works conducted by Stravinsky and three conducted by others; every Stravinsky recording gets a better rating than any of the others.

40 Leo Smit, 'A card game, a wedding, and a passing', *Perspectives of New Music* 9/2–10/1 (1971), 92–3.

41 It sounds as if Smit had been watching *Fantasia*, but images of birds proliferate in later accounts of Stravinsky's stage presence: see, for instance, George Rochberg, (untitled), *Perspectives of New Music* 9/2–10/1 (1971), 32–3, and J. K. Randall, 'Stravinsky in person', *Perspectives of New Music* 9/2–10/1 (1971), 134. Something of this quality can be seen in the many published photographs of Stravinsky conducting, but perhaps most eloquently in Milein Cosman's drawings (Hans Keller and Milein Cosman, *Stravinsky Seen and Heard* (London: Toccata Press, 1982)).

42 Taruskin (*Text and Act*, 97–8) elaborates a similar argument, again in relation to *The Rite*, further developed in Fink, '"Rigoroso"', 323–4.

43 Fink, '"Rigoroso"', 317, 318–23.

44 The date is given in Stravinsky, *An Autobiography*, 129, but contradicted in Stravinsky and Craft, *Expositions and Developments*, 144–5, where Stravinsky says that he first conducted *The Rite* in 1928 for the Columbia recording, and in concert in 1929. Both accounts place the first concert performance in Amsterdam.

45 Fink, '"Rigoroso"', 324.

46 These two sentences are condensed from Nicholas Cook, *Analysing Musical Multimedia* (Oxford: Oxford University Press, 1998), 196–202, where references may be found, but for the authoritative account see Richard Taruskin, *Stravinsky and the Russian Traditions: a Biography of the Works Through* Mavra (Oxford: Oxford University Press, 1996), chaps. 12–13; for a more concise one, see Hill, *The Rite*, especially chap. 7.

47 White, *Stravinsky*, 574, 577.

48 Stravinsky and Craft, *Expositions and Developments*, 145.

49 In direct contravention of the stipulations in *Poetics of Music*: 'The sin against the spirit of the work always begins with a sin against its letter and leads to the endless follies which an ever-flourishing literature in the worst taste does its best to sanction. Thus it follows that a *crescendo*, as we all know, is always accompanied by a speeding up of movement . . .' (124). This recording was made with the Walther Straram Orchestra (Toscanini's favourite orchestra when in Paris).

50 See the tables in Hill, *The Rite*, 124, and, for more detail, Fink, '"Rigoroso"', 356.

51 Igor Stravinsky and Robert Craft, *Dialogues and a Diary*, enlarged edn (London: Faber and Faber, 1968), 108.

52 Hill, *The Rite*, 123.

53 Fink, '"Rigoroso"', 347.

54 The 1960 recording of *Petrushka* (Stuart's no. 92) is available as part of the 'Recorded legacy' set (Sony Classical SMK 46293). Philip's comparison of recordings from the 1920s and 1930s by Stravinsky, Coates, Malko and Stokowski does, however, show that Stravinsky's range of tempo variation, even in 1928, was lower than that of his contemporaries; Philip, *Early Recordings and Musical Style*, 31–3.

55 Stravinsky, *An Autobiography*, 101.

56 Stravinsky and Craft, *Conversations*, 117–23.

57 Ibid., 118.

58 Ibid., 119.

59 Ibid., 20.

60 Stravinsky, *Themes and Conclusions*, 226.

61 This expression, Stravinsky explains, has 'attained a myth-like status comparable to "the rosy-fingered dawn" in Homer' (ibid., 131). Some of Stravinsky's other references to Karajan were less kind.

62 Stravinsky and Craft, *Dialogues and a Diary*, 90.

63 Stravinsky and Craft, *Expositions and Developments*, 113. The reference is presumably to Bruno Walter, whose rehearsal

of movements 1–3 of Mozart's 'Linz'
Symphony, K. 425, was included on the
two-LP set 'The birth of a performance',
Philips ABL 3161–2.
64 Ibid., 56; see also Stravinsky and Craft,
Conversations, 38. Other conductors whom
Stravinsky heard in St Petersburg include
Nikisch and Richter, while in Berlin he heard
Weingartner, who became 'a near idol of mine
in my youth' (Stravinsky, *Themes and
Conclusions*, 225).
65 Natalie Bauer-Lechner, *Erinnerungen an
Gustav Mahler* (Vienna: E. P. Tal, 1923), 46,
quoted in translation by Philip, *Early
Recordings and Musical Style*, 37.
66 Philip, *Early Recordings and Musical Style*,
233.
67 From Gray's *A Survey of Contemporary
Music* (London: Oxford University Press,
1927), quoted in Hill, *The Rite*, 100–1.
68 The best formulation, quoted by Taruskin
(*Text as Act*, 117n.), comes from Nicolas
Nabokov ('Stravinsky now', *Partisan Review* 11
(1944), 332): 'Look at any one of
[Stravinsky's] bars and you will find that it is
not the measure closed in by bar lines (as it
would be in Mozart, for example), but the
monometrical unit of the measure, the single
beat which determines the life of his musical
organism.'
69 Stravinsky and Craft, *Expositions and
Developments*, 87–8, where Stravinsky not only
lists his repertoire but also registers an
unrealised ambition to conduct Beethoven's
Symphonies 1–4 and 8, and *Fidelio*. Live
recordings of music by other composers
are included in Stuart, *Igor Stravinsky*,
Appendix C.
70 'Igor Stravinsky Edition: Symphonies'
(Sony Classical SM2K 46294). Curiously,
Stravinsky suggested recording *The Sleeping
Beauty* in 1929 within the terms of his
Columbia contract, but the offer was not
taken up; see Stuart, *Igor Stravinsky*, 8.
71 'Igor Stravinsky Edition: Ballets vol. II',
SM3K 46292.
72 Respectively, nos. 7, 99 and 182 in Stuart,
Igor Stravinsky; reissued as 'Stravinsky: The
Rite of Spring and The Firebird' (Pearl
GEMM CD 9334), 'Igor Stravinsky Edition:
Ballets vol. I' (Sony Classical SM3K 46291),
and 'Igor Stravinsky Edition: Ballet Suites'
(Sony Classical SMK 46293). Fig. 9.1, which
is adapted to take account of the two different
openings, is based on an average tempo for
each section (not on beat-by-beat analysis);
it should be noted that this method conflates
the effects of tempo proper with those of
caesurae.

73 Stravinsky and Craft, *Expositions and
Developments*, 147.
74 Fink, '"*Rigoroso*"', 313.
75 Hill, *The Rite*, 137.
76 Tempos are taken from Hill's chart (ibid.,
124), but with the metronome marking at
rehearsal number 57 corrected from 168 to
166. Hill points out that any such values can
only be approximate (ibid., 120), because they
depend in part on the method of
measurement; for consistency I have
therefore left his values for the 1960
performance of the Introduction to Part 2
unchanged, despite the divergence between
them and Table 9.1.
77 Philip, *Early Recordings and Musical Style*,
234.
78 Stravinsky and Craft, *Dialogues and a
Diary*, 82–90, and Stravinsky, *Themes and
Conclusions*, 234–41.
79 Concert Hall CM 2324 (stereo LP).
80 According to Hill's chart, the winner,
by a wide margin, is Craft's 1962 recording,
of which Stravinsky inexplicably writes,
'The tempo is correct' (*Dialogues and a Diary*,
85).
81 Stravinsky, *An Autobiography*, 137.
82 Stravinsky and Craft, *Conversations*, 118.
83 A sense of this transformation is conveyed
by Soulima Stravinsky in Ben Johnston, 'An
interview with Soulima Stravinsky',
Perspectives of New Music 9/2–10/1 (1971),
15–27.
84 Stravinsky and Craft, *Conversations*, 119.
85 Stravinsky and Craft, *Dialogues and a
Diary*, 122.
86 Stravinsky, *Themes and Conclusions*, 139.
87 Ibid., 228.
88 Taruskin, *Text and Act*, 129.
89 Ibid., 117.

10 Stravinsky as devil: Adorno's three critiques
1 T. W. Adorno, *Philosophie der neuen Musik*
(Tübingen: J. C. B. Mohr (Paul Siebeck),
1949), in *Gesammelte Schriften*
(Frankfurt/Main: Suhrkamp Verlag, 1975)
vol. 12, ed. Rolf Tiedemann and Klaus
Schultz. Eng. edn: *Philosophy of Modern Music*,
trans. Anne G. Mitchell and Wesley V.
Blomster (London: Sheed and Ward, 1973).
2 Schoenberg in a letter to Rufer in 1949
wrote: 'it is disgusting, by the way, how he
treats Stravinsky. I am certainly no admirer of
Stravinsky, although I like a piece of his here
and there very much – but one should not
write like that.' Cited in H. H.
Stuckenschmidt, *Schoenberg: His Life, World
and Work*, trans. Humphrey Searle (London:
Calder, 1977), 508.

3 Célestin Deliège, 'Stravinsky–ideology –
language', *Perspectives of New Music* 26/1
(Winter 1988), 83.
4 Robert Craft, 'A bell for Adorno', in
Prejudices in Disguise (New York: Knopf, 1974),
91–102.
5 T. W. Adorno, 'Stravinsky: a dialectical
portrait', in *Quasi una fantasia*, trans. Rodney
Livingstone (London: Verso, 1992), 147.
6 Carl Dahlhaus, 'Das Problem der "höheren
Kritik": Adornos Polemik gegen Strawinsky',
in *Neue Zeitschrift für Musik* 148/5 (1987),
9–15.
7 Peter Bürger, 'The decline of the modern
age', trans. David J. Parent, *Telos* 62 (Winter
1984–5), 117–30.
8 Jean-François Lyotard, 'Adorno as the devil'
[1973], trans. Robert Hurley, *Telos* 19
(1974/5), 127–8.
9 See Thomas Mann, *Doctor Faustus*, trans.
H. T. Lowe-Porter (Harmondsworth:
Penguin, 1968), 231–7.
10 T. W. Adorno, 'Die stabilisierte Musik'
[1928], *Gesammelte Schriften*, vol. 18, ed. Rolf
Tiedemann (Frankfurt/Main: Suhrkamp
Verlag, 1984), 721–8.
11 T. W. Adorno, 'Zur gesellschaftlichen Lage
der Musik' [1932], in *Gesammelte Schriften*,
vol. 18, 729–77. English version: 'On the
social situation of music', trans. Wesley
Blomster, *Telos* 35 (Spring 1978), 128–64.
12 See my *Adorno's Aesthetics of Music*
(Cambridge: Cambridge University Press,
1993), 102–5.
13 T. W. Adorno, 'Die stabilisierte Musik'
[1928], p. 725 (my translation).
14 At the beginning of *Philosophy of New
Music* Adorno cites a significant passage from
Walter Benjamin's *The Origin of German Tragic
Drama*: 'Philosophical history as the science
of origins is that form which, from the most
far-flung extremes and apparent excesses of
development, allows the emergence of the
configuration of the Idea, characterized as the
totality of all possibilities for a meaningful
juxtaposition of such opposites.' *Philosophie
der neuen Musik*, 13 (my translation).
15 *Philosophy of Modern Music*, 181.
16 Ibid., 171.
17 Ibid., 142.
18 Ibid., 144.
19 Ibid., 159.
20 Ibid., 173.
21 Ibid., 157n.
22 Adorno, 'Stravinsky: a dialectical portrait',
148–9.
23 Ibid., 150.
24 Bürger, 'The decline of the modern age',
119.
25 'Stravinsky: a dialectical portrait', 150–51.
26 Dahlhaus, 'Das Problem der "höheren
Kritik"'.
27 Jonathan Cross, *The Stravinsky Legacy*
(Cambridge: Cambridge University Press,
1998), 234.
28 Ibid., 234–5.
29 Adorno, *Philosophy of Modern Music*,
216–17.
30 Adorno, 'Stravinsky: a dialectical portrait',
152.
31 Apparently Beckett had reservations about
Adorno's interpretation of his *Endgame*. See
James Knowlson, *Damned to Fame: the Life of
Samuel Beckett* (London: Bloomsbury, 1996),
478–9.
32 T. W. Adorno, 'Trying to Understand
Endgame', in *Notes to Literature*, vol. 1, trans.
Shierry Weber Nicholsen (New York:
Columbia University Press, 1991), 268.
33 Adorno, 'Stravinsky: a dialectical portrait',
173.
34 Adorno, 'Trying to Understand *Endgame*',
243.
35 See my essay, 'Adorno's aesthetics of
modernism', in *Adorno, Modernism and Mass
Culture: Essays on Critical Theory and Music*
(London: Kahn and Averill, 1996), 51.
36 'Stravinsky: a dialectical portrait', 174.
37 Ibid., 174.
38 T. W. Adorno, *Minima Moralia* [1951],
trans. Edmund Jephcott (London: Verso/New
Left Books, 1974), 49.

11 Stravinsky in analysis: the anglophone traditions

1 Igor Stravinsky, *Chroniques de ma vie* (Paris:
Denoël and Steel, 1935–6). Trans. anon. as *An
Autobiography* (New York: Steuer, 1958); repr.
with corrections by Eric Walter White
(London: Marion Boyars, 1975), 53.
Stravinsky's italics.
2 Jonathan Cross, *The Stravinsky Legacy*
(Cambridge: Cambridge University Press,
1998), 14.
3 Igor Stravinsky, *Poetics of Music, in the Form
of Six Lessons*, trans. Arthur Knodel and Ingolf
Dahl (Cambridge, MA: Harvard University
Press, 1947), 6.
4 *Poetics*, 80–1.
5 Igor Stravinsky and Robert Craft,
Expositions and Developments (London: Faber
and Faber, 1962), 101–2. Their italics.
6 Richard Taruskin, 'Stravinsky and the
subhuman. A myth of the 20th century: *The
Rite of Spring*, the tradition of the new, and
"the music itself"', in *Defining Russia Musically*
(Princeton: Princeton University Press, 1997),
360–85; 382.
7 Ibid., 379.
8 Ibid., 367.

9 The influence of Stravinsky's objectivity and its relation to Schoenberg's ideal of structural autonomy is discussed in Rose Rosengard Subotnik, *Deconstructive Variations: Music and Reason in Western Society* (Minneapolis: University of Minnesota Press, 1996), 148–76.

10 Edward T. Cone, 'Stravinsky: the progress of a method' [1962], in Benjamin Boretz and Edward T. Cone (eds), *Perspectives on Schoenberg and Stravinsky* (rev. edn New York: Norton, 1968), 155–64; Arthur Berger, 'Problems of pitch organisation in Stravinsky' [1963], in Boretz and Cone, *Perspectives*, 123–54; Pierre Boulez, 'Stravinsky remains', in *Stocktakings from an Apprenticeship*, trans. Stephen Walsh (Oxford: Clarendon, 1991), 55–110. Boulez's essay, written in 1951, was first published in French as 'Stravinsky demeure', in Pierre Souvtchinsky (ed.), *Musique russe*, 2 vols (Paris: Presses universitaires de France, 1953), vol. 1, 155–224, and first appeared in English in 1968.

11 Declared by Boulez in 'Schoenberg is dead [1952]', in *Stocktakings*, 209–14.

12 Milton Babbitt, 'Remarks on the recent Stravinsky' [1964], and Claudio Spies, 'Notes on Stravinsky's *Abraham and Isaac*' [1965], 'Notes on Stravinsky's *Variations*' [1965], and 'Some notes on Stravinsky's Requiem settings' [1967], all in Boretz and Cone, *Perspectives*: 165–85, 186–209, 210–22, 223–49 respectively.

13 Richard Taruskin, *Stravinsky and the Russian Traditions: a Biography of the Works Through* Mavra (Oxford: Oxford University Press, 1996). The case for a wider European context for Stravinsky is put by Pieter C. van den Toorn in *Music, Politics, and the Academy* (Berkeley: University of California Press, 1995), chap. 7 ('A case in point: context and analytical method in Stravinsky'), 179–219.

14 Olivier Messiaen, *The Technique of my Musical Language*, trans. John Satterfield (Paris: Alphonse Leduc, 1956), vol. 1, 59–60; vol. 2, Exx. 312–28.

15 Berger, 'Problems of pitch organisation', 132.

16 Taruskin, *Stravinsky and the Russian Traditions*, 266. A concise discussion of octatonicism in Stravinsky and Rimsky-Korsakov is contained in Louis Andriessen and Elmer Schönberger, *The Apollonian Clockwork: on Stravinsky*, trans. Jeff Hamburger (Oxford: Oxford University Press, 1989), 228–35. See also Anthony Pople, 'Early Stravinsky', this volume, p. 66.

17 A full explanation of the basics of octatonic theory is given in Pieter C. van den Toorn, *The Music of Igor Stravinsky* (New Haven: Yale University Press, 1983), 31–72.

18 Van den Toorn is 'inclined to agree with Arthur Berger that the Stravinskian stamp is advantageously defined with reference to the octatonic pitch collection, whether inferred singly or in terms of some kind of octatonic-diatonic penetration', ibid., 41.

19 See ibid., chap. 10, 271–320. Stravinsky's interest in the sonority and symmetrical properties of the major-minor tetrachord is reported in Allen Forte, *The Harmonic Organization of 'The Rite of Spring'* (New Haven: Yale University Press, 1978), 33, n. 7, and is associated with the trope of the bell in Andriessen and Schönberger, *The Apollonian Clockwork*, 272–4.

20 See, for example, Taruskin's discussion of Rimsky-Korsakov's 'harmonic exploitation' of the octatonic scale, in particular chromatic chord progressions ascending and descending in minor thirds (i.e. through the diminished tetrachord). *Stravinsky and the Russian Traditions*, 255–306.

21 Stravinsky, *Poetics*, 32.

22 Forte, '*The Rite of Spring*', 29.

23 Notably in the correspondence between Forte and Taruskin published in *Music Analysis*, 5/2–3 (1986), 313–37. Forte is also implicated in Taruskin's rejection of formalist approaches to *The Rite* by Elliott Antokoletz, *Twentieth-Century Music* (Englewood Cliffs, NJ: Prentice-Hall, 1991) and Pieter C. van den Toorn, *Stravinsky and 'The Rite of Spring': the Beginnings of a Musical Language* (Berkeley: University of California Press, 1987). The conflicts and similarities of the views of Forte, van den Toorn and Taruskin are discussed in Anthony Pople, 'Misleading voices: contrasts and continuities in Stravinsky studies', in Craig Ayrey and Mark Everist (eds.), *Analytical Strategies and Musical Interpretation: Essays in Nineteenth- and Twentieth-Century Music* (Cambridge: Cambridge University Press, 1996), 271–87; 271–7.

24 Forte, '*The Rite of Spring*', 28.

25 For precision and concision, pitch-class (pc) collections are designated throughout this chapter using Forte's set names, as listed in *The Structure of Atonal Music* (New Haven: Yale University Press, 1973), Appendix 1, 179–81. In this case, set 4–17, '4' indicates that the set is a tetrachord, '17' simply that it is seventeenth in the list of tetrachords; the pc list [0,3,4,7] expresses the basic form of the set using the numerical notation of pcs (C = 0, C♯ = 1, etc.) and indicates that in its (abstractly defined) prime form this set comprises C, E♭, E♮ and G. In an actual composition, of course, the set would usually

appear in transposition and inversion, while retaining its identity as the major-minor tetrachord.

26 Forte, '*The Rite of Spring*', 32. Similarly, Forte analyses extracts from Stravinsky's works (up to the *Three Songs from William Shakespeare*) alongside music by Schoenberg, Berg, Webern, Bartók, Busoni, Ives, Ruggles, Skryabin and Varèse.

27 Any one of the three distinct forms (van den Toorn's Collections I–III) of the octatonic scale naturally selects eight of the twelve chromatic pcs; if the pc content of a passage can be accounted for by a single collection, then a relatively exclusive harmonic focus is in operation. Any two collections cover the total chromatic, holding invariant a diminished tetrachord (set 4–28 [0,3,6,9]); potentially, then, any passage in which twelve pcs are present may be described as octatonic, but this becomes a structural description only when the two collections can be shown to be (a) discrete and (b) interactive (as, for example, when chords belonging to separate collections alternate and are perhaps connected by their invariant diminished tetrachord). In a very general sense, this is van den Toorn's procedure in *Stravinsky*.

28 See Cone, 'Stravinsky', 156.

29 These concise definitions are taken from the glossary of Taruskin's *Stravinsky and 'The Rite of Spring'*, 1677–9. The principles are considered at length on 951–66.

30 Jonathan Kramer, 'Moment form in twentieth-century music', *Musical Quarterly* 64 (1978), 177–94; 'Discontinuity and proportion in the music of Stravinsky', in Jann Pasler (ed.), *Confronting Stravinsky: Man, Musician, and Modernist* (Berkeley: University of California Press, 1986), 174–94; and *The Time of Music: New Meanings, New Temporalities, New Listening Strategies* (New York: Schirmer, 1988), 221–85. Kramer's approach is the point of departure for two original, structurally sensitive studies by Marianne Kielian-Gilbert: (1) 'The rhythms of form: correspondence and analogy in Stravinsky's designs', *Music Theory Spectrum* 9 (1987), 42–66 (centred on the second of the *Three Pieces for String Quartet* and the 'Soldier's March' from *The Soldier's Tale*); and (2) 'Stravinsky's contrasts: contradiction and discontinuity in his neoclassic music', *Journal of Musicology* 9 (1991), 448–80 (on the *Concertino* for string quartet, the first movement of the Symphony in C and the Octet).

31 See also Cross, *The Stravinsky Legacy*, chap. 2 ('Block forms'), 17–79, which traces this Stravinskian formal inheritance in Varèse, Messiaen, Stockhausen, Tippett and Birtwistle.

32 Kramer, 'Moment form', 177–88 *passim*. Proportional analysis is an essential mode of relation in Kielian-Gilbert's 'The rhythms of form' and is developed further in Akane Mori's 'Proportional exchange in Stravinsky's early serial music', *Journal of Music Theory* 41 (1997), 227–59, which applies and extends Kramer's concepts to formal design, the relation of voices and text setting in *Canticum Sacrum*.

33 Stravinsky, *Poetics*, 30–32.

34 Arnold Schoenberg, *Fundamentals of Musical Composition*, ed. Gerald Strang and Leonard Stein (London: Faber and Faber, 1967), 8. Schoenberg's conception of structure gives priority to 'developing variation', a more profound conception of transformation than Stravinsky's 'similarities': for the teleological theorist, the latter would correspond to Schoenberg's 'variants' ('changes of subordinate meaning, which have no special consequences', p. 8).

35 Taruskin, 'Stravinsky and the subhuman', 366. See also Taruskin, *Stravinsky and the Russian Traditions*, 1125–6, on Stravinsky's reception of the ideas of Bergson and Souvtchinsky.

36 See Stephen Kern, *The Culture of Time and Space 1800–1918* (Cambridge, MA: Harvard University Press, 1983); Mark Antliff, *Inventing Bergson: Cultural Politics and the Parisian Avant-garde* (Princeton: Princeton University Press, 1993); and Martin Jay, *Downcast Eyes: the Denigration of Vision in Twentieth-Century Thought* (Berkeley: University of California Press, 1993), 186–209.

37 Bergson, *Time and Freewill: an Essay on the Immediate Data of Consciousness* [1889], trans. F. L. Pogson (London: Allen and Unwin, 1910), 109.

38 Following Boulez's 'Stravinsky remains', theoretical treatments of rhythmic and metrical structure in Stravinsky customarily begin by consolidating spatial conceptions in the play of even and odd durations (Boulez's 'rational' and 'irrational' values), symmetry and dissymmetry, and layered rhythmic structures, in which separate rhythms unfold in various strata of a composition. Cross's survey of analyses of rhythmic innovations in *The Rite* by Boulez, van den Toorn (*Stravinsky and 'The Rite of Spring'*, 137–43) and Taruskin (*Stravinsky and the Russian Traditions*, 958–64) emphasises the flexibility and 'exchange' of rhythmic cells in the work, the interplay of ostinato and repetitive asymmetrical or syncopated rhythms, and the vertical

opposition of rhythmic regularity over a regular metre; see *The Stravinsky Legacy*, chap. 3 ('Structural rhythms'), 81–104. Van den Toorn's *Stravinsky and 'The Rite of Spring'* contains the most developed theoretical account of Stravinsky's rhythmic practices, divided in two 'dimensions': (1) 'the repetition of a single reiteration, fragment, line or part'; (2) 'the registrally fixed repetition of fragments, lines or parts which repeat according to *varying* and hence "separate" or "independent" rhythmic-metric patterns' (p. 216, his italics). Countering the received idea of Stravinsky's rhythm as a fully emancipated parameter of music, van den Toorn focuses on the ways in which rhythmic invention, while discretely organised, interacts with pitch structure. This is also the intention of Jonathan Kramer's analysis of *Symphonies of Wind Instruments* in which 'moments' and 'submoments', constructed from integrated cells of pitch and rhythmic material, are controlled by a diatonic-chromatic linear progression (*The Time of Music*, 221–85). However, the conflict of immobility and process in the rhythmic organisation itself and between the two parameters (rhythm and linear pitch structures) is difficult to resolve if integration is the analytical goal. Alexander Rehding's 'Towards a "logic of discontinuity" in Stravinsky's *Symphonies of Wind Instruments*: Hasty, Kramer and Straus reconsidered', *Music Analysis* 17/1 (1998), 39–67, perceptively explores this problem in Kramer, alongside analyses by Joseph N. Straus, from 'The problem of prolongation in post-tonal music', *Journal of Music Theory* 31/1 (1987), 1–21, and *Remaking the Past: Musical Modernism and the Influence of the Tonal Traditions* (Cambridge, MA: Harvard University Press, 1990), and Christopher Hasty, from 'On the problem of succession and continuity in twentieth-century music', *Music Theory Spectrum* 8 (1986), 58–74. Rehding seeks a logic of discontinuity that avoids the stylistically dissonant 'organicist' approach of László Somfai ('Symphonies of Wind Instruments (1920): observations of Stravinsky's organic construction', *Studia musicologia Academiae Scientarum Hungaricae* 14 (1972), 355–83) while proposing various modes of 'overall coherence', culminating in the syntheses of the final chorale. The primary stylistic feature to emerge from these studies is that Stravinsky's 'block forms' contain initial cellular fusions of pitch and rhythmic variables which can be distributed and transformed separately in subsequent

'blocks' and eventually achieve a re-synthesis or, to adapt a phrase from *Poetics*, convergence in a state of repose.

39 Taruskin, *Stravinsky and the Russian Traditions*, 1648–75.

40 Spies, 'Stravinsky's Requiem settings', 237, n. 6.

41 My evidence is biographical and circumstantial. Andriessen and Schönberger emphasise the importance to Stravinsky of some Italian music (especially Gabrieli) and of Venice, the city in which he is buried (*Apollonian Clockwork*, 7–10). They also hear unspecified 'reference to other Requiems from musical history' (8). Stravinsky himself referred to echoes of *Il Trovatore* heard by some in *Apollon musagète* and *Perséphone*, neither accepting nor rejecting these associations; see Igor Stravinsky and Robert Craft, *Dialogues* (London: Faber and Faber, 1982), 34.

42 Joseph N. Straus, *Remaking the Past*. Straus applies a version of Harold Bloom's Freudian theory of the 'anxiety' of poetic influence to a wide range of modernist music, including Stravinsky's, in order to reveal a dimension of reinterpretation in relation to eighteenth- and nineteenth-century tonal models. Primarily, the issue bears on Stravinsky's neoclassical music. See also van den Toorn, *Music, Politics and the Academy*, chap. 6 ('Neoclassicism revised'), 143–78, in which Straus's arguments are reviewed in the context of recent literature on the topic, and Cross, *The Stravinsky Legacy*, chap. 6 ('A fresh look at Stravinsky analysis'), 193–225, for analyses of the Symphony in C and the Symphony in Three Movements in the light of Straus and theories of the 'moment'.

43 *Requiem Canticles* is based on two series (see Spies, 'Stravinsky's Requiem settings', 233–7). Stravinsky's serial procedures are discussed in: van den Toorn, *The music of Stravinsky*, 427–55; Milton Babbitt, 'Stravinsky's verticals and Schoenberg's diagonals: a twist of fate', in Ethan Haimo and Paul Johnson (eds), *Stravinsky Retrospectives* (Lincoln, NE: University of Nebraska Press, 1987), 15–35, and 'Order, symmetry and centricity in late Stravinsky', in Pasler, *Confronting Stravinsky*, 247–61; Charles Wourinen and Jeffrey Kresky, 'On the significance of Stravinsky's last works', in ibid., 262–70; Paul Schuyler Phillips, 'The enigma of *Variations*: a study of Stravinsky's final work for orchestra', *Music Analysis* 3/1 (1984), 69–89; and Joseph N. Straus, *Stravinsky's Late Music* (Cambridge: Cambridge University Press, 2001). See also Straus, 'Stravinsky the serialist', in this volume.

44 Since Stravinsky's technique of rotation is applied to the hexachords, not to the complete row, pitch repetitions are produced between the a and b hexachords of all the IR forms except IR0a and IR0b, which are mutually complementary (as in traditional serialism).

45 These two exceptions are produced by Stravinsky's deployment of the hexachords and verticals. The absence of G♮ (pc 7) in *Huic ergo* (bars 250–54) is compensated by the presence of this pc as the last note of bar 249 and in the vertical (Vb5) in bar 255. Similarly, the absence of D♮ and E♭ (pcs 2 and 3) in the *Amen* is mitigated by the presence of these pcs at the end of phrase 6 (bars 260–61). It is clear, though, that Stravinsky's serial logic is directed towards the system created by the rotation of hexachords and verticals and does not insist axiomatically on the (Schoenbergian) requirement to keep all twelve pcs in play.

46 The verticals are labelled according to the hexachord from which they are derived. 'Vb1' refers to the first vertical generated from IRb, and so on (see Table 11.4).

47 Igor Stravinsky and Robert Craft, *Conversations with Igor Stravinsky* (London: Faber and Faber, 1959), 24. Stravinsky goes on to say that 'I hear harmonically, of course, and I compose in the same way I always have' (25). Taruskin's view is that Stravinsky's 'late serial music is probably the most essentially harmonic – in the literal, vertical, chordal sense of the word – of any that may be found within the borders of the dodecaphonic realm' (*Stravinsky and the Russian Traditions*, 1652–3); but this is true only literally, vertically and chordally. In their different ways, Berg and Webern, for example, construct and exert a tight control on the vertical dimension of their serial music (the Scherzo of Webern's String Quartet, Op. 28, is a classic instance of an 'essentially harmonic' conception). The most recent considerations of Stravinsky's serial harmonic logic are Joseph N. Straus's indispensable essay on this topic, 'Stravinsky's "construction of the twelve verticals": an aspect of harmony in the serial music', *Music Theory Spectrum* 21 (1999), 43–73, his chapter 'Harmony', in *Stravinsky's Late Music*, 141–82, and 'Stravinsky the serialist' in this volume. Straus argues that 'the evolution of solutions to the problem of writing serial harmony during this period can be understood, at least in part, in terms of evolving solutions to the problem of writing serial harmony' ('Stravinsky's "construction"', 43). He identifies Stravinsky's most original contributions to serial theory as (1) the 'Lacrimosa'-type 'verticals of rotational

arrays' (authoritatively theorised in Babbitt's 'Stravinsky's verticals', and 'Order, symmetry, and centricity'); and (2) the verticals in four-part arrays, 'a layering of four series from which twelve chords are created as vertical slices through the array' (45).

48 The construction of this doubled five-verticals array foreshadows the five-chord arrays in the Postlude of *Requiem Canticles*, in which five different chords (piccolo, flutes, piano, harp) alternate with other chord sequences (celesta, bells, vibraphone), three of which contain five verticals.

49 As noted above, the whole-tone scale intersects with the octatonic collections, but its distinctive character tends to dominate its octatonic content. Table 11.7 reveals that Stravinsky seems intent on avoiding the anomalous whole tone: in the music (bars 250–53) 4-25 is split into set 3-8 (bar 250) and the dyad F♯/C (bar 253); when the dyad D♯/A♯ (bar 250) is placed beneath 3-8, this whole-tone trichord is incorporated into the diatonic/chromatic set 5-30.

50 For example, the 5-Z38 (10, 1, 4, 5, 6) of Vb3 (bar 233) contains A♯, C♯, E, F, F♯, of which the segment A♯, C♯, E, F♯ (10, 1, 4, 6) belongs to octatonic collection III. This segment can also be interpreted as an F♯^{7} chord, but no priority is given to this tonal formation here.

51 In *Stravinsky and the Russian Traditions*, 1661–2 and Ex. 20, Taruskin analyses the C♮ and G♮ (bar 232) as the point of transition from octatonic collection II (bars 229–31). Although this is broadly accurate, the presence of E♯ in bar 233 (Vb3, 5-Z38) lies outside collection III and transforms the sonority. It is an exaggeration to claim that 'the harmony produced is nothing other than a *Petrushka* chord (excepting the E sharp . . .)' (1662), since the chord sounds nothing like the (octatonic) *Petrushka* chord: the theoretical explanation here is reductive in the sense that it does not address the aural effect of the chord in bar 233, nor the difference within the octatonic similarity of the chords compared. Taruskin also claims that the 'Lacrimosa' progresses regularly through simultaneities of collections II and III; again, this is reductively true, but the multiple of instances of foreign notes generated by the interaction of the various rotational schemes means that the movement is not quite as systematically controlled as Taruskin's brief analysis makes it appear.

52 Igor Stravinsky and Robert Craft, 'Change of life', in *Themes and Episodes* (New York: Knopf, 1966), 23–4.

53 Milton Babbitt, 'Stravinsky's verticals', 16.

54 Stravinsky, *Poetics*, 35.

55 Ibid., 37. Stravinsky encapsulates the function of pitch centres in the concept of 'polarity' which may apply to a sound, an interval or a 'complex of tones'; see *Poetics*, 36. The structural processes implicit in polarity were explored initially in Berger's 'Problems of pitch organisation', 135–41, in particular the contradiction inherent in the concept that if a sonority (Stravinsky's 'complex of tones') is to be polarised then single-pitch polarity would have to be either withheld or polarised within the sonority. Further ramifications of Berger's discussion are considered in Marianne Kielian-Gilbert, 'Relationships of symmetrical pitch-class sets and Stravinsky's metaphor of polarity', *Perspectives of New Music* 21 (1982–3), 209–40, and pursued in extracts from the *Three Pieces for String Quartet*, *The Rite of Spring* (Introduction) and the Octet ('Tema con variazione'). She argues that polarity exists when two or more versions of a pc set class exhibit a structure symmetrical around a pc or dyad that remains invariant when one or more of the sets is transposed (for example, C–D–F–G [0, 2, 5, 7] and F–G–B♭–C [5, 7, 10, 0]); this creates 'inversional balance or complementation'. Under these conditions, polarity of a sonority (a set class) can co-exist with single-pitch polarity, as long as the single pitch is the invariant centre of symmetry for the various transpositions and configurations of the sonority. Kielian-Gilbert's conception of polarity theorises a particular ('inversional') configuration of Straus's analysis of harmonic polarity in Stravinsky's centric music according to a theory of 'tonal axis', defined as 'a nucleus of pitches' that (a) consists of overlapping major and minor triads (for example, E–G–B–D), (b) must function as a referential sonority, and (c), in contradistinction to a 'unified' major or minor seventh chord, must embody a conflict or polarity between its two constituent triads (e.g. E–G–B and G–B–D). These latter triads, for example, fulfil Kielian-Gilbert's conditions for inversional complementation ([4, 7, 11] and [7, 11, 2]). See Joseph N. Straus, 'Stravinsky's tonal axis', *Journal of Music Theory* 26 (1982), 261–90.

56 See Theodor Adorno, *Philosophy of Modern Music*, trans. Anne G. Mitchell and Wesley V. Blomster (London: Seabury Press, 1973), 138–40. The structural and aesthetic effects of hypostatisation are considered at length in Cross, *The Stravinsky Legacy*, chap. 7 ('Conclusions: Stravinsky, Adorno, and the problem of non-development'), 227–41.

57 Adele T. Katz, 'Stravinsky', in *Challenge to Musical Tradition: Toward a New Concept of*

Tonality (London: Putnam, 1947), 294–349; Felix Salzer, *Structural Hearing* (New York: Charles Boni, 1952; corrected edition, New York: Dover, 1962); and Allen Forte, *Contemporary Tone Structures* (New York: Columbia University Bureau of Publications, 1955), 25–38, 128–38, 150–53, 187–92.

58 Salzer, *Structural Hearing*, 219 and Ex. 427.

59 Heinrich Schenker, 'Further considerations of the Urlinie II', in William Drabkin (ed.), *The Masterwork in Music*, vol. 2, 17–18. See especially 17, Fig. 31. Some ramifications of Schenker's analysis are discussed in Robert Morgan, 'Dissonant prolongations: theoretical and compositional precedents', *Journal of Music Theory* 20 (1976), 49–91.

60 Salzer, *Structural Hearing*, 194.

61 Ibid., 218.

62 Ibid., Ex. 472.

63 Arnold Whittall, 'Music analysis as human science? *Le Sacre du printemps* in theory and practice', *Music Analysis* 1/1 (1982), 33–53; 51. The function of dissonance in Stravinsky is explored further in 'Tonality and the emancipated dissonance: Schoenberg and Stravinsky', in Jonathan Dunsby (ed.), *Models of Musical Analysis: Early Twentieth Century Music* (Oxford: Blackwell, 1993), 1–19.

64 Salzer, *Structural Hearing*, 191.

65 Roy Travis, 'Towards a new concept of tonality?', *Journal of Music Theory* 3 (1959), 257–84.

66 On this theoretical issue, see Joseph N. Straus, 'The problem of prolongation', and 'Voice-leading in atonal music', in James Baker, David Beach and Jonathan Bernard (eds), *Music Theory in Concept and Practice* (Rochester, NY: University of Rochester Press, 1997), 237–74; see also Arnold Whittall, 'Music analysis as human science?', 41–9.

67 Katz, 'Stravinsky', 337.

68 Ibid., 340; see also 341–7. Katz addresses the issue that concerned Schoenberg in the early 1930s, in reaction to Ernst Kurth's *Grundlagen der lineare Kontrapunkt* (Bern, 1917). Both Katz and Schoenberg argue against the notion that counterpoint in extended tonality, atonality or serialism can proceed entirely 'linearly' without harmonic logic or control. See Schoenberg, 'Linear counterpoint' and 'Linear counterpoint: linear polyphony', in *Style and Idea*, ed. Leonard Stein, trans. Leo Black (London: Faber and Faber, 1975), 289–95 and 295–7 respectively.

69 In *Contemporary Tone Structures* (1955), Forte's analysis of the 'Larghetto' from *Les cinq doigts* and the whole of *Petrushka* also produces linear structures (generated by

'specific single tones') unfolding independently and dissonantly, a technique that 'results in tensions between the individual lines, thus providing a compositional resource of great potential' (137). Like Katz, Forte rejects the implication that such lines exemplify so-called 'linear counterpoint' and maintains that 'vertical coincidence at important structural points is manifestly an important consideration' (137). This harmonic logic, which takes the form of departure from and return to referential sonorities, does, however, remain somewhat attenuated in the analyses. The tension between the linear and vertical is an unresolved theoretical problem in *Contemporary Tone Structures*, but finds a radical solution in Forte's pc set theory (see above) predicated on the Schoenbergian-atonal concept of the 'unity [or parametrical identity] of musical space'. Subsequently, Forte extended the scope of pc set theory to admit the linear projection of pc sets, a type of non-tonal prolongation applied to sections of *The Rite* and *Petrushka*: see Allen Forte, 'New approaches to the linear analysis of music', *Journal of the American Musicological Society* 41 (1988), 315–48.

70 See Joseph N. Straus, 'A principle of voice-leading in the music of Stravinsky', *Music Theory Spectrum* 4 (1982), 106–24, 'The problem of prolongation', and 'Voice-leading in atonal music'; Arnold Whittall, 'Music analysis: descriptions and distinctions' (Inaugural lecture in the Faculty of Music, King's College London, 1982); Anthony Pople, 'Misleading voices', 277–87.

71 My term 'centrum' is intended to differentiate Stravinsky's pitch centres from the tonic function in common-practice tonality.

72 See Straus, 'The problem of prolongation', 13–21. In 'Voice-leading in atonal music', Straus refines the associational model, adopting David Lewin's principle of transformational networks in order to define more precisely the relationship of the associative sonorities.

73 In their prime forms, set classes 6-Z25, 5-16 and 5-19 are supersets of 4-Z29, as follows: 6-Z25 [5,6,8,0,11,3] contains 4-Z29 as [5,6,8,0] requiring a theoretical transposition down five semitones to the prime form of 4-Z29 [0,1,3,7]; 5-16 [0,1,3,4,7] contains 4-Z29 [0,1,3,7]; 5-19 [0,1,3,6,7] contains 4-Z29 [0,1,3,7].

74 Although it is difficult to hear the linear projection of 4-Z29 in the high piccolo register, I would maintain that the linear 4-Z29 is a structural event, projected in this case both horizontally and registrally, and that its inaudibility is a striking image of structural alienation; see Adorno, 'Stravinsky: a dialectical portrait', in *Quasi una fantasia*, trans. Rodney Livingstone (London: Verso, 1992), 145–75; 146.

75 The association of the G♮s in the voice (bar 263) and trombone (bar 265) is strong but disturbed by the final vocal A♮ and the trombone's G♯. As I hear the passage, there is no structural closure on the G♮ unison (ic0) but a cadential reiteration of ic1 (G♮/G♯) that keeps in play the chromatic interference with the centrum.

76 See also Jeffrey Perry, 'A "requiem for the requiem": on Stravinsky's *Requiem Canticles*', *College Music Symposium* 33–4 (1993–4), 237–56, for a culturally-nuanced discussion of the tension between tonal implication and serially-controlled centricity in the work (especially the 'Libera me'). The complexity of incipient tonal structure in a short serial work by Stravinsky (*Anthem*: 'The dove descending breaks the air' [1962]) is analysed and demonstrated in Arnold Whittall's 'Music analysis: descriptions and distinctions' and Anthony Pople's 'Misleading voices'. The types of harmonic duality and ambiguity they identify are also present, though differently balanced and configured, in Stravinsky's later neoclassical music. Kofi Agawu's 'Stravinsky's *Mass* and Stravinsky analysis', *Music Theory Spectrum* 11 (1989), 139–63, isolates a 'residue of conflict' even at the deepest levels of tonal structure of the Kyrie of the Mass (1948) and concludes that a dual hearing of tonal process is necessary, specifically 'an underlying tonal structure of G, which then refers back to a more surface phenomenon, the "arpeggiated" tetrachord, 4-23' (161). This duality of structure is strikingly similar to that of the 'Lacrimosa' (the G♮ centrum and projected chromatic set), except that in the later work the duality of the constituents achieves a greater degree of integration (or 'unity') since G♮ is polarised *within* set 4-Z29. Agawu's case for 'the benefit of […] two essentially contradictory perspectives in order to gain the richest sense of structural procedure in the piece' (161) is confirmed in a recent, harmonically sensitive study by Chandler Carter, 'Stravinsky's "special sense": the rhetorical use of tonality in *The Rake's Progress*', *Music Theory Spectrum* 19 (1997), 55–80. Carter's methodologically pluralist analysis of four sections of the *The Rake's Progress* – using voice-leading and motivic analysis, pc set theory and post-tonal linear theory – seeks the mediating features of the

diverse tonal 'styles' within the opera but resists the temptation to resolve such conflict formalistically into a synthesis or harmonic consistency. With the aid of theoretical formulations that begin to revitalise the metaphors of pitch focus and tonal perspective in Stravinsky, Carter proposes (and demonstrates convincingly) that tonality in the work is used 'to create the opera's décor', a context inhabited by 'the play of a variety of musical impulses – tonal, bitonal, motivic, chromatic, set-class transformational – all sounding within the context of tonal backgrounds of varying degrees of aural immediacy' (78–9).
77 Adorno, 'Stravinsky: a dialectical portrait', 174.
78 See n. 30.
79 See n. 76.
80 Andriessen and Schönberger, *The Apollonian Clockwork*, 6. See also Andriessen in chap. 13 of this volume.

12 Stravinsky and the critics
1 Igor Stravinsky and Robert Craft, *Conversations with Igor Stravinsky* (London: Faber and Faber, 1959), 107.
2 François Lesure, *Igor Stravinsky: Le Sacre du printemps. Dossier de presse* (Geneva: Minkoff, 1980), 90–91.
3 Scott Messing, *Neoclassicism in Music: From the Genesis of the Concept through the Schoenberg/Stravinsky Polemic* (Ann Arbor: UMI Research Press, 1988), 134.
4 Leonid Sabaneyeff, *Modern Russian Composers*, trans. Judah A. Joffe (New York: International, 1927), 71.
5 Lesure, *Dossier de presse*, 85.
6 Sabaneyeff, *Modern Russian Composers*, 65.
7 Ibid., 64.
8 Boris Asaf'yev, *Kniga o Stravinskom* [A Book about Stravinsky] (Leningrad: Triton, 1929; repr. Muzyka, 1977); English translation by Richard F. French (Ann Arbor: UMI Research Press, 1982).
9 Mikhail Druskin, *Igor' Stravinskiy: lichnost', tvorchestvo, vzglyadï* (Leningrad: Sovetskiy kompozitor, 1974); English translation by Martin Cooper as *Igor Stravinsky: his Personality, Works and Views* (Cambridge: Cambridge University Press, 1983).
10 Viktor Varunts, ed., *I. Stravinskiy – publitsist i sobesednik* [I. Stravinsky as publicist and conversationalist] (Moscow: Sovetskiy kompozitor, 1988). *I. F. Stravinsky, Perepiska s russkimi korrespondentami. Materialï k biografii* [I. F. Stravinsky. Correspondence with Russian correspondents. Materials for a

biography], ed. Viktor Varunts, vol. 1: 1882–1912, vol. 2: 1913–1922 (Moscow: Kompozitor, 1997, 2000); both volumes contain as Appendix II notices and critical articles in the Russian press about works by Stravinsky for the appropriate years. Two further volumes are in preparation.
11 Boris de Schloezer, *Igor Stravinsky* (Paris: Claude Aveline, 1929), 191.
12 Lesure, *Dossier de presse*, 34.
13 Ibid., 23.
14 Pierre Souvtchinsky, 'Introduction: Domaine de la musique russe', in Pierre Souvtchinsky (ed.), *Musique russe*, 2 vols (Paris: Presses universitaires de France, 1953), vol. 1, 21.
15 Jean Marnold in Lesure, *Dossier de presse*, 37.
16 David Bancroft, 'Stravinsky and the "NRF" (1910–20)', *Music and Letters* 53/3 (1972), 277.
17 Ibid.
18 Lesure, *Dossier de presse*, p. 38.
19 Theodor W. Adorno, *Philosophie der neuen Musik* (Tübingen: Mohr, 1949); Eng. trans. as *Philosophy of Modern Music*, Anne G. Mitchell and Wesley V. Blomster (New York: Seabury Press, 1973), 188.
20 Lesure, *Dossier de presse*, 27–8.
21 Ibid., 49.
22 Ibid., 51.
23 Ibid., 74–5.
24 Ibid., 71.
25 Bancroft, 'Stravinsky and the "NRF" (1920–29)', *Music and Letters* 55/3 (1974), 267.
26 Bancroft, 'Stravinsky and the "NRF" (1910–20)', 283.
27 Paul Collaer, *Strawinsky* (Brussels: Équilibres, 1930), 135.
28 André Schaeffner, *Stravinsky* (Paris: Rieder, 1931), 91.
29 Richard Taruskin, *Stravinsky and the Russian Traditions: a Biography of the Works through Mavra* (Oxford: Oxford University Press, 1996), 1598.
30 Jean Cocteau, *A Call to Order*, trans. Rollo H. Myers (London: Faber and Gwyer, 1926), 62.
31 Lesure, *Dossier de presse*, 81.
32 Messing, *Neoclassicism in Music*, 130.
33 Igor Stravinsky, *Selected Correspondence*, ed. with commentaries by Robert Craft, 3 vols (London: Faber and Faber, 1982–5), vol. 1, 217n.
34 Arthur Lourié, 'Neogothic and neoclassic', *Modern Music* 5/3 (1928), 3.
35 Ibid., 4.
36 Arthur Lourié, 'La Sonate pour piano de Strawinsky', *Revue musicale* 6/10 (1925), 101.
37 Schloezer, *Igor Stravinsky*, 110.

38 Lourié, 'Neogothic and neoclassic', 7.
39 Artur Lur'ye [Arthur Lourié], 'Dve operï Stravinskogo' [Two operas by Stravinsky], *Vyorstï* 3 (1928), 125.
40 Arthur Lourié, 'Le *Capriccio* de Strawinsky', *Revue musicale* 11/103 (1930), 355.
41 Igor Stravinsky and Robert Craft, *Expositions and Developments* (London: Faber and Faber, 1962), 113.
42 Pierre Boulez,*Orientations*, ed. Jean-Jacques Nattiez, trans. Martin Cooper (London: Faber, 1986), 355–6.
43 Bancroft, 'Stravinsky and the "NRF" (1920–29)', 270.
44 Bancroft, 'Stravinsky and the "NRF" (1910–20)', 279.
45 Stravinsky, *Selected Correspondence*, 1/157.
46 Schloezer, *Igor Stravinsky*, 9.
47 Ibid., 36.
48 Ibid., 144.
49 Ibid., 78.
50 Ibid., 108–9.
51 Stravinsky, *Selected Correspondence*, 2/497.
52 Deborah Priest, ed., *Louis Laloy (1874–1944) on Debussy, Ravel and Stravinsky* (Aldershot: Ashgate, 1999), 306.
53 Collaer, *Strawinsky*, 52.
54 Ibid., 61.
55 Ibid., 108, 129–30.
56 Ibid., 115–22.
57 Ibid., 163.
58 Ibid., 33.
59 André Schaeffner, *Stravinsky* (Paris: Rieder, 1931), 5–6.
60 Igor Stravinsky, *Chronicle of my Life* (London: Gollancz, 1936), Foreword.
61 Schaeffner, *Stravinsky*, 91.
62 Ibid., 101.
63 Ibid., 118.
64 *Selected Correspondence*, 3/227.
65 Lesure, *Dossier de presse*, 105.
66 Ibid., 110.
67 Herbert Fleischer, *Strawinsky* (Berlin: Russischer Musikverlag, 1931), 'Vorwort'.
68 Ibid., 42–3.
69 Ibid., 111–12.
70 *Selected Correspondence*, 2/271–2.
71 For a qualification of this view and a fuller account of Adorno's understanding of Stravinsky, see Max Paddison's chapter in this volume.
72 Lesure, *Dossier de presse*, 91.
73 Bancroft, 'Stravinsky and the "NRF" (1920–29)', 261.
74 Lesure, *Dossier de presse*, 151.
75 Ibid., 153.
76 G. W. Hopkins and Paul Griffiths, 'Boulez, Pierre', in Stanley Sadie (ed.), *The New Grove Dictionary of Music and Musicians,*

2nd edn. (London: Macmillan, 2001), vol. 4, 98.
77 Boulez, *Orientations*, 18.
78 Boulez, 'Strawinsky demeure', in Souvtchinsky, *Musique russe*, vol. 1, 221.
79 Roman Vlad, *Stravinsky* (Rome, 1958); trans. Frederick and Ann Fuller (London: Oxford University Press, 1960; 2nd edn 1967), 178.
80 Ibid., 224.
81 Stravinsky, *Selected Correspondence*, 2/376n.
82 Stravinsky and Craft, *Expositions and Developments*, 111.
83 Stravinsky, *Selected Correspondence*, 2/343.
84 Ibid., 344.
85 Stravinsky, *Themes and Conclusions* (London: Faber and Faber, 1972), 202–5, 214–17.
86 Ibid., 209–14, 219–20.
87 Stravinsky, *Selected Correspondence*, 2/99–101.
88 Messing, *Neoclassicism in Music*, 154.
89 Ibid., 193.
90 Jonathan Cross, *The Stravinsky Legacy* (Cambridge: Cambridge University Press, 1998), 103–4.

13 Composing with Stravinsky

1 Louis Andriessen and Elmer Schönberger, *The Apollonian Clockwork: on Stravinsky*, trans. Jeff Hamburg (Oxford: Oxford University Press, 1989), 6.
2 A version of this essay was first published in Dutch under the title 'Met Stravinsky naar de eenentwintigste eeuw' in the programme book of the Vlaams-Brabant Festival 2000, 19–21.
3 Arnold Schoenberg to Josef Rufer, quoted in Malcolm MacDonald, *Schoenberg*, p/b edn (London: Dent, 1987), 29.
4 Pierre Boulez, 'Schoenberg is dead', in *Stocktakings from an Apprenticeship*, trans. Stephen Walsh (Oxford: Clarendon, 1991), 214.
5 T. W. Adorno, 'Stravinsky: a dialectical portrait', in *Quasi una Fantasia*, trans. Rodney Livingstone (London: Verso, 1992), 172.
6 Igor Stravinsky and Robert Craft, *Conversations with Igor Stravinsky* (London: Faber and Faber, 1959), 133
7 This idea is more fully explored in Jonathan Cross, *The Stravinsky Legacy* (Cambridge: Cambridge University Press, 1998).
8 Richard Taruskin, *Stravinsky and the Russian Traditions: a Biography of the Works Through Mavra* (Oxford: Oxford University Press, 1996), 1677.
9 Stephen Walsh, 'Stravinsky', in Stanley Sadie (ed.), *The New Grove Dictionary of Music*

and Musicians, rev. edn (London: Macmillan, 2001), vol. 24, 557.

10 'Stravinsky's influence can be seen ... in a specific *attitude* towards already existent material.' Andriessen and Schönberger, *The Apollonian Clockwork*, 100.

11 The conversation took place at the home of Louis Andriessen in Amsterdam on 12 February 2001.

12 Andriessen and Schönberger, *The Apollonian Clockwork*, 101.

14 Stravinsky and us

1 Robert Craft, 'Introduction: a master at work', in Igor Stravinsky and Robert Craft, *Retrospectives and Conclusions* (New York: Knopf, 1969), 3.

2 Igor Stravinsky and Robert Craft, *Expositions and Developments* (London: Faber and Faber, 1962), 164.

3 Michel Georges-Michel, 'Les deux Sacres du Printemps', *Comoedia* (11 December 1920), cited in Truman C. Bullard, 'The first performance of Igor Stravinsky's *Sacre du Printemps*', PhD diss., University of Rochester, 1971, vol. 1, 3.

4 See André Schaeffner, *Strawinsky* (Paris: Éditions Rieder, 1931), 43, n.1; also 'Table des planches', 217, Pl. 21.

5 Stravinsky and Craft, *Expositions and Developments*, 169

6 See Taruskin, *Stravinsky and the Russian Traditions: a Biography of the Works Through Mavra* (Oxford: Oxford University Press, 1996), chaps. 4 and 12.

7 See Bernice Glatzer Rosenthal, 'The transmutation of the symbolist ethos: mystical anarchism and the revolution of 1905', *Slavic Review* 36 (1977), 616.

8 Stravinsky and Craft, *Expositions and Developments*, 114–15; the original 'overpublicized bit about expression' (as it is described there) is from Stravinsky's autobiography (*Chroniques de ma vie*) in its anonymous English translation as *An Autobiography* (New York: Simon and Schuster, 1936), 83.

9 The term *panromanogermanic* comes from Prince Nikolai Sergeyevich Trubetskoy's Eurasianist tract *Yevropa i chelovechestvo* (Sofia: Rossiysko-Bolgarskoye Knigoizdatel'stvo, 1920), a book published by Stravinsky's friend Pyotr Suvchinsky (Pierre Souvtchinsky).

10 Boris de Schloezer, 'La musique', *La Revue contemporaine* (1 February 1923); quoted in Scott Messing, *Neoclassicism in Music: From the Genesis of the Concept through the Schoenberg/Stravinsky Polemic* (Ann Arbor: UMI Research Press, 1988), 130.

11 See *Stravinsky and the Russian Traditions*, 1486–93.

12 Letter to Charles-Ferdinand Ramuz (23 July 1924), in Robert Craft (ed.), *Stravinsky: Selected Correspondence*, 3 vols (New York: Knopf, 1985), vol. 3, 83.

13 As embodied in the title to his collected essays, *A Call to Order*, trans. Rollo H. Myers (London: Faber and Gwyer, 1926).

14 Quoted in Deems Taylor, 'Sound – and a Little Fury' (review of the American premiere under Leopold Stokowski), reprinted in *Of Men and Music* (New York: Simon and Schuster, 1937), 89–90.

15 Pieter C. van den Toorn, *Stravinsky and 'The Rite of Spring': The Beginnings of a Musical Language* (Berkeley: University of California Press, 1987), 1.

16 'Sacre', in N. K. Roerich, *Realm of Light* (New York: Roerich Museum Press, 1931), 188.

17 Stravinsky and Craft, *Expositions and Developments*, p. 115; quoted in van den Toorn, *Stravinsky and 'The Rite of Spring'*, 18. In the last sentence, where van den Toorn quotes Stravinsky as saying 'form', the original text, on both occasions, has 'the form'.

18 Van den Toorn, *Stravinsky and 'The Rite of Spring'*, 19.

19 Van den Toorn, 'Politics, feminism, and music theory', *Journal of Musicology* 9 (1991), 276.

20 Letter received 20 September 1951; printed in Robert Craft, *Stravinsky: Chronicle of a Friendship, 1948–71*, rev. and expanded edn (Nashville: Vanderbilt University Press, 1994), 65.

21 Dorothy Lamb Crawford, *Evenings On and Off the Roof: Pioneering Concerts in Los Angeles, 1939–1971* (Berkeley: University of California Press, 1995), 64.

22 Vera Stravinsky and Robert Craft, *Stravinsky in Pictures and Documents* (New York: Simon and Schuster, 1978), 422.

23 Ibid.

24 The lecture was first published in the *Atlantic Monthly* (December 1982) under the title 'On a misunderstood collaboration: assisting Stravinsky'; this version was reprinted (under the title 'Influence or assistance?') in Robert Craft, *Present Perspectives* (New York: Knopf, 1984), 246–64 (the anecdote in question appearing on pp. 252–3). A second version, set down in a letter to Joan Peyser, was published by the latter in 'Stravinsky–Craft, Inc.', *American Scholar* 52 (1983), 513–22.

25 As reprinted in Eric Walter White, *Stravinsky: the Composer and his Works*

(Berkeley: University of California Press, 1966), 430–31.

26 First published in 1928 directly on the Aeolian piano roll of the ballet, this analysis is discussed in *Stravinsky and the Russian Traditions*, 587–98.

27 Craft, *Chronicle of a Friendship*, 75.

28 'Rencontre avec Stravinsky', *Preuves* 2/16 (1952), 37.

29 Letter of 27 July 1932, in Arnold Schoenberg, *Letters*, ed. Erwin Stein, trans. Eithne Wilkins and Ernst Kaiser (Berkeley: University of California Press, 1987), 164.

30 Milton Babbitt, 'Remarks on the recent Stravinsky', as reprinted in Benjamin Boretz and Edward T. Cone (eds.), *Perspectives on Schoenberg and Stravinsky* (Princeton: Princeton University Press, 1968), 171.

31 Ibid.

32 Programme note on the Cantata, as reprinted in White, *Stravinsky*, 429 These words are a virtual paraphrase of Stravinsky's explanation, in *Chroniques de ma vie*, of his fascination with Russian folk verses during the years of the First World War: 'What fascinated me in this verse was not so much the stories, which were often crude, or the pictures and metaphors, always so deliciously unexpected, as the sequence of the words and syllables, and the cadence they create, which produces an effect on one's sensibilities very closely akin to that of music' (Stravinsky, *An Autobiography*, 83). These are the words that immediately precede the famous sermon ('that overpublicized bit') on music and expression.

33 Craft, *Chronicle of a Friendship*, 89 (entry for 26 December 1952).

34 See the Alain Nicolas auction catalogue *Autographes–Livres–Documents* (Paris: Librairie Les Neuf Muses, 1993), lot no. 196.

35 Igor Stravinsky and Robert Craft, *Conversations with Igor Stravinsky* (Garden City, NY: Doubleday, 1959), 78.

36 ' "Dear Bob(sky)" (Stravinsky's letters to Robert Craft, 1944–49)', *Musical Quarterly* 65 (1979), 412–13; Craft, *Stravinsky: Selected Correspondence*, vol. 1, 346–7. A facsimile of the uncensored letter was displayed, and the quoted passage read aloud, by Charles M. Joseph in 'Ellipses, exclusions, expurgations: what do Stravinsky's letters really say?', a

paper presented at the 58th Annual Meeting of the American Musicological Society in Pittsburgh, 7 November 1992.

37 David Allenby, 'Judge for yourselves', *Musical Times* 137 (June 1996), 25.

38 Quoted in Jacob Drachler, 'The case of the Stravinsky Cantata', *Midstream* (August/September 1971), 37.

39 Its substance was incorporated into a footnote on p. 304 of Lillian Libman, *And Music at the Close: Stravinsky's Last Years* (New York: Norton, 1972). Pieter van den Toorn relied on this evidence, as well as the passage to which it was appended, in which Libman characterised reports of Stravinsky's anti-Semitism as 'ridiculous fiction' that 'could hardly have entered the scope of his thought', in declaring the matter unworthy of pursuit. See van den Toorn, 'Will Stravinsky survive Postmodernism?', *Music Theory Spectrum* 22 (2000), 121. I know of no comparable case, at least in the refereed professional literature, where the word of a press agent is invoked in order to justify the foreclosure of inquiry. Such subscholarly credulity is impressive testimony to the continuing regulative force of the Stravinsky myth, and its deleterious effect on scholarship.

40 See Igor Stravinsky, *Poetics of Music in the Form of Six Lessons* (Cambridge, MA: Harvard University Press, 1947; repr. 1970), 163.

41 The situation is admittedly somewhat complicated by the fact that Holst's setting, unlike Stravinsky's, is used in Anglican services, where a different set of audience expectations, and a different set of premises regulating audience behaviour, are in force. For a discussion of them, see Harold Copeman, *Singing the Meaning* (Oxford: published by the author, 1996). But at an Anglican service there would also presumably be no Jewish ears to offend.

42 In his 1995 recording of the Cantata for Music Masters, Robert Craft did change 'The Jews on me' to 'My enemies', according to the suggestion embodied in Lillian Libman's letter to Jacob Drachler. The change was silent, however, and the problem unaddressed.

43 See 'Jews and geniuses: an exchange', *New York Review of Books* (15 June 1989), 58; *Chronicle of a Friendship*, 107–8 (entry for 16 March 1954).

Select bibliography

Adorno, Theodor W. *Philosophie der neuen Musik.* Tübingen: J. C. B. Mohr (Paul
    Siebeck), 1949. In *Gesammelte Schriften,* vol. 12, ed. Rolf Tiedemann and
    Klaus Schultz. Frankfurt/Main: Suhrkamp, 1975. Trans. Anne G. Mitchell
    and Wesley V. Blomster, as *Philosophy of Modern Music.* London: Sheed and
    Ward, 1973

—. 'Stravinsky: a dialectical portrait'. Trans. Rodney Livingstone, in *Quasi una
    fantasia.* London: Verso, 1992, 145–75

Agawu, V. Kofi. 'Stravinsky's *Mass* and Stravinsky analysis'. *Music Theory Spectrum*
    11 (1989), 139–63

Albright, Daniel. *Stravinsky: the Music Box and the Nightingale.* New York: Gordon
    and Breach, 1989

Andriessen, Louis, and Elmer Schönberger. *The Apollonian Clockwork: on
    Stravinsky,* trans. Jeff Hamburg. Oxford: Oxford University Press, 1989.
    Originally published as *Het apollonisch uurwerk: over Stravinsky.* Amsterdam:
    Uitgeverij De Bezige Bij, 1983

Asaf'yev, Boris. *A Book About Stravinsky,* trans. Richard F. French. Ann Arbor:
    UMI Research Press, 1982. Originally published under the name Igor Glebov,
    as *Kniga o Stravinskom.* Leningrad: Triton, 1929; repr. under Asaf'yev's name,
    Muzyka, 1977

Babbitt, Milton. 'Remarks on the recent Stravinsky' [1964]. In Boretz and Cone
    (eds.), *Perspectives on Schoenberg and Stravinsky,* 165–85

Berger, Arthur. 'Problems of pitch organisation in Stravinsky' [1963]. In Boretz
    and Cone (eds.), *Perspectives on Schoenberg and Stravinsky,* 123–54

Boretz, Benjamin, and Edward T. Cone (eds.). *Perspectives on Schoenberg and
    Stravinsky.* Princeton: Princeton University Press, 1968. Rev. edn, New York:
    Norton, 1972

Boulez, Pierre. 'Strawinsky demeure' [1951]. In Pierre Souvtchinsky (ed.),
    Musique russe, 2 vols. Paris: Presses universitaires de France, 1953. Vol. 1,
    155–224. Trans. Stephen Walsh, as 'Stravinsky remains', in *Stocktakings from
    an Apprenticeship.* Oxford: Clarendon, 1991, 55–110

Carter, Chandler. 'Stravinsky's "special sense": the rhetorical use of tonality in *The
    Rake's Progress'. Music Theory Spectrum* 19 (1997), 55–80

Chew, Geoffrey. 'Pastoral and neoclassicism: a reinterpretation of Auden's and
    Stravinsky's *Rake's Progress'. Cambridge Opera Journal* 5 (1993), 239–63

Cone, Edward T. 'Stravinsky: the progress of a method' [1962]. In Boretz and
    Cone (eds.), *Perspectives on Schoenberg and Stravinsky,* 156–64

—. 'The uses of convention: Stravinsky and his models'. *Musical Quarterly* 48
    (1962), 287–99

Craft, Robert. *Stravinsky: Chronicle of a Friendship, 1948–1971.* New York: Alfred A.
    Knopf, 1972. Rev. and expanded edn, Nashville: Vanderbilt University Press, 1994

—. *Igor and Vera Stravinsky: a Photograph Album (1921–1971)*. London: Thames and Hudson, 1982

—. *A Stravinsky Scrapbook 1940–1971*. London: Thames and Hudson, 1983

—. *Present Perspectives*. New York: Knopf, 1984

—. *Stravinsky: Glimpses of a Life*. London: Lime Tree, 1992

Cross, Jonathan. *The Stravinsky Legacy*. Cambridge: Cambridge University Press, 1998

Druskin, Mikhail. *Igor Stravinsky: his Personality, Works and Views*, trans. Martin Cooper. Cambridge: Cambridge University Press, 1983. Originally published as *Igor' Stravinskiy: lichnost', tvorchestvo, vzglyadï*. Leningrad: Sovetskiy Kompozitor, 1974

Fink, Robert. '"*Rigoroso* ($\bullet = 126$)": *The Rite of Spring* and the forging of a modernist performing style'. *Journal of the American Musicological Society* 52 (1999), 299–362

Forte, Allen. *The Harmonic Organization of 'The Rite of Spring'*. New Haven: Yale University Press, 1978

Griffiths, Paul. *Igor Stravinsky: The Rake's Progress*. Cambridge: Cambridge University Press, 1982

—. *Stravinsky*. London: Dent, 1992

Haimo, Ethan, and Paul Johnson (eds.). *Stravinsky Retrospectives*. Lincoln, NE: University of Nebraska Press, 1987

Hill, Peter. *Stravinsky: The Rite of Spring*. Cambridge: Cambridge University Press, 2000

Hyde, Martha M. 'Neoclassic and anachronistic impulses in twentieth-century music'. *Music Theory Spectrum* 18 (1996), 200–35

Johnston, Ben. 'An interview with Soulima Stravinsky'. *Perspectives of New Music* 9/2–10/1 (1971), 15–27

Keller, Hans, and Milein Cosman. *Stravinsky Seen and Heard*. London: Toccata Press, 1982

Kielian-Gilbert, Marianne. 'The rhythms of form: correspondence and analogy in Stravinsky's designs'. *Music Theory Spectrum* 9 (1987), 42–66

—. 'Stravinsky's contrasts: contradiction and discontinuity in his neoclassic music'. *Journal of Musicology* 9 (1991), 448–80

Lederman, Minna (ed.). *Stravinsky in the Theatre*. New York: Da Capo, 1949

Lesure, François. *Igor Stravinsky: Le Sacre du printemps. Dossier de presse*. Geneva: Minkoff, 1980

Libman, Lillian. *And Music at the Close: Stravinsky's Last Years: a Personal Memoir*. New York: Norton, 1972

Messing, Scott. *Neoclassicism in Music from the Genesis of the Concept through the Schoenberg/Stravinsky Polemic*. Ann Arbor: UMI Research Press, 1988

Oliver, Michael. *Igor Stravinsky*. London: Phaidon, 1995

Pasler, Jann (ed.). *Confronting Stravinsky: Man, Musician, and Modernist*. Berkeley: University of California Press, 1986

Pople, Anthony. *Skryabin and Stravinsky 1908–1914: Studies in Theory and Analysis*. New York: Garland, 1989

—. 'Misleading voices: contrasts and continuities in Stravinsky studies'. In Craig Ayrey and Mark Everist (eds.), *Analytical Strategies and Musical Interpretation:*

Essays in Nineteenth- and Twentieth-Century Music. Cambridge: Cambridge University Press, 1996, 271–87

Rehding, Alexander. 'Towards a "logic of discontinuity" in Stravinsky's *Symphonies of Wind Instruments*: Hasty, Kramer and Straus reconsidered'. *Music Analysis* 17/1 (1998), 39–67

Schaeffner, André. *Strawinsky*. Paris: Éditions Rieder, 1931

Schloezer, Boris de. *Igor Stravinsky*. Paris: Claude Aveline, 1929

Claudio Spies. 'Notes on Stravinsky's *Abraham and Isaac*' [1965], 'Notes on Stravinsky's Variations' [1965], and 'Some notes on Stravinsky's Requiem settings' [1967]. In Boretz and Cone (eds.), *Perspectives on Schoenberg and Stravinsky*, 186–209, 210–22, 223–49

Straus, Joseph N. 'A principle of voice-leading in the music of Stravinsky'. *Music Theory Spectrum* 4 (1982), 106–24

—. 'Stravinsky's tonal axis'. *Journal of Music Theory* 26 (1982), 261–90

—. *Remaking the Past: Musical Modernism and the Influence of the Tonal Tradition*. Cambridge, MA: Harvard University Press, 1990

—. 'Stravinsky's "construction of twelve verticals": an aspect of harmony in the serial music'. *Music Theory Spectrum* 21/1 (1999), 231–71

—. *Stravinsky's Late Music*. Cambridge: Cambridge University Press, 2001

Stravinsky, Igor. *Poetics of Music in the Form of Six Lessons*, trans. Arthur Knodel and Ingolf Dahl. Cambridge, MA: Harvard University Press, 1947. Originally published as *Poétique musicale*. Cambridge, MA: Harvard University Press, 1942

—. *Chroniques de ma vie*, 2 vols. Paris: Denoël & Steel, 1935–6. Trans. anon. as *Chronicle of my Life*. London: Victor Gollancz, 1936. Repr. as *An Autobiography (1903–1934)*. New York: Steuer, 1958. Repr. with corrections by Eric Walter White. London: Marion Boyars, 1975

—. *Stravinsky: Selected Correspondence*. Ed. and with commentaries by Robert Craft, 3 vols. London: Faber and Faber, 1982–5

Stravinsky, Igor, and Robert Craft. *Conversations with Igor Stravinsky*. London: Faber and Faber, 1959

—. *Memories and Commentaries*. London: Faber and Faber, 1960

—. *Stravinsky in Conversation with Robert Craft*. Harmondsworth: Penguin, 1962

—. *Expositions and Developments*. London: Faber and Faber, 1962

—. *Dialogues and a Diary*. Garden City, NY: Doubleday, 1963. Enlarged edn, London: Faber and Faber, 1968

—. *Themes and Episodes*. New York: Knopf, 1966

—. *Retrospectives and Conclusions*. New York: Knopf, 1969

—. *Themes and Conclusions*. London: Faber and Faber, 1972 (combined repr. of *Themes and Episodes* and *Retrospectives and Conclusions*)

—. *Dialogues*. London: Faber and Faber, 1982 (reissue of 'Dialogues' from *Dialogues and a Diary*)

Stravinsky, Vera, and Robert Craft (eds.). *Stravinsky in Pictures and Documents*. London: Hutchinson, 1979

Stuart, Philip. *Igor Stravinsky – The Composer in the Recording Studio: a Comprehensive Discography*. New York: Greenwood Press, 1991

Taruskin, Richard. *Stravinsky and the Russian Traditions: a Biography of the Works Through* Mavra. Oxford: Oxford University Press, 1996

—. *Defining Russia Musically.* Princeton: Princeton University Press, 1997

Van den Toorn, Pieter C. *The Music of Igor Stravinsky.* New Haven: Yale University Press, 1983

—. *Stravinsky and 'The Rite of Spring': the Beginnings of a Musical Language.* Berkeley: University of California Press, 1987

—. 'Context and analytical method in Stravinsky'. In *Music, Politics, and the Academy.* Berkeley: University of California Press, 1995

—. 'Neoclassicism and its definitions'. In James M. Baker, David W. Beach and Jonathan W. Bernard (eds.), *Music Theory in Concept and Practice.* Rochester, NY: University of Rochester Press, 1997

Vlad, Roman. *Stravinsky,* trans. Frederick and Ann Fuller. London: Oxford University Press, 1960. 2nd edn, 1967; enlarged 3rd edn, 1978. Originally published in Italian (Rome: 1958)

Walsh, Stephen. *The Music of Stravinsky.* Oxford: Oxford University Press, 1993

—. *Stravinsky: Oedipus Rex.* Cambridge: Cambridge University Press, 1993

—. 'Stravinsky's symphonies: accident or design?'. In Craig Ayrey and Mark Everist (eds.), *Analytical Strategies and Musical Interpretation: Essays in Nineteenth- and Twentieth-Century Music.* Cambridge: Cambridge University Press, 1996, 35–71

—. *Stravinsky: a Creative Spring: Russia and France 1882–1934.* London: Jonathan Cape, 1999

—. *The New Grove Stravinsky.* London: Macmillan, 2002

Watkins, Glenn. *Pyramids at the Louvre: Music, Culture, and Collage from Stravinsky to the Postmodernists.* Cambridge, MA: Belknap Press, 1994

White, Eric Walter. *Stravinsky: the Composer and his Works.* London: Faber and Faber, 1966. 2nd rev. and expanded edn, 1979

Whittall, Arnold. 'Music analysis as human science? *Le Sacre du printemps* in theory and practice'. *Music Analysis* 1/1 (1982), 33–53

Index of names and titles